MAN AND HIS RELIGION

MAN AND HIS RELIGION

Aspects of Religious Psychology

GIORGIO ZUNINI

With a foreword by Sean O' Riordan

GEOFFREY CHAPMAN
LONDON DUBLIN MELBOURNE 1969

Geoffrey Chapman Ltd
18 High Street, Wimbledon, London SW 19

Geoffrey Chapman (Ireland) Ltd
5–7 Main Street, Blackrock, County Dublin

Geoffrey Chapman Pty Ltd
44 Latrobe Street, Melbourne, Vic 3000, Australia

This book was originally published in Italian under the title *Homo Religiosus* by Casa editrice Il Saggiatore, Milan, 1966

This book is set in 11 on 13 pt Times and printed in Great Britain by Clarke, Doble & Brendon Ltd, Plymouth

Contents

This book is dedicated to

GORDON W. ALLPORT,
OTTO KARRER
AND ALL MY TEACHERS AND FRIENDS

Preface

The title of this book is too ambitious; hence the delimitation indicated in the subtitle: 'Aspects of Religious Psychology'. The book is not, therefore, a complete treatise on religious psychology. Too many aspects have been left alone or dealt with in a purely marginal way; certainty and religious doubt, typology of religion, psychopathology of religion, conversion, mysticism, worship, prayer—the living expression of religion— all this would have called for ample treatment on its own. The guiding thread which unites the various chapters is perhaps the same one which guided William James: the study of human nature in the matter of religious behaviour.

Several chapters of this book have already been published in Italian in shortened form: chapters one, two and four in *Orientamenti pedagogici* (1963, 1964, 1965); chapter five in the Carlo Figini *Miscellanea* (Milan, 1964).

I should like to express my thanks to my colleagues, collaborators and students who, during my ten years at the University of Bari, encouraged me to do this work.

GIORGIO ZUNINI

Foreword

'To the psychologist,' wrote William James in Lecture I of *The Varieties of Religious Experience*, first published in 1902, 'the religious propensities of man must be at least as interesting as any other of the facts pertaining to his mental constitution.' The historical record of psychology bears out this assertion. The psychology of religion is now over a hundred years old—which, for practical purposes, means as old as the science of empirical psychology itself. In the present work Father Zunini does well to remind us of the pioneering work of Wilhelm Wundt in this field—and he rightly calls Wundt 'the founder of modern psychology'.

By this time the body of psychological research bearing directly on the topic of religion is colossal. Father Zunini covers a great deal of it in his book, summarizing the various theories of religion advanced by successive psychologists and schools of psychology and employing these theories to develop and illustrate his own view of the matter. What makes his study a particularly valuable contribution to the literature on the subject is his refusal to isolate religion or religious experience from the totality of human life and human experience and his insistence on *man himself (homo religiosus)* as the subject and bearer of the specific kind of human experience he is discussing. Empirical psychology has not escaped the tendency of its historical predecessor, philosophical psychology, to single out particular elements of psychic life for specialized consideration in such a way as practically to reify them and set them up in autonomus compartments, sealed off from the surging, untidy, many-sided dynamism of human life itself. Abstraction of a precise theme of study from the generality of psychic life is,

of course, a precondition of scientific psychology; but the fact
that an abstraction has been made has to be kept in mind all
the time if justice is to be done to *man's* psyche. The part has
to be continually referred back to the whole: human sexuality,
the human 'search for glory' (in Karen Horney's phrase),
human religion, have to be continually referred back to *man*.
Father Zunini's religious psychology never loses sight of man
—that strange, complex being who has all gods and all devils
in his heart. The concreteness of his approach to the psychology
of religion imparts a quality of human insight and wisdom to
his writing on the subject that is often notably absent from
the abstractive excesses of Freud, Jung and others whom he
discusses at length in the present work—valuable as are their
contributions to religious psychology in many areas of this
complex field.

Firmly relating the psychic fact of religious experience to
man himself, Father Zunini is in a strong position to assess
the objective validity of this form of human experience. Is
religion, psychologically speaking, an 'illusion' (in Freud's
sense of the term) or a true response to some kind of transcendent reality? In simpler terms, is the religious man *(homo
religiosus)* right in his interpretation of things or is he just
childish, if not a little crazy? Father Zunini argues, on grounds
proper to psychology itself, that he is right and that an
irreligious interpretation of man's experience of himself and
his world is partial, stunted, basically inhuman, and moreover
exposed to unconscious invasions from a repressed and distorted need of 'divinity' in life (as Jung had already pointed
out in his article 'The Spirit of Psychology' in the *Eranos-
Jahrbuch* of 1946). Man is inescapably religious, just as he is
inescapably sexual, sociable, power-seeking and lots of other
things. It is the task of psychology to *recognize* man in all
these different but interconnected dimensions of his being—
including the religious dimension—and to make a correct
scientific analysis of them. 'Normal' and 'abnormal' forms of
religion will show up in such an analysis; but the normality of
religion itself will be an accepted datum, just like the normality

of sexuality or sociability or any other accepted sphere of psychic life.

Religiosità is Father Zunini's Italian term for the religious element in psychic life which can and should form the object of empirical investigation and analysis. He distinguishes it from religion in the credal sense which involves what William James calls 'a proposition of value' or 'a spiritual judgment'. This is a different *kind* of judgment from that involved in the assessment of the empirical facts of *religiosità*. It is a judgment of personal appreciation and appropriation—a *faith*-judgment of some kind. Obviously *religiosità* is present in religion but the converse is not necessarily true: unbelief too can have a strong component of *religiosità*. We have no word for *religiosità* in this sense in English. 'Religiosity' is a pejorative term—whereas what we want is a term as neutral as 'sexuality'. In the present translation *religiosità* has been rendered by such acceptable English terms as 'religious experience' (William James's term), 'the religious sense' or simply 'religion', where the context makes it clear that there is question of the psychological phenomenon indicated by *religiosità*.

A few passages in the book have been abbreviated in translation and others lengthened. This has been done after consultation with the author who supplied the extra material for the lengthened passages. The bibliography has been adapted to the needs of the English-speaking reader.

SEAN O'RIORDAN, C.SS.R.
Professor of Pastoral Psychology
Alphonsian Academy
Lateran University
Rome

1. The Religious Sense in Modern Psychology

William James: 'Religious experience' and 'human nature'

William James was invited in 1900-01 to give a series of lectures to the Gifford Foundation for courses in natural theology at the Scottish universities, but for health reasons he was obliged to postpone his trip to England for a further year. Meanwhile, in retirement and study, he prepared these lectures, which were published in 1902 under the title *The Varieties of Religious Experience*.[1] Thus is was that twelve years after the publication of *The Principles of Psychology*[2]—which appeared to have exhausted his output as a psychologist—William James made a name for himself by a work which has remained fundamental for the study of the religious sense. For its broad outlook and vigorous style this work is considered to be one of his best. The subtitle of this book: 'a study of human nature' is very meaningful. James made the following statement in a letter:

> The problem I have faced is a difficult one: first, to defend 'experience' against 'philosophy', as the real backbone of religious life in the world and second, to induce the listener or the reader to believe what I myself invincibly believe, namely, that however absurd all the manifestations of religion may have been (I mean the various beliefs and

[1] W. James, *The Varieties of Religious Experience*, University Books, New York, 1963. Also available as a Fontana paperback.
[2] W. James, *The Principles of Psychology*, William Barton, London, 1952.

1

theories), nevertheless religious activity as a whole is the most important function of mankind.

William James thus asserted that human nature cannot be understood unless the religious element is taken into consideration, and he had the courage to undertake to study it according to the criteria and methods which are used in the study of other psychic activities.

Is it possible to discover how people 'experience' or 'live' religion? We have direct experience of memories, feelings and tendencies, but how do we experience religion? How does it start and how does it change? William James begins by claiming that religious feeling must be considered as a genuine psychic activity which has still to be explained even when it is summarily judged as a psychic abnormality. He subsequently defines the field for the study of religious psychology and indicates the manner in which he intends to pursue his work. What he has to say in his first lecture interests us particularly, because after sixty years it is still completely modern. His decision and courage in facing up to this problem are admirable. In face of the Bible or of a religious personality (such as George Fox, founder of the Quakers), we can, he says, propose two orders of inquiry: first, how did they come about, what is their constitution, origin and history; or, 'what is their importance, meaning or significance now that they are once here?'[3] The answer to the one question is given in an *existential* judgment, that is, by describing the fact as presented to us, without attempting to evaluate it. To the second order of inquiry the answer is a *proposition of value*. William James declares that neither of these two species of judgment can be immediately deduced from the other. The fact that the books of the Bible reflect the type of civilization in which they were written, or the character of their authors, of itself tells us nothing of the religious teaching they contain. Similarly, the fact that George Fox is to be judged a psychopath from his writings and the evidence of his life says nothing of the value

[3] W. James, *The Varieties of Religious Experience*, p. 4.

of his religious practice and that of the 'Society of Friends' (Quakers) which he founded. The procedure which does not take these two orders of judgment into account is mistaken and irritating and oversimplifies the argument as follows: the Bible is a mythological work and George Fox is an eccentric; therefore what the Bible contains is of no value and the religion of the Quakers is the product of an unsound mind. This procedure is mistaken because judgments of value are deduced from existential judgments; and it is irritating because any being or object which we respect (and this applies also to religious customs) 'feels to us as if it must be *sui generis* and unique'.[4] Even a crab would be filled with a sense of personal outrage 'if it could hear us class it without ado or apology as a crustacean and thus dispose of it. "I am no such thing," it would say, "I am myself, myself alone." '[5] There is a keen sense of humour in this comparison which draws our attention to a situation almost invariably forgotten when we are filled with a holy zeal for classification and expect every pigeon-hole to contain what is written on our label and nothing else. Besides this prejudice which derives from classification, William James refutes another which derives from the origin or genesis of the fact to be studied, that is to say, the idea that very simple and elementary biological and psychological conditions dispense us from estimating the enormous repercussion which the fact itself has upon us. William James makes a determined attack on what he calls 'medical materialism',[6] the 'nothing but' mentality,[7] in which triviality and an arrogant parade of learning denote a deplorable lack of observation and critical sense. Not that William James despises the biological and psychological aspects of religion. On the contrary, the reader of his work can get the impression that James overestimates this aspect. He deliberately sets out to study the most striking and therefore unilateral manifestations of religion, in which there is a greater temptation to see abnormal and pathological conditions. The reason for this strategy is that just as in physiology

[4] *Ibid.*, p. 9.   [6] *Ibid.*, p. 13.
[5] *Ibid.*   [7] *Ibid.*, p. 12.

the functions of the various organs are revealed by the effects they produce on bodily health, so also, according to James, the tasks of the various psychological processes involved in the religious phenomenon appear more clearly: they are particularly developed and therefore cause an anomalous situation. But it would be fatal to stop short at this situation if we intend to understand their meaning, which depends on the general repercussion rather than on the origin of the anomaly. The work done and the capacity by means of which it was done is all that matters, and it does not matter very much if the one who accomplishes it is in other respects singularly deficient, or if he is eccentric or even mad in doing it. The psychiatrist Maudsley expresses this opinion which is approved by James.[8]

In the proposition of value it is not the roots that count but the result. As regards the religious fact, however, some conditions such as illness, which we ordinarily consider to be unfavourable, prepare the way for a better understanding of religious feeling than do other conditions judged to be favourable, such as an excellent state of health.

What subjective facts are to be considered properly religious? It is very hard to decide, because according to William James there are no exclusively religious facts, but all psychic facts can assume a religious tone. Excluding the external ritual manifestation of religion from his study, James intends to deal with the more clearly personal aspect and he holds that this has prevalently affective characteristics. Everything is religious to which we feel impelled to respond solemnly and gravely, in face of a primal, 'divine' reality.[9] There is a difference between moral and religious 'experience'. The former is based on an effort while the latter appears to be a gift.

Moral behaviour implies a tension in order to keep to a certain way of life, and it is accompanied by a sense of fear in face of difficulty and uncertainty. But in religious behaviour there is a need for dedication, for renunciation, a need to be led by something different from ourselves, and this is accompanied by a sense of security and serenity. The happiness which

[8] *Ibid.*, p. 19.　　　[9] *Ibid.*, p. 38.

accompanies religious experience is distinguished from other forms of happiness in ordinary life, since the latter are 'reliefs'[10] occasioned by our escape from some evil or by our having satisfied a desire, while religious happiness, which does not ignore evil, is rather an inclination to sacrifice. From the emotional point of view religious consciousness is very rich since it is able to face up to evil and overcome it.

Psychology, which confines itself to the observation of facts experienced by the subject, is unable to state whether realities of a different order correspond to these. However, psychology would not exist if those who experience psychic facts and also those who study them did not consider that they had a reality in the conscious mind. The objects of consciousness may be present to the senses or merely to our thought. In both cases they determine a decision on our part. This happens also with the religious phenomenon. There is a sense of presence, though differently felt, and there is decision, though of a different kind from decisions taken in other areas of experience.

William James outlines two different attitudes toward religious feeling, which are in a certain sense antithetic: 'healthy-mindedness' and the attitude of the 'sick soul'.[11] I am afraid that these two expressions, taken by themselves, are not sufficiently clear. Perhaps we are nearer to his idea when we describe the first attitude as carefree and optimistic and the second as melancholic and pessimistic. With some people the conviction prevails and even becomes exclusive that the world is good and that what we consider as evil can be overcome or is even non-existent. James brings together in this category some very different men, like St Francis who sings the beauties of creation, J. J. Rousseau, Diderot, B. de S. Pierre, who preach the return to nature, and Walt Whitman who repeats incessantly: 'men, life, death and all things are good'. A curious comparison, for St Francis was certainly neither blind to evil nor indifferent to suffering, but still a very meaningful one. In reality there are optimists who are so set on seeing good at all costs that the mere admission of something evil would mean

[10] *Ibid.*, p. 49.   [11] *Ibid.*, pp. 78, 127.

the collapse of their mentality. This attitude may be either
spontaneous or voluntary. In the second case it becomes
theoretical, abstract and hostile to anything that contradicts it.
It is intolerant and needs to defend itself. In its extreme consequences it even becomes cruel and absurd. The opposite to
this attitude is found in the 'sick soul', typical of persons 'who
cannot so swiftly throw off the burden of the consciousness of
evil, but are congenitally fated to suffer from its presence'.[12]
To these the optimism of the 'healthy-minded' appears blind
and superficial. On the other hand they themselves are despised
by the optimist who judges them to be ill and unfitted for life.
Which side does James take? That of the sick souls.

> It seems to me that morbid-mindedness ranges over the
> wider scale of experience and that its survey is the one that
> overlaps. The method of averting one's attention from
> evil . . . is splendid as long as it will work. . . . But it breaks
> down impotently as soon as melancholy comes; and even
> though one be quite free from melancholy one's self, there
> is no doubt that healthy-mindedness is inadequate . . .
> because the evil facts which it refuses positively to account
> for are a genuine portion of reality; and they may, after all,
> be the best key to life's significance.[13]

Actually the person who is familiar with adversity and suffers
from evil has a greater understanding for others. 'If religious
intolerance and hanging and burning could again become the
order of the day, there is little doubt that, however it may
have been in the past, the healthy-minded would at present
show themselves the less indulgent party of the two.'[14] This
statement of James is not outdated if we consider that faith in
science has more religious characteristics than may appear
and that a humanitarian ideal can be transformed into a policy
of oppression and elimination for those who do not accept it.
   The religious sense therefore presents itself not only as a
calm and spontaneous outlook on life, but in its deeper
manifestations implies a conflict between the recognition of an

---

[12] *Ibid.*, pp. 133-4.   [13] *Ibid.*, p. 163.   [14] *Ibid.*

evil and its reacceptance in a higher order. William James speaks of the 'once-born souls' and of sick souls which need to be born over again to reach that state of unification which is characteristic of religious feeling. Here there is a process of painful interior conflict which can be resolved gradually by lysis or suddenly by a crisis.

James devotes two long lectures to conversion, which presents the more extreme and dramatic aspects of religious feeling. He traces the process which leads up to conversion, its actual coming about and the subsequent process of settling down. A new orientation of all personal activity is involved.

Two lectures (XIV and XV) are also devoted to holiness, in which he recalls and comments upon many aspects of the lives of the saints. He points out a certain note of exceptionality or 'extravagance'. Are the men who follow the ordinary norms of life right, or are the saints nearer to the truth? An answer is not possible. Here we realize how complex and mysterious is the interweaving of ideals and realizations. An ideal type (knight or saint) brings with him a note of unity which is idealized and not actually available to the full. The behaviour of the saints would be the most perfect conceivable behaviour in an environment in which all were already saints, but in surroundings where saints are few and many are the opposite, this behaviour is bound to be out of place. Yet it is the saints—even though their emphasis on an ideal is one-sided—who do much more to make the world a tolerable dwelling-place than do those who present it in strictly objective and utilitarian terms. In this sense the saints constitute a genuine and creative social force.

Mysticism with its mysterious and fascinating manifestations is often discredited as a fantastic notion in opposition to facts and logic. Yet there is no people in which it fails to appear and no form of civilization, even one which has little religion, in which it does not show itself. It includes personal experiences of which the subject is unable to give a faithful verbal account but which have a cognitive content and an unrestrainable influence on behaviour. It is a field of experience quite different from the usual fields, completely new and full of charm, but only to those who enter it and not to others. At all events, mysticism is also an argument against the all-sufficiency of rational procedures.

In his lecture on *Philosophy* William James tackles the problem whether subjective experiences are based on real occurrences. He holds that affective activity and feeling prevail in the beginning and that reason is employed merely to find arguments to justify this feeling. Philosophy can do little to demonstrate the existence of God and still less to establish his attributes. James refers to the English empirical tradition and to the pragmatism of the American, C. S. Peirce, of whom, according to his biographer Perry, he gives a mistaken interpretation. The core of James' doctrine, expressed in current language, is: 'Beliefs do not, as most people would suppose, work because they are true, but are true in that they work. (James had a curious fondness for these paradoxical reversals —compare his theory that we are frightened because we run and angry because we strike).'[15]

In his concluding lecture James enumerates the characteristics of the religious sense which are based on the following beliefs: that the visible world is part of a more spiritual universe from which it draws its chief significance; that union or harmonious relations with that higher universe are our true end; that prayer or inner communion with the spirit thereof— be that spirit 'God' or 'law'—is a process wherein work is really done, and spiritual energy flows in and produces effects, psychological and material, within the phenomenal world. 'Religion includes also the psychological characteristic of a new zest which adds itself like a gift to life . . . an assurance of safety and a temper of peace. . . .'[16] James adds that in illustrating these characteristics by documents he has been 'literally bathed in sentiment',[17] and that the 'science and religions' from which the afflatus of personal sentiment is

[15] M. Knight, *William James*, Penguin Books, London, 1954, p. 50.
[16] W. James, *The Varieties of Religious Experience*, pp. 485-6.
[17] *Ibid.*, p. 486.

lacking is not an equivalent to living religion. It is true that scientific thought has 'deanthropomorphized' the imagination, substituting measures and formulae for living experience and for this reason it gives a picture of the world which is foreign and unreal. But 'as soon as we deal with private and personal phenomena as such, we deal with realities in the completest sense of the term. The cosmic objects, so far as the experience yields them, are but ideal pictures of something whose existence we do not inwardly possess but only point at outwardly, while the inner state is our very experience itself.'[18]

Therefore

it is absurd for science to say that the egotistic elements should be suppressed. The axis of reality runs solely through the egotistic places—they are strung upon it like so many beads.[19] To describe the world with all the various feelings of the individual pinch of destiny, all the various spiritual attitudes, left out of the description . . . would be something like offering a printed bill of fare as the equivalent for a solid meal.[20]

It is only by acknowledging religious questions as genuine that we can understand them. They are not the survival of a primitive mentality driven into the background by scientific thought. James goes on to say that religious activity, because of its extraordinary influence on action and endurance, must be classed among the most important biological functions of mankind. Apart from purely objective utility, we must ask ourselves whether, under all the discrepancies of the creeds, there is not a common nucleus to which they bear unanimous testimony. James answers in the affirmative: all religions have characteristics in common. First of all there is an uneasiness, 'a sense that there is something wrong about us as we naturally stand',[21] and in the second place a solution, a sense that we are saved from the wrongness by having recourse to higher powers. But man 'becomes conscious that this higher part is conterminous

[18] *Ibid.*, p. 499.   [20] *Ibid.*, p. 500.
[19] *Ibid.*, p. 499.   [21] *Ibid.*, p. 508.

and continuous with a *more* of the same quality, which is operative in the universe outside of him, and which he can keep in working touch with, and in a fashion get on board of, and save himself when all his lower being has gone to pieces in the wreck'.[22] But is this *more* of the same quality merely our own notion or does it really exist? If so, in what form does it exist? Does it act and what is the possibility of union with it? In answering these questions, all the divergencies between the various religions come to light. James therefore prefers to deal with what they have in common rather than with what distinguishes them. He asserts that 'the *subconscious self* is nowadays a well-accredited psychological entity',[23] referring to an essay by Myers in 1892 where it is written that 'Each of us is in reality an abiding psychical entity far more extensive than he knows—an individuality which can never express itself completely through any corporeal manifestation. The Self manifests through the organism; but there is always some part of the Self unmanifested; and always, as it seems, some power of organic expression in abeyance or reserve.'[24] It is in this subconscious self that contact takes place between the conscious self and that *more* with which we feel ourselves connected in religious experience. The expression of these over-beliefs is very varied. But 'confining ourselves to what is common and generic, we have *in the fact that the conscious person is continuous with a wider self through which saving experiences come*, a positive content of religious experience which, it seems to me, *is literally and objectively true as far as it goes*'.[25]

Christians, says James, indicate this *more* by the name of God; God is real because he produces real effects. The subconscious is a way which opens up and opens us up to different worlds.

---

[22] *Ibid.*
[23] *Ibid.*, p. 511.
[24] F. Myers, in *Proceedings of the Society for Psychical Research*, vol. VII, p. 305, quoted in James, *op. cit.*, p. 512.
[25] *Ibid.*, p. 515.

Sigmund Freud: the 'neurosis of humanity'

Although Sigmund Freud liked to call himself an atheist, he was interested in the question of religion and his interest was so recurrent and insistent in the various periods of his activity that it cannot be considered as just marginal or devoid of a considerably personal note. His last book, the English translation of which he awaited anxiously and had the satisfaction of seeing published before he died, deals with religion. There are four essays in which he deals *ex professo* with the religious problem: *Obsessive Acts and Religious Practice* (1907); *Totem and Taboo* (1912-13); *The Future of an Illusion* (1927); *Moses and Monotheism* (1938).[26] But important references to religious problems are also to be found in *Group Psychology and the Analysis of the Ego* (1921), *Civilization and its Discontents* (1930), as also in *The Moses of Michelangelo* (1914).[27]

In his study of obsessive acts and religious practices Freud declares that he is not the first person to have been struck by the resemblance between them. The obsessive neurotic carries out with meticulous exactness a series of acts which are apparently futile and altogether meaningless, but which he cannot neglect without becoming a prey to anguish. From slight manifestations, such as an excessive attention to the arrangement of things in his room before he goes to bed, he passes on, in the more serious forms, to a succession of inconsistent and apparently absurd acts of which the meaning and the cause can only be discovered by very accurate investigation.

[26] Dates in the text refer to the original German editions. The original titles are: *Zwangshandlungen und Religionsübungen, Zeitschrift für Religionspsychologie*; *Totem und Tabu*; *Die Zukunft einer Illusion*; *Der Mann Moses und die Monotheistische Religion*. All quotations from the writings of Sigmund Freud in the present work are taken from The Standard Edition of *The Complete Psychological Works of Sigmund Freud*, Hogarth Press, London, in 24 volumes, 1953-. *Totem and Taboo* is also available in English as a paperback (Routledge, London, 1950).

[27] S. Freud, *Massenpsychologie und Ich-Analyse*; *Das Unbehangen in der Kultur*; *Der Moses der Michelangelo*.

Usually these acts are repeated in private. Religious ceremonial also consists in a succession of gestures to be performed
punctually and where one is safe from all external disturbance,
and transgression produces a sense of guilt. The religious
ceremonial is distinguished by the fact that it is performed in
public, and by a stereotyped succession of actions which one
is often unable to explain, but which are justified as symbols.
Notwithstanding this fact, the link between obsessive actions
and ceremonial is revealed by psychoanalytical methods which
show how both serve important interests of the personality
and express events or thoughts highly charged with emotion.
Four aspects appear to be common to obsessive acts and ceremonial. 1) The gestures are performed without knowledge of
their meaning and are justified by a fictitious explanation.
2) There is a sense of guilt involving the idea of chastisement,
an expectant anxiety and a defensive attitude. 3) The suspen-
sion of an infantile instinctual impulse, which remains active in
the unconscious, determines a specific scrupulosity, which
charges the action with anguish. Hence the inner conflict
cannot be resolved and the obsessive actions are replaced by
prohibitions in great number. 4) Finally, there is a tendency to
arrive at a compromise between need and action and to turn
what is important and essential into an absolutely secondary
detail. 'An obsessive neurosis,' says Freud, 'presents a travesty,
half comic and half tragic, of a private religion.'[28] He concludes that 'in view of these similarities and analogies one
might venture to regard obsessional neurosis as a pathological
counterpart of the formation of a religion, and to describe that
neurosis as an individual religiosity and religion as a universal
obsessional neurosis'.[29] For my own part I should like to point
out that these definitions are based on a particular religious
act (ceremonial) which is taken to be the complete expression
of religion. After a mainly formal comparison with obsessional
neurosis, they conclude with a formulation of principle in

[28] S. Freud, *Obsessive Acts and Religious Practice*, in Standard Ed.,
vol. IX, p. 119.
[29] *Ibid.*, pp. 126-7.

psychopathological terms. But this foundation seems too weak to support a building of such large dimensions.

In *Totem and Taboo*, on the basis of the programme indicated in the subtitle: 'Some Points of Agreement between the Mental Life of Savages and Neurotics', Freud seeks in the history of mankind the situation which gave rise to universal obsessional neurosis, or religion, in the same manner in which he sought the cause of individual neurosis in the precocious impressions of infancy. He accepts Darwin's hypothesis that primitive men lived in small hordes, each of which was subject to the tyranny of the eldest male member, and he also accepts Atkinson's idea that this patriarchal regime ended in the revolt of the sons who killed the father and ate him. Freud follows the totem theory of Robertson-Smith. The brothers, victorious over their father, renounced the women on whose account they had killed their father. They then imposed exogamy and families were subsequently organized according to matriarchal law. But to the sons the father was still an object of jealousy (for possession of the mother), and also an object of fear. As a social convention an animal was chosen to symbolize the father. This was the totem, the protecting spirit which was not to be disturbed or killed. But once a year one of these animals was slain and eaten in common in a celebration in which all were obliged to take part since it signified liberation from paternal tyranny and the beginning of a new moral and social order. According to Freud, religious practices go back to this initial situation in the history of mankind, just as obsessional neurosis goes back to emotional traumas in early childhood. Freud himself recognized that the historical documentation on which he built had been the subject of much argument and had even been contradicted. He pleaded that he was not an ethnographer but a psychoanalyst who had the right to draw from ethnographical data what he needed for his psycho-analytical work. This is a strange excuse, not infrequently used by Freud in other circumstances. *Totem and Taboo*, therefore, was to be considered a kind of historical parable which could have been true, to illustrate the formation of the superego which Freud found in the individual. The force of the parable was to survive even though its historicity was shown to be doubtful.

In going back to the sources of things, Freud also intended to be a builder. He showed himself in this light in his book *The Future of an Illusion*, in which he envisaged the possibility of a religion no longer founded on obscure and obsessive impulses but on scientifically verified convictions. Religion was defined as 'illusion'. Error could be contradicted by proof. For example, Aristotle's statement that worms are born of dung was an error. Illusion, on the other hand (such as Christopher Columbus' conviction that he had found a new route to India), springs from intense desire (and from this point of view is close to delirium). It is a more or less valid satisfaction of the desire itself and for this reason can neither be proved nor disproved. Since the scientist must also aim at happiness and well-being for himself and for others, he must point to a religion which frees men from the burden of ritual prescriptions. It is significant that throughout the entire book there is a spirit of revolt, a yearning for freedom, and an unconditional trust in science which increases our mastery over the world and must regulate our lives. 'Science has shown us by numerous and significant triumphs that it is no illusion.' Freud did not confine himself therefore to emptying religion of its content by demonstrating its instinctual origin and considering it an obstacle to progress and freedom. He went on to prophesy a scientific religion which would set men free from the yoke of fears and prescriptions and which would not be a mere illusory gratification of desires but a real conquest of happiness.

It is evident from his last book *Moses and Monotheism* that the religious problem continued to torment Freud until his death. He himself related the vicissitudes of this work which he had several times thought of publishing but which he only decided late in life to present to the public. Starting from a conjecture of Sellin, he maintains that Moses was not a Jew by birth, but an Egyptian, unable to speak Hebrew, a priest of the most strictly monotheistic form of sun cult. Moses became the leader of the Jews, imposed strict monotheism upon them and convinced them of God's special assistance. But the burden of his law was a heavy one and he was assassinated in the desert by the Jews. After his death and after a period of 'latency' his image returned and imposed itself on the Jews as the representation of God himself; Moses and monotheism were but one thing. From the assassination of Moses the monotheistic religion of the Jews derived not only a spiritual elevation but a rigidity of ritual observance which has characteristics in common with obsessional neurosis. This strange book—strange because of Freud's hesitation and tenacity in regard to its publication and also because of the historical untenableness of its suppositions—aroused indignant protests not only from Christians but also from Jews, who described it as 'the voice of one of the most fanatical Christians in his hatred of Israel, and not the voice of a Freud who hated and despised such fanaticism with all his heart and strength'.[30] When a Jewish scholar, A. S. Yahuda, visited Freud in 1938 and reminded him that Sellin himself had withdrawn his interpretation of Moses, Freud shrugged his shoulders and replied: 'It might be true all the same',[31] just as had happened in the case of *Totem and Taboo*.

Moreover, Freud himself acknowledged his uncertainty in regard to the facts and spoke initially of his *Moses* as a 'historical tale'. The outstanding fact, though, is that the supposition of Moses' assassination enabled him to create a parallel, a 'homology' (to borrow a term from comparative anatomy) between the origin of individual neurosis and the origin of neurosis in humanity, that is, religion, even in the noble and exalted form it assumed in the Jewish people. Parricide is at the root of both. Moral conscience and religious feeling are born of the sense of guilt. Thus with his *Moses* Freud put the finishing touches to his doctrinal conception, with a theme which had already been outlined forty years

[30] E. Jones, *Sigmund Freud: Life and Work*, Hogarth Press, London, 1957, vol. III, p. 396.
[31] *Ibid.*, p. 400.

earlier, when he wrote in 1904: 'A great part of the mythological view of the world which reaches far into the most modern religions, is nothing other than psychological processes projected into the outer world.'[32] In 1910, in his study of Leonardo, he wrote: 'Psychoanalysis has made us aware of the intimate connection between the father-complex and the belief in God, and has taught us that the personal God is psychologically nothing other than a magnified father; it shows us every day how young people can lose their religious faith as soon as the father's authority collapses. We thus recognize the root of religious need as lying in the parental complex.'[33] That his attitude towards religion remained unchanged to the end of his life is obvious from the 'ironical modesty', as Bally calls it, with which Freud defended himself against a remark of L. Binswanger, in a letter of 1936:

> Naturally I still don't believe you. I have always dwelt only in the ground-floor and basement of the building. You assert that when one changes one's viewpoint, one can also see upper stories in which such distinguished guests as religion, art, etc. reside. You are not the only one in that; most cultivated types of *homo natura* think the same. In that you are the conservative, I am the revolutionary. Had I only another life of work in front of me, I should dare to offer even those highly-born people a home in my lowly dwelling. I have already found one for religion after I came across the category 'neurosis of mankind'.[34]

C. G. Jung: the divine 'imprint'

Carl Gustav Jung approached Freud and became his admiring and admired disciple when he had already carried out personal

[32] S. Freud, *The Psychopathology of Everyday Life*, quoted in Jones, *op. cit.*, p. 578.

[33] Quoted in Jones, *op. cit.*, p. 379.

[34] Quoted in Jones, *op. cit.*, p. 218. Also cited in G. Bally, *Einführung in die Psychologie Sigmund Freuds*, Hamburg, 1961, p. 14.

research on 'so-called occult phenomena', 'dementia praecox' and 'free associations'. His research in the field of 'free associations' is particularly important since it suggested the term 'affective complex' to denote certain states of mind which determine a noteworthy delay in responses in free associations without the subject being able to account for the phenomenon. Jung met Freud personally for the first time in 1906. He became Freud's friend and collaborator and accepted his fundamental ideas and methods, but at the same time he maintained his independent judgment. This ripened into a theory of his own which he set forth in his book *Psychology of the Unconscious* in 1912,[35] and which Freud judged to be incompatible with his own doctrine. Jung's final separation from Freud dates from this time. But what concerns us here is to follow up Jung's ideas on religious feeling. In a pamphlet published in 1909, entitled *The Significance of the Father in the Destiny of the Individual*,[36] Jung fully accepts Freud's point of view as regards the origin of religious feeling.

What we see enacted on the stage of world history happens also in the individual. The child is guided by the power of the parents as by a higher destiny. But as he grows up, the struggle between his infantile attitude and his increasing consciousness begins. The parental influence, dating from the early infantile period, is repressed and sinks into the unconscious, but is not eliminated; by invisible threads it directs the apparently individual workings of the maturing mind. Like everything that has fallen into the unconscious, the infantile situation still sends up dim, premonitory feel-

[35] C. G. Jung, *Wandlungen und Symbole der Libido*, Vienna, 1912, first published in English under the title *Psychology of the Unconscious* in 1917 and republished in 1952. It appears under the title *Symbols of Transformation* in the *Collected Works of C. G. Jung*, Pantheon Books, New York, vol. V. Unless otherwise stated, all quotations from the writings of C. G. Jung in the present work are taken from the above edition of his *Collected Works*.
[36] C. G. Jung, 'Die Bedeutung des Vaters für die Schicksal der Einselnen' in *Jahrbuch für Psychan. und Psychopath. Forschungen*, 1912, republished in Zurich, 1949. In *Collected Works*, vol. IV, pp. 301 ff.

ings, feelings of being secretly guided by otherworldly influences. . . . These are the roots of the first religious sublimations. In the place of the father with his constellating virtues and faults there appears on the one hand an altogether sublime deity and on the other hand the devil.

In a new edition of this work in 1949 Jung expressed himself as follows:

Freud was of the opinion that all 'divine' figures have their roots in the father-image. It can hardly be denied that they do derive from this image, but what we are to say about the father-image itself is another matter. For the parental image is possessed of a quite extraordinary power; it influences the psychic life of the child so enormously that we must ask ourselves whether we may attribute such magical power to an ordinary human being at all. Obviously he possesses it, but we are bound to ask whether it is really his property. Man 'possesses' many things which he has never acquired but has inherited from his ancestors. He is not born as a *tabula rasa*, he is merely born unconscious.

In the first of these passages, written when he gravitated in Freud's orbit, Jung accepts the doctrine 1) that religious feeling is the projection of the parental image, 2) that it is the sublimation of the affective tie repressed in the unconscious which binds the child to his parents, 3) that what takes place in the development of the individual is repeated in the history of mankind. In the second passage, written many years after his separation from Freud, Jung does not retract the statements already made but prefers to ask a question: what is the exact relationship between representations of the divinity and the father-image? And the question is followed by two statements: 1) the parent-image has an extraordinary power; 2) man possesses many things he has inherited from his ancestors. Between these two positions we find the entire evolution of Jung's doctrine.

In the volume *Psychology of the Unconscious* Jung breaks

away from the biologico-sexual conception of the libido to which Freud remained anchored all the time. He extends the symbolical interpretation, which was to be stressed more and more in his subsequent writings, to the point of presenting libido as a primordial energy which is expressed not only in sexuality but in all man's psychic manifestations. Hence, while for Freud every moral, aesthetic and religious sublimation is sexuality in disguise, for Jung it is an original, genuine and separate manifestation, since for him libido is pure energy without any biological connotation and it serves all sorts of different activities. The question then arises as to how this energy is channelled and guided. In order to form an image of his parents the child needs sensory stimulations which come to him from them. But the image is not a mere objective impression: it involves a large affective content which can only be acquired in actual experience: the image represents the parents as the child has seen and heard them. The child projects his experience, the image, upon his parents and also upon other people, without being aware of the duality of factors (objective and subjective) which have played a part in forming the image itself. In the course of analysis Jung noticed that he was constantly confronted by images which could not be restricted to personal situations and he also observed the recurrence of identical operative patterns in dreams, symbolic figures and myths, and all this in persons pertaining to quite different civilizations and social conditions.

For example, the course of the sun and the phases of the moon express the myth of periodicity and renewal. It could be objected that this myth is merely an ingenuous attempt to explain the natural facts. It is true that without the sun there would be no solar myth, but it is also true that without the interpretative contribution there would be no myth either. There must therefore be a constant psychic orientation, a regulation of energy according to a single plan, a definite primordial regulator, an archetype which is imprinted on the representations to which it gives a symbolic vesture. Thus the father considered objectively does not suffice to explain the father-image. Far more important is the unconscious pattern which constitutes him as father by giving him a symbolical significance which is not identical with that of the mere objective sensory datum. Here we are in the presence of the archetype.

> Behind submerged 'memories' of events in the individual's lifetime lies a racial heritage manifested in archetypal figures. Behind the particularized physical mother's womb lies the archetypal womb of the great Mother of all living; behind the physical father the archetypal Father, behind the child the *puer aeternus*; behind the particular manifestation of the procreative sexual libido lies the universal creative and re-creative Spirit. The second of all these pairs appears, not as a phantasy-substitute for the first; but rather does the first appear as a particular manifestation and symbol of the second. The way is now open to us, for instance, no longer to conceive God as a substitute for the physical father, but rather the physical father as the infant's first substitute for God, the genetically prior bearer of the image of the All-Father. God is less a Big Father than the physical father a little god.

This is how Jung's idea is summarized by his pupil, Father V. White.[37] It should be noted that while this transition from symbol to myth and archetype can appear hazardous and fantastic, it is fundamentally consistent with Freud's outlook. He was so anxious to go back up the river of psychic activity to its sources that he skipped the dry patches where, in his opinion, the water runs beneath the river bed. If a patient relates a fact of his early childhood which did not take place or if a historian questions the existence of the primitive horde and primitive parricide, the psychoanalyst confronted by the 'psychological reality' of trauma and filial aggression must look for a cause, and the primitive cause indicated 'could be the true one'. Jung goes beyond the biological fact to grasp its

[37] V. White, *God and the Unconscious*, Regnery, Chicago, 1954, pp. 56-7. Also available as a Fontana paperback.

meaning and finds this in symbol, myth and archetype. He too is in search of the sources of psychic activity and pursues this search on a similar basis to that of Freud.

The fact that the archetype is expressed in apparently varied but substantially identical forms both in the life of the individual and in the history of mankind leads Jung to assert the existence of a collective unconscious in which the archetypes are the energetic dominants. These influence the individual unconscious. The archetype is therefore inherited, it is pre-existent to the actual experience which it moulds and upon which it imposes itself inevitably and with irrepressible force; it is the organ of the psychic organism, as indispensable for the functioning of the latter as is a physical organ for the functioning of the biological organism. Like the physical organ it is the product of a history which has gone on since the dawn of life. When the archetypal connection between collective unconscious and individual unconscious is wanting, the sources of life are cut off and the result is chaos. Neurosis and psychosis are desperate and futile efforts to restore the order which has broken down. In his book *Psychology of the Unconscious* Jung starts from the autobiographical account of a schizophrenic patient which appeared in a French review under the pseudonym of Miss Miller, in order to point out how inconsistent phantasies take on form and order when compared with certain myths; but the meaning of these has been lost for the mental patient who finds himself alone and oppressed in a world turned upside down. The patient must rebuild for himself a conception of the world, a *Weltanschauung*, and find again a meaning for life. The religious myth, according to Jung, despite the deceptiveness of symbols (he is alluding here to the infantile attachment to the form of the symbol which must be overcome by understanding its meaning), 'is one of man's greatest and most significant achievements, giving him the security and inner strength not to be crushed by the monstrousness of the universe'. Jung believes that faith must be overcome by understanding. We should then keep the beauty of the symbol, but we should be free from the depressing effect of subjection to faith. This, according to Jung, should be the psychoanalytical treatment for faith and for lack of faith. The word 'faith' in this context, as far as we can see, indicates blind and constraining acceptance. Jung, like Freud, feels the need of liberation, by understanding, however, and not by negation. Jung was obliged later on to find a solution to this problem: if religion is not an epiphenomenon but a necessary and inevitable expression of psychic dynamism and if, on the other hand, the existence of a personal God is inadmissible on strictly psychological grounds, how is it to be conceived and how is it to be? The answer is that religion is an irreducible psychic process which must however lead to moral autonomy. His study of religious myths leads Jung to believe that they have a common background and that institutional religions are symbolism arranged as a system. But this leads to a progressive impoverishment of religious experience and causes formalism to prevail over what is genuine. On the other hand, in the development of the individual there is a liberation from the projection of the paternal archetye of the real father on to an entity outside the human world. Here we have the psychological reason (says Jung) why men have always needed demons and cannot live without gods. The idea of God is a psychological function of an irrational nature—which has nothing whatever to do with the question of God's existence. The human intellect can never answer this question, still less give any proof of God. Moreover, such proof is superfluous, for the idea of an all-powerful divine Being is present everywhere, unconsciously if not consciously, because it is an archetype.[38] Jung therefore remained decidedly agnostic for a long time even after his separation from Freud, although he insisted on asserting that 'religion is psychologically true' in his writings up to 1937. In that year, in three lectures delivered at Yale University and published under the title *Psychology and Religion*,[39] some developments in his thought make their appearance. Religion

[38] C. G. Jung, *Collected Works*, vol. VII, p. 70.
[39] C. G. Jung, *Psychology and Religion, Collected Works*, vol. XI, p. 8.

is defined as a mental attitude in which there is 'a careful consideration and observation of certain dynamic factors that are conceived as "powers", spirits, daemons, gods, laws, ideas, ideals or whatever name man has given such factors in his world as he has found powerful, dangerous or helpful enough to be taken into careful consideration, or grand, beautiful and meaningful enough to be devoutly worshipped and loved'. It can be seen that Jung, although holding fast to his position, recognizes that the operative characteristics of the archetypes are those described by Rudolf Otto in his study of the phenomenology of the 'sacred', as 'momenta' of the *numinosum*: the feeling of dependence, of majesty, of mystery, of attraction, of increased energy. Personal experience therefore attributes an external cause to the sense of the sacred. The conscious mind feels passive; it experiences the action of the sacred more than it produces it. For this reason Jung defines religion as 'the attitude peculiar to a consciousness which has experience of the *numinosum*' and in order not to stray from the psychological field, he describes this action upon consciousness, this prompting—which for him is almost merged in the concept of God in current language—by the name of 'the Self', indicating by this term the total ego, the absolute centre of the ego and the unconscious which surpasses them, includes them and sustains them. Hence Jung speaks of religious experience as a 'state of grace'. 'It matters little,' he says, 'what the world thinks of religious experience. Anyone who has had it possesses an inestimable treasure and a wellspring which gives an elevated meaning to life.' We may remark how these words re-echo a motif frequently found in William James.

Jung continued to be keenly interested in religious symbolism not so much for strictly religious reasons as for the fruitfulness of its results. While Freud stops at consideration of the symbol as the libido in disguise, Jung maintains that it expresses the entire psychic dynamism. Some drawings made by a female patient which were startlingly similar to symbols used by alchemists—although the patient knew nothing of alchemy—induced Jung to study the question more deeply in his work

Psychology and Alchemy in 1944[40] and to state his position with reference to alchemical symbols and religious symbols. He repeats that as a scientist and psychologist he can only speak of the representation of God, the symbolism of which reveals more of the man who speaks than of the God of whom he speaks. This occurs also in the case of alchemical symbols. Both are archetypal projections. In this book we find a passage which is now famous, in which the characteristics of religious activity are thrown into bold relief, but with greater understanding of what the believer means when he speaks of God.

'Accordingly when I say as a psychologist that God is an archetype,' he writes,

I mean by that the 'type' in the psyche. The word 'type' is, as we know, derived from τύπος, 'blow' or 'imprint'; thus an archetype presupposes an imprinter. . . . The competence of psychology as an empirical science only goes so far as to establish on the basis of comparative research, whether for instance the imprint found in the psyche can or not reasonably be termed a 'God-image'. Nothing positive or negative has thus been asserted about the possible existence of God.[41]

Then he adds:

The religious point of view, understandably enough, puts the accent on the imprinter, whereas scientific psychology emphasizes the 'typos', the imprint—the only thing it can understand. The religious point of view understands the imprinter as the working of an imprinter; the scientific point of view understands it as the symbol of an unknown and incomprehensible content. Since the 'typos' is less definite and more variegated than any of the figures postulated by religion, psychology is compelled by its empirical material to express the 'typos' by means of a terminology not bound by time, place or milieu. . . . For this reason I have found myself obliged to give the corresponding archetype the psychological name of the 'Self'.[42]

[40] C. G. Jung, *Psychology and Alchemy, Collected Works,* vol. XII.
[41] *Ibid.,* p. 12.   [42] *Ibid.,* pp. 17-18.

Obviously Jung's constant endeavour is to keep the study field of the psychologist separate from the affirmations of the religious man, even if this involves laborious explanation and a complicated terminology. We find in him the recurring theme that psychology can make no religious statements even though in fact it has often claimed the power to do so. We also find in him the admission that religious facts can be validly explored by methods other than those of psychology. Actually it is not easy to distinguish the psychologist from the theologian in Jung himself.

Jung, like Freud, chose a biblical subject for one of his last books, *Answer to Job*.[43] As in the case of Freud's *Moses*, biblical scholars raise serious objections to the validity of the ideas expressed in the book. Actually it is a strange type of book which can only be justified by the fact that it expresses the subjective reaction of its author. In Jung's interpretation of the Book of Job God appears as an oriental despot puffed up with his own omnipotence and intentionally blind to the injustices he inflicts on the just man, Job. Job, on the other hand, is the wise man who knows that in God omnipotence must go hand in hand with wisdom and justice and is certain that God will vindicate him. But God, instead of listening to Job's pleadings, overwhelms him by a display of his omnipotence which allows of no question. Job bows down and is silent.

The man Job shows himself to be morally superior to God. It may be that Yahweh has now seen his own weaknesses, that is, the poor content of the idea of God which has prevailed up to now. This idea must be changed: 'Yahweh must become man precisely because he has done man a wrong.'[44] 'This time it is not the world that is to be changed; rather it is God who intends to change his own nature.'[45] The answer to Job is this: the Incarnation, God's becoming man, with men becoming

[43] C. G. Jung, *Answer to Job*, Routledge and Kegan Paul, London, 1954.
[44] *Ibid.*, p. 69.
[45] *Ibid.*, p. 56.

aware of the depths of God. This incarnation is not, however, fulfilled in the human life of Christ, for Christ 'was not an empirical human being at all' but rather a demigod, as far as his office of mediator appears in his acceptance of death where 'God has experience of mortal being and undergoes what he caused his faithful servant Job to suffer'. There is a further incarnation in the descent of the Holy Spirit, by which 'God is generated in created men', and which reaches its summit in the apocalyptic vision of the Woman who gives birth to a divine son: 'the female prototype in contrast to the male prototype'. The dogma of the Assumption, recently defined by the Catholic Church, is judged by Jung to be the most important religious event since the Reformation, and Mary is the symbol of the unification of all opposites in God: the masculine and feminine components, divine and human, conscious and unconscious. Thus the real answer to Job's questioning is effected in history. This strange interpretation becomes more comprehensible when we take into account that here also Jung is referring not to a change in God understood as an objective reality, but to the change in the conception of God taking place in the Jewish-Christian tradition. But even from this point of view Jung leaves us with the impression that he is voicing a personal interpretation based on a pre-existent idea. We encounter the preponderance of a mentality and a method over historical objectivity and religious experience itself.

In attempting to explain the recurrence of particular states of mind and their repercussion which is often disproportionate to the actually identifiable cause, depth psychology has gone back over the history of mankind to localize the critical point at which religious behaviour was established. Freud has recourse to parricide and totemism; Jung to the archetypes. This implies a shift from individual psychology to social psychology, from the study of what can be observed in the individual to what is apparent in a group: and consequently succumbing to the temptation to interpret what is individual in terms of what is collective. This is particularly evident in Jung (collective unconscious); but neither is it far from Freud's mentality. In his last book *Moses and Monotheism* the following expressions are to be found:

It is not easy for us to carry over the concepts of individual psychology into group psychology; and I do not think we gain anything by introducing the concept of a 'collective' unconscious. The content of the unconscious, indeed, is in any case a collective, universal property of mankind. For the moment, then, we will make shift with the use of analogies. The processes in the life of peoples which we are studying here are very similar to those familiar to us in psychopathology but nevertheless not quite the same. We must finally make up our minds to adopt the hypothesis that the psychical precipitates of the primaeval period became inherited property which, in each fresh generation, called not for acquisition but only for awakening. In this we have in mind the example of what is certainly the 'innate' symbolism which derives from the period of the development of speech, which is familiar to children without their being instructed, and which is the same among all peoples despite their different languages.[46]

Freud expresses doubts as to the utility of the path taken by Jung and he confirms his own attachment to psychopathology. But fundamentally he seems to be merely re-echoing what has been said by Jung. It is not surprising, then, that with the very rapid progress made in social psychology in the last twenty years and with the repercussion of psychoanalytical interpretations, a psychological outlook has developed which stresses the study of social behaviour as an essential condition and even as a creative and normative factor of individual behaviour.

W. Wundt and E. Durkheim: the defence and apotheosis of society

Since religion finds both individual and collective expressions, it has to be considered from the latter point of view also. This

[46] S. Freud, *Moses and Monotheism, Standard Ed.*, vol. XXIII, p. 132.

is not an absolutely new idea. Although it may appear that psychology developed primarily as the study of the individual on his own and subsequently of the individual in society, it was evident from the beginning that the two kinds of study could not be conducted separately. A witness to this fact is the founder of modern psychology, William Wundt, who as far back as 1862 divided psychology into two branches, physiological psychology and the psychology of peoples, and proposed to divide his scientific activity between the two. The composition of his ten volumes *The Psychology of Peoples*, undertaken after his works on physiological psychology, engaged him until his death.

According to Wundt there is no discontinuity between the two fields of psychological study notwithstanding his assertion that physiological psychology in the laboratory is absolutely inadequate for the study of complex processes such as thought which belong to the field of the psychology of peoples, where psychic processes inaccessible to experimental investigation are activated. The elementary processes of sensations are grouped to form associations, but this synthesis comes about in the manner in which a sensation is incorporated into the 'apperceptive mass' (Herbart), that is to say, the mass of associations already acquired which are to a great extent the product of the culture in which a person lives. The 'apperceptive mass' includes the language, habits and ideas of the 'people's psyche', or *Volkseele*. Wundt, according to G. W. Allport, would have been very much at home in modern discussions on 'social perception'.[47] As regards the development of religion, Wundt has a theory of his own connected with the animism of Tylor, and which attaches great importance to the personification of nature. Primitive men had no belief either in God or in many gods, but they believed in 'demons' (and by this expression he means spiritual agents of any kind, without a definite formulation). They felt the need to defend themselves against harm

[47] G. W. Allport, 'The Historical Background of Modern Social Psychology' in Lindzey, *Handbook of Social Psychology*, Addison-Wesley, London, 1959, pp. 3 ff.

which they feared from the souls of the dead and from the influences of the living. The primitive form of prayer is conjuration, and defensive magic is in the forefront. This first form of animism, devoid of belief in personal deities and devoid of worship, therefore lacks religious content. Animism was followed by animalism (or animal worship) of which totemism (worship of the animal ancestor) is the earliest manifestation. With totemism are linked prohibitions, taboos; and from the totem is derived the belief in demons (the more definite form) and in gods. Simultaneously men arrived at active magic in order to influence the gods in their favour. The 'civilizing heroes' who helped the people in difficulty or introduced new arms or utensils, or governed wisely, were transformed into gods: the idea of God originated in that of the civilizing hero. Freud also has recourse to this type of conception of primitive religion, although he interprets it with undeniable if questionable ingenuity.

Emile Durkheim, the founder of the French sociological school, exercised a stronger influence than Wundt on social psychology, although he was not strictly a psychologist. Durkheim established a clear distinction between physiological, psychic and social activity. He stressed the irreducibility of conscious thought to the functioning of the nervous system: 'this can at most explain the elementary sensations, but how can it be capable of explaining associations and thought which are regulated by the principle of similarity when there is no muscular mechanism to produce this similarity?' On the other hand individual psychic activity is not sufficient to explain social activities which surpass what the individual can give and which impose themselves on him: 'just as it is impossible to specify the contribution of each cerebral cell to an image, so too it is impossible to specify the contribution of an individual to the collective performance'.[48] Man has two types of consciousness, a consciousness of private experience and a consciousness of the experiences attributed to the social

[48] E. Durkheim, 'Représentations individuelles et représentations collectives' in *Revue de Métaphysique*, 1898.

grouping of men. This grouping produces thoughts, customs and habits which are external to and independent of ourselves, but which nevertheless constrain us and oblige us to cooperate. Religion is precisely a collective performance upon which the individual is dependent and according to Durkheim it constitutes the axis of society. He also considered the problem of origins to be fundamental and he explained it on the basis of evolutionary principles: primitive societies lend themselves more readily to the study of the religious phenomenon since they present it to us in less complex terms and reveal its various developmental stages.

This is the epistemological criterion of Durkheim's great work *The Elementary Forms of Religious Life* which carries a significant subtitle: 'Totemism in Australia'.[49] Totemism is considered to be the most archaic form of religion because the social organization of the early Australians, based on the clan, is the most primitive and the simplest known to us. The family is derived from the clan. Every totemist population is divided into different clans and all members of a clan consider themselves related as they believe they are descendants of the same ancestor (an animal of which the clan bears the name). Kinship does not therefore derive from consanguinity but from the clan's magic relationship with a certain species of animal. Although totemism seems to consist in the worship of a single animal or even of an object, 'what we find at the origin and basis of religious thought are not determined and distinct objects and beings possessing a sacred character of themselves; they are indefinite powers, anonymous forces, more or less numerous in different societies, and sometimes even reduced to a unity'.[50] But totemism is far from possessing the idea of God as supreme being and has merely a concept of impersonal powers very similar to those 'physical forces whose manifestations the sciences of nature study'.[51] How is it possible to bridge the enormous gap between a harmless animal which constitutes

---

[49] E. Durkheim, *The Elementary Forms of Religious Life*, Allen and Unwin, London, 1915.
[50] *Ibid.*, p. 200.   [51] *Ibid.*, p. 200.

the totem and the religious forces which are so strong and binding in their action upon individuals?

> But how has this apotheosis been possible? . . . to its members society is what a god is to his worshippers. In fact, a god is, first of all, a being whom men think of as superior to themselves, and upon whom they feel that they depend. . . . Now society also gives us the sensation of a perpetual dependence . . . it demands that, forgetful of our own interests, we make ourselves its servitors, and it submits to us every sort of inconvenience, privation and sacrifice, without which such life would be impossible.[52]

A god is not only an authority to which we are subordinate but also a power from which our own strength is derived. One who has been obedient to his god is convinced that the god is on his side and so he faces the world with confidence and redoubled energy. Social activity makes the same claims on us: not only does it call for sacrifices, privations and efforts on our part . . . but it permeates us and organizes itself within us, becoming an integral part of our being, raising it up and making it greater. 'Religion,' concludes Durkheim, 'is society transfigured and symbolically conceived', and it is true and lasting like society. 'Hence, in substance, there are no false religions. All are true in their own way since all of them reflect, although in different ways, different conditions of human existence.' As is obvious, Durkheim's formulation of the principle of the creative and normative fuction of society in the sphere of religion could not be more categorical.

Among the interpretations of religion, the three which we have outlined here (William James' theory, depth psychology and sociology) are the most important and they indicate various and partially complementary ways of studying the phenomenon of religion. In the wake of William James especially, whose interpretation is broader and more in keeping with the complexity of psychological life, a number of other authors have

[52] *Ibid.*, pp. 206-7.

dealt with the question of religion as a whole, though they bear in mind both the valuable and the defective contributions of other schools of thought. Among these are J. B. Pratt, R. H. Thouless, P. E. Johnson, G. W. Allport, L. W. Grensted and W. H. Clark. Allport's study is particularly effective and stimulating. Our task would be too complicated if we were to examine all these authors for the purpose of obtaining a general view of the study which modern psychology has made of religion. Besides it would tend to obstruct our view rather than clarify it.

It will perhaps be more useful to say something about approaches to the religious problem made in terms of the principles of the various schools of psychology which have an undeniable influence on the methods and mentality of psychologists today.

Functionalism, Behaviourism, and Gestalt Psychology: learning theories and 'requiredness'

In 1896 John Dewey severely criticized the psychological 'atomism' which was in great favour at the time. He declared that neither stimuli nor combined stimuli, nor individual nor combined reflexes constitute action, but that stimuli and reflexes assume a meaning only through the action in which they are incorporated. To the study of 'psychic contents' (the structuralism of Wundt and Titchener) he opposed the functionalism of psychic activities: the contents acquire a meaning in terms of the activity in which they are embodied. The activities of the organism are directed to the physical and social (human) environment and they are constituted in this interaction or 'transaction'. The action of a player in a football match is understood not from his single acts but from their relation with those of the other members of the team. In the social relationship psychic experience reaches its fullest expression. At a later date Dewey devoted himself particularly to education, understood as an interpersonal relationship, and paid little attention to developments in psychology. As regards the religious sense, Dewey effectively stressed its presence in cases of real commitment to an aim or an ideal: the religious attitude made up of loyalty and dedication can characterize the artist, the scientist, the citizen, the parent; proceeding fundamentally from affective and emotive activity, it can exercise a unifying influence on all expressions of psychic life. According to Dewey every full experience is connected with an interpersonal relationship and is social. For this reason he does not accept religious formulations based on supernatural principles, because they distract attention from human relations or are opposed to them. He is a promoter of a 'common faith' that imbues with the same emotional impulse man's devotion to the needs of love, compassion, justice and freedom which are common to all human beings.[53] John Coe, author of a book on the psychology of religion, follows Dewey in his functionalist theory of religion and in his transition from religious psychology to religious education.[54] In his appreciation of the deep and unifying resonance of emotion, in establishing a close connection between the religious and the social sense, and in his work for the secularization of religion and for the education of the religious sense, John Dewey has mapped out some paths which are being followed up in American psychology.

Behaviourism, as its name indicates, is the study of behaviour, that is, the study of what the individual does in a given situation as a result of two fundamental conditions: the situation or stimulus and the response. Stimulus and response together determine behaviour. In behaviourism as formulated in the first place by Watson, everything remotely 'mentalistic' is eliminated. Only those facts capable of being observed and tabulated are considered and it is presupposed that behaviour is supple, not to say indefinitely and indefinably variable. As formulated subsequently by Hull, behaviourism admits the existence of 'needs' as determinants of behaviour and lays down two ruling principles: first, the reduction of the need when it has been satisfied by the behaviour which it has stimulated so

[53] J. Dewey, *A Common Faith*, Yale New Haven, 1934.
[54] J. Coe, *The Psychology of Religion*, Chicago, 1916.

that it tends to diminish or even disappear completely, and secondly, the principle of reinforcement which means that a preferential value is given to responses that meet with success. Biological and therefore innate needs are primary (hunger, thirst, sex); secondary needs are those which are determined by a particular situation. While primary needs are few, secondary needs can be numerous and are the result of a learning process.

> Certain signs such as frowns and other kinds of threatening movements, as well as certain words (overt threats) through their association with attack, acquire the power of evoking flight reactions. . . . Thus words acquire a certain real power to punish, and so to deter, transgressors. And since the statement that a person has transgressed in a certain way is associated with punishment, and since such a statement is a moral judgment, it comes about that the overt passing of an adverse moral judgment becomes a deterrent to forbidden acts. In a similar manner, the passing of a favourable moral judgment becomes a secondary reinforcing agent fostering desirable action.[55]

Morality and religious life are therefore to be interpreted as the result of a learning process: the repetition of attitudes of reverence, fear, admiration, delight, which have been manifested in certain circumstances and which one has learnt to repeat precisely by repeating them.

B. F. Skinner observes that

> We have no reason to be disturbed that the basic process through which an efficient government 'keeps the peace' is exemplified under far less admirable circumstances in the use which the bully or gangster makes of his power to punish. It is not the technique of control but the ultimate effect upon the group which leads us to approve or disapprove of

---

[55] C. L. Hull, 'Value, Valuation and Natural Science Methodology' in *Philosophy of Science*, vol. XI, 1944, p. 137, cited in R. B. Brandt, *Ethical Theory*, Prentice-Hall, Englewood Cliffs, N.J., 1959, p. 138.

any practice. . . . The place of religion in modern life cannot be clearly understood without considering certain processes which are employed outside the field of religion proper for very different purposes. . . . Behaviour is classified, not simply as 'good' and 'bad' or 'legal' and 'illegal', but as 'moral' and 'immoral' or 'virtuous' and 'sinful'. It is then reinforced accordingly. . . . The reinforcers portrayed in Heaven and Hell are far more powerful than those which support the 'good' and 'bad' of the ethnical group or the 'legal' and 'illegal' of governmental control, but this advantage is offset to some extent by the fact that they do not actually operate in the lifetime of the individual.[56]

Religious control is obtained by warning against sin, by the prescription of particular practices, by appealing to supernatural powers, by imposing a form of obedience and self-control which guarantee a certain line of conduct even in the absence of the religious 'agent'. 'The religious agency may come into conflict . . . with economic, educational or governmental agencies. . . . A limit to religious control is imposed by the extent to which the controllee will submit . . . and this may restrict the scope of the agency.'[57] Skinner himself, who used pigeons for his experimental researches into the nature of experience, declares that he observed an 'active conditioning' in the hungry pigeon which in expectation of food performs a 'rite' of bowing.

The bird behaves as if there were a causal relationship between its behaviour and the presentation of food, although such a relation is lacking. There are many analogies in human behaviour. Rituals for changing one's luck at cards are good examples. A few accidental connections between a ritual and favourable consequences suffice to set up and maintain the behaviour in spite of many unreinforced

[56] B. F. Skinner, *Science and Human Behaviour*, Macmillan, New York, 1953, pp. 350-3.
[57] *Ibid.*, p. 358.

instances. The bowler who has released a ball down the alley but continues to behave as if he were controlling it by twisting and turning his arm and shoulder, is another case in point.[58]

Skinner defines this behaviour of the pigeon as superstition. We are to conclude that the learning process is the fundamental process of psychic activity.

O. H. Mowrer is another founder of the school of thought which built up learning theories on the basis of experimentation on animals. In one of his books on learning theory and symbolic processes, however, he takes up a more independent position. One of the last chapters of this work contains an excellent review of the studies on animal behaviour which are a prelude to those on man: individual and social learning, 'animal language', learning by imprinting, domestication, socialization and the structure of groups. However, the conclusion is a very reserved one:

> If, in the present book, learning theory appears to have achieved some degree of maturity at the level of the 'animal model', we must remain modest indeed in face of the large, infinitely more challenging problem: that of showing the continuity, if continuity there be, between those psychological processes which are common to man and beast and those capacities and concerns which we see only at the human level.[59]

Among these latter capacities and concerns Mowrer mentions religion. He asserts that he is confident that a unitary doctrine can eventually be reached but that, while we should by all means endeavour to ratify the precepts elaborated down through the centuries for a broader life of the spirit by a deeper analysis of the principles which are valid for biological adapta-

---

[58] B. F. Skinner, *Cumulative Record*, Appleton, New York, 1961, pp. 407-8.

[59] O. H. Mowrer, *Learning Theory and the Symbolic Processes*, John Wiley, London, 1960, p. 419.

tion, we must remember that this is no more than an attempt to solve the religious problem. To assert that the problem does not exist, he adds, is an expedient that 'cannot be used indefinitely by a science which aspires to a comprehensive knowledge of man'.

Behaviourism asserts an indefinite possibility of association between stimuli and responses. As against this theory Gestalt psychology asks: 'Why are these associations actually formed instead of others which are equally possible?' It has established the principle that consistency between situation and experience is a preliminary condition for the formation of an association and therefore for learning. Behaviour is guided by an understanding of relations, and hence we can judge not only whether it is intelligent or not, but also whether it is normal or not. A person who knows how to apply arithmetical principles but does not use them in an appropriate manner, or a hungry person who throws food away, is behaving inconsistently. In perception, the Gestalt psychologists argue, we see a number of things grouped in a certain way and we cannot see them arranged in any other way. All peoples have grouped in more or less the same manner the stars of the various constellations: they have discovered a consistency of form in them. In emotion there is also a consistency between the situation and the emotion itself. A dangerous situation arouses fear and an unexpected event produces surprise: the emotion rises up spontaneously without preparation or effort and we have the clear impression that, given the circumstances, this should be so. The same thing holds for the norms which regulate our actions. 'It is understandable,' writes Asch,

that rewards and punishment produce desire and fear, but there is no way of seeing how they can produce the experience of 'should'. . . . Authority can produce fear or anger; yet, however peremptory, it is as powerless to introduce into the human mind the distinction between a just and and unjust act as it is to establish a discrimination between red and green. . . . Social forces cannot import ethical judgments into the individual. . . .

At a given period of development the child is a being that feels the stresses and handles the concepts of right and wrong. He does so when he can comprehend the relation between a motive and an act and between an act and its consequences.[60]

There is a 'requiredness' in the relationship between situation and action. Wertheimer writes:

One 'ought' not to snatch food from a hungry child. If one has a brick and a piece of bread and is facing a hungry man and a man building a house, one 'ought' to give the bread to the hungry man, the brick to the house-builder. Nor is this a matter of personal preference. One may dislike the hungry man and still see the rightness of giving him the bread, just as one can add up one's bank balance and get a result very different from what one would like.[61]

We cannot 'produce' a certain interior experience (admiration, gratitude, devotion). We can merely arrange the conditions in which it must have its origin spontaneously and consistently. We may consider, like Hull, that the child assumes the role of his father either openly or in his imagination, and finds satisfaction in this. 'In doing so,' writes Hull, 'the child takes on the parental role, at least momentarily, with all the feelings, attitudes, values and actions that he attributes to the person who actually occupies the role.' But the Gestalt psychologists remark: 'True, the child can imitate what the parents do and say, perhaps even mimic their gestures, but how can he imitate their feelings, attitudes and values? There can be no prescription for these, nor can they be brought about by merely reproducing the behaviour of the parents.' W. Köhler has

[60] Solomon E. Asch, *Social Psychology*, Prentice-Hall, Englewood Cliffs, N.J., 1952, pp. 356-7.

[61] M. Wertheimer, 'Some Problems in the Theory of Ethics' in *Social Research*, vol. II, 1935, pp. 353-67.

written a book entitled *The Place of Value in a World of Facts*[62] and more recently (1958) gave a series of lectures in the Gifford Foundation on the religious problem, which has unfortunately not yet been published. Hence, while we are familiar with the Gestalt psychologists' approach to the problem of values, we cannot yet state their exact attitude to the religious problem. We may suppose, though, that they insist on the character of 'requiredness' of a religious attitude, particularly in certain circumstances.

We shall only make passing mention of the use of quantitative methods in the study of religious activity. These methods can only reach the expressive aspect of religion but they cannot penetrate subjective experience. The followers of this method, remarks Thouless, who was himself one of its pioneers,[63] sometimes write as if there were no other valid method for the study of religion. The statistical method has its uncertainties no less than the older methods based on comparatively unsystematic observation. Many conclusions depend on the manner in which the data are collected and on the initial hypotheses which ought in turn to be subjected to a statistical examination. Be that as it may, although these studies deal only with a marginal area of the subject, they serve to illustrate some aspects of religious experience.

Positions and problems

Since the purpose of this chapter is informative, I do not feel obliged to enter on a critical examination of the various theories mentioned. However, a few considerations will not be out of place by way of conclusions.

William James, although he had a predilection for the study of religious experience in exceptional cases, is distinguished by a singularly broad outlook and by a fine sensitivity to

[62] W. Köhler, *The Place of Value in a World of Facts*, Liveright, New York, 1938.
[63] R. H. Thouless, *The Psychology of Religion*, Cambridge Univ. Press, New York, 1936.

religion as a personal experience. Freud and Jung also began with abnormal and mainly pathological cases and based their interpretations entirely on the analysis of the unconscious. Using presuppositions drawn definitely from pathology and with reference to Jewish-Christian culture and to totemism, Freud stressed mainly the negative aspects of religion. Jung, with a more open outlook, went beyond the psychopathological data, but he had recourse to general principles which are difficult to define (psychic energy) and to a cosmopolitan religious symbolism: he insists continually on the constructive aspect of religion. The sociological and anthropologico-cultural interpretation sees religion as a social product, a social exigency, which man reflects as in a mirror. The development of religion is seen as an evolutionary process, passing from the simple to the complex, according to Darwin's theory, regulated by competition, selection and adaptation. Among the psychological schools, behaviourism favours learning theory, the learning being sustained by 'reinforcement' and satisfaction, while Gestalt psychology focuses its attention on the termination of dynamic processes of search for consistency and structuration. Each of these general theories presents a particular set of principles which it has reached by observation in a specific field. William James' theory is perhaps the broadest because James is not ashamed to consider himself a philosopher as well as a psychologist. Depth psychology is an extension of psychopathology, behaviourism of the study of learning processes, especially in animals, and Gestalt psychology of the study of perception. Sociology continually transposes psychic processes from the social collectivity to the individual and back again. It would almost seem that there is in each instance an obstinate insistence on the study of particular aspects of religion by methods which have proved successful in other fields of research, while the problem of what religion signifies in man's psychic activity is shelved. This is understandable when we consider that in speaking of 'religious psychology' it would be necessary to specify each time *which* psychology and *which* religious activity is meant. Actually things begin to take clear shape only when religious activity is accepted as a psychological fact, as a typical human way of being, and when we study how it occurs, how it develops and changes and how it is expressed—and all this by psychological methods: *psychologica, psychologice.* Consequently religious psychology has its limitations, and the contribution which can be made by the various theories based on the emphasizing of particular aspects is also limited. It must also be recognized that the exclusiveness of the various theories inevitably counterbalances their worth when they pass on from individual facts to form a global concept. James, Freud, Jung and Durkheim (and, within their own limits, also Watson, Hull and Wertheimer) deserve respectful admiration for having given us interpretations of the facts which raise problems of principle. It is original thinkers and men endowed with intuition rather than mere collectors of information who have been the pioneers in the history of science.

A meaningful note constantly recurs in all the different theories proposed. Against the background of a certain reluctance on the part of psychologists to speak of religion, some extreme attitudes stand out in bold relief. Among these is the tendency to substitute a scientific conception of the world and of life for the usual religious forms, and the aspiration towards a happy existence freed from the encumbrances of established religions. But are not these characteristics—a concept of life and liberation from constraint, together with total commitment of oneself—the very characteristics of religious activity? The psychologist who deals with religious experience or declares that he does not want to deal with it, or combats it openly, is in danger of becoming an adept in 'psychological religion' (for which even the unlettered are extremely avid). Surrounded by the halo of science he seems to furnish the explanation to problems which face every man and seems to set men free from the burden of these problems. When we recall that in the case of almost all the great psychologists their interest in psychology coincided with painful personal conflicts, we can see more clearly why psychology can fascinate people in circumstances in which this power usually falls to the lot of religion.

In modern psychology some convergent characteristics are evident in all the different schools when the subject of religious experience is considered. An almost exclusive priority is attributed to the affective datum in religion while the rational element is minimized. Stress is placed on the 'psychic reality' of the religious datum[64] and on its confinement to the person who experiences it. The biological and utilitarian function of religious experience is given prominence. There is recourse to a 'polytheism' of directing entities (personal and collective unconscious, society) which the subject cannot know. A distinction is made between individual and social evolutionary stages corresponding to biological and historico-ethnological processes of development in order to explain the enormous influence of religion, despite the unverifiability or the absurdity of rational justifications of religion. All this aims at bridging the wide gap that exists between the empirically demonstrable, limited, changeable, irrational conditions and the characteristics of universality, comprehensiveness and necessity proper to religion. Finally, there is a clear assertion of the biological, personal and social relativism of religious experience.

Are these assertions to be considered conclusive and immutable? We should be doing an injustice to science if we answered in the affirmative. It is more consistent to consider that they ought to be tested further in order to discover what is durable and what is ephemeral in them. Is religious activity a by-product of refusal of psychic activity or a genuine and inevitable quality of this activity? Is it an artificial product of the environment and of society or does it imply personal spontaneity and commitment? Is it a divisive or a unifying manifestation of personal psychic activity? Does it indicate psychic development or psychic regression? Can science become a religion? Is religion a mere projection of individual needs, or does it point to realities beyond those accessible to

[64] W. James: 'True belief is a belief that works.' C. G. Jung: 'Das was wirkt, ist wirklich.'

the senses? Here we have a series of questions presented as alternatives, rather for the purpose of emphasizing the acuteness of the religious problem than to elicit a categorical and unilateral reply. As is invariably the case, antagonisms serve a good purpose and are, in fact, the prerequisites for the establishment of a proper balance. It is this balance that we must discern and achieve in our present field of study.

2. Religion : Genuine and Spurious

Religion and neurosis[1]

When Freud defined religion as an obsessional neurosis of mankind he was referring in particular to the ritual aspect, the regular performance of religious practices which when neglected gives rise to anguish and a sense of guilt. He maintained that the origin of religion in the individual was the Oedipus complex and that collective religious activity originated in the ancestral parricide. He prophesied that these forms of religion would disappear and that a new religion would be established, no longer based on obscure impulses but on scientifically proved convictions. Taken as they stand, these statements are remarkably feeble. Formalist religious practice certainly exists, but on the other hand we have the undeniable existence of broad and fruitful religious conviction. The proof which Freud draws from his analysis of the individual is difficult to interpret and his assertions with reference to pre-history have been questioned or even denied by ethnologists, while religion on a scientific (or psychoanalytic) basis is just as great an 'illusion' (i.e. a conception born of intense desire and of partial satisfaction of the desire) as the one whose disappearance he predicts. We might also ask ourselves how it is that Freud, who criticized and demolished religion so ruthlessly and took pains to declare himself an atheist from his youth—with an ingenuousness which he considered rational and scientific—at the same time, as one of his admirers, G.

[1] In this chapter in which we are discussing qualities shared by morality and religion the two terms sometimes appear to be equivalent and interchangeable. The qualities which distinguish morality from religion will be stressed at a later stage.

44

Zillboorg, has pointed out, reveals many religious elements in his attitudes. If nothing else, there is his faith in psychoanalysis.[2] But the insistence with which Freud busied himself about religion, pointing out some of its negative aspects and some aspects of its individual and social development, indicates that his contribution is not to be undervalued, although it is mainly critical and unfavourable to religion. Indeed, he could well have opened up a new path in this field, although he himself failed to follow it. We intend for the moment to refer chiefly to his equation: religion = obsessional neurosis. The fact that he used a technical term taken from psychiatry, that is, from the treatment of individuals (sick persons) who behave differently from others (healthy persons), goes to show that just as there is neurotic religion we must also expect to find a healthy form of religion. If this opposite is lacking, what can be the meaning of a definition as broad as that of 'universal obsessional neurosis'? Charles Odier has endeavoured, precisely on the psychoanalytical plane,[3] to reach a distinction between false, unhealthy values (moral and religious) and genuine ones. He refers especially to the third chapter of *The Ego and the Id*,[4] in which Freud deals with the ego and the superego. Odier remarks how Freud uses indiscriminately the three terms superego, ideal ego and ego ideal, which today have different meanings.

The superego, according to Freud, is the result of complicated processes of identification which with the disappearance of the Oedipus complex mark a pause in development of the libido (beginning of the latency period). 'Psychoanalysis has been reproached time after time,' he writes, 'with ignoring the higher, moral, supra-personal side of human nature.' Freud refutes this accusation and points out that the problem did not arise until psychoanalysis began to deal with repressed

[2] G. Zillboorg, *Freud and Religion*, Newman Press, Westminster, Maryland, 1958.

[3] Ch. Odier, *Les deux sources consciente et inconsciente de la vie morale*, Neuchâtel, 1947.

[4] S. Freud, *The Ego and the Id*, Standard Ed., vol. XIX.

material. 'But now that we have embarked upon the analysis of the ego,' he writes, 'we can give an answer to all those whose moral sense has been shocked and who have complained that there must surely be a higher nature in man.' 'Very true, we can say, and here we have that higher nature, in this ego ideal or superego, the representative of our relation to our parents. When we were little children we knew these higher natures, we admired them and feared them; and later we took them into ourselves.' 'The ego ideal,' Freud continues,

> is therefore the heir of the Oedipus complex, and thus it is also the expression of the most powerful impulses and the most important libidinal vicissitudes of the id. By setting up this ego ideal, the ego has mastered the Oedipus complex and at the same time placed itself in subjection to the id. . . . What has belonged to the lowest part of the mental life of each of us is changed, through the formation of the ideal, into what is highest in the human mind by our scale of values. . . . As a substitute for a longing for the father, it contains the germ from which all religions have evolved. The self-judgment which declares that the ego falls short of its ideal produces the religious sense of humility to which the believer appeals in his longing. As a child grows up, the role of father is carried on by teachers and others in authority; their injunctions and prohibitions remain powerful in the ego ideal and continue, in the form of conscience, to exercise the moral censorship. The tension between the demands of conscience and the actual performance of the ego is experienced as a sense of guilt. Social feelings rest on identifications with other people, on the basis of having the same ego ideal. Religion, morality and a social sense—the chief elements in the higher side of man,—were originally one and the same thing.

The distinction between them came about later in the course of phylogenesis: religion and moral restraint developed through the process of mastering the Oedipus complex itself, and social feeling through the necessity of overcoming the rivalry that remained between the members of the younger generation.

It appears, from this passage of Freud, that adult religion and moral restraint are a simultaneous overcoming and survival of the processes of the id. 'By setting up this ego ideal, the ego has mastered the Oedipus complex, and at the same time placed itself in subjection to the id.'

Odier observes that there is clear evidence here of Freud's manner of reducing psychic phenomena to individual and ontogenetic psycho-biological processes. 'Freud,' he says, 'subjects them to a vast psycho-biological reduction and he has a right to do so.'[5] We may certainly be permitted to remark that it remains to be seen if a reality corresponds to this reduction or merely an artificial product. Odier, for his part, concludes that Freudian doctrine does not close the door conclusively on the study of values, but encourages us to take up this study again on the psychological plane. He maintains that in addition to opposition on the conscious plane between being and ideal (between what we are and what we would like to be) there is a second opposition, in the unconscious, between superego and moral conscience, and particularly between the superego and the true ideal in general. Hence his theory, expressed in the title of his book *Les deux sources consciente et inconsciente de la vie morale*. The latter source is the deeper and more hidden one; it is the more necessary one and comes first in order of time. 'We cannot speak of *values* until the moment at which the ego tries to take or actually takes a step outside the limited sphere of the *functions*, that is, outside the sphere of biological, instinctual and affective needs on the one hand, and—in the social sphere—its own interests on the other hand.'[6] 'Functions,' according to Odier, 'are selfish means inspired by conscious or unconscious motives to satisfy a need or to realize an individual tendency, regardless of the moral or spiritual consequences involved.'[7] Thus the convergence of values and functions is not necessary and may indeed be wanting. In this way false values are born—those proceeding either

[5] Ch. Odier, *op. cit.*, p. 40.   [6] *Ibid.*, p. 55.   [7] *Ibid.*, p. 56.

from the functions or from an unconscious motivation. 'Does not the mention of false values suggest that true values exist? Who could claim to "serve" the latter effectively without abolishing or dismissing the former?'[8] Odier admits that some psychologists have been carried away to the extent of 'reducing' true as well as false values to mere processes or to biological or cultural conditions. The psychoanalyst, he says, proceeds to a different type of reduction which is in a certain sense the opposite of the preceding one and which by reducing 'the false values to their proper function, contributes to reintegrating the true values in their newfound specific quality'.[9] Obviously this is a programme which indicates a modest clearing process, an elimination of what is 'false' so that what is 'genuine' may appear more clearly. But in point of fact it amounts to a categorical assertion that psychoanalysis is capable of finding a remedy where all the great moral counsellors and religious thinkers have failed. These have not found the remedy because they have only observed the conscious aspect of false values and shown up their fraudulence; they have failed to discover the unconscious cause which is inaccessible to the subject himself. The psychoanalyst, on the other hand, has been able to locate this cause in the superego where he can probe it.

According to Odier, therefore, a healthy moral life implies two principles: 1) the absence or non-intervention of unconscious moral processes (and therefore non-activity of repressed tendencies and of the superego); 2) the autonomy of the ego and of the moral conscience (and therefore freedom from all influence of the superego). Unhealthy moral life is synonymous with the ego's lack of autonomy in relation to the superego. But it should be noted that this is a psychological and not a specifically moral criterion, since a person who possesses full autonomy can also make bad use of it. Hence 'the concept of moral health does not coincide with that of moral perfection'. Moreover, the absence of unconscious morality does not imply a high degree of conscious morality. This depends on the quality of the ego and on its positive virtues and 'not on the

[8] *Ibid.*, p. 95.   [9] *Ibid.*, p. 97.

negative fact that it is not subject to any influence from the superego'.[10] I must say that it is precisely here that the problem lies. It is not clear how psychoanalytical doctrine can help, centred as it is upon the predominance of the unconscious. The synoptic table of the constituent elements in the two moral systems presented by Odier can almost appear to be a handbook by which to distinguish the two types of morality. But it seems to be psychoanalytical in conception and terminology in the column dealing with unconscious morality, while adopting the language and standards of traditional moral philosophy in the column referring to moral and religious consciousness. This dichotomy of moral behaviour undeniably represents progress in comparison to Freud's definition of religion as a universal neurosis. At least it recognizes the existence of genuine morality and religion as opposed to morality and religion possessing neurotic characteristics. But in reality, according to Odier, absolutely genuine religion is the exception rather than the rule: there are very few cases in which there is no intromission of the superego and in which this intromission is recognized and combated. The vast majority of men are, he holds, in the 'neurotic' category, situated between the healthy few and the decidedly sick, the obviously neurotic. This vast mass of 'moral neurotics', made up of persons whose disorders range from milder to more serious forms, are apparently satisfactorily adapted to life, but actually they are ruled by the unconscious impulses of the superego rather than by motives of which they are aware and which they consciously either accept or reject. The vast majority of men are moral and religious more by impulse than from conviction: and the impulse is very often disguised by a pseudomoral formalism in which they are seeking the satisfaction of a need rather than aiming at an ideal. Finally, since moral health is a quality possessed by very few, 'moral neuroticism' can only be defined in relation to something more clearly outlined, more pathological than itself, that is, by comparison with neurosis. Obviously this further step taken by Odier in comparison to

[10] *Ibid.*, p. 150.

Freud still remains in the pathological field and proceeds all the time in the same direction: moral and religious instability is a condition in which the subject needs treatment of a psychoanalytical nature before he can rise to the higher level of moral and religious health. Substantially Odier maintains that it is only when the psychotherapist has cleared the ground of the weeds produced by the superego that a trule moral conscience can develop. This position is far from satisfactory. The psychotherapist, who has come forward with the modest proposal of preparing the way, in point of fact declares himself indispensable: he wants to take command of the whole situation. If the majority of men are 'moral neurotics', nothing good can be expected in the way of morality and religion until the psychoanalyst has accomplished a comprehensive reclamation of the ground since it is only analytical procedure that can determine whether a given moral or religious behaviour is genuine or spurious. The psychoanalyst is thus transformed into a general 'discerner' of spirits. A serious aspect of this theory lies in the fact that the state of 'moral neuroticism' is the condition of a sick person, of a person who must therefore place himself in the hands of another, who must abdicate in order to be authorized to govern in his own house. This situation is extraordinarily favourable to that flight from personal responsibility (jauntily attributed to character, to one's parents, to family environment or to social pressure) which, if it is not already a sign of neurosis, is likely to lead to it. But even under these conditions, is psychoanalysis—so able and ingenious in the work of demolition—really capable of furnishing the means of rehabilitation? The first to doubt this was probably Freud himself. Concerned as he was about the genesis of the 'complex', he spoke of therapeutic suggestions as a combination of common sense and ordinary rules.[11] Besides,

[11] E. Strauss, a psychiatrist who also practised psychoanalysis, writes: 'A successful Freudian analysis results only in a person "*making* good", in the current American sense; the idea of his *being* or *becoming* good, or even *doing* good, does not come into the picture. How could it in a system which is rigidly closed to ideas of moral value? Again, how could it in accordance with a scheme that has abolished the concept of

no psychoanalyst can predict whether and in what way recovery will take place once the 'complex' has been eliminated. Persons who submit to psychoanalytical treatment may obtain relief, but when they have been able to adjust they must still face up to the same difficulties as those people who were not in need of this treatment. Freud has nothing constructive to offer here. The 'treatment' itself actually encourages a tendency to submit blindly to the guidance of others, while what is required for moral and religious life is clear judgment and conscious independent decision. It remains to be seen if the psychoanalytical theory, even as formulated by Odier, does not constitute a help merely in cases where curative measures are really required. The initial statement that the pathological state is the ordinary one and the normal state the exception compels us to interpret the facts according to the typical schemas of Freud who had a predilection for turning situations upside down. While we maintain that the moral principle precedes transgression, that respect for paternal authority precedes parricide and that guilt precedes anxiety, Freud appears to prefer to invert all this. For him the moral conscience derives from transgression, paternal veneration originates in rebellion against the father and guilt derives from anxiety.

With regard to genuine morality and religion, Odier, who presents them in such a 'simple' schema, loses touch with reality (like the philosopher of the 'categorical imperative') and is compelled to confine himself to very rare cases, since ordinary human experience, even among the most privileged of men, does not take place under ideal conditions and produce the best possible results. If in those very frequent cases which

the conscience and replaced it with the idea of the superego? . . . I do not deny the validity of the Freudian concept of the superego. Far from it. I regard it as a most useful concept, but as one which loses half its value unless it has the idea of the conscience with which to contrast it. . . . In the course of analysis, an analysand appears to be enabled to distinguish between true and false guilt, but when he turns to Freudian philosophy for a definition of true guilt, he finds that there is really no such thing and that all guilt is a psychic miasma which can be dissipated by further analysis' (E. Strauss, *Reason and Unreason in Psychological Medicine*, H. K. Lewis, London, 1953, p. 14).

Odier calls cases of 'moral neuroticism' the subject's routine, conformist or adaptive behaviour is swarming with false values, and if moral and religious insensibility can be detected under cover of unconscious motives effectively disguised, then we must ask ourselves if conscious possibilities, dicernible by the observation of our own behaviour, are always totally lacking as a foothold towards genuine moral effort. May not the admission that we do not always attain to what we aim at contain a higher moral value than the attitude (unhappily so narcissistic) of the person who examines himself complacently and with approval? It is moreover dangerous to stress merely the conditions of behaviour and to pride oneself on 'human understanding' while avoiding an objective judgment of the facts, for none of us can say for certain how we would act in given circumstances. Moberley remarks in regard to delinquents that 'it is disastrous to lead a man to believe that he is more sinned against (by the verdict) than sinning (by his crime) and to imply that strenuous moral effort on his own part is unnecessary'.[12] It is equally disastrous to spread the conviction that a widely practised but in fact merely apparent morality is due to unconscious motives alone and that it should therefore be treated by psychoanalysis like an illness of which the patient suffers the effects without being responsible for the cause. The restlessness and anxiety of 'morally neurotic' persons should not be explained too readily as a neurotic disorder. In a number of cases, at least, its origin can be traced to a former violation of moral and religious principles inadequately evaluated by the morally neurotic person himself. We may finally ask ourselves if the unmasking of the neurotic symptom as an illusory spectre and the insistent criticism and challenging of the superego (Freud loved to compare himself to the devil, the tempter, in this respect) does not involve the risk of producing moral chaos and an exaggerated sense of guilt. To envisage two such important human activities as moral and religious consciousness only from the pathological point

[12] W. Moberley, 'Responsibility', *Riddell Memorial Lectures*, 1951, Seabury Press, Greenwich, Conn., 1956, p. 24.

of view and to seek to reduce them to psycho-biological causes, as Freud and his followers have done, leads inevitably to a misunderstanding of principle, even if it throws light on some genetical aspects of the question.

A clinical interpretation of religious behaviour by psychoanalytical methods and standards is presented by N. Mailloux and L. Ancona.[13] Their thinking is closely linked with that of Freud for whom they express admiration and with whom they agree, though with some reservations. Conflicts with a religious content are not always to be judged as neurotic phenomena and they occur in a particular domain which is irreducible to the dynamism of the libido, although not removed from its disturbing influence. This domain is called 'religious' and is judged to be one of the four fundamental areas of psychic life, the other three being sociability, sexuality and the existential character of human life. Freud's stages of psychosexual development are accepted by Erikson, whose formulation of them is, however, broader and more in harmony with the complexity of the situation we are considering. In correspondence with the phases which Freud calls oral, anal and phallic, Erikson formulates the stages of reception, power to retain and expel, and active penetration of space, which are the expression of 'critical needs' characteristic of the different phases. Mailloux and Ancona distinguish between an immature religious sense, expressed in infantile types of behaviour, and a mature religious sense which has succeeded in breaking free and achieving independence. Employing concepts derived from Anna Freud and Erikson, they describe immature religious activity as dependent on the adaptive mechanism of the ego: projection-introjection in the first stage; intellectualization and rationalization in the second; evasion, removal and sublimation in the third. In the case of mature religious activity or religion in the true sense, Mailloux and Ancona state that 'observation is rather difficult' and that it appears as a 'phenomenon of

[13] N. Mailloux and L. Ancona, 'Interpretazione clinica del comportamento religioso' in *Contributi dell'Istituto di Psicologia dell'Università Cattolica*, Catholic University of Milan, 1958, no. XXI.

interior life whose external manifestations are moderate and well-balanced and are intermingled with the everyday occupations of the maturely religious person'. Here we have a repetition of the situation already noted by Odier: what is pathological is more easily defined than what is normal and what is normal can only be defined by traditional and rather general criteria or by philosophical and moral criteria rather than by a well-defined psychological system. This leads the psychologist to deal to a greater extent with instinctual factors which are more easily recognizable and more amenable to therapeutic treatment. Since neurotic elements can survive even in mature religious activity, the task of the psychologist is to enable the patient to discern the dynamic unfolding of his personality and to help him in the process of readjustment. But Mailloux and Ancona also recognize that it is extremely difficult for the psychologist to establish in each case the limits between genuine and spurious religious feeling. The ultimate judgment in this matter is not one that the psychologist can make. It is a judgment that the subject himself must make, aided by the theologian and the moral counsellor, since the subject himself is the person directly involved. This is certainly true. But traps lie in wait for the unwary in this field. Few people realize how difficult this constructive task is, especially when the subject, under neurotic constraint, finds it very hard to come to decisions and when the complexity and delicacy of the religious problem have not been glimpsed by those whose task it is to act as guides, whether they be psychologists, moral counsellors or theologians.

Normality and abnormality[14]

Freud's framing of religion in psychopathological terms and the consequence drawn by Odier, namely, that an unhealthy

[14] For a more complete treatment of this problem see: H. Müller-Suur, *Das Psychisch-Abnorme*, Berlin, 1950; G. Bally, *Der Normale Mensch*, Zurich, 1952; Fr. Duyckaerts, *La notion de normal en psychologie clinique*, Paris, 1954; K. Jaspers, *General Psychopathology*, University of Chicago, 1963.

religious activity presupposes a healthy one, oblige us to make an excursus into the meaning of the opposing terms normal and abnormal, healthy and sick, which every psychologist, as Jaspers says. is bound to come up against at least once in his life. Here we are dealing with a crucial question, since it is an inevitable one, and whatever answer is given to it, whether explicit or implicit, involves questions of principle. It is usual to assert nowadays that abnormal pathological states provide us with an enlargement—which can therefore be more easily observed and studied—of normal states, while normal states escape our notice precisely because they appear so natural and spontaneous in the course of unobstructed normal processes. One who is quite familiar with abnormal pathological states should also be well acquainted with normal states, since he has identified and defined their characteristics. The question then arises as to what is normal and what is abnormal, and the reply tends invariably to take the following form. Since a clear and conclusive comparison is not possible because the abnormal is an enlargment, a distortion and an independent expression of what can only with difficulty be distinguished in the more uniform and harmonious setting of the normal, we cannot establish two absolute standards separated by inviolable boundaries. We must rather visualize a continual transition from normality to abnormality through slight variations which only become apparent when they accumulate and constitute a real obstacle to adjustment and to daily life. Normal and abnormal have no meaning in themselves but only in their consequences. It is a question of quantitative rather than of qualitative difference. This manner of reasoning goes back to Darwin's theory of evolution in which the transition from one living species to another takes place by tiny, gradual changes, in which only the sufficiently adapted forms of life survive, that is, those which emerge victorious from the struggle for existence. Galton, who lived in this atmosphere of thought, expressed the theory in mathematico-statistical terms, using what Gauss had brought out in his errors graph: the normal is to be defined as that which happens more frequently; the abnormal is that which happens less frequently and which tends to revert to average (law of regression). The index of correlation (R, denoting regression) gains in significance the nearer it approaches to average. The psychophysics of Fechner, who attributes the variety of sensations to the accumulation of elementary sensations, belongs to the same order of ideas. There is a continual process of transition as when a spectrum of white light is broken up into its elementary components. Just as light and darkness are relative to the eye which perceives them, the normal and the abnormal are relative to possible and tolerable forms of existence in a particular environment. After having explained the difference between normal and abnormal in quantitative terms, it becomes necessary to derive one from the other while at the same time distinguishing between them; and since the abnormal is less frequent but more easily recognizable than the normal, the initial situation is reversed. The abnormal is taken as the norm or measure of the normal. This is particularly apparent in Odier, where very few cases of genuine moral and religious life are cited and where the vast majority of cases dealt with are described as falling into the category of 'moral neuroticism'. Before the second world war, when interminable inconclusive discussions on disarmament were in progress at the League of Nations in Geneva, since some thought that disarmament consisted in not manufacturing weapons (but leaving the way open for their illegal importation) and others declared that it consisted in having plenty of weaponry to guarantee the peace by frightening the enemy (weaponry which could, if necessary, be actually used), the English minister, Sir John Simon, was asked what was the difference between armament and disarmament. He replied: 'I do not know what the difference is, but I recognize it. I cannot define an elephant, but I recognize one perfectly well.' A humorous sally, but one which contains a truth that is overlooked by over-subtle reasonings which end in sophisms. Actually among psychopathologists and psychologists there is no shortage of protests against the shelving of this problem of the normal and the abnormal: it is recognized as a source of much fruitless discussion. An able psychiatrist, H. C. Rümke, has expressed himself on this point very clearly and decidedly on various occasions, particularly during the First International Congress on Mental Health, held in Toronto in 1954. He declared:

> I do not believe I am exaggerating in saying that here we are touching upon the central problem, upon a good part of which depends the solution of all problems in the two fields (mental hygiene and mental health). It is no less than the question of the relationship between sickness and good health. . . . It is precisely when health becomes more than the absence of illness that the problem arises. From then on, it is impossible to protect and promote health in combating illness. It becomes necessary to know the laws of health, the bases on which they are founded and the forces which control them. Now, these forces and these bases are not known to us. We do not know what is essentially health.[15]

According to Rümke, Freud has taught us a lot. He showed us half of the road to be followed in the treatment of neuroses but he has told us nothing of psychic health. To the usual argument that there exists between health and illness an almost imperceptible progressive transition and that consequently an understanding of neuroses is in itself an understanding of man, Rümke retorts:[16]

> No, that is exactly what I do not accept. This transition is not proven. . . . This is one of the temptations, I believe, to which psychiatry might succumb. It is my firm conviction that the understanding of the sick man's disturbances hardly contributes to the understanding of the normal man. Too often we

[15] Cf. H. C. Rümke, 'Solved and Unsolved Problems in Mental Health' in *Mental Hygiene*, vol. XXXIX, no. 2, April 1955, pp. 182-3.

[16] Freud's description of his clinical cases is particularly fascinating; there is keen observation and originality while his style is distinctly dramatic although restrained. Still, according to the testimony of Ernest Jones, Freud was known to have a poor knowledge of men and a strong tendency to over-simplification; for him things were 'either black or white'.

confuse the psychically disturbed life with the greatest depths
of being—this is a professional malady typical of psychiatry.
Doubtless we catch a glimpse of unfathomable depths;
doubtless at one time or another (but not often!) the depths
and the heights of human possibilities become visible to us,
but these are pathological depths and heights. The artist
discloses and shapes the most profound life, not the
psychiatrist. This life never appears in a mentally ill man,
but appears in supreme moments of the normal man. These
moments are of short duration. Soon life falls back to the
ordinary level, a level more or less satisfying according to
the temperament in question. Going down again, life shuts
itself and that is precisely the characteristic sign of normal.
The life of the mentally ill remains open, yawning; remains
visible, shameless, clarified in a strange manner, insane. The
pathological case lacks form and style. It becomes evident
that the difference between illness and normality is a problem
of form. The psychiatrist who by his psychiatry believes
himself to be a connoisseur of men runs the risk of badly
judging normal man and he is not seeing that which is miss-
ing in the one who is ill. And it is precisely the question to
find that which he lacks, that which is absent, that is to say,
the great human qualities of love and creativity.

Rümke is obviously thinking here of the typical mental patient,
the psychotic; but what is to be said of the neurotic in whom
the traces are so slight that they appear quite normal, while
his behaviour appears strange and can be considered abnormal?
Here the problem becomes more difficult, for Rümke speaks
of a 'neurotic understudy' which can take the place of the
normal person, causing neurotic symptoms to appear although
the totality of the characteristics which belong to a neurotic
personality and give it its particular tone is not present.
'Neurosis offers us a copy of human suffering, but we note the
absence of something. Or, to make use of another image, the
piece of music is not rendered by an artist of real talent, but by
an understudy of inferior quality.' The irritating quality of

artificiality or falsehood which is found in the neurotic is not
without significance. On the other hand Rüke has shrewdly
pointed out that the insistence of psychoanalysts on neurotic
mechanisms has caused us to lose sight of the 'pathological
elements of normality itself'. Under these conditions it is not
the symptoms or the content of consciousness—which can be
unexpectedly bizarre even in a normal person—that constitutes
abnormality. Rather it is their general organization, the form
they assume. 'If we were to base our judgment on the content,
we should have to declare mentally ill the majority of the men
we take to be normal. Inversely, the content does not enable
us to diagnose between the sick and the normal, even though
some of this content may lead us to suspect the presence of
certain illnesses.' Sickness is therefore characterized by a
manner of being rather than by the enlarged, disproportionate,
autocratic manifestations of certain presumed 'elements' which
are common also to a healthy condition. The mental life of a
normal man can be very upset without our having the right
to declare him mentally ill. 'It is an offence against human
dignity to call its struggles and failures an illness.' The life of
man is distinguished precisely by the struggle or conflict
inherent in it, which is a condition of its development and
enrichment. Psychogenic factors such as those described by
psychoanalysis and 'psychodynamics', are certainly involved.
But this does not mean that we must subject every worried man
to psychoanalytical treatment. Rümke declares that only a small
percentage of the mentally ill are capable of deriving benefit
from this treatment. Modern psychoanalysis seems to have
forgotten the existence of spiritual powers which elude any
biological description. Among the normal man's qualities is
his undeniable possession of a scale of values which is not
merely a means to 'come to terms' with his environment but is
also a source of spiritual energy. 'I do not believe,' says Rümke,
'that science will ever attain an understanding of that which
is at the bottom of aspiration, of straining towards an ideal.
On the other hand, I am convinced that it will penetrate more
and more into the problem of that which makes man blind

towards ideals, of that which presents an obstacle to their recognition.'

Sante De Sanctis, in his book *La conversione religiosa*, had already expressed ideas very similar to Rümke's.[17] De Sanctis takes a firm stand against the reduction of the religious sense to a psychopathological condition, while he admits that there is almost invariably a religious element in mental illness. At the same time he asserts the legitimacy of a form of religious psychology based on the criteria of normal psychology, provided the limits of this discipline are acknowledged and that no attempt is made to express value judgments which are outside its province. He expresses admiration for Freud's genius, but disagrees with him in maintaining that the unconscious presupposes consciousness, in other words, the capacity to note and interpret the impulses that proceed from the unconscious (although the possibility of error in this process is not excluded). The conscious mind is therefore the locus where the instinctual objectification and control of impulses take place. It is not a mere epiphenomenon. In this light sublimation, while possessing unconscious roots, really takes place when elaborated by the conscious mind. In other words it is more than 'transparent' sublimation, in which unconscious motivations are dimly perceptible. Consciousness and unconsciousness are therefore reciprocally integrated in the cognitive and volitive activity which expresses the uniqueness of the normal person. On the other hand, according to De Sanctis, partial tendencies which can make a transitory appearance in the person of sound mind, take command in mental illness and establish themselves there, sometimes in anarchical independence. De Sanctis declares that 'semeiology and positive mental pathology almost invariably offer us the capacity to distinguish in individual cases between the genuine mental patient and the one who is not deranged or is only apparently and momentarily in this state'. He adds that 'insanity relates to consciousness and not to the unconscious: the same potential material can

[17] S. De Sanctis, *La conversione religiosa*, Bologna, 1924, pp. 197-8.

take a sane form in one personality and an insane one in another. In moments of unconscious and automatic mental activity a person may make wise and original statements which he is unable to translate into action if his mental condition is unsound.'

G. W. Allport, in a relatively recent work on normal and abnormal personality, points out that by describing generically as normal a person whose behaviour corresponds to a definite rule, and abnormal one who departs from it, we often confuse two different and sometimes opposite norms: the statistical norm and the moral norm.[18] The first of these norms relates to what is habitual, and it is quantitative; the second refers to value, and is qualitative. Psychology seems to prefer the first of these norms but often has recourse to the second one as well. Despite their apparent precision, statistical reports on normality seem to be increasingly inadequate. One wonders today whether regression to the average, or rather regression to mediocrity, does not show up precisely what is least conducive to human efficiency, to human 'normality'. One wonders if the mediocre man is not exposed more than others to mental illness, to delinquency, to the servitude of dictatorships. It is not the more usual, the more frequent facts, but the capacity of human nature which can furnish us with a standard by which to judge the healthy or normal personality. Thus the psychologists have set out to find new standards of normality and abnormality in the strictly naturalistic field: human characteristics as opposed to those of animals (Shoben); the need for social development and cohesion (P. Halmos); adjustment, reduction of tension, homoeostasis. But these criteria, besides being partial, are unsatisfactory precisely because they do not express values. How are we to establish what human qualities are good or bad? How are we to know that growth and social cohesion are an expansion and not a diminution of human capacities? How are we to know that the simple gratification of needs, for the most part limited ones, represents

[18] G. W. Allport, *Personality and Social Encounter*, Beacon Press, Boston, 1960.

bliss and not unhappiness?[19] Even personality inventories (those compiled by Maslow and Allport, for example) reveal the same defect: they do not automatically justify the description of some characteristics as valuable and of others as negative.

Dealing with the problem of continuity between normal and abnormal behaviour, Allport maintains that if we take symptoms into account there is in fact a continuum running from normal to abnormal and that when tests and scales are employed the results arrange themselves into a continuous graph. But, he thinks, this continuum is found only in the domain of symptoms. The processes underlying these symptoms are not continuous. For example, there is a substantial difference, a difference of polarity, between facing the world and its problems (which is intrinsically a good thing and one that ought to be done) and escape or withdrawal from the world (which is intrinsically an unhealthy process). Extreme withdrawal and flight constitute psychosis. But, we may ask, do not all of us seek to escape from what thwarts or upsets us? Certainly we do, and what is more important, our flight can often be not only recreational but genuinely constructive, as happens in the case of some daydreams. Still, the process of escape can be harmless only if the dominant process is that of facing up to life, of contrasting flight with reality ('reality testing'). Left to itself the process of flight is disastrous. In the psychotic this process has got the upper hand while in the normal person the process of facing up to reality, the 'testing of reality' prevails. According to this criterion other processes can be listed which of themselves lead to abnormality (as, for example, repression, defence mechanisms, uncontrolled impulsiveness, regression to earlier phases, petrifaction), processes which may be grouped under the title 'katabolic functions'. In

[19] 'Nothing is so unbearable to man as to be at a standstill, without passion, business, amusement, occupation. 'Tis then he feels his nothingness, his foolishness, his insufficiency, his dependence, his emptiness. Forthwith there will issue from the depth of his soul ennui, blackness, gloom, chagrin, vexation, despair' (Pascal, *Pensées*, translation by H. F. Stewart, Pantheon Books, New York, 1950, p. 57).

opposition to these we have other processes which are constructive rather than reductive or merely conservative, the 'anabolic functions' (such as a sense of reality, self-objectivization, integrative action of the nervous system, capacity for abstract thought, progress in individualization or the stressing of individuality, tolerance of frustration). The katabolic functions might be compared to the unhealthy process of some diseases (such as diabetes, tuberculosis, thyroiditis) which can to some small extent be normalized provided they are counterbalanced and dominated by anabolic constructive processes. Normal life is characterized by the preponderance of the anabolic functions and abnormal life by that of the katabolic processes. Allport also points out that in the empirical approach to the problem of normality and abnormality, based on the characteristics which are attributed to one or the other, and which can be grouped into inventories or anabolic and katabolic processes, there can be observed, despite the verbal difference, a congruence of meaning which nobody has yet fully succeeded in expressing. It is also significant that each type of psychotherapy aims at a particular goal: for the behaviourists it is efficiency; for the sociologists, group cohesion; from Fromm, productivity; for Frankl, meaning and responsibility; for non-directive therapy, growth; for K. Goldstein, self-realization. As is obvious, the nature of each kind of therapy is expressed by the stress placed on a certain value, even if it should be the case that a given therapy embodies a confluence of different values rather than a stress on one value exclusively.

Allport ends up by stating that psychological researches cannot solve the problem of normality and that they open out into the problem of morality because they are unable to justify values by purely psychological standards. The moral counsellor receives from the psychologists the contribution of facts more closely connected with the moral problem than might be imagined.

We are indebted to Allport for a valuable empirical and descriptive distinction between two types of religion: extrinsic and intrinsic. He writes:

For many people, religion is a dull habit, or a tribal investment to be used for ceremony, for family convenience, or for
personal comfort. It is something to *use* but not to *live*. It
may be used to improve one's status, to bolster one's self-
confidence. It may be used as a defence against reality, and
as a divine sanction for one's own formula for living. Such
a sentiment assures me that God sees things my way. In
theological terms, the extrinsically religious person turns to
God but does not turn away from self. This type of extrinsic
relations, one's domestic life, one's quandaries, guilt and

'By contrast,' continues Allport,

intrinsic religion is not instrumental. It is not a means of
handling fear, a mode of sociability and conformity, a
sublimation of sex, or a wish-fulfilment. . . . One's ethnic
relations, one's domestic life, one's quandaries, guilt and
ultimate ontological anxiety are all handled under a comprehensive commitment, partly intellectual but more
fundamentally motivational. It is integral, covering everything in experience, making room for scientific fact and
emotional fact. It is a unifying orientation. Such religion
does not exist to serve the person; rather, the person is committed to serve it.[20]

We may conclude that while a schematic, conceptually rigid
distinction is not possible between normal and abnormal,
healthy and sick, genuine and spurious, two situations and two
fundamentally different attitudes must be recognized. Just as
we inevitably think in antithetic categories (just and unjust,
beautiful and ugly, good and bad) which break up and seem to
disappear in a logico-intellectualist arrangement, but which
hold out tenaciously and reappear in other forms when they
are suppressed, so also in the case of religion we find it impossible to define the authentic and the counterfeit but are obliged
to acknowledge their presence. Thus the problem of antithetic

[20] G. W. Allport, 'Mental Health: A Generic Attitude' in *Journal of
Religion and Health*, vol. IV, no. 1, October 1964, pp. 13-14.

categories arises in a particular form in the field of religious activity. In this connection let us glance briefly at the impressive synthesis of a philosopher who started out with the method of scientific analysis in which the principle of evolution seems to demolish the validity of psychological intuition, but who ended by asserting that psychological intuition itself is the starting-point for the interpretation of the facts. The philosopher in question is Henri Bergson.

Static and dynamic religion

When we speak of the two sources of moral and religious life, as Odier has done, we are necessarily brought back to Bergson's great work which preceded Odier's and bears a very similar title: *The Two Sources of Morality and Religion*.[21] Odier rightly observes that his own theory is a different one: he is referring to the Freudian unconscious and to conscious morality, while Bergson is referring to social pressure and mysticism. If some motives of Bergson's first source may be common to both writers, those of Bergson's second source, according to Odier, undoubtedly belong to the supernatural plane. Bergson's work is so valuable and so brilliant that we must mention it briefly in the present context where we are endeavouring to see religion in the proper light, asking ourselves if it is satisfactory to explain it by the play of antagonistic forces. Bergson begins by asking himself what constitutes the core of what we call obligation, of the feeling that a thing must be done, while the alternative also exists of being able to leave it undone. Physical and biological causality knows no such alternative. In the history of the world of living things an evolutionary bipartition has come about. On the one hand the anthropoids, and particularly insects, have developed towards deterministically organized social patterns (so much so that the members can be appropriately compared to the cells of an

[21] H. Bergson, *The Two Sources of Morality and Religion*, Henry Holt and Co., New York, 1935. Also available in an Anchor paper-back edition.

organism rather than to individuals in human society). On the other hand the vital impulse has been directed towards forms capable of greater independence although still united by social needs. Man expresses this situation to the maximum degree. Instinct and intelligence are two different ways by which life establishes itself, but both involve an element of obligation. If Nature has willed, at the apex of the evolutionary line leading to intelligence, to leave a certain latitude to individual choice, she has also arranged that social regularity should prevail here by means of the process of habit-formation. Habit assumes an obligatory function similar to that of instinctive regulation. Thus there comes into being a force that Bergson calls 'the totality of obligation', the concentrated extract or quintessence of the thousands of special habits we have contracted in order to conform to the thousands of particular demands of social life.[22] The nucleus of obligation therefore proceeds from 'social pressure' and aims at the preservation of society itself. When danger threatens, obligations can be turned upside down. 'We need only think of what happens in time of war. Murder and pillage and perfidy, cheating and lying become not only lawful, but are actually praiseworthy.'[23] The stratum of justification attributed to moral conduct is overthrown by the social instinct which lies at the basis of social obligation. A society of this type is necessarily shut up in itself and reacts violently to any change which upsets its order. Escape is possible, but at the price of estrangement from society, accompanied by a sense of anguish. In this way what is of pure obligation is clearly established, but a rigid and static morality is the result. Many times in the course of human history there have been irruptions of new life, incarnated in exceptional men by whom others were carried away in a vital impulse which overcame social constraint itself. Bergson sees here another source of morality and religion, irreducible to the former because it has opposite characteristics. The difference is not one of degree but of kind, just as an open geometrical figure is different from a closed one. Here there is not question of pressure but of liberation.

[22] *Ibid.*, p. 18.   [23] *Ibid.*, p. 23.

The first type of morality is a social morality, the second a human morality. The former is the one we think of when we feel a natural obligation to do something. The other is love, dedication and transcendence, expressed in a simple and all-embracing activity. According to Bergson we become most familiar with the second source of morality and religion by drawing near to the great mystics of the Jewish-Christian tradition, in which mystical experience also impels to action. While the first source issues from the social instinct and is therefore infra-intellectual, the second proceeds from contact with the life-giving impulse and is therefore supra-intellectual. Bergson insists on the fact that there is no possibility of transition from the one type of morality to the other (and the same holds good for religion). He points out, however, that each type is an ideal limit. Actually the two streams flow side by side even though one appears to prevail over the other. But both the infra-intellectual, social impulse and the supra-intellectual or mystical one are worked over by man's reason which tends to introduce universality into purely static or infra-intellectual morality and a sense of obligation into purely dynamic or supra-intellectual morality. In regard to religion particularly, Bergson writes: 'The spectacle of what religions have been in the past, of what certain religions still are today, is indeed humiliating for human intelligence. . . . Religion has been known to enjoin immorality, to prescribe crime.'[24] What is the origin of this clinging to the irrational? '*Homo sapiens*, the only creature endowed with reason, is also the only creature to pin its existence to things unreasonable.'[25] Even civilized man is not immune from certain forms of irrational faith. Without a doubt, man who enjoys the privilege of reason but at the same time bears the burden of being unable to find an answer to many questions which arise in his mind, and who is aware of the fragility of his existence, has an instinctive need to know and to rule. This is why he 'fabulates', filling his world with absurd personalities, and this is the origin of magic, by which he imagines he is bending the world to his will. This

[24] *Ibid.*, p. 92.   [25] *Ibid.*

myth-making is the consequence of his need to protect his life. It is a biological process which is reflected on the psychological plane in the form of religion, just as individual interaction and social pressure are reflected in the form of obligation. This kind of static religion is 'a defensive reaction of nature against what might be depressing for the individual and dissolvent for society in the exercise of intelligence'.[26] 'The myth-making function, though not an instinct, plays in human societies a part exactly corresponding to that of instinct in animal societies.'[27] The antithesis of this is 'dynamic religion', in which man makes contact again with the life-giving and creative impulse and passes from a state of fear, a shut-in state, to one of love, which opens up and is receptive and active at the same time, and is capable of seeing all humanity in the individual man. This pure mystical intuition is certainly 'a rare essence that is generally found in a diluted form but even then it still gives to the substance with which it mingles its colour and fragrance'.[28] But when it calls, there is

in the innermost being of most men the whisper of an echo. Mysticism reveals, or rather would reveal to us if we actually willed it, a marvellous prospect: we do not and in most cases we could not will it; we should collapse under the strain. Yet the spell has worked, and just as when an artist of genius has produced a work which is beyond us, but which makes us feel how commonplace were the things we used to admire, in the same way static religion, though it may still be there, is no longer what it was, above all, it no longer dares to assert itself, when truly great mysticism comes on the scene.[29]

Here too religion is gripped as in a vice between two contrasting and irreducible demands: the demand of what Bergson calls 'closed morality' and of what he calls 'open morality'. Extreme cases in the unalloyed state are rare (especially where 'open' religion is concerned) and intermediate states are more

[26] *Ibid.*, p. 194.
[27] *Ibid.*, p. 196.
[28] *Ibid.*, p. 202.
[29] *Ibid.*, p. 203.

numerous. The statement of two distinct principles remains, however, and the far from negligible fact of an intermediate situation. It is worth our while to make a few comments at this point. Bergson declares that social pressure is felt by the individual in the form of a 'sense of obligation'. This statement, as Copleston points out, is ambiguous. It might mean that social pressure is an empirical, non-ethical fact which causes in us the peculiar (that is, specifically ethical) feeling of obligation. The case would be analogous to that of a man who had feelings, say, of great happiness and peace under a drug. On the other hand the statement that social pressure is felt by the individual in the form of an obligation might mean that this feeling is one of social pressure directed to the performance or non-performance of action, in the sense that consciousness of the obligation is consciousness of the social pressure. Asch discusses the same problem extensively.[30] In either case, what is this new, 'moral' aspect which is superimposed on the pressure? Here we are faced with the various senses in which Bergson appears to use the term 'obligation', since he includes under it mere social conventions and the valuation of morally binding acts. Instead of making a *prima facie* observation of the sense of obligation, so as to establish its characteristics, Bergson tends to look for its cause and he then calls this cause 'obligation'. This confusion of cause and effect is a mistake. Copleston says:

> We can determine, for instance, the physical causes of our perception of colours, but it does not follow that these causes can appropriately be called colours. The matter is more than a 'mere question of words'. If we wish to say that the State developed out of the tribe, it is none the less misleading to speak of the State as a tribe or of a tribe as a State. If it could be shown, for example, that the affection of friendship was a sublimation of sexual desire, it would none the less be misleading to call friendship sexual desire; for it would conceal important differences. And whether we

[30] S. Asch, *Social Psychology, op. cit.*

understand by Bergson's 'pure obligation' social pressure or the habit of contracting habits, it is misleading to call it obligation in the context of an ethical enquiry.[31]

In actual fact, to reduce the moral obligation to social pressure signifies explaining morality by eliminating it from the discussion entirely.

As regards the distinction between closed and open forms of morality and religion, we may remark that in defining the closed forms as religions of 'obligation' and the open forms as religions of 'invitation', stress is certainly laid on the greater possibility of escape from the open forms than from the closed forms. But invitation also implies a choice, a decision, an act by which the subject is perhaps committed to a greater extent than he is by social pressure. If we pass on from the establishment of the fact (rigidity and aberrations in the closed forms, freedom and creative activity in the open forms) to a judgment of values, and judge the closed religions to be inferior and the open ones of greater worth, there is danger of overlooking the fact that the open forms also, if undisciplined, can be harmful. This becomes evident in certain forms of isolation from society and certain forms of fanaticism. It must also be said that the form itself needs a means of expression, and whether this is new or utilizes pre-existing material it cannot escape from being 'closed'. 'Dictionaries and grammars,' writes Mathieu,

do not constitute a second source of literature side by side with inspiration. . . . Just as there are not two literatures, but only one good literature which expresses something unitary in words, and bad literature which strings together words and sentences according to an exterior technique—so too there are not two moralities, but a single morality which is the inventor of forms. . . . The writer is faced with words and rules of grammar and syntax already established, and he does not succeed in his work merely because he follows

[31] F. C. Copleston, 'Bergson on Morality', *Proceedings of the British Academy*, 1955, vol. XLI, pp. 255-6.

these, but because he uses them to express a new creative impulse.[32]

Even if there are two or more paths by which people come to have moral convictions, observes Copleston, this does not prove that there is not *one* human morality which can be known in different ways and into which various individuals and different societies can have varying degrees of insight.

These reservations seem necessary when Bergson makes obligation coincide with social pressure (and thereby reaches the conclusion that there are two irreducibly different forms of religion), as also when he speaks of two sources with opposite characteristics. But we must also appreciate some other statements of Bergson which have opened an effective counter-attack on positions whose rigidity had seemed to be impregnable. We recall Bergson's opposition to the reduction of the simple to a sum of imperceptible transitions. References to the negation of movement when it is studied by merely mathematical standards (the paradox of Zeno); to the reduction of 'seeing' to the total of a number of elementary stimulations of the eye; to making an imprint coincide with the displacement of particles which, under pressure of the hand, have arranged themselves in such a way as to produce the image of a stamp or seal—these are comparisons and examples which recur frequently both in *Creative Evolution* and in the *Two Sources*. Bergson's statement is strong: movement exists, the act of seeing is simple, the imprint possesses a quality of its own.

If we think only of the interval and the various points, infinite in number, which we still have to pass one by one, we shall be discouraged from starting, like Zeno's arrow.... But if we step across the intervening space, thinking only of the goal or looking even beyond it, we shall easily accomplish a simple act and at the same time overcome the infinite multiplicity of which this simplicity is the equivalent.

[32] V. Mathieu, *Bergson: il profondo e la sua espressione*, Ed. di Filosofia, Turin, 1954.

The psychic experience of moving, of seeing, of recognizing does not coincide with the fragmentariness of the elements, but is the only thing that enables us to unify them in a reasonable way. Religious experience also has a clearly unifying character. This is perhaps the most significant result of Bergson's work on the data of consciousness and it is one of the reasons why the evolution of organisms cannot be explained by theories such as those of Darwin and Spencer, but involves a life-giving impulse, a creative evolution. It seems to me that Bergson's spark of genius is to be found here. Even if there is a continuum of transitions or moments, there is a discontinuity of facts. It is therefore in the aggregate qualities, in their close relationship, in their 'form' that the continuum is broken, as Rümke and Allport have said, echoing Bergson. The distinction of qualitative as well as quantitative differences is therefore restored.

Openness and withdrawal

All that has been said leads to another distinction—that between openness and withdrawal, which is liable to be misunderstood and must therefore be made with certain reservations (already mentioned). Between these two situations there is an insurmountable barrier. The parabola and the ellipse, although delimited by curved lines, are irreducible one to the other. Withdrawal signifies static necessity, openness the possibility of development. Minkowski declares that 'the open indicates something alive; the closed no longer does so, it is opaque'.[33] We might add that what is closed, or dead, still possesses qualities which could characterize the open or living, but it has lost what is essential, namely impulse. Here we realize that the contrast between open and closed is indispensable in order that impulse may be maintained and that the points of gradual transition may be surmounted. From this point of

[33] E. Minkowski, 'Psychiatrie, psychothérapie: relations avec le malade et le grand publique' in *Annales Medico-Psychologiques*, October 1953.

view, although there is opposition between the open and the
closed, it is not a reciprocally exclusive opposition, as Bergson
sometimes seems to indicate, but an opposition of co-existence,
in reciprocal, joint antagonism. Minkowski, then, would seem
to have hit the mark when he pleads for a recognition of

> the very character of human life, which while made up of
> adaptation and alleged equilibrium, also involves—we were
> about to say fortunately—untimely and upsetting forces
> which are often the source of quite positive reactions,
> including creative power. These forces are also the origin of
> the appeal to the individual to deal on his own as best he
> can with these forces. . . . Natural human weaknesses must
> be taken into account. They are far from being a sign of
> neurotic need, as K. Horney seems to think when she
> enumerates neurotic needs, so deceptively similar to natural
> human weaknesses. It is necessary to re-establish the rights
> of this notion of human weakness.

'There is no such thing as a sky without clouds or a sea without waves,' continues Minkowski.

> An upset can also be caused by excessive adaptation, exces-
> sive equilibrium, by excesses of pragmatism, rationalism or
> prosiness. The same applies to 'affective maturation' which
> fortunately involves some residua of the infantile mind:
> the excess of adultism is only another excess added to others.
> Mental life is not a pure source . . . it is made up of
> innumerable heterogeneous factors which it is impossible to
> separate—contradictions, internal conflicts, etc. It does not
> present a simple aspect. There is a beginning of degradation
> in the 'nervousness' of every life. The mistake lies in giving
> undue prominence to degradation. For despite all this
> heterogeneity we arrive at intention, action and progress. . . .
> Intention, act and reaction cannot be separated psycho-
> logically from this mobile and obscure foundation from
> which they proceed unless we want to treat them as abstract
> concepts. There are two sources or perhaps ultimately only
> one—that to which conscious life is related in its progress.

The acts of seeking, tending, building and aspiring stand out in relief against this progression: here we have the foundation of every human life.

I have taken the liberty of quoting this long passage because it would be difficult to express more clearly and effectively the conclusion of much discussion on normality and abnormality. Morality and religion, as psychic activities, are included in this framework of heterogeneity, of simplicity, of constructiveness, and when they are removed from it they lose their harmonious vitality and appear in a false light. This is why the reductive position of Freud does not satisfy us, nor that of Odier which is certainly more liberal. There is a healthy religious activity and an unhealthy one, but completely healthy or completely unhealthy religion are abstract concepts which do not authorize us to deny the religious activity of men in general. At best we find in men 'that touch of the pathological which exists in the normal', and if the worst comes to the worst we still find in them a genuine need to refer to something outside themselves and the valuable experience of the insecurity of human existence. When William James, with his predilection for extreme cases, contrasts the religion of perfect mental balance with unhealthy religion and attributes a much more efficient vitality to the latter, he repeats a meaningful paradox: the superiority of the man who feels a problem acutely compared to superficiality of the man who does not see it at all in his anxiety to avoid the slightest damage to his own well-being. Morality and religion which are felt merely as constraint or which do not involve trial and effort, already show that they are not authentic. To stop at this point and reduce morality and religion simply to neurotic mechanisms shows failure to understand their most substantial aspect. This explains why such misrepresentation is painful to those whose religious convictions are based on what is substantial. It also explains why it is attractive to those who already have a tendency to abdicate and escape from themselves. It is moreover to be noted that while pseudomoral and pseudoreligious manifestations take place in neurotics, deriving from a different cause, there are also genuinely religious neurotics why by means of their personal experience itself, sometimes past, sometimes still in progress, bring us face to face with strong, calm and convincing religious activity which is the very opposite to the rigidity and egoism of the neurotic. As I write these lines I am thinking of Father Vincent McNabb, admired and loved as one of the noblest of souls by men like Chesterton and Belloc, but who, in the life of him written by Father F. Valentine, comes out as a serious case of neurosis. We may well ask ourselves, then, whether the analytical method is really the indispensable panacea, as Odier believes, and if we are to relegate to the background the great religious truths expressed in the severe language which Jesus used against the Pharisees.

In advanced religious life there is a note of human greatness and tragedy that is unknown to science. 'If King Oedipus had suffered from the Oedipus complex, his fate would not have been a tragedy, but a *historia morbi*,' writes Rümke. 'If Oedipus was suffering from an Oedipus complex in the neurotic sense, if we were to see in his adventures the effects of neurosis, he would be greatly to be pitied, but he would not have become a great tragic figure. The tragedy moves us by its human tone, so different from that of neurosis.' Rümke observes that in Sophocles' tragedy there is much more than the clinical picture of neurosis. First of all, we have the ambivalent reaction of his parents towards Oedipus, destined by them to die. Then there is the tragedy of Jocasta whom we should consider just as neurotic as Oedipus. The problem of guilt and punishment is disconcerting: unconscious crime, innocent guilt, or were Oedipus and Jocasta aware of what they were doing? The same sense of bewilderment is experienced by anyone who considers the terrible possibilities to which his life is exposed. Is it really neurotic to consider incest to be horrible? Ought it not to be considered normal to judge parricide the most terrible of disasters? No, says Rümke, none of the principal actors here is neurotic. Yet there are analogies between the fate of Oedipus and the events of the Oedipus complex. But, argues

Rümke, these are likenesses which do not remove the difference: the happy life of the couple for eighteen years and the characters of both Oedipus and Jocasta are anything but neurotic. Unlike the stunned apathy of the pathological patient, 'the tragic personality as presented to us by Aeschylus and Sophocles, by Shakespeare and Dostoievsky,' writes R. Cantoni, 'is not fascinated by death and nothingness. He is moved by strong passions, he wants to live and assert his own personality instead of shutting himself up in desolate contemplation of ruin and death. Tragic experience is not merely destructive and annihilating but is even to a great extent reconstructive and edifying, when man finds out by this means, beyond all alibi or escape, the character and meaning of his presence in the world.'[34]

In religious activity with its impulses and its weaknesses, along with a note of serious and deep commitment we hear another note, majestic and serene. Here we have something different from the insistent monotony of a torment where escape is sought under any form whatsoever. In a stormy sky a bright patch will sometimes appear, so immensely serene and calm that it survives in the soul even when the storm is renewed or when daily life takes on the appearance of a drab and futile succession of little acts which submerge us in a harsh cold scepticism from which we try to escape by stifling our emotions. Rümke synthesizes this state of affairs in the 'principle of openness and withdrawal' which we have already seen indicated by Allport. A veneer of 'neurotic withdrawal' may conceal a genuine moral and religious process but cannot suppress it. When either attitude, openness or withdrawal, becomes absolute, the result is abnormality. A state of continual withdrawal is stagnation while one of continual expansion is dissipation.

Normality is to be found in the rhythmic and harmonious antagonism between expansion and withdrawal. Rümke observes that this rhythm has a biological parallel. We inhale

[34] R. Cantoni, 'Il tragico come problema filosofico' in *Rivista di Filosofia*, LIV, no. 1 (Jan.-Mar. 1963), pp. 37-38.

and expel the air. We accept and refuse nourishment. The body is kept alive by rhythmic pulsations; the muscles are subject to contraction and relaxation, the nerves to tension and repose. During the entire course of our life we are alternately awake and asleep. We expand and withdraw in relation to ourselves, in relation to others and to the world. If there is to be expansion or opening it must necessarily be preceded and followed by closing or withdrawal. The very 'opening' when it fails to allow of a subsequent 'closing' becomes rigid and static, like a permanent hole.

Religion and morality pure and unalloyed probably do not exist even in the most perfect men. They constitute an ideal state which is beyond our reach. Although we distinguish two sources, the river which flows into our consciousness is a single one, more or less turbid. Even the most limpid river carries some detritus which helps to form the river bed and channel the waters. A stagnant and muddy swamp always contains a little water which can be purified by the sun. It is true, of course, that when the river's flow is obstructed there must be a rechannelling to prevent stoppage and the danger of flooding. The psychiatrist must intervene in this case. When unconscious motives have become an obstacle to normal psychic life he may succeed in providing a remedy. Processes like morality and religion which are so essential to human life, so strong in their effects yet so fragile from the point of view of stability, are inevitably exposed to degeneration, neither more nor less than other human possibilities. Dedication degenerates into a calculating attitude; faithfulness into conformism; beauty and art into fashion. Here too it is a question of form and rhythm rather than of raw material. This is why we have dwelt on the subject—perhaps at too great length—to demonstrate the fallacy of reductive and quantitative interpretations. Even if these interpretations appear to have finished off the religious concern of men in its narrow institutionalized manifestations, religion is liable to reappear in the most unexpected and disconcerting forms. With reference to Jewish religious life as it appears in the impressive poetry of the Psalms, C. S. Lewis has written: 'There, despite the presence of elements we should now find it hard to regard as religious at all [imprecation, etc., as already mentioned], and the absence of elements which some might think essential to religion, I find an experience fully God-centred, asking of God no gift more urgently than his presence, the gift of himself, joyous to the highest degree and unmistakably real.'[35] Is there not a spark of this mysterious presence and tacit petition in the religions of all peoples and in all men, even when they declare they have no religious belief and are taken at their word?

It is impossible to establish absolute norms by which to judge whether religion is genuine or spurious. But this does not mean that religion is to be reduced to a biological process disguised under the most varied and vexed forms. It is possible to distinguish, though, in which cases religion appears more limpid and in which more turbid, to recognize it as more genuine or more spurious. But in both cases the only indication is that of characteristic meaning, of a 'general attitude' to a Mystery, largely independent of ideological and moral principles (which, however, it cannot forgo). Religion can in a certain sense be described as ambivalent, because of its deeply human tone and its openness to that which surpasses man.

---

[35] C. S. Lewis, *Reflections on the Psalms*, Harcourt, Brace and Co., New York, 1958, p. 52. Also available in a Fontana paperback edition.

3. The 'Natural History' of Religion

Archetype, symbol and myth according to C. G. Jung

When Jung points out that the power of the father-image is out of proportion to its sensory components even when these are highly charged with emotion, and considers it necessary to have recourse to the individual's ancestral inheritance in order to explain it, he is in agreement with Freud. But when he claims that a primitive imprint or archetype is transmitted and attributes to the libido a mere energetic content devoid of any sexual character, he takes a step which cuts him off definitely from Freud, since he is now asserting the primordial genuineness of experiences other than the sexual. When he subsequently asserts that the archetypes are irreducible to the child's personal situations, that they appear with singular tenacity in symbols, dreams and myths so that they must belong to a collective unconscious: when he observes that the archetype converges towards the *numinosum* and claims that religious experience is a primitive, general and irreducible one; and finally, when he points to the existence (psychological, not ontological) of an archetype possessing divine qualities, the 'Self', which imposes itself on consciousness, he is reversing the situation from which he started. It is not the father-image which produces by projection the God-image, but the archetype which is projected on to the father and bestows divine qualities on his image. The heavenly father is no longer the image of the earthly father, but the earthly father is the image of the heavenly one.

These considerations could seem to be the result of a complex theoretical conception which is then applied to the facts. At first sight Freud's interpretation appears more consistent and straightforward: attraction, conflict, introjection, identification, projection of the father-image. This may be true. But it remains to be explained how from the fact that a sensory representation is invested with affect, following the primitive pattern of pleasure and pain, an image can emerge possessing characteristics which are so different in themselves and which can be traced neither to sensory data nor to affective causes. The power of this image and its qualities of greatness, power, mystery and fascination are quite the opposite of the real father's actual characteristics and seem to point to the superimposition of a primordial pattern upon a sensory representation. Binswanger arrives at a conclusion similar to that of Jung: 'The bond which binds the child to the father is neither the example nor the starting-point of the God-father thought, but the reverse. The fact that the child is receptive to the child-father idea is the result of a typically ideal existence of the child-father idea born of our relation to God.'[1] V. Frankl also comes close to this position, although he does not accept the archetype but supposes a personal relationship. The problem of archetype, symbol and myth cannot therefore be overlooked and a vast number of studies have been devoted to this question.

We began with Jung and perhaps it will be useful to explain his doctrine more fully. Jung has taken the term 'archetype' from the *Corpus Hermeticum* and from the writings of pseudo-Dionysius. The etymology points to the meaning: *arche*: beginning; *typos*: norm, imprint or figure. St Augustine (to whom Jung refers) also speaks of archetypes as 'ideae principales, formae quaedam vel rationes rerum stabiles atque incommutabiles quae ipsae formatae non sunt, ac per hoc aeternae'.[2] He is referring to Platonic ideas, but the qualities indicated (stable and immutable principles and forms) are in agreement with the archetype as conceived by Jung. The mean-

---

[1] L. Binswanger, at the Groningen Psychological Congress, cited in H. C. Rümke, *The Psychology of Unbelief*, Rockliff, London, 1952, p. 30.

[2] Augustine, *De Diversis Quaestionibus*, PL, vol. XL.

ing, however, is different. St Augustine was speaking of eternal ideas in the divine mind, whereas Jung had in mind those psychic elements which are constant in all men independently of individuals, because they exist apart from all personal experience and are therefore to be referred to a collective unconscious. (Note the curious comparison between Jung's collective unconscious and the divine mind of Leibniz and the ontological philosophers, according to whom individual men have a direct intuitive perception of these ideas and contemplate them in the divinity.)

Like Freud, Jung found himself obliged to build up a psychic organism and the archetypes are precisely the psychic organs. The form of these archetypes, according to Jung, is comparable to the axial systems of a crystal which predetermines, as it were, the crystalline formation in the saturated solution, without itself possessing a material existence. This existence first manifests itself in the way the molecules arrange themselves. The axial system determines the structure but not the concrete form of the individual crystal and just so the archetype possesses an invariable core of meaning that determines its manner of appearing always only in principle, never concretely.[3] This theory is also very close to that of Goethe who set out to find primordial images (Urbilder) which are actualized in animal and plant forms.[4]

We have already mentioned that Jung, who accepts unconditionally the principle of ontogenetic recapitulation of phylogenetic development, sees in the archetypes the result of progressive acquisitions of the human species. He asserts that this takes place in man because he possesses neuropsychic dispositions which enable him to form equivalent images— equivalent because these maintain the same meaning although they employ different materials. Jung specifies that 'the archetype does not proceed from physical facts but describes how

[3] J. Jacobi, The Psychology of C. G. Jung, Yale University Press, 1954, p. 57.
[4] Cf. E. Dacqué, Natur und Erlösung, Munich, 1933; C. Singer, A Short History of Biology, Oxford, 1931, pp. 215-17.

the psyche experiences the physical fact'.[5] The physical world, the environment, is the stimulus (Leibniz would call it the occasion) for the projection into it of the archetypes (as the developing liquid brings out pictures on photographic plates): and 'the psyche often behaves so autocratically that it denies tangible reality or makes statements that fly in the face of it'.[6] That which we observe in the symbol is precisely the enormous preponderance of the archetype over the raw fact. Now

in the dream, as in the products of psychoses, there are numberless interconnections to which one can find parallels only in mythological associations of ideas. . . . Had thorough investigation shown that in the majority of such cases it was simply a matter of forgotten knowledge, the physician would not have gone to the trouble of making extensive researches into individual and collective parallels. But, in point of fact, typical mythologems were observed among individuals to whom all knowledge of this kind was absolutely out of the question, and where indirect derivation from religious ideas that might have been known to them, or from popular figures of speech, was impossible. Such conclusions forced us to assume that we must be dealing with 'autochthonous' revivals independent of all tradition, and consequently, that 'myth-making' structural elements must be present in the unconscious psyche.[7]

The variety of symbols is quite extensive. 'The human figures are father and son, mother and daughter, king and queen, god and goddess. Theriomorphic symbols are the dragon, snake, elephant, lion, bear and other powerful animals, or again, the spider, crab, butterfly, beetle, worm etc. Plant symbols are generally flowers (lotus and rose). These lead on to geometrical figures like the circle, the sphere, the square, the quaternity, the clock, the firmament and so on.'[8] But it is not a question

[5] C. G. Jung and K. Kerényi, *The Archetype and the Unconscious*, in *Collected Works*, vol. IX, part 1, p. 154.
[6] *Ibid.*
[7] *Ibid.*, p. 152.
[8] *Ibid.*, p. 187.

of mere images, even thought distorted. Each one is charged with meaning and indicates an action; and in this they are the expression of an archetype, although an archetype may be expressed by various symbols represented by images.

The archetype of the conflict between light and darkness can be expressed by the myth of the sun-hero who escapes from the dark bosom of Mother Earth and plunges into it again at the end of each day, or in the myth of the fight with the dragon. It is to be remarked how in the myth the symbols become 'dramatis personae', that is, the myth expresses something that is lived. 'What else is the myth of the night sea voyage, of the wandering hero, or of the sea monster, than our timeless knowledge, transformed into a picture, of the sun's setting and rebirth?'[9] The number of archetypes is limited, since they are outlines of action corresponding to man's typical but limited possibilities, and the total of the archetypes is the total of all the latent possibilities of the human psyche. A particular emotional intensity corresponds to them, so much so that in the moments in which an archetypal situation presents itself, the subject appears to be seized by a superhuman power. Nor is it possible to resist the action of archetypes with impunity, for they behave 'exactly like neglected or maltreated physical organs or organic functional systems'.[10] Neurosis and psychosis are the consequences of an archetypal transgression, which seeks to reappear in a deviant form. Symbols and archetypal experiences are the patrimony of all religions. The petrifaction of religious formalism and also the technico-rationalist mentality curtail the possibilities of connection between the clear conscious part of the mind and the obscure, unconscious part, thus cutting it off from the source of life.

Jung's position can be outlined more or less as follows. The existence of patterns of reference and of action shared by men of all races and religions leads us to believe in a psychic organization according to primitive types (the archetypes). This organization of sensory data and affective impulses is so much

[9] J. Jacobi, op. cit., p. 62.
[10] C. G. Jung and K. Kerényi, op. cit., p. 157.

D

more decisive than the raw, objective datum that it appears to contradict the latter. The result of this organization (the symbol), which astounds us by its irrationality, contains and expresses a vital and insuppressible psychic meaning. Psychic dynamism is therefore attained and understood by means of the archetypal organization rather than by a man's environment and the messages he receives from it. Mental disorder enters in when the archetypes are prevented from operating or meet with opposition. The archetypes appear in a particularly exacting manner in religious activity and hence religion is a normal psychic activity and indeed fulfils the indispensable task of maintaining a right balance. When the religious sense weakens or is expressed in a one-sided manner, the door is opened to neurosis.

Religious behaviour and art among primitive men

We now propose to look at the problem of myth from other points of view, beginning with its expression in primitive man.

The history of man upon earth is a very long one when compared to the brief life of the individual, and documents for its reconstruction become more and more rare and difficult to interpret as we go back towards the sources.[11] Despite this fact, says Marrett, 'traces of religion and all the major institutions of mankind persist until they fade out altogether precisely at the point at which man himself fades out also'.[12] The first

[11] In establishing whether skeletal remains are of men or of monkeys, palaeontologists are guided by the presence or absence of handmade objects along with the bones, that is, by traces of human activity in the form of tools, carved objects, or evidence of fire. The earliest traces of a magico-religious concept, according to von Koenigswald, are the probable practice of cannibalism and skull worship by Sinanthropus (G. H. R. Koenigswald, *Die Geschichte des Menschen*, Berlin, 1960). But reliable and meaningful documentary evidence appears in the Middle Palaeolithic Age (animal worship, offerings of first fruits, funeral rites with provision of foodstuffs for life beyond the tomb), and we have definite magico-religious manifestations in the Upper Palaeolithic Age (grottoes of Tuc d'Audobert and Lascaux).

[12] E. O. James, *History of Religions*, English Universities Press, London, 1956, p. 211.

signs of religion (objects of worship, sculpture, paintings, remains of tombs) go back to the most recent period of the Stone Age. Some scholars believe that traces have been found in China, at Chou-Kou-Tien, of skull worship practised about four hundred thousand years ago, that is to say, three hundred thousand years before Neanderthal man in Europe buried his dead. The most significant documents of early man's activity relate to the period between fifty thousand and one hundred thousand years ago, that is, to the final interglacial period which came with the last glacial (Würmian) expansion. The remains of utensils indicate considerable technical ability in the preparation of instruments intended for a particular purpose and owned by individuals personally (also to be found in tombs). Paintings and sculptures denote an ability to represent things perfectly and realistically. The images of animals are quite recognizable and absolutely true to life, so much so that the likeness of an elephant covered with hair was not understood by the first discoverers and was taken to be a fantastic representation. But at the end of the last century, when some mammoths were discovered in Siberia, perfectly preserved in the ice, it was recognized that these drawings were true to life.

This realistic note is not however sufficient to explain another aspect of the most ancient objects made by man's hand and the most primitive representations he designed. Particularly interesting are the designs, especially those depicting animals, engraved on bone or which appear on the walls of caverns or in the form of little statues. On both slopes of the Pyrenees, towards France and towards Spain, well-preserved frescoes have been discovered in several grottoes. At Font-de-Gaume, near Les Eyzies in the Dordogne region, a long tunnel leading into a grotto appears at a certain point to be blocked by stalactites and beyond this barrier the grotto walls are painted, terminating in a perfect reproduction of a rhinoceros painted in red ochre. This arrangement of paintings leading to the most important representation situated in a particularly secluded spot is repeated in other grottoes also.

At Niaux the chamber adorned with frescoes is distant about

three-quarters of a mile from the entrance and separated from it by a lake. Proceeding into the depths of the grotto one reaches a recess where there is a representation of a wounded bison surrounded by designs depicting the projectiles and weapons with which it was attacked. These are evidently hunting scenes. But why were they portrayed? Seemingly they cannot be attributed to the mere need to manifest artistic talent. In these grottoes there is no trace of households or human dwellings. The placing of the designs in inaccessible and secluded spots rather points to the fact that propitiatory sorcery relating to hunting was practised there. The animals depicted are especially those which were used as food.

Sometimes the images of animals are found one on top of another, palimpsests which show that the place was destined for magical practices. Moreover, the hunting scenes depicted on bone or on the horns of a reindeer, fashioned into weapons, conferred on these the value of amulets and were intended to guarantee the efficacy of the instrument with which the animals were attacked. In the grotto of Tuc d'Audobert, which is also in the Pyrenees, in addition to the pictures on the rock, imprints were found of barefooted artists who had penetrated into a side grotto difficult of access to depict in clay a male bison pursuing a female of the same species. Other footprints crossing and recrossing were evidently produced during a sacred dance, probably in the course of a fertility ritual.

It is not likely that the social organization of palaeolithic man was totemistic, like that of the early Australians, since not one but several animals are depicted. The magico-religious interpretation of palaeolithic paintings, however, is now certain. Stone Age man, who lived in a nomadic state and fed upon the products of the chase, believed he could improve his conditions of life not only by technical means and stratagems (weapons, hunting excursions) but by religious actions which might bring him success in his hunting and an increase in the number of his children.

Another representation discovered at Tuc d'Audobert is very meaningful—a human face with a long beard, the eyes and beak of an owl, a lion's claws and a horse's tail. This has been interpreted as the effigy of a dancing sorcerer. Similar figures have been found in other grottoes. Even if this interpretation is incorrect, a figure of this kind goes to show how primitive man associated men and animals in the events of his life.

Important evidence of the mentality of the men of earliest times appears in their burial places, of which some traces have survived. Characteristic of the Stone Age are tombs covered with red ochre or red clay. It is believed that these men considered blood to be the vital fluid, the loss of which meant death. They believed that if it were possible to put fresh blood into the dead man, he would come back to life. Hence the addition of red ochre to the tombs, signifying a renewal of life: a magical act aimed at restoring life to the dead body. In the tombs, besides this ochre, shells are to be found strung together to form necklaces, probably amulets. Many skeletons of the Stone Age have been found bent double. Some see in this a symbol of rebirth, since it reminds them of the position of the foetus in the womb, but this supposition seems a daring one when we consider how little these primitive men knew of anatomy. It has been suggested that the dead were bent over into this position before they became rigid, to prevent their spirits from going about to molest the living. Along with these bones, stone weapons have been found and bones of the animals that were used for food.

A custom of which we have earlier traces still is the preservation of skulls (which it is believed were separated from the trunk with flint knives), all of them placed with the face towards the east and plunged in red ochre. In 1939 a man's skull (race of Neanderthal) was discovered in a grotto on Monte Circeo (between Rome and Naples), placed in a ritual position in a space enclosed by a circle of stones. It is thought that the brain had been extracted to serve as sacred food which conferred courage and fertility. In 1940 the 'Palaeolithic Sistine', as it was called by H. Breuil, was discovered at Lascaux.

The first evidences of men's activity in the Stone Age indicate their ability as builders and artists and also give us some idea of their mentality, their characteristic relationship with the world with regard to the problems of nutrition (hunting), increase (fertility) and survival after death (burial places). This relationship is not expressed in material form but as an action upon occult and mysterious powers, in sharp contrast with the significance that merely sensory experience could have bestowed on the events of hunting and mating.

In the case of survival, the contrast becomes particularly clear, because no rebirth or resurrection was ever witnessed. This is a clear indication that a psychological need was superimposed on the results of sensory data, even though belief was acquired by learning and transmitted in traditions. The tenacity with which this interpretation was sustained is also significant. While depth psychology has accustomed us (too much) to seek unconscious causes rather than their expression on the surface, we must also admit that the existence of particular human needs, bodily needs but also psychic and religious needs (longing for safety, attraction, fear, protection in the face of unknown powers), already appears quite clearly in primitive man. It is these needs which bestow order on his world and give it a meaning.

In the Neolithic or later Stone Age, when men had passed from nomadic to sedentary life, when they cultivated plants, reared cattle and established themselves in fixed abodes, the expression of religion took on a different form and was gradually differentiated and enriched. Provision of food supplies for the inclement season, storage of seed for the following year, domestication and rearing of animals, transport by wheeled vehicles, the use of fire and so forth: in all these activities man became aware of his ability to rule but also of his limitations and his dependence on higher powers. He sought to propitiate these powers by communications of a religious nature. He created sacred emblems and temples; he dedicated particular persons, days or circumstances to these higher powers. All this shows that man in the later Stone Age already recognized the existence of a spiritual world, and that this idea was already institutionalized and incorporated in his social customs. As a psychological reality the spiritual world is an indestructible element of life.

It is only in comparatively recent times that written documents emerge in history to throw a clearer light on the interpretations of the world expressed by the various religions in myths and prayers.

Myth

'The first man,' writes Kerényi, 'has not yet been discovered by science. Rather is he the true object of mythology.'[13] This statement is not an ironical one, as if to say: 'where science stops imagination takes over; the less we know the more we chatter'. It expresses the conviction that myths, apart from their historical import—whether or not they took place in the precise way in which they are presented—have a value and an importance of their own. According to Malinowski's definition they are 'the statement of a primitive, a great and an important reality upon which the life and destiny and activity of mankind depend'.[14]

Obviously we are very far from the meaning attributed to the word 'myth' in modern language, which represents it as a fantastic construction with no real equivalent. The eighteenth-century Illuminati considered myth to be a 'mystification', a falsehood sustained for selfish motives, a vulgar imposture. The Romantics, on the other hand, present it as the source of human culture, art and poetry. Rationalist and Positivist philosophers regard myth as a primitive phase in the development of human history, destined to disappear when it reaches the more perfect phases of reason and science. Hegel and Comte express themselves approximately in this way.

At the close of the last century, J. J. Bachofen advanced an original interpretation and evaluation of myth. 'The memory

[13] K. Kerényi, 'Der Erste Mensch' in *Lebendiges Wissen*, Wiesbaden, p. 224.
[14] B. Malinowski, *Crime and Custom in Savage Society*, Littlefield, New Jersey, 1959.

of real happenings which befell the human race,' he said, 'is deposited in myths. We are not dealing with fiction here but with events which really took place. These are experiences of the human race, the expression of histories which were really lived. History has brought to light greater events than even creative imagination could invent.'[15] This interpretation met with wide approval from the naturalists (E. Dacqué), anthropologists (Malinowski, Frobenius), philosophers (E. Cassirer and R. Guardini), scholars in the field of the history of religion (Jensen, Eliade) and of psychology (C. G. Jung). In his *Preface to the Scientific Study of Mythology*, compiled in collaboration with Kerényi, Jung writes: 'The primitive mentality does not *invent* myths, it *experiences* them. Myths are original revelations of the preconscious psyche, involuntary statements about unconscious psychic happenings and anything but allegories of physical processes. . . . Myths have a vital meaning. Not merely do they represent, they *are* the psychic life of the primitive tribe.'[16]

As we have seen, Jung connects myths with archetypes. Kerényi remarks that myths in their later formulation express an idea which is centred in the mythological characters, but that when we endeavour to penetrate further everything concerning the character disappears to give place to a broader and wider experience. All that is connected with the name of the character vanishes and an emotional situation emerges. In myth we find 'the evidence of something which in comparison with an idea is obscure, but in comparison with blind sensations is nevertheless similar to an idea—the revelation of something which is still shut up like a flower-bud. The oldest mythological ideas are, as a matter of fact, like buds.'[17] Myth is therefore the expression of a subjective experience, transmitted from generation to generation. When scholars speak of myth nowadays they are referring—with some divergency as to details—to this typically human artefact. Just as he prepared

[15] J. J. Bachofen, *Das Mutterrecht*, Basle, 1897, p. 24.
[16] C. G. Jung and K. Kerényi, *op. cit.*, vol. IX, part I, p. 154.
[17] *Ibid.*

utensils to meet his daily needs, primitive man in order to understand the world and give it a meaning had recourse to his inner experience and invented myth.

The 'first man' is a mythological theme and similarly 'primitive man' was first of all a myth and only at a later stage did he become the object of study. It has been shrewdly remarked that primitive man was first imagined and then discovered. When scholars began to study the life, environment and activity of primitive human beings, they were disconcerted to find how different their 'world' (or rather the world as early man saw it) was from our own. Our European world seems to be regulated by unchangeable laws of thought—the instrument we use to discover and describe it—and by the rules of logic. But this seems to be absent from the manner of thinking of primitive men, where we find representations which to our minds are inconsistent and contradictory. This is the reason why myths have been judged to be fantasy, more akin to dreams than to what we call 'reality'.

Durkheim interpreted myths as an inadequate effort to understand the world and to explain man's part, or rather his participation, in it. Lucien Lévy-Bruhl thought at one time of a prelogical mentality which was unaware of the contradictions between what it said and what experience placed before its eyes, a mentality 'which experience could not penetrate'. He considered that between our mentality and that of primitive man there was an abyss, a qualitative difference. But in his last writings, the *Carnets*,[18] he no longer upheld this 'prelogicism' but asserted the existence of thought which was not directed to the world of things but to the 'mythical' world: a thinking which was not expressed in practical but in interpretative activity. In fact primitive man in his 'technical' creations adheres more closely to reality than civilized man, and has perhaps a richer and more realistic perception of reality. The works of his hands, his buildings, all his practical activities are regulated by principles identical with our own and point to the presence of productive thought. But when we observe his

[18] L. Lévy-Bruhl, *Les Carnets*, P.U.F., Paris, 1949.

conception of the world we find, side by side with a strange lack of logical consistency, a particularly lively affective expression. He 'knows' less but 'feels' more and his feeling eludes presentation in cognitive terms, just as enjoyment of a piece of music eludes the technical description of the notes of which it is composed.

According to Lévy-Bruhl early man penetrated vitally into the mysterious world of mystical experience, the 'source of emotions', he writes, 'that penetrate the innermost depths of imagination and heart: fear, hope, respect, submission and subsequently confidence and love. In a word, we have here the whole emotional range pertaining to religious experience.'[19] For Lévy-Bruhl, therefore, primitive man's participation in the world, his connection with it, his 'sense' of the world is primarily mystical and affective and only secondarily of a logical character.

The later position assumed by Lévy-Bruhl, according to van der Leeuw, led to diminution of the difference between the thinking of primitive man and that of the man of today until it finally disappeared altogether. The revaluation of primitive thought reaches its acme today with Claude Lévi-Strauss. In his book *La Pensée Sauvage*[20] he attributes a practical and even systematic knowledge to many peoples who were considered to have little or no intellectual capacity. With regard to totemism, Lévi-Strauss declares that it cannot be explained as the adoption of a feared or venerated animal by a group, either for practical motives or from fear, but that it corresponds to precise intellectual needs. 'The alleged totemism is no more than a particular expression, by means of a special nomenclature formed of animal and plant names (in a certain code, as we should say today), which is its sole distinctive characteristic, of correlations and oppositions which may be formalized in other ways . . . by oppositions of the type sky/earth, war/peace, upstream/downstream, red/white, etc.'[21] Anthro-

[19] *Ibid.*, p. 262.
[20] C. Lévi-Strauss, *La Pensée Sauvage*, Plon, Paris, 1962.
[21] C. Lévi-Strauss, *Totemism*, Beacon Press, Boston, 1963, pp. 88-9.

pology reveals a 'homology of structure between human thought in action and the human object to which it is applied'.[22] Thus, according to Lévi-Strauss, 'if religious ideas are accorded the same value as any other conceptual system, as giving access to the mechanism of thought, the procedures of religious anthropology will acquire validity, but it will lose its autonomy and its specific character'.[23] To put it briefly, thought is the supreme need of primitive man and of modern man. Here we are at the opposite pole from the reduction of religion to an emotional fact. But here, too, its reduction to an obligatory product of the intellectual order leaves unsolved the problem of the meaning and value of religion in human life.

Myth is not, however, lacking in a logic of its own, even though it clashes with what we are accustomed to call logical thinking. H. Frankfort points out that 'prelogical thinking' involves the use of logical categories not for the purpose of reasoning but for 'highly emotional acts'.[24] In face of the phenomenal world, primitive man assumes an attitude which is the result of his need to understand rather than the result of a technical stimulus. This attitude is due rather to the urge to regulate his emotions judiciously than to attempt to analyse them. It springs rather from the need to assert himself even in face of a hostile world than from the need to reach an abstract, detached and impersonal thought-system. Myth, as is unanimously pointed out by scholars in this field, is not greatly concerned with practical life but deals with things which concern man more closely: his sense of solitude, his need of support, his need to communicate with other beings. In a word, it deals with the reason for his life and his destiny. It might be said to be more metaphysical than physical.

Frankfort has indicated several characteristics of mythopoetic thought. It lacks our distinction between the subjective and the objective. We say that the sun rises and sets, that we see a

[22] *Ibid.*, p. 91.
[23] *Ibid.*, p. 104.
[24] H. Frankfort, *Before Philosophy*, Penguin Books, Harmondsworth, Middlesex, 1954, p. 19.

colour or that we dream of a person who is dead. These are subjective experiences, but we also make other statements which we describe as objective: the earth revolves around the sun, colour is produced by vibrations of a certain wave-length, the person of whom we dream is present to us by a different process from that by which we perceive a living person. Primitive man does not divide up his perception in this way. That which appears to him *is*. Thus for him there is no clear-cut division between the living and the dead. 'The whole of mythical thought,' writes Cassirer, 'may be interpreted as a constant and obstinate negation of the phenomenon of death.'[25] Ancestor worship (in China, in ancient Rome, among the American Indians) shows 'in a clear and unmistakable manner that we have here come to a really universal, an irreducible and essential characteristic of primitive religion'.[26] So also for primitive man there is no clear division between the symbol and the object it signifies, between the name of a person and the person himself. Even a portion of an object does for the whole object: *pars pro toto*: a person's shadow, his hair, his clothing. Hence the conviction that the ritual act is a real action.

Primitive man tends to consider real the things which are merely fashioned by his own mind. In the same way he tends to objectify what we call abstract concepts: he conceives justice, courage and eloquence as substances which can be stolen. Life and death are also visualized as concrete substances. 'Here we meet the paradox of mythopoetic thought,' writes Frankfort. 'Though it does not know dead matter and confronts a world animated from end to end, it is unable to leave the sphere of the concrete and renders its own concepts as realities existing *per se*.'[27] As to the category of causality, primitive thought naturally recognizes the relationship of cause and effect in a concrete situation, but it cannot accept our view of an impersonal, mechanical and lawlike functioning

[25] E. Cassirer, *An Essay on Man*, Yale University Press, 1964, p. 84.
[26] *Ibid*., p. 85.
[27] H. Frankfort, *op. cit*., p. 22.

of causality. It looks, not for the 'how' but for the 'who' when it looks for a cause. It addresses itself not to inanimate objects but to personalized objects: the weather which wants or does not want to rain, the river which wants to rise or refuses to rise, the stone which wants or does not want to move. We understand individual phenomena by what makes them manifestations of general laws. But what early man experiences most strongly is the individual character of the event. Why should *this* man die *thus* at *this* moment? We can only say that in certain physiological conditions death must occur, while the primitive man wants to find a specific and individual cause. This man dies because he wants to die. This explanation may appear incompatible with the objectification of death already mentioned, that is, the consideration of death as a material substance inherent in the one who dies. But death considered emotionally is the act of a hostile will. The same applies to other events such as illness or sin. Despite the fact that they are substantialized (and therefore combated as antagonistic substantializations) they express a hostile will. The personification of the gods answers the primitive man's need for causes to explain the visible world.

On the whole the thinking of primitive peoples about a succession of facts emphasizes the beginning and the end without seeking a connection between the intermediate facts. Accordingly, in cases where we would only see an association of images, mythopoetic thought finds a causal cohesion. Its error is one of excess rather than defect where the principle of causality is concerned. The 'filling', to use Bartlett's terminology, put in between the initial situation and the final one is accomplished without critical attention to intermediate 'fillings'. The changes effected are thus reduced to transformations or metamorphoses.

When we turn to the category of 'space', here too we find that the primitive man does not conceive it as an abstract relationship between different objects. He refers instead to concrete directives and concrete figures: high and low, east and west, linked up with an emotional value (heaven and hell, life and death), experienced as familiar or foreign, as hostile or friendly. The affective tone again prevails over the tangible reality. The category 'time' is not a succession of moments or a uniform duration. As Cassirer has remarked, there is a 'biological time' resultant on the various phases of life: childhood, adolescence, maturity and old age, each separated from the next by a crisis marked by a ritual. Likewise the succession of the seasons and the movements of the heavenly bodies 'are not viewed as "natural" processes in our sense. When there is change, there is cause; and cause, as we have seen, is a will.'[28] But another interpretation also presents itself to the primitive mentality: the varying length of day and night, the ever-changing spectacles of sunrise and sunset, and the equinoctial gales do not suggest a tranquil, automatic succession of phases but a conflict in which man himself is involved because of the close connection of his living conditions with these events. Time, therefore, to the mind of primitive man indicates a diversity of events, willed and in conflict, but not a succession of inevitable and independent moments.

Fundamentally, in myth man does not meet nature as a hostile or at any rate an indifferent mechanism, but as a being with whom he feels he has an intimate relationship; not as a *thing* in contrast with his *person*, but as a *person* facing his own person, as a You in relation to a Me. His thought is genuine thinking. It goes beyond the empirical aspect and settles in forms which appear contradictory to the modern mind but which admirably express his needs and hence his nature. We may therefore venture to conclude that myths reveal an attitude of self-assertion and participation, of existence and commitment, which is characteristic of religious activities.

The scientific process—based on the splitting up of the perceptive datum into ever smaller elements until it seems to vanish into nothingness—has achieved incredible results, but it presents us with a world so different from the one we experience as men that mathematical abstraction alone can explore it. The mythical process, on the other hand, based on the

[28] *Ibid.*, p. 33.

meeting between the perceptive datum and emotional experience, has a genuine quality of human experience, but it vanishes into nothingness when it becomes 'fabulation'. Bergson said that this is the inevitable retaliation of the need to live on the destructive effect of the intelligence. Actually it is symptomatic that the function of 'fabulation' raises its head imperiously every time the intelligence is denied free movement by some unexpected event or by the awareness of its incapacity to reach the all and to grasp it. On the other hand, it is also symptomatic that mythical thinking is not absent even from what are considered to be quite unbiased forms of thought. It is a human note, 'a touch of nature', as Shakespeare would say, which reflects the deep human need of meaning, union with and participation in a world which analysis presents to us as devoid of meaning, fragmentary and hostile or indifferent. The ideologies of our times (progress, science, social justice) are largely mythologies with their heroes, their conflicts and their reconciliatory conclusions. It is also a significant fact that when Freud adopted towards reality an attitude which was intended to be scientific and which, in point of fact, was perhaps mainly intuitive, he found no other way of expressing it than by recourse to myth. In fact he created a fresh myth, with all the characteristics typical of myths: objectivization of psychic powers, conflict between them, intervention of the subject under the guidance of the analyst to resolve the combat and direct it towards a useful purpose. J. Bruner describes psychoanalysis as 'a theatrical theory of the personality'.[29]

What are the relations between myth and religion? Bergson distinguishes two types of religion: static and dynamic. Static religion is historical religion produced by social pressure and by 'fabulation', and stabilized in forms handed down from one generation to the next. Dynamic religion springs from an attraction, from an inner call which breaks through conventional forms and seeks its freedom. He maintains that myth pertains to the first type and personal religion to the second.

[29] J. S. Bruner, 'Freud and the Image of Man' in B. Nelson, *Freud and the Twentieth Century*, London, 1938.

It may be observed, however, that since we are facing two forms of religion having partially antithetic characteristics, static religion must necessarily have a dynamic beginning. If it has ultimately come to be firmly established, it must have been active and impetuous in the initial stages. Otherwise it could not have spread and gained the upper hand in society.

The distinction made by Jensen between two phases in the formation of the myth is therefore very important: the expressive phase and the phase of application.[30] The formulation of myth is the result of an irresistible impulse, while its application proceeds when it has already been regulated. These processes are both so forceful that it is impossible to see from the first phase what will happen in the second. Conversely, it it difficult to reconstruct from the second phase the genuine meaning of the first. Cassirer also speaks of compenetration rather than of dichotomy: a myth is initially a religious expression and religion even in its higher manifestations contains mythical elements. Cassirer moreover remarks, with reference to the static religion indicated by Bergson, that the power of tradition is not absolute and totalitarian even for primitive man, since a life in which individual activities are eliminated because completely absorbed in those of the group 'seems to be rather a sociological or metaphysical construction than a historical reality'. Malinowski supports the same thesis, asserting that in even the lowest stages of culture there are traces of something more than conventional forces. If we remove from the word myth its derogatory meaning (that is, of something untrue) and insist on its essential meaning (deep-felt and lively expression of a genuine experience), a mythical idea will necessarily enter into every religious concept: a genuinely human idea, not an idea that has been dehumanized by logical formulae. This quality is found in vigorous religion in our own times also.

[30] A. E. Jensen, *Myth and Cult among Primitive Peoples*, University of Chicago Press, Chicago and London, 1963.

Magic

Myth is a more affective than logical expression of man's conception of the world, the reflection in the human mirror of a reality which is close to it. Magic, on the other hand, expresses the human need to exercise mastery, to possess and subject to its desires all that is opposed to them. Man is no mere spectator, but a *dramatis persona*.

Leo Frobenius tells how, in the course of a journey in tropical Africa, he was accompanied for a week through virgin forest by a number of pygmies, several men and one woman. One evening there was a shortage of food and he asked the men to bring him an antelope. They expressed astonishment and one of them finally replied that they would have done so willingly but that it was too late. It would be necessary to prepare for this hunt and they would therefore go the following day. Frobenius' curiosity was aroused by this reply, so he rose before dawn and hid in a spot where he could observe their behaviour in the place agreed on the previous evening. With the first streaks of dawn the men appeared, accompanied by the woman. Crawling on hands and knees, they advanced as far as a small clearing on rising ground, where they prepared a level patch of earth. Here a man drew something on the ground with his finger while the others, including the woman, murmured formulas and prayers. Then all remained there in silence. The sun rose above the horizon. A man with an arrow in his bent bow approached the patch of bare ground. After a few minutes the sun's rays fell on the drawing traced on the earth. Quick as lightning the woman raised her arms towards the sun, yelling some incomprehensible words. The man shot his arrow at the drawing. Then all the men dashed into the surrounding thicket while the woman returned to the camp.

Frobenius examined the spot where all this had taken place. On the earth was traced the image of an antelope, about three feet long, with the archer's arrow fixed in the neck. That afternoon the men returned carrying a male antelope which had been killed by an arrow in the neck. They returned to the rise with a bowl of antelope's blood and some of the hair. They plastered these on the image and cancelled it, as Frobenius learned later from one of the men who had drunk too freely of palm wine. Frobenius could find out nothing about the formulas, but the men declared that the antelope's blood would have killed them if they had not performed this magic rite.[31]

'In this simple story,' observes Edgar Dacqué, 'lies the key to the explanation, for a long time only dimly perceived, of the designs traced on rocks and on bones by primitive man.'[32] Man in the primitive state is convinced of his ability to act upon things around him, by physical means but also by psychological means. Perhaps he does not distinguish between them, as occurred in the episode just narrated; he uses both means, believing them to be complementary instead of exclusive of each other. It is significant that the magic rite is accompanied by fear of retaliation by the animal and by the use of a magic process to avert this danger. It shows primitive man's deep sense of participation with other creatures and his personification of them. But what could induce him to see in the prefiguration the act he would subsequently perform—a superficial and absurd idea to our minds—and to see it, not as a plan or guide, but as a real and true anticipation, or better as an efficacious prefiguration?

Someone has said that when the hunter performs magic rites on the effigy of his prey he does not do so because it is a symbol of the reality but because to him the image and the object it represents are absolutely identical. There is no difference between the likeness and the real thing. Jensen, who mentions this view, asks: 'But did the hunter, then, draw the image and take it to be a real animal? Imagine the consequences of such a statement. Would the hunter be tempted to eat the image as he would a real animal, to skin it, to use its bones? How disappointed the hunters would be next day if they did not find meat. . . . If the hunter does not eat his effigy

[31] L. Frobenius, *Das Unbekannte Afrika*, Munich, 1921.
[32] E. Dacqué, *Urwelt, Sage und Menschheit*, Munich, 1931, p. 238.

it is because he distinguishes it from the real animal with which he is familiar.' Jensen concludes that categorical statements such as the one he criticizes are anything but infrequent in the writings of scholars who make a study of primitive man. Then he adds: 'For a long time we have been obliged to acknowledge that in the economic and technical field primitive mankind achieved astonishing results and evaluated them according to measures used by rational men. But on the planes of mental and spiritual activity, in art and especially in religion, we deny that they were rational at all.'

For primitive man the employment of demonic powers (by which we mean forces which are not physical but spiritual) coincides with the use civilized man makes of physical forces. That which to primitive man is the demon which gives life to lightning or causes a landslide, modern man calls 'electricity' or 'gravity'. But these are names to indicate forces which remain a mystery, just as the demon is a mystery to primitive man. E. Dacqué writes:

> The hunter's magic rite and ceremonial 'was more than a dance around an arrow stuck in the ground, more than a mechanical and fantastic pummelling of the fetish. It was the employment of natural powers to produce a desired circumstance or banish a dreaded one—similar to what we do when we take an iron rod and bind it with wire into which we introduce electric current, transforming the iron rod into a magnet. Both of these things . . . have a real effect: they bind the spirits of nature which we today—in language which is still symbolical, like that of primitive man—call natural forces. Both of these procedures are 'magic'. . . . A human being of some thousands of years ago, to whom our mathematical signs and physical knowledge would be incomprehensible, would see in our formulas nothing but superstition.[33]

Dacqué goes to the opposite extreme by declaring that to primitive man the likeness and the animal to be killed are

[33] *Ibid.*, p. 31.

identical. He maintains that there is identity of procedure in incantation and scientific experimentation. Actually both are an intervention of man in the world, but the second procedure would not have supplanted the first—despite the incredible tenacity of magical practices—if in a certain field of action it had not demonstrated a more certain and more constant efficacy. But it is a significant fact that the magical conception has been transferred to scientific thinking, exalting the omnipotence and exclusive validity of science in all forms of human activity, even when the scientific explanation fails to unravel the mystery of nature, but draws the attention of open-minded people to this mystery or disguises it in a verbal interpretation. 'Power over the world' is the source of energy both in magic and in science.

Does this mean that magic is to be considered a primordial form of science? Yes and no. Yes, in the sense that it is a first taking possession of the world with the conscious desire to modify it. No, in the sense that it remains shut up in itself and places a barrier to intellectual effort. But it is also true that science, in its turn, is not immune from this same danger of cornering and exclusivism. This danger exists in so far as science prepares for man a world in which technical progress alone has absolute rights and other human needs are simply ignored or directly combated. Bergson is right when he writes:

> Let there be no talk, then, of an era of magic followed by an era of science. Let us say that science and magic are both natural, that they have always co-existed, that our science is very much more extensive than that of our remote ancestors, but that these ancestors must have been much less given to magic than non-civilized men today. We have remained, at bottom, what they were. Driven back by science, the inclination towards magic still survives and bides its time.[34]

By reason of its investigation of hidden things, its certainty of being able to influence the course of events, and because of

[34] H. Bergson, *op. cit.*, p. 162.

its faith in its own practices, magic has been considered to be a primitive form of religion. Undoubtedly it possesses some religious features which we find surviving even in the more developed religions. But despite all this we must point out, with Bergson, that magic also possesses antithetic characteristics. Magic is above all egocentric, not to say egoistical: it is the externalization of the will to influence events according to one's own desires and in one's own favour. If a higher power is invoked, it is in order to obtain the protection and cooperation of this power. Magic in itself is exercised on an impersonal materialized means, as is the 'mana' of the Melanesians, the 'orenda' of the Iroquois, the 'Wakanda' of the Sioux and so forth.

According to Hubert and Mauss, magic is inseparable from the concept of 'mana'. But Bergson is of the opposite opinion. He holds that the concept of 'mana' exists because man believes in magic.[35] To the egoism, tyranny and impersonal powers of magic religion opposes antithetic attitudes: admiration, supplication of a mysterious 'You', even if this is personalized in various deities, and, even in many forms of polytheism, recourse to an undefined, mysterious, supreme Being. We therefore understand how the higher forms of religion fight against magic as being the degradation to the material level of an effort which ought to be devoted to spiritual values. Ritual forms certainly persist which have the semblance of magical rites, but their tone is completely different and suggests bringing man closer to God instead of making God submit to men. It must also be recognized that the danger of falling into the formalism of magic is present in all religions.

We are led to conclude that magic and religion spring from a common origin—the acknowledgment of man's participation in a world ruled by mysterious powers—but that religion stresses admiration and dedication and proposes higher ideals, while magic aims at acquisition and domination. Some anthropologists seem to be convinced of a 'continuity' between magic and religion. Frazer holds that religion grew from the discovery

[35] *Ibid.*, p. 155.

that magic had failed and from the idea that the world obeys higher laws than those imposed by men. This is a rather artificial hypothesis, as Cassirer points out. There is no evidence that a magical era was succeeded by a religious era. But we can readily believe that even in magic, especially in its initial expressive phase, a religious note was not lacking, an element which was suffocated later when it assumed rigid forms in practice.

The sacred and the profane

Myth and magic appear to be expressions of man's fundamental need to look out upon an orderly world—the need for a cosmos and the horror of chaos—and the need to play in this world not merely a passive but an active role. There is a characteristic affective tone which corresponds to this need, namely, man's sense of the 'sacred'. It is by no means easy to define this sentiment, any more than it is easy to define other human sentiments. The most effective manner of placing it in relief is to observe it in contrast with its opposite, the sense of the profane. Against a background of things with which we are quite familiar (the profane), there are others which stand out and claim our attention by reason of the aura of mystery and greatness and power which surrounds them, and which we find overwhelming but at the same time attractive (the sacred).

According to Rudolf Otto there is experience of the sacred when a man is faced with some overpowering and fascinating mystery and when he feels in this situation the presence of 'something' completely different from himself, from other men and from the world—a situation of dependence, of remoteness and also of attraction.[36] The 'sacred' as Rudolf Otto describes it presents itself as *tremendum* (awful) and *fascinans* (fascinating), *majestosum* (overpowering) and *numinosum* (mysterious).

[36] R. Otto, *The Idea of the Holy*, Penguin Books, Harmondsworth, Middlesex, 1959.

Otto has made very evident the subjective, affective aspect of the 'sacred' but he has not sufficiently appreciated the objective aspect. There is a distinct contrast between sacred and profane, even when the sacred absorbs the profane and the profane over-whelms the sacred. The sacred belongs to a world beyond, the profane to this world: one belongs, we may say, to a divine world and the other to a human world. That something 'com-pletely different' which arouses a sense of the sacred is under-stood as objective, independent and powerful, as something that is shared.

Religion, which enters into all human activities and expresses itself through them, is also directed towards all objects, all situations and every mood of man. The religious attitude of man and the religious tonality which distinguishes a sacred universe from a profane one refer to a wide variety of objects: material objects, world events or social events, invisible beings. We therefore have manifestations of the sacred (hierophanies) in all kinds of places and in all kinds of activity, individual or social, economic or political. This is a statement of fact, independent of the reasons for which it has come about and been established. A stone, a tree, a hill, a building; the beginning of puberty, marriage, wars, burial; the king, the nation—all can be 'invested' with religion and be considered as manifesta-tions of the sacred.

Every hierophany, says Mircea Eliade, represents a paradox. 'By manifesting the sacred, any object becomes *something else*, yet it continues to remain *itself*. . . . A *sacred* stone remains a *stone*. . . . But for those to whom a stone reveals itself as sacred, its immediate reality is transmuted into a supernatural reality.'[37] 'If, in a primitive society, some tree or other is regarded as the "Tree of the World", it follows that, thanks to the religious experiences which originated that belief, it is possible for the members of this society to attain to a meta-physical understanding of the Universe; for the symbolism of the Tree of the World has revealed to them that a particular

[37] M. Eliade, *The Sacred and the Profane*, Harper, New York, 1961, ch. 1.

object may signify the whole of the cosmos.'[38] Thus, 'an object becomes sacred in so far as it reveals itself as belonging in some way to a different order of being'.[39] Every evidence of the 'sacred' reveals some modality of the sacred (it is a hierophany) and some attitude of man towards it.[40] These statements of Eliade, I should think, can be accepted even apart from his general conception of religion. We have mentioned them because they show clearly the transformation in meaning brought about by the religious sense.

It is therefore not an indifferent matter that the men of a certain civilization practise one religion or another or declare that they practise no religion. For individuals and for social institutions religion fulfils a normative function. When life has a particular meaning in its salient moments, behaviour must also follow as a consequence. The primordial needs of nutrition and procreation, like the need for a dwelling-place, cultivation of the fields, erection of temples and rotation of the seasons are all full of religious significance for primitive man. The case is very different in modern civilization, where human needs are studied in order that men may deal with them by a series of technical measures to ensure that they be more surely and easily satisfied. It seems as though man can thus free himself from absurd and irksome constraint. We who belong to Western civilization are living in a profane and deconsecrated world, but we are proud of technical achievement which subdues it for our use and we boast of being free and of being masters of the world. Yet the religious need does not disappear. Today there is a faith, more or less valid, in man's ability to build up a world in which everything will be easier and better. But technical progress reveals itself as a deity no less exacting and mysterious than the gods of ancient times.

Religion is not limited to a representation of the world and

---

[38] M. Eliade, *Myths, Dreams and Mysteries*, Harper, New York, 1960, p. 19.

[39] M. Eliade, *Patterns in Comparative Religion*, Sheed and Ward, London and New York, 1958, p. 17.

[40] *Ibid.*, p. 2.

of the drama of man's journey on earth. It makes demands on human beings, since it shows them how they are to act. Scholars speak of the widespread conviction among men concerning an initial era, a divinized 'history', which preceded the history of man himself. It is in this primordial era that myth takes place. The myth is there at the source. Not only is it the explanation of what follows, but it assumes the significance of a paradigm, an outline of what is to be reproduced in human history. Hence the commitment of man to carry out or to represent (in the etymological sense of the word, meaning renewal of the action) what is enacted in the myth. It is precisely in this phase of application that the myth becomes systematized and begins to be bound up with institutions. Its compelling pressure on the individual nevertheless remains very strong and it is reinforced by the participation of the community.

Religion moves towards a goal, towards a conclusion to be reached, and it therefore looks towards the future with a sense of urgency, while adapting itself with difficulty to delays. Every religion has its own eschatology, its own apocalypse. There is a myth which deals with origins, but there is also a myth relating to the ultimate destiny of man. This is to be observed in all the great religions but it appears most strikingly in religious sects. It is significant that even political and social movements (especially in the initial revolutionary phase) present the 'new order' as imminent or even already actualized. The messianic character of Russian Communism has been pointed out repeatedly.[41]

Worship is the realization of myth in actions performed by the individual or by the community. In a primitive society it gives living and expressed meaning in a very clear way to a personal experience which is also closely bound up with the community. The individual therefore has a sense of religious responsibility which can be quite serious, because upon what

[41] Cf. N. Berdiaev, *Le fonti e lo spirito del comunismo russo*, Corticelli, Milan, 1945; W. Nigg, *Das Ewige Reich*, Zurich, 1944; G. Guariglia, *Il messianismo russo*, Studium, Rome, 1956.

he does or fails to do will depend what is to happen. Once more, he is no mere spectator but an actor.

Custom and morals: taboo

On the one hand a certain religious belief communicates order to the world and a meaning to life and appears to have a necessary function in a given civilization. It constitutes a reference chart for the guidance of social life and has therefore a clearly useful function in establishing and preserving social life. But on the other hand we must not close our eyes to the harsher aspects of religion which can and do exist, or to the manner in which its constrictive force can exceed what we are accustomed to describe as the 'moral order'. Faith in a divine regulator or fertility finds expression not so much in idyllic ceremonies as in orgies, sacred prostitution and cannibalism. Faith in the primitive construction of the world by a god lies at the roots of construction sacrifices, the slaying of infants or young girls to draw down the favour of the gods upon a new dwelling or a temple. War is a repetition and a renewal of the eternal event portrayed in the myths, and the death of those who take part in it or the killing of the vanquished is looked upon as a sacred act. This is a terrible yet inevitable aspect of religion which brings us face to face with a disconcerting problem. Religion is undoubtedly one of the most potent forces which stirs within man and morality and obligation are closely bound up with it. Jensen considers that widely different and even contrasting moral attitudes such as we find in primitive man and modern man—which have become customary among various peoples in such a vast range of nuances as to make the brain reel—can all be traced to the same origin. Living according to a higher order (the divine order of primitive man) is quite different from the habitual order, because, primarily, it is achieved by direct perception and without any intervention of the intellect, and secondly, because it cannot be evaluated by any utilitarian standards.[42]

[42] Cf. A. E. Jensen, op. cit., pp. 34 ff.

I may be allowed to state the matter more exactly. That morality differs from intelligence is certain, but it does not by any means follow that the intellect has no part in the moral act. Jensen himself denounces the disastrous prejudices of theories which claim that primitive man was not yet 'man' as we know him.[48] That the moral element is not to be measured by utilitarian standards appears to me to be quite exact, since the moral element remains firm all the time irrespective of benefit or detriment to the subject concerned.

Linked up with the moral element we find prohibition or taboo. Even for the early Australians taboo implies the totem. No prohibition exists which is not connected with an antagonistic power, and both totem and taboo have a clearly sacred character, apart from the mythology to which they belong. It seems to me that the importance of this fact has been insufficiently appreciated from the psychological point of view. The conception of the world which draws boundary lines between prohibited and permitted things is a sacred one. These limits resemble to some extent the political frontiers between various states, which we should term arbitrary if they did not correspond to actual facts. These delimitations may appear to us so varied and variable as to tell us nothing of their original meaning. But they undoubtedly reflect a fundamental structure of man, who looks out on a limitless world and cannot do otherwise than take his place in it. This implies both a manner of behaving and a conception to justify this behaviour. This necessarily leads to the identification of protective and hostile powers in a manner that is typical of the 'sacred'.

Cassirer has brilliantly demonstrated the long path mankind has had to travel to free itself from the merely customary prohibition, 'to abrogate this complex system of interdictions . . . to discover a positive power . . . of inspiration and aspiration . . . to turn passive obedience into an active religious feeling'.[44] But here too we are not altogether immune from the danger of stopping short at the prohibition, just as

[43] *Ibid.*, p. 271.
[44] E. Cassirer, *op. cit.*, p. 108.

it would be hazardous for us to say that the religious practice of primitive man contains no element of inspiration and aspiration. Our own civilization is swarming with taboos although it likes to proclaim itself free from them. We are unaware of them because they are all around us. Here, however, we have a difference: we have deconsecrated these taboos and we call them norms and social conventions, but this does not mean that we are free from them.

The reduction of primordial needs to biological necessities likewise fails to deprive these of a certain aura of ideality, although this has lost all religious tone. Nowadays the stress is placed with exasperating monotony on the crude biological fact. Study and research are encouraged in this field by increasing the attractions and minimizing the responsibilities involved. This is particularly the case where sex is concerned. To primitive peoples sexuality appears as a

> direct manifestation of the sacred in the life of the universe
> . . . and hence in a certain sense it becomes symbolical. Even
> when the sexual act is not formulated in cosmological terms,
> that is, when it is not identified as *Hierosgamos* or sacred
> marriage, it is no less loaded with religious symbolism. . . .
> It is by virtue of its sacred character that the orgy occupies
> such an important place in the vegetation festivals.

All the excesses of an unbridled collective sexuality are explained as 'assimilation of the sexual act in the union of heaven with Mother Earth'.[45]

It is significant that this sacred meaning of sexual union is strongly defended and given great prominence by two modern writers who have concentrated their attention on sexuality: Havelock Ellis and D. H. Lawrence. It would appear that Freud, on the other hand, did not sufficiently appreciate it. The instinctive urge is not the only component of sexuality, and its insertion into a sacred order could be wrongly interpreted as the effect of a sense of guilt which does not accompany the frustration of other instinctual urges. There must be an earlier

[45] M. Eliade, in *Etudes carmelitaines*, 1952.

tendency than the sexual one by which it is overcome in its physiological actualization and becomes a symbol. An analogous process of symbolization must take place to transform the sensory impression exercised by the father in the paternal image and to diffuse a religious aura around some of the contents of the unconscious. Things being so, we must conclude that religion is the most primitive urge of psychic activity since it constantly organizes and directs it. When religion grows weak, confusion and bewilderment are the result. It should also be remembered that 'consecration' takes place in conscious activity and that the consistency of behaviour is certainly not to be defined as rationalization, since it expresses a vital experience. The religious impulse emerges as an exclusively human characteristic. This is evident from its expansion, which is quite different from that of sexuality, circumscribed as this is by the satisfaction of a need. Sexuality in animals has produced none of the manifestations typical of man, either from the constructive point of view (art, morals, religion) or from the point of view of deficiency (neurosis).

Religion, then, inevitably comes into view whenever we observe the 'human world'. It shows itself either in the form of subjective experience or in concrete expressions, as is already evident in the very earliest religious manifestations of which traces remain or which still survive among primitive peoples today and also among civilized peoples. We find a religious-intellectual interpretation of the world in myth. We observe man's attempt to approach the higher powers, either to subdue them (magic) or to adore them. In religion we have a prospect in which sacred and profane are intertwined and yet distinct, with the prescription of what should be done and of what is prohibited. Religion can become petrified in formalism, but it can also evolve in the direction of more coherent and spiritual expressions. In so far as it prescribes and prohibits, religion is interwoven with morality; but it can also extend to manifestations which may appear profane and which are sometimes opposed to morality. Its pervasive quality, its personal and social penetration, even when its points of reference remain vague, exercise a stimulus on the individual and on groups which is all the more impelling the less the subject is aware of it. The importance of this stimulus must not be minimized. Religion is the incentive which causes the men of all epochs to face Mystery. It is the sign, the indicator of the presence of a world which man's eyes do not behold but which is as clearly announced to him as the world to which he has access by means of his senses. That is why the 'natural history' of man is also the history of his religious sense. 'There is no opposition between man, in so far as he is "civilized man", and *homo religiosus*,' writes van der Leeuw. 'Indeed there is a close connection between the "no" which man says to nature and this awareness of the Something Else. The origin of civilization is religious.'[46]

To judge religion to be a strange residue of the past, a 'childish survival', a fossilized remnant to which we are still unreasonably attached, is to misunderstand a primordial and genuine power in man which contains all possibilities of construction and destruction. An uncultivated religious sense or one that remains so because it fails to declare itself and hides under other names is the greatest danger for man. This is amply demonstrated in the history of mankind by a succession of the most absurd errors and monstrous cruelties. Is man, then, incurably religious and the victim of his religious sense? No, because while religion reveals his misery, it keeps constantly alive his yearning for God.

[46] G. van der Leeuw, *L'homme primitif et la religion: étude anthropologique*, Alcan, Paris, 1940.

4. Religion and Society

It has been shrewdly remarked that if a fish started to study its environment, the last thing it would notice would be the water. Thus 'the last thing of which human beings have really become aware, in their long history of studying themselves, has been the intimate way in which they express the social world of which they are a part'.[1] Although this statement is an exaggeration, it contains some truths which are too often overlooked. In point of fact, many scholars have considered religion be be a private affair of the individual and no more.

It is a noteworthy fact that in the development of psychological and sociological studies the religious factor has been treated as a matter of secondary importance. From the psychological point of view, moreover, it it particularly difficult to state the social implications of religion since it is not merely a matter of pointing out the characteristics of a particular kind of behaviour, but of showing how it is lived by the individual or how it expresses a personal experience. Besides, although we cannot prescind from the manifestations of religion in beings who live together in society, it is one of the typically human activities which are falsified when they are reduced to biological and sociological terms.

The symbolic thought expressed in religious myth already has a meaning for the one who conceives it, but also for the individuals to whom it is communicated. It is therefore closely connected with processes of discernment, evaluation, commit-

---

[1] L. K. Frank, quoted by G. Murphy, *An Introduction to Psychology*, Harper and Brothers, New York, 1951, p. 518.

ment and action which are not confined to the individual but are at the same time social processes. The individual is committed in this field because he shares the life of others. In our anxiety to establish what is genuinely personal we continue to wonder what the individual would do in conditions of complete isolation. We fail to consider that no man comes into a world completely uninhabited by men and that by isolating him we are creating an unnatural and absurd situation. When we observe religion under normal and natural conditions of development the social environment cannot be overlooked.

Society and religion

Let us begin by glancing at the judgments pronounced on religion by sociologists, by those scholars, that is, whose principle purpose is the study of society and subordinately the study of man as a constituent element of society. Sociology first began to take shape in France as a naturalist science in the atmosphere of the Encyclopaedists and Illuminists.

Montesquieu (1689-1755) in *The Spirit of the Laws* examined the various religious beliefs as mere facts and endeavoured to discover their function in society. Condorcet (1743-94) asserted that social facts are as natural as those studied by the inorganic and organic sciences and that the same methods used in physics and biology are therefore applicable to them. Social laws are rigorous and must be formulated in mathematical terms to allow the building up of a social world from which religious fables are to be banished. Count Henri de Saint-Simon (1760-1815) has been described as one of the precursors of totalitarianism, because of his faith in social laws, in progress, in the programming and palingenesis of mankind, supported by a religious enthusiasm of which his disciples became the interpreters by founding a religious sect which lasted only a short time. (*Nouveau Christianisme* is the title of one of his last books.)

In point of fact, Saint-Simon acknowledged the inevitability of religion under one form or another and predicted a religion which would be consistent with science. Auguste Comte (1798-1857), who was Saint-Simon's secretary for some time, wrote in his *Course of Positive Philosophy*: 'I believe I must venture today to use the new term "sociology" which is the exact equivalent to the expression "social physics" which I already introduced. My intention was to designate by a single name this complementary portion of natural philosophy which pertains to the positive study of the fundamental laws proper to social phenomena.'[2] The paternity of the new science is thus attributed to Comte, since he gave it a name and indicated its purpose. To the rigid inevitability of social laws Comte adds a philosophy of history: every society is regulated by a law of development and passes through three successive stages of improvement: the theological stage, the metaphysical stage and the scientific stage. An admirer of the Catholic Church, Comte nevertheless prophesied its decline and cherished the hope that a secular church would be founded.

Emile Durkheim (1858-1917) views religion in the setting of social determinism as an indispensable 'function' of society which makes its appearance in every social group. In the gods men adore society, and religion is the matrix in which laws, sciences and arts are formed. Durkheim, too, predicts a secular and rationalist religion. 'It has always seemed odd to me,' writes Evans-Pritchard, 'how these three men [Saint-Simon, Comte and Durkheim] combined a deterministic philosophy, a belief in the regeneration of the human race as an inevitable evolutionary process, with an almost fanatical reforming zeal and at times a vituperative indignation towards all who differed from them.'[3]

English sociology was influenced by the utilitarian and elementarian mentality of the early nineteenth century and accepted without reserve the principle of evolution as formulated by Darwin for the biological sciences. Herbert Spencer

[2] J. Leclerq, *Introduction à la sociologie*, Louvain-Paris, second edition, 1959.
[3] E. E. Evans-Pritchard, 'Religion and the Anthropologists' in *Blackfriars*, April 1960, p. 107.

E

may be considered its founder.[4] He too was convinced of the existence of laws which regulate society, difficult to formulate because of their complexity. Spencer stresses the analogy between the organism and society already proposed by Hobbes: the digestive system is constituted in society by agriculture and industry; the circulatory system by commerce and finance; the nervous system by the State and the government; the House of Lords fulfils the functions of the cerebral cortex, the Commons the functions of the elongated medulla! We cannot help being amused by this analogy, even though Spencer, to be fair to him, acknowledged its limitations. But—in parenthesis—we may be allowed to smile today when the terminology of Freud's psychosexual stages is applied to society. The same principle has obviously continued to be dominant up to the present day.

Religion, according to Spencer, is false and futile: the study of society constitutes a sounder basis of life (because scientific) than moral philosophy. God, if he exists, is unknowable: religious practice is a symbolical projection of dependence on those who hold power. Darwin's principle of the struggle for existence produced enormous repercussions and was formulated by Spencer as the 'principle of the survival of the fittest'. Thus a single factor of progress is introduced, since the survival of organisms adapted to the environment and the struggle and the elimination of those unsuited to it would explain the establishment and continuance of suitable and efficient organisms.

Today the supreme validity of this principle has begun to be questioned. Darwin's inclusion of man in the general classification of animals, in the group of primates, led to research into the evolution of psychic characteristics from animals to man. Hence, especially through the work of enthusiastic popularizers and by reason of an undue rigidity on the part of theologians, the conviction grew that religion, precisely because of its variability of expression, was an inferior form of thought, destined to disappear in the struggle against science. The comparative study of religions, which culminated in the

[4] H. Spencer, *The Principles of Sociology*, Appleton, New York, 1900.

monumental work of Frazer,[5] is an indication of this mentality. Religions are very different one from another, but they have some features in common. One religion dies and another takes its place, but all of them are deemed to be products of the imagination and devoid of any scientific foundation. Peoples pass through three phases: magic, religion and science. Magic is already a kind of rudimentary science which disappears when true science is established on the basis of observation and verification of facts. The religions of the second phase contain elements already found in magic. The general attitude of Frazer is agnostic and hostile to religion.

Anglo-Saxon sociology conceived religion as the result of a progressive selection between fantastic, widely different and chaotic elementary concepts, until a certain institutional homogeneity is reached which subsequently selects to its own advantage those elements alone which are compatible with what it already possesses. German sociology was distinguished by the assertion of a directive principle, 'the spirit', which is objectivized in progressively more perfect forms. In Hegel's philosophy there is a single, absolute, divine directive mind which is manifested in the course of history. Development, 'becoming', is the result of the struggle between opposing forces (the dialectic process) which operate upon individuals and cannot be reduced to the psychic activity of individuals. Hegel also considers religion to be an inferior form of knowledge, suited to primitive peoples and children and destined to be replaced by science and philosophy.

Karl Marx is closely linked with Hegel although his thinking took its own course with the critical revision of Hegel's *Philosophy of Right*. 'My investigations,' wrote Marx,

led to the result that legal relations such as forms of state are to be grasped neither from themselves nor from the so-called general development of the human spirit, but rather have their roots in the material conditions of life. . . . The

---

[5] J. G. Frazer, *The Golden Bough*, first published 1890; second edition, 12 vols, London, 1911-15, supplement, London, 1936; abridged edition, Macmillan, London, 1922 (also available as a paperback).

general result at which I arrived and which, once won, served as a guiding thread for my studies, can be briefly formulated as follows: In the social production which men carry on they enter into definite relations that are indispensable and independent of their will; these relations of production correspond to a definite stage of development of their material forces of production. The sum total of these relations of production constitutes the economic structure of society—the real foundation on which rises a legal and political superstructure and to which correspond definite forms of social consciousness. The mode of production in material life determines the social, political and intellectual life processes in general. It is not the consciousness of men that determines their being, but, on the contrary, their social being that determines their consciousness.

Ferrarotti, in quoting this passage from the Preface to *A Contribution to the Critique of Political Economy* (1859), remarks that 'this is an admirable summing-up of the essential nucleus of Marxist doctrine. This is the economic interpretation of history, which is not to be understood in a limited sense or in a vulgarly materialist sense, as some commentators have done.'[6]

Actually Marx is an author whose thinking is so rich that it can be distorted for purposes of propaganda and be given considerably different shades of meaning. All the more so, as Ferrarotti goes on to say, since

there are ambiguities in the formulation of Marxist doctrine, which in the first place makes the 'mode of production' the basis of the 'processes of social, political and spiritual life', but later on, in the same sentence, points to the 'social being' of man as the determining factor of his consciousness. We are therefore faced with a dual conception of the determin-

---

[6] F. Ferrarotti, 'Storia della Sociologia' in *Storia delle Scienze* (edited by N. Abbagnano), U.T.E.T., Turin, 1962, vol. III, part 2, p. 904. Quotations from Marx are taken from *Karl Marx, Selected Works*, Lawrence and Wishart, London, 1945, vol. I, pp. 355-6.

ing factor: the *mode* of production and the social *being*. Later on Marx was to make the revolutionary social being coincide with the notion of 'general class' or 'proletariat', a mythical instrument to remove the burden of former society from the shoulders of the new society. Sociological analysis is to make way for a 'historical mission' of a prophetic type.[7]

From all this we can understand how the assertion that other human activities are built on material relations and that 'social being' determines consciousness has spread abroad the conviction that Marx bases his doctrine on social 'becoming'. In this light religion is seen as a superstructure which protects the interests of a certain class against the interests of another. The slogan 'religion is the opium of the people' can then be understood.[8] The Marxist attitude towards religion is hostile or at best provisionally tolerant, while it is not itself immune from a form of 'prophetism' with clearly religious tones.

The thinking of Max Weber (1862-1920), considered to be one of the founders of sociology, is also deeply rooted in German philosophy. Weber endeavours to get over the barrier between the natural sciences *(Naturwissenschaften)* and the spiritual sciences *(Geisterswissenschaften)*—between the sciences dealing with facts and those dealing with values— which had arisen in the Hegelian tradition, by declaring that both proceed from a conceptual contrivance which fixes the selective criterion and indicates the general direction of research. For Max Weber, therefore, the problem of method and the study of values as visualized by the individual concerned and as indicated by his consequent behaviour, are fundamental in sociology. We can understand, then, why, in a work which has become famous, he stressed the correspondence

[7] F. Ferrarotti, *op. cit.*, p. 906.

[8] This phrase in its original context *(The Holy Family)* has a less brutal meaning. 'Religious poverty is on the one hand the expression of real poverty and on the other the protest against real poverty. Religion is the lament of the oppressed creature, the heart of a heartless world, just as it is the spirit of a spiritless age. It is the opium of the people.' In this sense the phrase expresses a heartfelt protest against the spiritual indifference of certain classes towards human suffering.

between puritanism (which looked on wealth as a reward from God to the righteous man) and the birth and development of capitalism, especially in Protestant regions. The economic process ought to be said to depend on the *values* instead of these being considered to be superstructures. Max Weber declared that he himself was neither anti-religious nor irreligious but that where religion was concerned he felt himself to be absolutely *unmusikalisch.*[9]

[9] A certain parallelism in theories can be noted in the historical development of psychology and sociology in Germany. German psychology began with Wundt, who set himself to discover and systematize the elementary psychic processes. This research dealt mainly with the content of consciousness. In opposition to Wundt we have Brentano, who was more concerned with psychic processes than with contents. At a third stage, against this double study of contents and acts, Gestalt psychology asserted the primordial unity of reciprocal relations between the elements in question, and the necessity of a certain configuration to give a meaning to the parts. Side by side with, but in contrast to, these lines of research which had as their common denominator the aim of providing an explanation of psychic facts, another method aimed at providing an understanding of facts *(verstehende Psychologie).* According to this last theory, while we can explain psychic facts we cannot arrive at a knowledge of their nature except by a special method, namely, that of 'understanding', a process which consists in finding the connecting thread running through a number of heterogeneous and apparently contradictory phenomena. This line of thought proposed by historical philosophers (Dilthey) and psychiatrists (Gruhle, Jaspers) culminates in the formulation of schemes of comprehensibility or types (Spranger).

Sociology busied itself for a long time (Tönnies, 1855-1936) with the distinction between community and society, and with fundamental types of society. As to the definition of sociology, Simmel (1858-1918) remarks that it turns to facts which are already the object of other sciences, such as economics, history and politics. For this reason it cannot but consist in the study of reciprocal relations between objects already studied in the other sciences. Its concern is with the social 'form' of objects elsewhere studied in isolation. It is a fact that there are characteristic forms of grouping and of social relations (the formation of parties, conflict, limitation, etc.) in the most varied social groups (political, scientific, commercial, religious, etc.). 'Simmel aspires to a geometrical sociology. Just as geometry determines pure forms applicable to any content whatever and fixes its laws, similarly sociology determines the laws of social life applicable to all its concrete manifestations' (J. Leclerq, *Introduction à la sociologie, op. cit.*). Here we have a Gestalt sociology. Finally, we find in Max Weber (1862-1920) a

It may prove useful to point out here a few features which the various European sociological schools have in common. There is the assertion that certain valid social laws exist in the same way as there are physical laws; the theory of a conflict of social forces which determines the development and progress of society; the tacit or recognized analogy between society and a living organism; the philosophy of 'becoming' or of history which distinguishes various stages of development and considers the earlier phases (religious phases) less perfect and destined to be supplanted by the later phases; the possibility of control over social forces so as to facilitate and improve human existence; the prediction of a social palingenesis in which man, just as he has dominated Nature, will become the planner and master of future society. Finally, we have the assertion that the existence and rights of society take precedence over individual existence and rights.

Religion is admitted to be an undeniable fact but is stripped of the aura of impenetrability and mystery which withdraws it from human control. It is generally deemed to be an illusion, useful in the interests of social cohesion, but certainly exercising its mastery over human conduct by touching what is most vulnerable and irrational in man, namely, his need for security. Religion is therefore considered to be a hindrance to progress, which is to be furthered by a knowledge of social laws and by their judicious application. Science is presented as the liberator that sets men free from religious superstitions and as the guarantor of true well-being. Hence the inevitable struggle of science against religion on the social plane for the achievement of progress.

Obviously these recurring motifs are quite heterogeneous, some of them taken from physics, others from biology, others from philosophy and others again from what we may call a

sociology of understanding of which Hofstätter sees the prototype in the psychology of understanding. Social facts are so complex that it is only by intuition of the system of values which is their mainspring that the original aspect of the various phenomena can be grasped. We have to try to find an ideal model of reference, even if only a provisional one which can be modified by subsequent approximations.

fragmentary psychology. A religious note is sounded continually, either by the condemnation of religion in general as illusion and fanaticism, or by the prediction of better things to come provided there be unconditional commitment on the part of those who aim at a social ideal. Faith in progress and a return to the ideas of justice, equality and improvement have, as Pareto pointed out, a religious tonality rather than the strictly impersonal and scientific one demanded by a science that proposes to model itself on the physical and biological sciences.

Sociology as presented in the chief systems, each sustained by a single principle—intellectual development (Comte), 'social laws' (Saint-Simon), justice (Proudhon), the material relations of life (Marx)—and aiming at a global conception of society, has made way, in the period between the two world wars, for an empirical sociology. This concentrates on research in more circumscribed fields which can be more clearly defined and dealt with by a more exact method. Thus we have surveys on Polish peasants in Europe and America by Thomas and Znaniecki, the study of the human factor in industry by Elton Mayo, studies on 'social stratification and mobility' by P. Sorokin, surveys on family groups in various cultures, on social 'roles' and so forth: researches conducted according to statistical, historical and typological methods with an interdisciplinary approach, that is to say, with reference to data acquired by related sciences (particularly anthropology and psychology).

When sociology passes from the description of social forms to the dynamic forces which produce them, its 'adventure' is fascinating. But it is also difficult, complex and dangerous, since it must have recourse to other sciences whose results are not always definite and reliable and which in any event are only partial. As far as psychology is concerned, the precise situation is that sociology has recourse to psychological theories which are useful and promising but which are still in course of elaboration. Hence, despite the enormous collection of data, the need for systematic arrangement and interpretation of these facts is increasingly felt, the need for some doctrinal principles. The synthesis proposed by Parsons, Tolman and Shils,[10] which links up with the doctrines of Durkheim and Max Weber, with neo-behaviourism and with 'microsociological' research, is undoubtedly an important event in the history of sociology, even though it has awakened perplexity and has aroused certain reactions—which are actually a sign of its importance.

Social psychology and religious sociology

This long yet inadequate excursus on sociology has taken us far from our true problem. But it was necessary in order to enable us to understand—apart from the social aspect of religion—how the development of sociology has determined the growth of that particular branch of psychology which deals with relations between individuals, namely, social psychology.

The beginnings of social psychology may be placed about the year 1908, with the publication of two books, one in America and the other in England. The first of these, entitled *Social Psychology*, by E. A. Ross, mirrors the interest of a sociologist in psychological problems. The second, *Introduction to Social Psychology*, by W. McDougall, reveals the need experienced by a psychologist formed in the German 'experimental' school under the guidance of G. E. Müller to extend his vision towards a psychology dealing with interhuman relations and towards a sociology anchored in biological presuppositions. With his doctrine of the instincts McDougall opened up possibilities of encounter and collaboration between psychologists and sociologists. His offer was not welcomed by either group of scholars, yet we must acknowledge him to be a pioneer of social psychology.

Actually, certain differences of object and method between psychology and sociology determine two distinct fields of study. Psychology deals with the individual and with subjective facts, that is, with things experienced by the individual. Sociology

[10] T. Parsons, E. C. Tolman and E. Shils, *Toward a General Theory of Action*, Harvard University Press, Cambridge, Mass., 1952.

deals with the relations between individuals in so far as they have a task to fulfil in society, and also between groups of individuals. Take the example of proceedings in a court of law. From the psychological point of view interest is focused on what is experienced by the individual in the situation under consideration: his manner of reconstructing the facts, the emotions, sentiments, motives and behaviour of each one— judge, accused, counsel for the defence, clerk of the court, etc. From the sociological point of view what counts is the existence of a law, its formulation, the legal action taken with reference to the community. The individual is the actor of a part or 'role'. Psychology studies the actor, while sociology studies the performance which is bound up with the actor but at the same time independent of his person. The actor can be replaced and therefore experience the situation in a very different way. So far so good. But we come to a point where the two aspects meet. An action is social precisely because the individual experiences it and carries it out and this is the reason why we have social psychology. On the other hand, there is something already preconstituted, a 'culture', in which the individual is necessarily involved and for this reason we have sociology. But while the psychologist attributes the social action to the individual, the sociologist relates it to the social structure. The passage from psychology to sociology is the *pons asinorum* of social psychology.[11]

A generally acceptable definition of social psychology might be the following: 'an attempt to understand and explain how the thinking, feeling and behaviour of individuals are influenced by the actual, imagined or implied presence of other human beings'.[12]

All problems of general psychology are therefore taken up once more from another point of view. On the part of many

[11] E. E. Evans-Pritchard, *Social Anthropology*, Cohen and West, London, 1960.
[12] G. W. Allport, 'The Historical Background of Modern Social Psychology' in Lindzey, *Handbook of Social Psychology*, Cambridge, Mass., 1954, vol. I, p. 5.

scholars there is a considerable effort, especially in the initial stages, to find a unitary explanation and a universal theory: imitation, gregariousness, individual or mass suggestion, the pursuit of utility and enjoyment, the desire for power. But even in more recent authors there is a similar tendency towards a univocal explanation: anxiety, frustration, sexuality, guilt feelings, cognitive organization, conditioning, reinforcement, social 'role' and 'assumption' of roles, communication—each of these explanations has claimed or is claiming a more or less complete monopoly in the treatment of social problems.

It is superfluous to remark that less talented scholars are satisfied with making a bunch of picklocks from all these theories which they then proceed to use with evident satisfaction and with a certain dexterity to explain the mysteries of individual and social psychology. We have only to glance at the catalogue of these principles of interpretation to realize that any one of them can claim to explain the religious sense: the need to feel oneself protected and not to diverge from the habits of the social group, which stimulates the conviction of supernatural help; the projection of the father-image on to an unknown being and deference to this being in order to overcome anxiety; again, projection of unappeased sexual needs on to this being; the primordial tendency to 'withdraw' or to make a good show even with fictitious structures; the irrepressible impulse to find a reason of some sort for even the most absurd facts; the action of the social group by means of a process of conditioning or reinforcement to satisfy the fundamental survival needs of the group itself; learning the various roles which individuals must assume in social life and which correspond to the requirements of the social group. Religion is thus acknowledged as a fact which can be manifested in certain typical forms of behaviour, the distribution and intensity of which are measured by observation and statistical methods.

It is easy to flatter oneself that the religious problem can be solved by an exclusively social approach. According to Durkheim, social facts are characterized by generality (extension to the persons in the group), by transmissibility and obligation. This is true of language and also of religion. Since social facts are accessible to observation and measurement the behaviourist psychological method is found most suitable, as it allows us to observe and evaluate behaviour. Then again, in the study of religion, the character of irrational obligatoriness seems to be rightly interpreted by depth psychology. Hence religious social psychology is in danger of becoming a sociology of religion, or else of presenting a preconceived interpretation of religion in behaviourist-psychoanalytical terms. The sociology of religion has developed to a great extent and is known as religious sociology, which could lead us to believe that it is a religious science. But this is by no means the case, for sociology is a profane science whose methods are totally independent of any religious concept and are applicable to the study of human groups in industry or agriculture, of ethnic groups and so forth. Excellent samples are to be found in the works of le Bras in France,[13] of Argyle[14] and Fogarty in England, of Father G. Grasso[15] and S. Samele Acquaviva[16] in Italy, and naturally in the works of many Americans.

As an example of the equivocation into which religious psychology can fall through a sociological approach, we might mention M. Argyle's book, *Religious Behaviour*. Here we find data collected during fifty years in England and America, displayed in a series of charts and graphs relating to environment, age, sex, personal traits, mental disorders, marriage, sexuality and so on. The first impression of absolute reliability is soon followed by a keen sense of disappointment at the paltry and often insignificant conclusions reached. The restriction of religion to the conditions in which it is manifested deprives the religious problem of its liveliest and most human aspect. Undoubtedly some interesting data are obtained, but to stop at these gives the impression that religious problems are being

[13] G. le Bras, *Etudes de sociologie religieuse*, Paris, 1955, 2 vols.

[14] M. Argyle, *Religious Behaviour*, Routledge, London, 1958.

[15] G. Grasso, *Ricerca sociologica e sociologia religiosa*, Alba (Italy), 1958; and in *Educare*, F.A.S., Rome, 1960, vol. II.

[16] S. S. Acquaviva, *L'eclissi del sacro nella civiltà industriale*, Ed. Comunità, Milan, 1961.

avoided rather than emphasized and explained. The evaluation of data in social psychology is anything but easy and anything but reliable.

Cultural anthropology

American 'cultural anthropology' according to the judgment of Christopher Dawson marks a certain progress in sociology, since it extends the study of social facts to include a study of man as the actor in these events.[17] As Kluckhohn writes, it makes a study of 'those forms and modes of behaviour which are the outcome of the meeting of universal human nature with historical events and which are realized in many very different cultures'. The concept of 'culture' (in the anthropological sense) relates to those 'selective ways' of feeling, thinking and reacting which distinguish one group from another, habits which are transmitted socially and acquired (with some degree of change, of course, as time goes on) by each new generation. A culture is not an accumulation of customs. It is not possible to grasp the network of selective principles without understanding the fundamental values involved, the cognitive assumptions and what the logicians call 'the primitive categories'. The way of life transmitted as the social heritage of each people does far more than provide a series of norms for the regulation of human relations and a series of skills for the satisfaction of human needs. Each different way of life has its own assumptions as to the end and purpose of human existence, the ways in which knowledge can be acquired, the manner of filing, as it were, each sensory datum for future reference, the things human beings have a right to expect from each other and from the gods, what is 'good' and 'right' or 'better' and 'worse', what is meant by fulfilment and by frustration.[18]

[17] C. Dawson, *Dynamics of World History*, Sheed and Ward, London, 1957.
[18] C. Kluckhohn, 'Anthropology and Psychology' in *Acts of Fifteenth International Congress of Psychology*, Brussels, 1957.

This presentation of cultural anthropology by Kluckhohn certainly does not err on the side of modesty. It claims for its province all that philosophers, psychologists, sociologists, ethnographers and politicians study and have studied. In the field of psychology there are in cultural anthropology sufficient 'pacific annexations' from psychology (selective ways of feeling, thinking and reacting; thought and sensory organization; learning, cognitive assumptions and so on down to the factors of gratification and frustration) to make the psychologist 'hate like a brother' the cultural anthropologist, to use an Arabic proverb.

Kluckhohn declares that around cultural anthropology and in connection with it there has developed 'that odd mixture of psychoanalysis, learning theory and anthropology known in the United States as the culture and personality movement'. The cultural anthropologist is faced with the fact that people of one 'culture' find it very difficult to believe that people of another culture can have a way of life so different from their own. This goes to show that a fair share of cultural acquisitions are irrational. In order to study them, the cultural anthropologist follows a method very similar to that of the psychiatrist: he seeks to discover the hidden thread which runs through all their various and inconsistent manifestations. Hence his fondness for psychoanalysis which provides him with a theory of human nature in non-rational terms.

The learning theories of psychology are also very useful to him. Cultural transmission rests on learning. The manner in which this learning is formulated by the majority of American psychological schools tends to eliminate biological heredity and rational processes to the greatest possible extent and to stress instead environmental influence through the stimulus-response mechanism. Finally, the personality, conceived as the total of the individual's characteristics, is shown to be profoundly conditioned by relations between individuals in a given group, where the individual must assume various roles and respond to the expectations of the others, or else remain isolated from the group. Hence the problem is to establish

how, from a 'basic personality' resulting from the compromise
between instinctual urges and social habits in early years, one
comes by means of the learning process to interiorize an
institutionalized culture and thus attain individual encultura-
tion and socialization. In this plan, as can be seen, the stress is
placed almost exclusively on environmental factors which can
be objectively observed, while the subjective elaboration of
culture is seen under the aspect of 'conformism to social
pressure'. In this way an attempt is made to explain how what
is extraneous to the individual becomes proper to him.

A 'culture' cannot be reduced to a mere total of independent
habits and customs. For this reason a comparative study of
the same custom in different cultures is meaningless. A given
culture, on the other hand, assembles and integrates reciprocally various customs in a characteristic way. As Ruth Benedict
says,[19] 'a culture, like an individual, is a more or less consistent
pattern of thought and action'. As in the case of the individual,
it passes through various phases of development, stabilization
and decadence. 'It is the same process,' she continues, 'by which
a style in art comes into being and persists . . .'[20] the only way
we can know the significance of the selected detail of behaviour
is against the background of the motives and emotions and
values that are institutionalized in that culture'.[21] Ruth Benedict
appeals to the concepts and terminology of German psychology: to W. Stern's *Struktur* and *Person*, to Koffka's *Gestalt*,
to Dilthey's *verstehende Psychologie*, to O. Spengler's 'cycles'.

There is a strong temptation to remark that it is only the
assimilative capacity of a cultural anthropologist that can
successfully reconcile in a single pattern such widely varying
and reciprocally intolerant psychological theories. Ruth
Benedict expresses her enthusiasm for Dilthey's *Typen der
Weltanschauung* and for O. Spengler's *Decline of the West*.[22]
She approves of the latter's delineation of two features of

---

[19] R. Benedict, *Patterns of Culture*, Mentor Books, New York, 1934,
p. 42.
  [20] *Ibid*., p. 43.   [21] *Ibid*., p. 45.
[22] O. Spengler, *The Decline of the West*, Knopf, New York, 1962.

Western civilization: the Apollonian concept of the ancient world based on order and the Faustian idea of the modern world based on conflict, which, however, appear more recently in less complex cultures than that of Europe. Each culture has its own 'cultural pattern' which is a condition for its life, just as the 'ideal pattern' of the systematic group to which it belongs is a condition of life for the living organism. Each culture is different from the next and the differences are quite striking. 'We might suppose,' writes Ruth Benedict,

> that in the matter of taking life all peoples would agree in condemnation. On the contrary, in a matter of homicide, it may be held that one is blameless if diplomatic relations have been severed between neighbouring countries, or that one kills by custom his first two children, or that a husband has right of life and death over his wife, or that it is the duty of the child to kill his parents before they are old. It may be that those are killed who steal a fowl or who cut their upper teeth first, or who are born on a Wednesday. Among some peoples a person suffers torments at having caused an accidental death; among others it is a matter of no consequence. Suicide also may be a light matter, the recourse of one who has suffered some slight rebuff, an act that occurs constantly in a tribe. It may be the highest and noblest act a wise man can perform. The very tale of it, on the other hand, may be a matter for incredulous mirth and the act itself impossible to conceive as a human possibility. Or it may be a crime punishable by law, or regarded as a sin against the gods.[23]

These widely varying and even contradictory manners of behaviour are justified in the cultural environment to which they belong. They are justified by cultural values, by the values that a given culture attaches to objects, persons or situations, thus determining the rule of conduct to be observed by the individual members of the community. Hence no value, not even a moral value, exists apart from the culture itself, no

[23] R. Benedict, op. cit., p. 41.

autonomous or 'absolute' value. What is right or wrong, good or bad, beautiful or ugly, depends entirely on the particular culture concerned. Even mental abnormalities which do not interfere with the course of social life may be considered abnormal in one culture and normal in another. Moral and religious values themselves may be appreciated in one culture and proscribed in another. War and pillage, slavery, vendetta, infanticide, even cannibalism can be considered a duty and extolled as heroic acts, provided they are socially acceptable and have a useful function in the type of culture concerned. Thus in the sexual sphere what is vice in one culture can be tolerated and even encouraged in another: sexual promiscuity, homosexuality and even prostitution (e.g. sacred prostitution).

This, in its essential lines and without going into the nuances, is the theory advanced by cultural relativism. Ruth Benedict maintains that

> the recognition of cultural relativity carries with it its own values, which need not be those of the absolutist philosophies. It challenges customary opinions . . . it rouses to pessimism because it throws old formulae into confusion. . . . As soon as the new opinion is embraced as customary belief, it will be another trusted bulwark of the good life. We shall arrive then at a more realistic social faith, accepting as grounds of hope and as new bases for tolerance the coexisting and equally valid patterns of life which mankind has created for itself from the raw materials of existence.[24]

The theory and conclusions of cultural relativism are so important that we cannot be dispensed from subjecting them to a brief critical examination.

Cultural relativism

That the norms regulating life differ greatly in various cultures and that people who belong to these groups accept them, adapt themselves to them or infringe them, is an undisputed fact. That

[24] *Ibid.*, p. 257.

these norms are the reflection of certain biological or environmental needs or of particular historical conditions which exercise a social function corresponding to the needs of the group (Malinowski), or constitute a structure of interdependent activities (Radcliffe-Brown); that they can be understood by means of a cultural pattern or theme (Benedict) or through the study of 'cultural values' (Kluckhohn), are interpretations which throw light on various aspects of a culture but reveal their inadequacy as soon as they claim a monopoly.

Cultural relativism embodies a truth, for every culture constitutes, as it were, an environment or indispensable frame in which human capacities develop even though they are limited and disciplined by this environment. We need only glance at our own lives to realize how they pursue their course in a network of human and social relations. From the psychological point of view a question nevertheless arises. Is it merely a matter of moulding individuals according to a pattern, of the imposition of external conditions which at a certain point are appropriated by the individual and felt to be his own needs? Or is there a convergence between personal needs and social habits? Could not this convergence be the essential condition that enables the norms to be accepted and appropriated as one's own? If so, the situation would be vastly different, for it would then be necessary to consider not so much that which the particular culture offers, but the reason why and the manner in which it is appropriated and the meaning it assumes for the individual. It would then be necessary to consider, in addition to those external norms which can be described and listed, the innate needs of the persons concerned, which are much less easily identified by mere observation and the arrangement of data. This possibility cannot be excluded a priori, nor can we avoid it with the usual excuse that we are only concerned with that which can be verified.

The variety of social norms, the open contradiction between some of them in the various cultures, and the denial of absolute norms valid for all cultures alike, are subjects that had already been dealt with before the advent of cultural anthropology.

We need only recall Herodotus and Plato in ancient times, and, in times nearer our own, H. Spencer and E. Westermarck.[25] But here too the more striking and unexpected fact (because it contradicts the principle that all men, because they are men, must be alike) has triumphed over the more ordinary one. The exceptional is more attractive than what is habitual. The more striking differences have been explored and described, but much less has been done to establish whether the conviction concerning a fundamentally essential human nature in all men is to be maintained or rejected conclusively. Cultural anthropology has thus been obliged to find a way of escape between its principle of a universal human nature and the contradictions between different cultures. How can there be a human nature if values do not exist that are common to all men? For this reason a more adequate appreciation of cultural convergences has become necessary.

As far as moral norms are concerned, the comparative method, which deals prevalently and almost exclusively with differences, leads to extreme and false conclusions. If no common norms or hardly any common norms were recognized, every scholar who set out to study a different culture would have to ask himself primarily whether the beings he meant to study were men or not. Actually the first explorers among primitive native peoples were faced with this very question, which only arises today in the case of the palaeo-anthropologist, who endeavours to interpret skeletal remains along with which there is no trace of man-made objects. But when behaviour and customs are carefully observed, it becomes evident that the moral differences consist in different interpretations and applications of common principles rather than in essential diversity. The religious situation in the various cultures is analogous to that of language. Enormous differences exist from one culture to another and even in a single culture in various stages of its development, but fundamental motifs common to all men are permanently present.

[25] E. Westermarck, *The Origin and Development of the Moral Ideas*, Macmillan, New York, 1906.

There is also the problem of terminology. With reference to palaeolithic and neolithic art, H. Breuil has pointed out the striking difference between them: the first being naturalistic and full of life, the second geometrical and conventional. A. Hauser in his *Social History of Art*[26] makes naturalism coincide with a profane view of the world, and geometrism with an outlook orientated towards the next world. This is questionable, to say the least of it, in view of the magical character of palaeolithic images. W. Hausenstein goes further and finds a correlation between geometrical style and Communism, since both manifest a tendency to equalize, to act authoritatively and to plan. Hauser rightly observes that these two concepts have a different meaning in art and in economy. Nothing is easier, he says, than to institute picturesque relations between sometimes contemporaneous social styles and forms, relations which, when all is said and done, rest on a metaphor: and nothing is more alluring than the glory to which these daring analogies appear to lead.[27]

In the comparisons made by certain cultural anthropologists the same defect is frequently evident, as when the same psychological terminology is used in the description of various cultures. When cultural anthropologists assert that the variety of customs implies an irreducible diversity of moral principles, they are glossing over a very important fact. R. Brandt observes that many of the examples adopted by Westermarck in support of cultural relativism merely tell us that various peoples favour or condemn adultery, falsehood, homosexuality and so forth.[28] But this is insufficient. The question is: how do these people conceive such acts? 'Do they eat human flesh because they like its taste, and do they kill slaves merely for the sake of a feast? Or do they eat flesh because they think this is necessary for tribal fertility, or because they think they will then partici-

---

[26] A. Hauser, *Social History of Art*, Routledge and Kegan Paul, London, 1951.

[27] *Ibid.*

[28] R. B. Brandt, *Ethical Theory*, Prentice-Hall, Englewood Cliffs, N.J., 1959.

pate in the manliness of the person eaten? Perhaps those who condemn cannibalism would not do so if they thought that eating the flesh of an enemy is necessary for the survival of the group.'[29]

In order to judge whether or not there is absolute incompatibility of moral principles it is also necessary to know how these principles are understood by the persons concerned, since behaviour alone does not tell us enough. The cognitive factor of the situation thus acquires decided importance. There are some situations in which, as the scholars of Gestalt psychology observe (Wertheimer, Duncker, Asch), the 'requiredness' of a certain behaviour becomes manifest.[30] The action corresponds to objective needs and is not merely the repetition of a preceding act of which the meaning is not understood, even though it has been 'rewarded'. Not only are approved patterns of behaviour accumulated by learning, but the subject must also recognize the suitability of this behaviour in a given situation. In this way the moral norm, even though rigidly fixed in a certain custom and transmitted by learning, has its origin in a need to give consistency to a disconnected, fragmentary situation in which meaning has been interrupted.

The moral norm can survive even when the original situation is changed. The word *addio* which originally must have expressed the wish to confide a beloved person to the care of a powerful Being (constituting a bridge for the friend about to face an unknown situation), has lived on. But it no longer retains this meaning in full and is merely a superficial expression of courtesy and affection. Similarly the salutation *ciao* has become very commonplace, although it originally meant 'I am your slave' *(sono tuo schiavo)*. The killing of a newborn baby or the elimination of a person incapable of fending for himself, which are condemned by those convinced of the human

[29] *Ibid.*, pp. 101-2.
[30] Cf. E. Wertheimer, 'Some Problems in the Theory of Ethics' in *Social Research*, 1935; K. Duncker, 'Ethical Relativity?—An Enquiry in the Psychology of Ethics' in *Mind*, 1929; S. Asch, *Social Psychology*, Macmillan, New York, 1906.

person's inviolable right to live, can be motivated by religious norms (sacrifice to a deity or introduction into a happy state) and by social customs. Moreover, more or less scientific reasons can also encourage today the use of contraceptives, euthanasia and the elimination of persons unfit for society or deemed to be dangerous. In this case, as in many others, the action is not evaluated in itself, but rightly or wrongly it is given a moral justification. Even Hitler at the outbreak of the second world war felt the need to declare that it was 'not moral' to tolerate offences against the German race any longer.

It could appear that we are returning along this path to the most primitive moral relativism, and that we are even making it worse by adding to social compulsion the aggravating circumstance of individual understanding. But here the question is a different one. We ask ourselves: 'Is there a primordial need for right and wrong, that is, for a moral norm?' The answer is unequivocal: the need exists but it is in danger of being wrongly stated and even becoming self-contradictory. Only in this way can we understand how different and apparently opposite modes of behaviour are the consequence, not of the absence of ethical principles, but of differences in conception and understanding.

The difference between treatment of the mentally deficient in the Middle Ages and at the present day depends upon a different appreciation of the situation. Similarly with regard to usury and the investment of capital. 'The relativistic argument, by failing to take into account the psychological content of the situation, equates things that are psychologically different and only externally the same.'[31] This is why the anthropologists have considerably mitigated the formulation of social relativism. In the first place they have also begun to study the cultural universals common to all mankind. Kluckhohn declares that

the search for genuine universal categories demands much skill as well as effort . . . there are certain 'precultural' conditions or limiting factors (e.g., the existence of two

[31] S. Asch, *op. cit.*, p. 377.

sexes) and there are certain universal psychological processes (e.g., sibling rivalry). There are certain universal cultural processes (e.g., diffusion and acculturation) and certain universal cultural forms (e.g., some panhuman values). . . . Finally, there are universal properties in all cultures which cannot (at any rate, as yet) be traced so firmly to biological needs of the human organism or to invariant elements in the human situation. For example, all cultures give their own cognitive and symbolic answers to the questions of what? how? why? and when?[32]

Elsewhere the same author writes: 'Every culture has a concept of murder, distinguishing this from execution, killing in war and other "justifiable homicides". The notions of incest and other regulations upon sexual behaviour, of prohibitions upon untruth under defined circumstances, of restitution and reciprocity, of mutual obligations between parents and children —these and many other moral concepts are altogether universal.'[33] And E. R. Linton says: 'A comparative study of a large number of cultures indicates that the basic values of all societies include many of the same elements. Differences increase as one moves toward the superficial end of the scale.'[34]

These comprehensive opinions expressed by two scholars who have declared themselves in favour of cultural relativism are extremely valuable, for they show that an exact understanding of it demands the recognition of some primordial values. Linton's distinction is particularly clear, since it shows us a sameness of fundamental values and variety in expressing them, just as language is common to all men while the terms it uses vary greatly. Linton's distinction moreover enables us to stress the difference between a value and a custom (custom

[32] C. Kluckhohn, 'Culture and Behaviour' in Lindzey, *Handbook of Social Psychology*, *op. cit.*, vol. II, p. 955.

[33] C. Kluckhohn, 'Ethical Relativity: Sic et Non' in *Journal of Philosophy*, LII, 1955, pp. 663-77.

[34] Cited in R. B. Brandt, *Ethical Theory*, *op. cit.*, p. 287. Cf. E. R. Linton, 'The Problem of Universal Values' in Spencer, *Perspectives in Anthropology*, University of Minnesota, Minn., 1954.

being understood here in all its variety, from firmly established customs to the variability of fashion), a difference which appears at times to be overlooked. When people speak of the variability of moral norms they frequently confuse genuine moral norms with mere traditional usage. This is easily explained, since to go against an established custom is easily noticeable by others and exposed to their judgment as well as to our own, while the transgression of a moral norm can pass unobserved. Wearing decidedly antiquated clothes, or putting one's feet on the table exposes one much more to the criticism and judgment of others than getting away with a lie or taking liberties with weights and measures and money in a business deal. One can even feel more humiliated and almost guilty on account of being unfashionably dressed than when one entertains hatred for another. From the subjective point of view, then, the transgression which produces distress is often more closely related to superficial values than to the deeper ones.

A further explanation is necessary with reference to the parallels between types of personality and types of culture and to the conclusion that 'Culture and personality are to be written in capital letters, personality and culture in small letters.' Here the old idea of Hobbes and Spencer reappears, the idea of identical processes in the organism and in society. It is taken up again by Spengler, insinuated by the psychoanalysts and accepted by the cultural anthropologists. Let it not be forgotten that analogy and identity are two very different things. Durkheim already pointed this out:

> The transition from the comparison of society with living organisms to the identification of the two signifies failure to acknowledge the specific character of social laws. Social facts, more complex individually than natural facts, respond to a teleological rather than a mechanical need. Sociology takes an intermediate stand between the 'sciences dealing with laws' and the 'sciences dealing with events'. It discovers rules and rhythms rather than laws.[35]

[35] E. Durkheim, in *Année sociologique*, II (1897-98), pp. 159-60.

Kluckhohn, while admitting that the parallels between culture and personality are striking, writes: 'The equation of culture with the personality of a society or of a personality as the subjective side of culture represents an unfortunate over-simplification. The former analogy leads to the brink of the "group-mind" fallacy. The latter is false because culture is far from being the only constituent of personality; a unique biographical heredity and idiosyncratic life history also enters in.'[36]

As to the exaltation of cultural relativism as a motive for reciprocal tolerance and better social adjustment, I am very, very sceptical. Would benevolent tolerance of the 'racial myth', for example, have been desirable? Yet it was a 'cultural pattern' consistent with the German mentality and side by side with persons who used it in their own shameful interests, others were not lacking who believed in it to the point of utter dedication. It was only when it had been vanquished that they realized what execrable crimes had been committed in its name. It ought rather to be said that when cultural relativism reaches the point of denying the existence of moral laws which are binding on all cultures, it is suddenly transformed into cultural absolutism without any possibility of control from within and can only be eliminated by violence. Unfortunately, autocratic cultural relativisms are not a thing of the past and tolerance of them only causes them to spread more widely and to become more tyrannical. Nothing but convictions founded on the inalienable values of man can place an effective barrier in their way. Besides, is the cultural relativist unaware that in his own judgment he himself is relative to his culture?[37]

Asch has pointed out 'the high phenomenal objectivity of our ethical judgments. We feel that we value as we do for

[36] C. Kluckhohn, 'Culture and Behaviour' in Lindzey, *op. cit.*, vol. II, p. 963.
[37] Ruth Benedict (1947), for instance, 'made an analysis of Japanese culture and although her conclusions about the Japanese mentality have since been challenged (Stoetzel, 1955), her observations proved very useful at the time of the American occupation' (J. C. Flugel, *A Hundred Years of Psychology*, Methuen, London, 1964, p. 323).

reasons connected with the situation, not merely because we are personally inclined to do so. As one writer aptly put it: "We all feel that we value a thing because it has value and not that it has value because we value it." [38] Firth writes that it is of the essence of moral standards (and these he thinks are required by every social system) that they are regarded as 'external, non-personal in their origin' and 'invested with a special authority' which 'demands that they be obeyed'.[39] This would explain the position of those psychologists who obstinately persist in considering norms merely as factors extraneous to the subject who only interiorizes them at a later stage. The situation is perhaps the reverse: the norms are externalized because they are considered to be inevitable. This would confirm the fact that moral judgment imposes itself not because men learn how to put it into effect, but because it is a primordial human necessity. The same considerations may be applied in the case of religion.

Membership of a group: prejudice

Cultural relativism is an aspect of the problem of 'belonging to a group'. For the gregarious animals the group is not a fictitious entity but a condition of life, and separation from the group has serious consequences for their individual behaviour and their very existence. Among birds and mammals in particular, attachment to the group determines a distinction between those of the same group (in a certain hierarchical order) and outsiders. Outsiders are accepted with difficulty and more often they are rejected or even killed. The note of extraneity can appear in the group itself. Tinbergen has observed this in colonies of sea-gulls, where individual birds behaved in an abnormal way or even withdrew from the rest or were treated by these as enemies. W. Köhler has described cases of intolerance and aggression among chimpanzees. M. Meyer

[38] S. Asch, *op. cit.*, p. 358.
[39] Raymond Firth, *Elements of Social Organization*, Watts & Co., London, 1952, pp. 186, 197.

Holzapfel relates several examples from which it emerges that animals which live in groups distinguish clearly between those who belong and those who do not belong to their group, and between followers and outcasts.[40]

On the other hand, K. Lorenz, with reference to monkeys' social defence, points out that 'every difference in rank is passed over when the horde of monkeys is menaced by a common enemy. Against beasts of prey most monkeys defend a companion, even their greatest rival, with a courage beyond compare.'[41] In a recent book[42] Lorenz maintains that aggression among animals has a clearly *arterhaltend* character, that is, it acts for the preservation of the species by elimination of the weak, by obtaining solidarity in the group and by encouraging the formation of defences. The continuity and development of the animal species (and consequently of individuals belonging to the species) are connected with the manner in which they come through the ordeal of aggression, especially in the case of those species which have a social organization. Social forms among animals are very numerous and we cannot yet venture on a theory valid for all. The attempt made by Lorenz is most interesting as regards the few animal societies he studied, but his general theory and the over-simplification of his application of it to man and his problems are quite perplexing.

As to human groupings, we must admit that they demand solidarity and the more or less accentuated exclusion of outsiders, unless these accept the norms of the group. Where these elements are lacking it cannot really be said that there is a group. Sociability as a biological fact is based on instinctual conditions and these persist also in man, who is able (to a certain extent) to understand their meaning and their consequences.

That which man calls loyalty, fidelity to the group, defence

[40] M. Meyer Holzapfel, 'Soziale Beziehungen bei Saugetieren' in *Gestaltungen Sozialen Leben bei Tier und Mensch*, Bern, 1958.
[41] K. Lorenz, *Verständigung unter den Tieren*, Zurich, 1953.
[42] K. Lorenz, *On Aggression*, Methuen, London, 1966.

against the common enemy, has instinctual presuppositions which can reappear with all their rigidity and irrationality. The awareness of belonging to a group is necessary. When it weakens or is lacking there are symptoms of the 'uprooting' and 'scattering of identity' (who am I? what meaning have I?) which accompany neurosis. On the other hand, pride of caste which is expressed in various nuances of family ambition, family honour, social position and membership of a religious group or a social class, can become the incentive to the most appalling iniquities. In wars in general and in religious and class wars, the instinctive inexorability which is latent in civil and religious institutions is unleashed. Yet in these very upheavals of the social order the element which distinguishes man from the animals—the capacity to fight against his instinctive irrationality—is consolidated and confirmed. Fidelity to an ideal, self-denial and mutual help appear in more critical moments. From this point of view it is possible to understand the inextricable tangle of contradictions in the history of man and of humanity which is reflected also in religion.

The earliest prescriptions of a religious and civil character in the Bible (the separation of these two fields is a modern innovation and is frequently equivocal), side by side with the imposition of solidarity in times of war against enemies, contain the precept of hospitality to the stranger and relief of the needy. In the other great institutional religions there is also something of the same kind, and the golden rule of not doing to others what you would not have them do to you is the greatest rule shared by all men. Precisely because it had been suppressed it was clearly stated in the Gospel. How, then, can we explain the contradictory expression in religion of tyranny and hatred side by side with unselfishness and love? There is only one answer. The religious sense, understood as dependence upon powers above man, is, as it were, a neutral force that can be linked with the most varied and contradictory actions. From the individual point of view it expresses man's merits and defects and from the social point of view those of the community. It develops consistently in a particular environmental and cultural situation, but it frequently clings to customs which outlive the circumstances which justified them, so that formalism can become more important than religious content. Under similar conditions it is inevitable that the demands of the group prevail over the tendency towards reciprocal help.

This paradox exists also in Christianity. Jesus Christ has shown, with unusual and perfect balance, the necessity of uniting *nova et vetera* and at the same time avoiding the 'patching of an old suit with new cloth'. He combated the stiff-necked attitude of the Pharisees to the point of falling a victim to it. He showed 'who is my neighbour' in the parable of the Samaritan outcast who went to the assistance of the wounded man while the priest and the levite passed him by. On the other hand, Jesus has insisted in the most vigorous manner on Christian unity and on the separation of Christians from the world, from the spirit of evil. But in the history of the Church innumerable divisions, heresies and the struggle against them, show how the most terrible human passions can be stirred up by a religious motive.

Religion, which brings man face to face with forces beyond his own capacities, carries both failings and virtues to their uttermost consequences. A cry of malediction against religion has not been lacking for the inexorable manner in which it divides men. In this rebellious outburst I am inclined to see the desperate lament of those who realize the impossibility of attaining the finest and greatest ideal: participation in the plenitude of all being, in God himself. On the other hand, is it not precisely the more deeply religious men who have revived man's aspiration towards good, who have broken down the barriers separating man from man and helped their fellows in the most disinterested manner? Where adherence to a religion is not exclusive participation in power groups and protective groups but a continual effort to overcome the constantly recurring selfishness of men, there is an irradiation of serenity and understanding which binds men closely together. If the paradox exists of a Christianity that preaches union among men and produces their separation, we also have the paradox of a Christianity which sounds the note of peace among men lacerated by discord, through its silent penetration rather than by elaborate speeches.

Closely connected with the distinction between adherents and non-adherents to a group we have the question of prejudice. An unfavourable judgment already exists before there has been any attempt to examine the matter and it even dispenses with this examination. There is a speedy appeal to judgments already formulated and diffused in the group and which are therefore almost invincible. Racial prejudice in particular has been the object of study. It is more widespread among adherents to religious groups than among people devoid of religious belief. This would seem to suggest that religion is at the root of prejudice. But the matter is not so simple. When we try to decide what type of religion produces prejudice, we note that it is predominantly a case of extrinsic legalistic religion in groups which have experienced strong opposition and find themselves for the most part in a state of social inferiority. We also notice that accentuated segregation of religious groups fosters prejudice, while cooperation for a common purpose attenuates it. But we also find that prejudice depends on the type of person who nourishes it rather than on the environment.[43]

From a substantial collection of studies by Adorno and his collaborators on the 'authoritarian personality',[44] which is in effect the personality which generates prejudice, the chief personal conditions conducing to prejudice are: subjection to parents masking interior rebellion; an excessively rigid moral outlook; the classification of others in two categories, the good and the bad; intolerance of ambiguity, that is, the inability to admit complex or inadequately defined situations; the attribution to external causes of what lies within the range of personal decision; preservation of a social order of any kind and, finally,

[43] G. W. Allport, *The Nature of Prejudice*, Addison-Wesley Inc., Cambridge, Mass., 1954.

[44] T. W. Adorno, E. Frenkel-Brunswick, D. G. Levinson and R. N. Sanford, *The Authoritarian Personality*, Wiley, New York, 1964.

a blind spirit of discipline. Adorno and his colleagues point out that these characteristics have been observed in persons holding very pronounced prejudices. It may be concluded that prejudice denotes a deficiency in the individual, that is to say, it provides a convenient solution for insufficiently solved personal problems. The ostentatious assertion that one is free from prejudice can itself be a sign that one is conveniently blind to the existence of prejudices. It is certainly true to say that prejudice is common to all men and that real strength of mind is required to overcome it. Here again we are faced with the harsh necessity of going against ourselves to give precedence to God, an exercise which belongs to the essence of religion but which no man is capable of performing to the full.

Culture and religion

With reference to 'culture', understood as a particular way of life influenced by environmental and historical conditions but necessarily linked with a fundamental conception which is expressed in all manifestations of a given culture, the question arises spontaneously as to the meaning of religion within the ambit of culture. I accept along with Bartlett the judgment of T. S. Eliot according to which 'no culture has appeared or developed except together with a religion', because 'whatever else may be true about the relations of religion and culture, it is obviously true that religion can appear as a lively issue for discussion only within the culture to which it has itself contributed in many ways'.[45] The discussion turns instead precisely on the reciprocal relations between religion and the culture concerned.

Is religion just one among many reactions of the cultural group to life's demands, or does it constitute one of the strongest wellsprings from which the stream of a given culture is fed and by which the characteristics and the course of this culture are shaped? This problem would appear to be very

[45] F. Bartlett, 'Religion as Experience, Belief, Action' in *Riddell Memorial Lectures*, Oxford Univ. Press, London, 1950, p. 3.

far from psychology had not the concept of culture been formulated at least to a large extent in psychological terms (see Kluckhohn). Here we have a whole gamut of answers. There are those who see religion as a strange social super-structure which is dying out by degrees and will disappear completely with the advance of science, particularly of psychology and sociology. Again, there are those who, like Spengler,[46] consider religion to be an aspect of a vital process in a given stage of development, a 'style' consistent with the spirit of the age *(Zeitgeist)*, and those who, like T. S. Eliot, assert that 'religion is culture and culture is religion'.[47]

All of these extreme opinions contain, as usual, a truth which is distorted when presented in an exclusive way. Scientific progress, which today seems to be identified with technical progress, has an enormous influence on the modern mentality and seems to ignore religious problems. But it is incapable of preventing them from springing up again. Besides, as we shall see later on, scientific progress itself is not exempt from clearly religious formulations. Consideration of religion as a cultural 'product' is therefore only comprehensible in the sense that every culture possesses a religious sense. But this does not mean that culture and religion are one and the same thing. Religious manifestations differ in various cultures and in various epochs. They take on the style and language of their respective cultures and periods, but the dress does not make the person who wears it.

In all primitive cultures we find, even though in crude and contradictory forms, an attempt to explain the mystery of the world and these conceptions are so powerful that they overthrow and suffocate explanations which are closer to reality and apparently more reasonable. Civil institutions themselves are also religious, with an aura of respect and sacredness which guarantees their efficiency and survival. While advanced cultures have a particular caste of men destined to represent

[46] O. Spengler, *op. cit.*
[47] T. S. Eliot, *Notes Towards the Definition of Culture*, Faber and Faber, London, 1948.

and transmit a religious tradition, in primitive cultures visionaries and prophets are honoured and respected as guides of the people. Priests have the task of instructing the people and organizing the sacrificial rites by which they propitiate the divinity and even obtain participation in the divine life. The king is the supreme political head, but his prestige is due to his religious character. The whole world of nature is also believed to be sustained by a divine order independent of man, who must bow down before it and consider it as the rule of social conduct. As Dawson rightly said, religion is the seed from which spring all the shoots of human civilization.[48]

It has been argued by Sir William Ramsay, E. Hohn and others that the origins of agriculture and of the domestication of animals, especially the ox, arose out of this [Sumerian] vegetation religion, so that in fact the art of agriculture was the fruit of the cult of the Mother Goddess and of the ritual imitation of the processes of nature, rather than the reverse. Certainly there is reason to suppose that the veneration of the Mother Goddess as the principle of fertility goes back to palaeolithic times, and thus far antedates the origins of agriculture.[49]

In the study of cultural development we encounter not only uniformity in social organization but also continual and conscious process of discipline. Language develops by a continual effort down through the centuries in order to establish a terminology and classifications. A generally accepted idea of reality, a common mental attitude towards life, have an active influence on social facts. 'In this way the intellectual factor conditions the development of every society. It is the active and creative elements in culture, since it emancipates man from the purely biological laws . . . and enables him to accumulate a growing capital of knowledge and social experience.'[50]

[48] C. Dawson, *Progress and Religion*, Sheed and Ward, London, 1938, p. 84.
[49] C. Dawson, *Religion and Culture*, Sheed and Ward, London, 1949, pp. 138-9.
[50] C. Dawson, *Progress and Religion*, op. cit., p. 80.

F

The various cultures have a certain course of development but this does not proceed with a steady rhythm. This fact has given rise to some impressive syntheses of a philosophical nature (such as those of Vico and Hegel) or of a more historico-naturalistic character. Famous among the latter is Spengler's work in which each culture is seen as an isolated event where the same characteristic style and spirit find expression in all human activity from the loftiest to the most humdrum and lowly. This spirit in turn indicates the phase through which the particular culture is passing in the irrevocable process of its vital parabola, from its origins to its full splendour and on to its decline. Spengler compares these phases to the seasons. In spring a new 'myth' appears, the vitality of which does not yet allow itself to be imprisoned in a logical system. In summer the culture becomes aware of itself and expresses itself in a philosophy. In autumn the development of social cohesion is threatened by rationalism and individualism. In winter only the hardened structures survive and here a 'culture' ends, giving place to a 'civilization' which is its fossilized counterpart, devoid of religious spirit and tending towards cosmopolitan expansion. Each culture stands by itself and evolves by an interior impulse. The development of a culture is in reality the life of a people which begins in the homeland that nourished it and spreads out later into a cosmopolitanism of uprooted beings. Western culture has reached this point. It has now exhausted its need for artists, philosophers and poets and requires instead technicians, financiers and organizers. This is the task of the German people (note that Spengler's work was written at the end of the first European war) while Russian culture is just beginning to appear.

Spengler's vision is one which has been fulfilled, even if only partially, in the events of two generations. The American anthropologist Kroeber sees in Spengler one of the inspirers of cultural anthropology because of his grasp of the characteristic quality of the various cultures, and Ruth Benedict has followed his fundamental concepts. In Spengler's cyclic determinism religion seems to have a more expressive than con-

structive function. It does not appear to have fundamental
continuity throughout the various cycles. This interpretation
is rather surprising since it would involve a complete rupture,
for example, between medieval Christianity and the Christianity
of modern times.

Another modern interpretation of cultural development is
presented to us in the monumental work of Arnold Toynbee.[51]
This author has carried out a comparative study on Western
and Eastern civilizations of the present day and their pre-
decessors. He does not follow Spengler in the assertion of
absolute and incontestable independence in the development
of each culture by means of internal movement and independently of relations with other cultures. He does not exclude
the presence of common elements in all cultures, nor does
he deny that science and ethics can surpass the limitations
of a given civilization. But he argues for the equivalence of
different cultures from the philosophical and moral point
of view and therefore accepts cultural relativism without
reserve.

One of Toynbee's critics has asked how the absolutism of
his judgments, especially in the first volumes of his work, is
to be reconciled with the cultural relativism of his theory.
Subsequently, however, in the final volumes, Toynbee abandons
the theory of equivalence in cultures. He no longer favours
the idea of cyclic development but visualizes progressive
development, a process of spiritual evolution, in four stages
(primitive societies, primary civilizations, secondary civilizations, higher religions). The higher religions are at the summit
of development and constitute a spiritual universality towards
which the growth of civilizations converges. Civilizations are
therefore in a subordinate relation to religion rather than one
of command. Although the higher religions are qualitatively
different, according to Toynbee, they are nevertheless to be
considered equivalent in the sense that they constitute various
paths by which mankind can set out and reach the Great

---

[51] A. Toynbee, *The Study of History*, 12 vols., Oxford University
Press, 1935-61. Also available as an O.U.P. paperback.

Mystery. 'Uno itinere non potest venire ad tam grande secretum' was the motto of the pagan Symmachus to prove the validity of various religions in opposition to St Ambrose. Toynbee makes this motto his own and professes himself a 'Symmachian disciple' of C. G. Jung, since he believes that the four great religions, Christianity, Islam, Hinduism and Buddhism, correspond to Jung's four types of fundamental 'psychic functions' namely, thought, sensation, feeling and intuition.

This debouching of a comparative study of civilizations into a theologico-psychological thesis is curious in the extreme. Even among admirers of the monumental work of the English scholar, there are few who agree with and many who criticize the solution he adopts. In the twelfth volume of his *opus magnum* entitled *Reconsiderations*, Toynbee weighs up criticisms and commendations of his work and also criticizes himself. A reviewer of this book writes: 'It would seem that what Dr Toynbee has mainly succeeded in doing is to exhibit what has been called *cette puissance de deduction qui est propres aux hommes d'une seule idée*. There may be many ideas, but the ruling passion here is to establish laws and make plans and schemes of all human things. He ends with the reminder that he stands with Lucretius, whose *De Rerum Natura* he is fond of quoting.'[52]

It is significant that a comparative study of civilizations conducted with great breadth and wealth of information should throw a clear light on the fundamental importance of the religious factor in the history of mankind and that the cultural relativism professed in the initial stages of the work should later be subordinated to a dynamic religious factor. 'The history of religion appears to be unitary and progressive by contrast with the multiplicity and repetitiveness of the histories of civilizations.'[53]

[52] J. J. Dwyer, 'Professor Toynbee's Apologia' in *The Month*, Dec. 1961, p. 339.
[53] A. Toynbee, *op. cit.*, vol. VII, pp. 425-6, cited in Dawson, *Dynamics of World History, op. cit.*, p. 397.

Is religion, then, to be looked on as a static, conservative force or as a dynamic factor of progress? Is it shut up in the phases indicated by Spengler or is it a great river fed by many tributaries and having its outlet in a single sea, as Toynbee visualizes it? This alternative is too categorical, as often happens in a work of synthesis when more attention is paid to the guiding threads than to individual data. 'Toynbee's great work is too telescopic and not sufficiently microscopic.'[54]

For the purpose of the present study which is more concerned with the psychological aspect or the actual experience of religion rather than with its historical development, it is worth while remarking that one of the outstanding characteristics of religion in any culture is that it refers to something surpassing the practical and utilitarian aspect of the culture itself and therefore imposes on this a particular norm. This might appear at first sight to be an external constraint—and the individual can feel it as such—but in reality it is inherent in the whole series of economic activities (by which I mean activities concerned with vital needs) which it nevertheless surpasses and directs. There is a transcendence in religion which differentiates it from other utilitarian activities, for men are aware that it points to a reality which is different from created things and from men themselves. It produces an awareness that 'the way of man is not in himself' but in forces extraneous to himself, as Franz Boas and Ruth Benedict have put it in their studies of primitive peoples. There is a sense of reality, the feeling of an objective presence (W. James): 'another world, another power, another being' (Dawson). This is not a merely negative experience, like Spencer's 'unknowable', nor is it 'the product of a tedious process of abstraction', as Engels has said.[55]

Religion is directed towards something that is considered no less real than the things we see and touch, something more powerful than these, an 'other' who commands respect and subordination. In this sense the religious factor, no matter

---

[54] C. Dawson, *Dynamics of World History*, *op. cit.*, pp. 403-4.
[55] C. Dawson, *Religion and Culture*, *op. cit.*, p. 133.

what its practical formulation may be, surpasses sensory experience and broadens our horizon even if this opens up on mystery. Obviously, therefore, when religion has grown up side by side with a culture, to which it gives a meaning and for whose institutions in inculcates respect, it constitutes a most potent cohesive factor. It might be compared to the earthen cup which God offered in the beginning to every people and from which they drank life, according to the Indian proverb recalled by Ruth Benedict. Cultural life is contained in the fragile yet enduring cup of religion. But religion is not on this account blindly conservative. Even movements of criticism and revolution have a religious afflatus, for they present an ideal to be attained which contrasts with existing conditions. If this positive and binding aspect is lacking, they immediately degenerate into unproductive criticism. What gives certain movements—not only religious but also political—a terrible power for the disruption of the constituted order is precisely the commitment to an ideal to be attained, a commitment which is felt to be imposed by a 'new order' which demands the abolition of the existing cultural norms. Revolutionary criticism places itself beneath the aegis of moral ideals (justice, freedom, prosperity) to the point of justifying even transgressions that are incompatible with any social order. Hence a culture finds itself in a state of continual tension because of conflicting religious forces and the victory of one force or the other leads to stagnation or to the collapse of the culture itself.

This interpretation of cultural religion, presented by Dawson, appears objective and well-balanced and enables us to avoid the dangerous identification of culture with religion, since it reveals their complementary character. At the present time we are living in a situation which is perhaps quite new in the history of mankind: 'a spiritual conflict in its most acute phase of social schizophrenia which divides the mind of society between an immoral desire for power served by inhuman technical methods, and a religious faith and moral idealism which no longer have any hold on human life. There must be a return to unity, a spiritual integration of cultures, if humanity is to survive.'[56] The disappearance of religion or its regression and concealment under wild forms is far more catastrophic than the 'neurosis of mankind', for it endangers the very existence of mankind.

What are the principal motifs, what is the recurring theme, in studies which deal with religion from the social point of view? Primarily, a certain rashness in basing research on observable facts which can be described, compared and even evaluated, facts which we might call 'religious ways of behaviour'. Very soon, though, the need for interpretation arises. Religion is seen as a constraint from without, exercised by superindividual entities, identifiable and definable in naturalistic terms such as the social group, society or culture, for the purpose of ensuring the existence and survival of these. Religion is therefore interpreted as a necessity for group cohesion capable of satisfying the needs of individuals, but also imposing certain restrictions upon them.

Since the obligatory character of religious prescriptions— sometimes absurd and completely opposed to individual aspirations—cannot be attributed to the individual, it must be attributed to society which alone is capable of imposing these prescriptions by means of its sanctions. Religious norms, there- fore, are not binding for all men, but only for those belonging to the group which imposes them in a given manner. There is an accentuation of psychological factors when, over and above the fact of 'social pressure', the widely varying forms which it assumes are taken into consideration. These are said to depend upon geographical and historical factors, but above all upon a particular manner of life and a particular interpretation of the world, said to be a 'culture'. There are striking analogies between culture and personality. Frequently we find that culture is interpreted anthropomorphically and in a terminology borrowed from individual psychology. This presents society as the pattern and the individual as shaped according to the pattern. In this conception religion is seen as one of the most

[56] Cf. C. Dawson, *Progress and Religion, op. cit.*, p. 217.

meaningful aspects of a culture and can even be identified with the culture itself.

We have already seen that the sociological interpretation offers a valuable approach to an understanding of religion in the forms in which it is manifested, but that it fails to grasp the meaning of religion. If social construction is to be effective it must be recognized by the individual members of the community as consistent with a given situation. Hence the consistency of the group presupposes a human individual with the capacity to understand, to choose a line of conduct and commit himself to follow it. Social pressure would be of no avail if it failed to produce a response in the persons concerned and if it failed to furnish the answer to a need on their part. The disconcerting differences in customs in the various cultures denote, it is true, a particular conception of life in each case, but they imply that men have many more characteristics in common than may appear at first sight. We have also observed that in an organic description of the various cultures it is easy and almost inevitable to slip into a terminology pertaining to the study of the individual and that in applying this analogically to the group (metaphor in the etymological sense) there is danger of absolutely arbitrary generalization.

In face of the psychologization of sociology we are inclined to wonder whether many characteristics attributed to society are not proper in the first place to the individual. We therefore ask ourselves whether the situation as seen by the sociologists ought not to be reversed. Should we not say that the group does not impose things on individuals, but that the individuals impose things on themselves? But this extreme position would also be quite erroneous. There must be a complementary and not an exclusive relation between individual and group. In this light religion appears as situated radically in the individual and developed in the social group. In animal societies, of which there is an immense variety, there undoubtedly exists a social organization, but there is not the slightest trace of religious behaviour. It is therefore not society as such which creates this behaviour. Society can merely offer or refuse the conditions in which religious behaviour can take place. Religion is moreover qualified by a distinctive characteristic, by the fact that it aims beyond the social bonds, reaching out to a mystery which it considers to be something real, even when religious behaviour assumes the strangest forms. Religion involves an overcoming of biological and social conditions. 'The individual whose interior horizon is limited to psychophysiological symbols cannot but consider the religious idea to be a foolish illusion and a nullity,' says Boutroux.[57] The same author enquires: when men appeal to society as the producer of values, to what society are they referring? Certainly they do not mean society as it really is, the society which does not offer the individual what religion attributes to the divinity. They are referring instead to an ideal society which is distinguished from the society we know by qualities which our society lacks completely although it considers these qualities indispensable. In its highest forms this 'ideal society', writes Boutroux,

tends to elevate to the highest grade compatible with human nature the cult of those spiritual things *which perhaps serve no purpose*: justice, truth and goodness. These products of thought which have no place in pure nature or which encumber it are considered by society to be of *supreme utility*. In a word, society imposes religion, it is inspired by religion and it is very far from manufacturing it. It is not a machine whose task it is to force the individual towards goals which he finds repugnant.[58]

[57] E. Boutroux, *Science et religion*, Paris, 1915, p. 201.
[58] *Ibid.*, p. 207. Talcott Parsons seems to come close to these ideas: 'It is not possible to agree with Durkheim's view that the ultimate "reality" in general symbolized in religious ideas is the reality "society" taken either as a concrete entity or as a factor in the latter. What is true is, rather, that it is in terms of what we call religious ideas that men attempt a cognitive apprehension of the non-empirical aspects of reality to which they are actively related . . . fundamental elements in the determination of men's actions in society. Ultimate-value attitudes, religious ideas and the forms of human action constitute a complex of elements in a state of mutual interdependence, to put the relation in Paretian terms' (T. Parsons, *The Structure of Social Action*, Collier-Macmillan Ltd, London, 1966, pp. 425-6).

5. The Psychology of Religious Experience

We now propose to deal with the question of religion as it is experienced by the individual. The subject directly concerned in religious experience is the human person and perhaps this is the reason why it is particularly difficult to discern the characteristics of this experience. But a psychological study of religion must necessarily return to the place of its origin and development.

If a visitor from another world happened to arrive on our planet, devoid of religion himself but endowed with human powers of observation and understanding—the strange type of observer pictured by some modern scientists—he would necessarily consider the religious behaviour of the men of all times as something unreasonable, absurd and even cruel. People who bow low before inanimate objects as if before another man who can capriciously decide whether they are to live or die; people who spare a ferocious animal that attacks them and who treat other harmless and unimportant animals with extreme respect; people who in orgiastic rites abandon themselves to the most repugnant licentiousness; people who seek to be venerated as beings endowed with limitless powers and demand that absolute homage be paid to their images; people who consider themselves obliged to kill others who do not accept their beliefs; who build magnificent edifices at the cost of immense sacrifice to honour an invisible being; who assemble in silent expectation or with lamentations and chants; who go apart from the human community to live in isolation under the poorest conditions and declare that they have reached a state of beautitude; who profess full and active dedication to ideals of goodness and justice; who lazily but tenaciously perform acts of dependence upon something or someone who cannot be seen, merely because it is the custom to do so, and who, protected by respectability, perform actions completely in contrast with the ideals they profess to serve. All these things are to be found in this world of ours and the long list of eccentricities and absurdities would afford a most discouraging picture of human possibilities if a religious character were not attributed to them and if we did not face up to the problem of what men really mean when they speak of religion.

What on earth have all these attitudes in common to entitle them to share the same designation? We might even come to the conclusion that precisely the variety and incongruousness of what are called religious manifestations constitutes conclusive and certain proof that a single genuine religious sense does not exist. We might conclude that such aberrant manifestations must be placed on the same level as other human incongruities and failings. In this case, though, they assume a particularly dangerous quality of obligatoriness, as has already been said. But the assumption of such a dogmatically negative position would signify failure to recognize another possibility. Could it not be that a typically human need (since religious behaviour is not to be observed in animals) exists, a need which gives rise to very many different forms of expression? It is precisely this second alternative which we intend to examine here, stimulated by the fact that the generic and therefore inexact designation of 'religious' necessarily attributed to widely varying kinds of behaviour must also point to a particular quality which distinguishes them from other types of human behaviour.

It is obviously quite difficult, not to say impossible, to form an idea of religion if we confine ourselves to objects or actions described as religious. It would seem that there is no being or happening or action which, in particular circumstances, may not assume a religious aspect. We are not dealing, therefore, with objects or situations, but with a particular attitude of man towards them. We cannot look for religion in things external to man; we must look for it in man himself. Religion is a particular manner of being. It signifies taking up a position, assuming an attitude which is reflected in all sorts of things. It is therefore a particular subjective experience.[1]

To study religious experience by the psychological method and terminology is to fix particularly rigorous limits, for it means isolating it, separating it from the person who lives it and also, let us say so quite frankly, from the one who observes it and who ought at least to some extent to live or relive it. The psychologist moreover approaches religious experience with the scholar's mentality, but also in the attitude of a man accustomed to a certain way of thinking. His position is therefore a particularly difficult one. 'From time to time it must appear as if I am taking sides,' says Bartlett in writing on religious experience. 'When this happens, I would myself remember and I would have all others realize that though I speak as a psychologist, I am also a man as other men. There are the things that I love and the things that I hate. I have my hopes and my fears and my longings that I must cherish. These will sometimes shine through. When they do, let them be taken for whatever they may be worth.'[2] The writer of the present work intends to adopt the same attitude, and adds that he is convinced that the reader will read and criticize more freely when faced with a person who cannot and does not wish to conceal his own convictions, rather than somebody who, beneath a semblance of open-mindedness, nourishes a factiousness which is all the more dangerous since it is disguised.

It is not easy to define religious experience, precisely because there is nothing to go by in the way of easily classifiable

---

[1] R. H. Thouless, in the recent reprint of his book *The Psychology of Religion* (Cambridge University Press, 1961), asserts that today he would replace the term 'religious experience' with 'religious behaviour'. I myself prefer the former term 'religious experience' since it stresses the subjective aspect which tends to disappear in the term 'religious behaviour'. An excellent collection of studies on this subject is to be found in 'Il problema dell'esperienza religiosa' in *Atti del XV Convegno del Centro di Studi Filosofici*, Gallarate-Brescia, 1961.

[2] F. Bartlett, 'Religion as Experience, Belief, Action', *op. cit.*, p. 4.

perceptible objects. But this is a disadvantage common to all psychic activities. Cognitive activity deals with things, but also with persons, concepts, affective states and actions. I recognize a chair or a friend, but also a number, boredom and the need to act. In the systematic expression of knowing, in science, I recognize the reciprocal relations between things and also the way in which I can cancel their phenomenal appearance so as to reconstruct them in a different form or for another use. I am aware that from a waterfall I can obtain, as well as stagnant water, the transformation of its mechanical force into electric power. Widely varying things one by one become the object of scientific knowledge. But affective activities can also be applied to all sorts of different objects and with antithetic effects: I can be afraid of lightning, of a man, of a snake or a spider, just as I can also view them with admiration, interest or indifference. Here it is not the object that counts but the emotion. The same applies to doing and willing: I can do many things, but I only do some of them and if I am compelled to do them I can be said to do them by compulsion and not on my own initiative.

Psychic activity, therefore, is in its manifestations undoubtedly directed towards something, it reaches out to something (Brentano's 'intentionality'). But in a certain sense it is independent of this something which it masters and utilizes for its own purposes. It is precisely this quality of 'reference' that distinguishes psychic phenomena. Now, as regards religious experience, this 'reference' is said to be transitory both in the expression of what is experienced and in what is presumed to determine the experience itself. Hence we must either conclude that in religious experience we are outside the range of psychological research or else postulate a particular psychic activity to be added to the rest. But the problem cannot be resolved so rapidly. In religious experience all those psychic activities by which we are usually obliged to 'facet' psychic activity as a whole are present: information, emotion, conation (in man: knowing, feeling and willing). Religious experience is distinguished by its typical structure, by its mode of being. It is normal psychic activity in its fulness and organized in a typical way. In what way?

We shall be able to answer this question more readily after we have examined the matter more fully. If we really require a temporary platform as a reference point, I should prefer to define religion from the psychological point of view in Pratt's words: 'Religion is the serious and social attitude of individuals or communities towards the power or powers which they conceive as having ultimate control over their interests and destinies.'[8] A further point must be clarified. In speaking of religious experience I am referring not only to exceptional events which have marked a real turning-point in a person's life, but also and especially to a habitual manner of evaluating things, and this moreover I intend to treat within the confines of development and even institutionalized religion rather than by a comparative survey of its various forms.

Individual factors

I shall begin with factors which may appear remote although this is not really the case. Bodily constitution and organic functioning, however much determined by heredity, still bears an individual imprint which is expressed even in histological and biochemical characteristics. Since psychic activity is necessarily connected with biological processes, the religious sense is also bound up with these. In a particular way affective intensity and tonality, speed or slowness in action, perceptive readiness and imaginative and symbolic elaboration, types and fluctuations of mood—all these are facts which enter into religious experience in the psychological network which we call 'temperament', and are to be considered constitutional and therefore predominantly inherited, although the relation between genetics and temperamental factors has not yet been sufficiently explained. It is unquestionable, in any case, that

[8] J. B. Pratt, *Religious Consciousness*, quoted in L. W. Grensted, *The Psychology of Religion*, Oxford University Press, London, 1952, p. 14.

religious feeling is differently coloured according to the type of person concerned and according to his age and condition in life (childhood, adolescence, maturity, old age; state of health, euphoria, depression, fatigue). It should be noted, however, that here we reach the limit beyond which we are faced with the question: how far do temperamental factors exert an influence and how far does the repercussion of a given psychic state extend? This is a question which in fact crops up continually in psychology and psychopathology.

Corresponding to general or particular physiological conditions, that is, according as such conditions are experienced as a need of the entire organism or of a single organ, we have various needs and tendencies which when intellectually structured are known as desires. Security and protection against danger, hunger, the sexual drive, tolerance or intolerance of physical pain or discomfort, the need for air, movement, rest and so forth, are described as viscerogenous needs and tendencies. They necessarily affect religious experience also, either obstructing or facilitating it (ravenous hunger, acute pain, intense fatigue; or, on the other hand, moderate or bearable hunger, a state of general well-being or even of tolerable general discomfort, of lethargy or of mild excitement). Psychologists frequently refer to these as primary needs, a term which is acceptable only in the sense that these needs are easily identifiable and always present, but it is very questionable if it implies that these are man's only authentic and primitive needs and that other needs are occasioned by their modification or transformation. They are certainly much more apparent in the child, because intellectual activity cannot yet control them, but this is a precise characteristic of childhood and does not imply that new elements cannot appear at a later stage which are not a product of biological, viscerogenous needs. Certain endocrine glands which are active in the child become less active in the adult. Besides, the child's living conditions are so different from those of the adult that the interaction between his organism and the surrounding world must necessarily be different, even though there exists for both child and adult a dividing line between the possibility and the impossibility of survival. It should however be added that certain needs which are present and reflexively actualized in the child become explicit and articulate later on in the adult. When we speak of the need for protection or nutrition in child and adult we are speaking of a biological continuity between the two, but we cannot disregard the psychological difference between them.

Undoubtedly, the viscerogenous needs appear before others in the development of the individual. In the child they present themselves as the only needs. But mere precedence in the appearance of these needs is not a sufficient reason for considering them the only ones to the exclusion of others and for judging the needs which make their appearance later to be a transformation of the earlier ones. The foetus already has a mouth and lungs but these do not serve to provide the body with food and oxygen until after birth. Even though the same need (nutrition) is satisfied, the manner in which this takes place in the child is so different from the way it occurs in the foetus as to be rightly considered something 'new'. Similarly in the child's psychological development such an enrichment of capacity takes place that the appearance of new needs different from the preceding ones ought not to strike us as strange. It ought rather to be said that the viscerogenous needs continue to exist, even though apparently dominated by other needs, and that it would be a mistake not to take account of them. It is not surprising that words indicating viscerogenous needs also serve to describe religious experience.

Side by side with the biological, viscerogenous needs we have others which we call psychogenous, that is to say, which imply the satisfaction of an exigency no longer pertaining to one or several organs but to the individual as a whole, to his entire person. Already in relations between individuals or in social relations something is manifested which demands more than a biological response on the part of the other person. A child could be artificially reared in a biologically perfect way, but according to some quite recent studies this would produce serious psychological repercussions (children reared in orphanages or hospitalized). As well as the problem of biological survival man faces that of psychological survival. There is the problem of satisfying certain needs of his being which are not merely organic. It is not enough for him to 'explore', he also needs to 'know', to distinguish the true from the untrue, good from evil, what is beautiful from what is ugly.

These elementary needs appear rather mysterious when critically examined, yet they exist. If some psychologists make herculean efforts (though not very convincing ones) to reduce them to needs of another order, nobody can deny that these needs are impelling, sometimes more impelling that organogenous needs. On these needs are based values, those principles which guide us in our appreciation of objects, situations and men. It is a significant fact that 'values' seem to be imposed from outside and are ordinarily objectified: truth, justice, beauty, goodness. Moreover, not all psychogenous needs are morally or socially desirable; for example, the need to dominate, the thirst for prestige, the urge to rebel, eagerness to repair one's losses and many other qualities of this kind. But it is very significant that in these cases the needs are not objectified but are seen as requirements of the ego and are not called values. Self-defence not only where one's life is in danger but where diminution or 'devaluation' of one's ego is involved, concern for the integrity of one's person, is a keenly felt need, sometimes excessively so, and produces a readiness not merely to defend ourselves but also to attack. On the other hand it is this very desire to 'take possession' that constitutes one of the essential qualities of personality and broadens its range of vision and action. Obviously this leads to a conflict both in the individual himself and in his relations with others.

In a word, it is these psychogenous tendencies which give to human existence its dramatic quality and its greatness. Even a superficial observer will recognize that these tendencies are also present in religious feeling which gives them a particular tone. Certain positive and negative values are involved in the religious sense, as well as a deep feeling of personal commitment, even if this is felt to be imposed from outside. We must therefore examine these psychogenous needs more fully.

The religious sense has appeared to many scholars as an emotional fact and hence they have concluded that religion is irrational, that the moment it is associated with reason it either collapses or becomes sterile and has no further influence over the person concerned. Hence it has been declared that the religious sense, being unable to justify itself with valid reasons, is sustained by fictitious reasoning, by 'rationalization', that is, the effort to explain the inexplicable.

It should be remarked at once that it is very dangerous to handle this process of 'rationalization' too freely, for while the objector who makes use of it believes he has demolished his adversaries' defences, he does not realize that he can be accused of just as much rationalization in his own arguments. In the sphere of religion, moreover, this risk is always present, both for the one who denies and for the one who upholds the validity of religion. It is true that the religious sense has a deep emotional resonance, but this does not necessarily mean that it is unsupported by valid reasons and must be jealously guarded to prevent the loss of its fragile but precious sentimental component. Emotivity is not separate from or arbitrarily independent of the situation in which it is manifested. It can, it is true, be independent, but this is not normally the case. It usually has a precise reference to the situation itself and acts as the spring which impels us to face this situation, stimulating us to seek a consistent explanation of it and leading us to adapt our behaviour to circumstances. This aspect of emotion, which is generally overlooked, was strongly stressed by Max Scheler who spoke of the 'intentionality' and the 'semantic value' of the emotions.[4] It is also dealt with by Solomon Asch who sees in the emotions the equivalent or counterpart of a configured system.[5]

The distinction which we ordinarily make between informative and emotional activity is more concerned, for systematic

[4] M. Scheler, *Liebe und Erkenntnis*, Bern, 1955.
[5] S. Asch, *Social Psychology, op. cit.*

reasons, with differences between the two activities than with their intermingling. There is no such thing as an affective activity which is not cognitive, nor is there any cognitive activity, however abstract, which does not rest on emotivity. In speaking, then, of the religious sense as a feeling, other psychologists in the wake of Shand and MacDougall mean the propensity to respond in a certain way to some objects, either physical or mental.[6] The feeling is the spring which propels us towards the object. Seen in this light, that is, in so far as the religious sense is taken to be a particular attitude—but not a mere 'feeling' separated from all other psychic activity and devoid of definite reference to an end—we can agree that emotivity is one of the more conspicuous notes of religion from the psychological point of view.

Cognitive activity

The question then arises as to how cognitive activity and what type of cognitive activity is involved in the religious sense. Bartlett has distinguished three types of thought: logical thought, which proceeds by deduction according to clearly formulated principles; scientific or naturalistic thought, which though working on data that cannot be defined, fills up the gaps by observation and experiment; and intuitive thought which, when faced by a disconnected and incomplete network of facts, finds the link between them by a 'jump'.[7] Bartlett in fact visualizes thought as a filling-up of gaps. He considers that in intuitive thought we are getting very near the basic conditions of religious experience. Even if we accept this point of view we must not forget that these forms of thought rarely exist in their 'pure state' and that we cannot depreciate intuitive thought as 'fantastic' in complete favour of logical and scientific thought. Indeed an intuitive moment is the inevitable companion of the latter types of thought and is even decisive. The 'productive thought' of the Gestalt school is the emergence of

[6] W. McDougall, *The Energies of Men*, Methuen, London, 1950.
[7] F. Bartlett, *op. cit.*, p. 9.

a structure from incoherent and contradictory data, not by trial and error or by deduction or verification, but by structuration and restructuration of the whole field.

Scientific thought is also guided by intuition, by a series of hypotheses or possible connections which are subsequently studied and verified in a methodical way, and it culminates in discovery when the link between isolated facts becomes evident. Frequently the intuition of this link imposes itself with irresistible clearness even before a precise statement or definition is reached. Bartlett observes that when there is intuition the proof is always seen—if we may be permitted the expression—in a revolutionary manner and he quotes this remark of the historian H. Butterfield: 'It is easy to teach anybody a new fact about Richelieu, but it needs light from heaven to enable a teacher to break the old framework in which the student has been accustomed to seeing his Richelieu.' It is unnecessary to recall the reception accorded to many scientific discoveries, even among specialists on such questions. This 'novelty' in interpretation makes it very difficult even for one who has had experience of intuition, especially religious intuition, to communicate it in an appropriate manner. He endeavours to describe it but does not succeed in translating it into common language. He is like one who 'attempts to paint a poem or to describe a symphony'.[8]

Another point must also be made clear. Our cognitive activity is not confined to physically definable objects (things or persons) but pertains to our moods and psychic activities also. We know that we are cheerful, sad or bored, just as we know that we are doing something or that we are passively compelled to do it. This type of information is more primitive and constant than information acquired by thought. We remember much better the irritation we felt in listening to a lecture than the subject of the lecture; and we feel (sometimes with a distress from which we try to escape) that we have done or omitted to do something, that we have endured it rebelliously or welcomed it with pleasure. Remark how in this type of

[8] *Ibid.*, pp. 10 ff.

information the affective aspect is accentuated although the information remains incontestable. All this goes to show that in religious experience, even though there is question here of a special kind of information and of a special poetic structure, the cognitive moment is nevertheless inevitable.

There is certainly danger of error, the possibility of using fictitious explanations (rationalization) instead of valid ones; but is there any field in which we are absolutely certain, free from all possibility of controversy or insinuation of error? Moreover, is it such a rare thing, even in the most regular and normal behaviour, to fall into rationalization to some extent? Some people even consider this a sign of psychic normality. Habitually cold thinking, implacably detached and too rigidly logical, would already indicate a rupture with one's surroundings and isolation from them. On the contrary, when the affective stimulus is lacking, the experience is also greatly impoverished. J. Leuba, in a famous passage quoted by William James, says that when there are no particular reasons for immediate interest in God, neither is there any effort to ask oneself what is the divinity and what does it mean. This is a crude and one-sided statement, yet it possesses an element of truth. So, too, when a religious conception is reduced to a concatenation of abstract reasonings, it loses all power to persuade, just as mathematical reasoning can impress one as rigorous and elegant but can produce a thrill of admiration only in exceptional men.

In religious experience, therefore, there is cognitive effort. It should be noted that this develops not only in face of exceptional events but also when our existence as men is examined and recognized instead of being passively accepted. It is lawful to ask ourselves what is our place in the world, but in pursuit of this information we are faced with such a dense and mysterious network of facts that we are bewildered and incapable of seeing any connection between them. How have I come into the world and why in that particular time and place? What am I among so many things, animate and inanimate, and among so many persons near and far? What am I myself with my store of habits and memories, occupied with the present but also reaching forward to the future, with my temperament, my emotions and passions? What am I doing here and what will this whole scenario mean when my life is done? What is my role in the cosmos? Foolish talk, says the man who likes to describe himself as realistic and practical. The trouble is that he himself is inconsistent with events and with himself, and when the clash comes he will be compelled to realize (although he will never admit it) that his 'realism' was mere illusion.

It will also be asked if we who live in this twentieth century should trouble to pose such problems, we who have a mania for speculating about useless things, while we live in houses where light, a suitable temperature, possibilities for communication and nutrition are all available, we who defend ourselves against sickness, who can move from one continent to another in a few hours and are convinced that we can harness nature in our service. The primitive man is said to be less sophisticated; he takes things as they come and is perhaps more fully satisfied.

It is not easy to find one's bearings among all these opinions which we hear expressed by people of all classes. It may be that being 'problematic', as it is the fashion to say, is a characteristic of modern man and that he often resolves his problems in a very miserable way, mainly by sticking in the mire of these problems and in a bored manner seeking futile satisfactions. But the question is, why does civilized man who enjoys all the advantages of civilization fail to flee from this sense of emptiness? His faculty of reason which has served him in mastering what he calls 'nature' and which places before him brief and isolated concatenations of events does not enable him to find an explanation of inconsistencies and absurdities in great number. On the contrary, it unfolds before his gaze, in consequence of his discoveries, a much more mysterious universe than that which the ancients had to deal with, and it leaves him without an answer to what concerns him most closely, namely, his own nature and destiny. When we consider too that the satisfaction of biological needs can be attained by some classes in civilized countries with comparative ease or even with an artificial exasperation and gratification of these needs (conveniences and 'amusements'), we realize that the relation between man and nature can be changed, but that it continues to subsist—even if it appears to be less exacting—and that it continues to present the same questions.

Undoubtedly in the so-called 'backward' civilizations men's relations with the 'mysterious universe' (Jeans) are more evident: birth and death, the rotation of the seasons, the harshness of living conditions, cataclysms and epidemics appear to primitive peoples as the expression of forces superior to their own and are given a consistency in myth and religion. How is it that the man of Western civilization, to whom technical progress would appear to have opened up unlimited possibilities and who is therefore inclined to judge religion as a very beautiful but evanescent fable—how is it that he himself is constructing other myths no less inconsistent and exacting? Why is he overcome by *taedium vitae*, or why does he come up against it again after a succession of gratifications which have turned out to be fleeting and fallacious?

We are led to believe that man's situation in the world as he sees it (through his cognitive activity) gives him an awareness of his impotence but also of his unsatisfied needs as he faces the Unknown. It is here that cognitive activity enters within the range of religion. Man could not be religious (or irreligious) if he did not possess the capacity to investigate and to know a capacity with which no other living creature is endowed.[9]

[9] L. Festinger began to elaborate his theory of 'cognitive dissonance' on the basis of a socio-psychological survey of a religious sect which prophesied the destruction of the world at a definite time not far off, and from his study of the reactions to the non-fulfilment of the prophecy. 'Two opinions or beliefs or items of knowledge are *dissonent* with each other,' he says, 'if they do not fit together—that is, if they are inconsistent, or if, considering only the particular two items, one does not follow from the other. . . . Dissonance produces discomfort and, correspondingly, there will arise pressures to reduce or eliminate the dissonance. Such attempts may take any or all of three forms. The person may try to change one or more of the beliefs, opinions or

Affect

Thus we come to study the repercussion, or rather the affective and emotive counterpart, in man of his awareness of the existence of forces shrouded in mystery which are decisive for him. The basic repercussion is a sense of bewilderment and fear as in any uncertain situation which may involve a threat to man's life. The ancients spoke of fear where modern man speaks of anxiety. I shall use the latter term for the moment, making it clear that by anxiety I mean the feeling of insecurity which grips us when we have no control over the development of a situation and cannot foresee how it will end, although we realize that it contains a threat to our existence. Since anxiety is connected with a cognitive process and more particularly with the process of thought, it is a specifically human characteristic, distressing on the one hand but stimulating on the other. 'A human existence devoid of anxiety, a sense of guilt and suffering, would lose its essential characteristics.'[10]

It should be added at once that these feelings proper to man can also signify intolerable constraint which restricts and impoverishes his life instead of deepening and broadening it. These are the sad pathological situations in which man alone among living creatures can find himself. But we should be

behaviours involved in the dissonance; to acquire new information or beliefs that will increase the existing consonance and thus cause the total dissonance to be reduced; or to forget or reduce the importance of those cognitions that are in a dissonant relationship.' Moreover, the increased cohesion and proselytism in the group express the need to reduce the dissonance by social support.

Festinger's method in this investigation (L. Festinger, H. van Riecken, S. Schachter, *When Prophecy Fails*, Harper and Row, New York, 1964, pp. 25-6) and also the extension of the concept of dissonance (L. Festinger, *A Theory of Cognitive Dissonance*, 1957, reprinted Stanford, 1962) have not escaped criticism. For our purpose it is important to note how Festinger stresses the motivational function of the cognitive aspect of religion.

For a fuller treatment of the question of religious sects, I suggest the well-known work of R. A. Knox, *Enthusiasm*, Oxford, 1950.

[10] G. Benedetti, 'Die Angst in psychiatrischer Sicht' in *Die Angst*, Zurich, 1959, p. 147.

shutting our eyes to human reality if we were to exclude anxiety, responsibility and suffering as abnormal. They can become abnormal, just as man's whole being is exposed to the most distressing alterations. By anxiety we do not merely mean trepidation in face of a possible danger (as when we are close to a beloved person who is seriously ill or when we face an event which can damage our own life), but also a state of insecurity which weighs upon us although we do not understand the reason of it. It is this second type of insecurity which leads to pathological forms of anxiety, with various characteristics and varying degrees of intensity. When this distress has reference, not to inanimate things or events, but to possible dangers in human society and the relations between ourselves and others, the anxiety assumes particular qualities, since it is directed towards what others intend to do rather than to what they are actually doing; there is question of clarifying by some interpretation or other what these others mean to us. It has been suggested that this type of anxiety should be called 'fear', but the term is perhaps too vague. There is also a more typically endogenous anxiety which refers to perplexity about decisions to be made or the distress occasioned by certain moods.

As has already been mentioned, these various forms of anxiety accompany the awareness of the precariousness of our existence, impelling us to seek security or an explanation. It is important to emphasize the manner in which the apprehension of danger stimulates our efforts to identify the danger itself more clearly (that is, to understand it), and to avoid it or defend ourselves against it. Flight (withdrawal, putting a distance between ourselves and the danger) is one of the most primitive reactions and lies at the bottom of many defensive tactics. But it is also possible for us to face the danger, to overcome it or turn it aside. Obviously we do not always succeed in this, but what is to be emphasized is the fact that anxiety can be at the root of efforts to withdraw and efforts to approach the danger.

All this can take place without any trace of the religious sense, but it necessarily enters into religious experience.

Precariousness and irrationality (by which I mean the inexplicability and contradiction of our conditions of existence) is manifested by a sense of anxiety which can be connected with clearly defined physical events (impressive natural phenomena, eclipses, earthquakes, famine) and with psychological states (sense of bewilderment, fear of all sorts of happenings, dread of death and nothingness). Our relations with others are also permeated with this uncertainty and insecurity in regard to even the closest and noblest affective bonds. But it is from this basis of our aspiration to certainty, from the impossibility of attaining it absolutely, and from disappointment and frustration of our hopes and efforts, that the recognition of our dependence on forces superior to our own emerges and is gradually established. Here we have one of the roots of religion.

The saying 'timor fecit deos' has come down to us from ancient times and we have heard modern prophets proclaim our liberation from the yoke of this fear (Feuerbach, Marx, Freud, Nietzsche, several existentialist schools). They assure us that religion is a spectre which intimidates men and makes them slaves, but vanishes as soon as reason is set free and realizes its own strength. Our destiny is not ruled by occult powers beyond our reach but by that which we ourselves as men can build. For the moment we can dispense ourselves from examining this enthusiastic substitution of reason for mystery which makes very little difference to the religious problem, since reason itself is terribly mysterious. We may remark, though, that where anxiety takes on a religious tonality some new and distinctive elements are added. As Rudolf Otto has pointed out, that which we experience religiously, the 'sacred', arouses in us opposing, ambivalent attitudes. On the one hand there is anxiety, the fear of the great Unknown (numinosum), on the other hand an irresistible attraction towards it (fascinosum).[11]

Hence, as well as a fear of mystery there is an impulse towards it. Besides, in the more typical forms of religious experience (perhaps the less frequent) there is an inevitable

[11] R. Otto, The Idea of the Holy, op. cit.

sense of a presence, considered by the person who experiences it to be stronger than our habitual sense of the reality in which we live. To a lesser degree and at times unnoticed, this sense is present in the simplest and most ordinary manifestations of religion. This brings us to another characteristic of religious experience, namely, the reciprocity of relations between the person and the 'sacred', the necessity of assuming an attitude towards it, the need for reciprocal communication. This also leads to the note of personification of the 'sacred' which is particularly accentuated in some religions but is never completely absent from any religion.

'No religious experience,' writes a modern historian of religions, Gerardus van der Leeuw, 'is a pure tendency. Man is not the only actor in the situation, but in one way or another God is acting too. A divine activity likewise sustains all religious phenomena, from the most primitive forms of religion up to Christianity, as well as all those religious movements which hide behind masks in our secularized civilization.'[12] Although it lies outside the field of a psychological approach to define the nature of the object towards which the religious sense tends and which sustains it, this judgment of van der Leeuw can be accepted by the psychologist, who is not expressing an opinion on the 'reality' of the world around him when he asserts that the paths by which the subject reaches a 'construction of the real', that is, 'sound experience' of a reality, are still dark and difficult. If by the word 'transcendent' we mean what is beyond reality, separate from it and not reached by way of the senses, then we can also accept the statement of another historian of religions, E. Benz, when he says: 'the religious sense is the response to the irruption of the transcendent'.[13] Hence, while religious anxiety can be compared only in a formal way to pathological anxiety, since no verifiable reference to an object appears in it, it differs substantially from pathological anxiety by reason of the sense of satisfaction which it finds

[12] G. van der Leeuw, *Phänomenologie der Religion*, Mohr, Tübingen, 2nd edition, 1956.
[13] E. Benz, 'Die Angst in der Religion' in *Die Angst, op. cit.*, p. 192.

in action (a fact already noted by James), and by reason of the interpretative consistency and formidable impulse towards activity, both contemplative and practical, which are found in it. The adjective 'formidable' is intended here in the fullest and strictest etymological sense, since religious feeling has driven man far beyond the possibilities of any other living creature—and unfortunately not always in the right direction. In many of the most sinister events in the history of individual men and of mankind as a whole, an element of religious feeling has not been wanting.

With reference to the anxiety connected with religious experience, we must make it quite clear that from the psychological point of view there is a gradation of intensity in relation to different individual constitutions, to developmental planes of psychic activity and to stages of personal self-organization, ranging from a religious expertise to religious insensibility. Similarly there are infinite varieties of emphasis in religious activity and of participation in it. Just as it would be wrong to deny the existence of music because some people listen to it and others do not and because some listen to one type of music and no other, so too we certainly cannot argue that man has no religious sense because there are many varieties of religious experience.

A brief excursus on anxiety as presented in psychological terms by Freud may perhaps be useful at this point. Cargnello has summed it up succinctly but very clearly.[14] Anxiety occupies a central place in Freud's doctrine, but it is difficult, not to say impossible, to gather from his writings a definition that reconciles his various ideas on anxiety. It will serve our purpose better to trace the development of these. One of Freud's first ideas was that anxiety was somatogenic: neurotic anxiety appears with extraordinary frequency in sexually frustrated persons: it is repressed libido. A second idea of his was that anxiety is an extremely distressing affective state which

[14] D. Cargnello, *Dal naturalismo psicoanalitico alla fenomenologia antropologica della Daseinsanalyse*, Ist. di Studi Filosofici, Rome, 1961.

tends to convert itself into pathological phenomena, both organic and psychic. It is no longer, then, merely an effect but also a cause of somatic disturbance. Freud's third idea (which can be dated from about 1920, when he wrote *Beyond the Principle of Pleasure*) presents anxiety as a form of reintegration of the psychic apparatus in so far as it enables psychic energy, which is in danger of remaining blocked in the trauma, to be discharged through collateral channels (troubled dreams). To restore his psychic integrity the individual must relive the anxiety of the traumatic situations he has experienced. A fourth idea of Freud's, found in his work *Inhibition, Symptom, Anguish*, was that anxiety is no longer to be seen as situated in an endopsychic conflict between two unconscious urges but in a relationship between different subjects at the time of early childhood, one of these subjects being the child, the others his father and mother.

According to Cargnello, Freud gradually abandoned an energetic conception in favour of the concept of interpersonal relations: Freud the theorist drew near to the Freud of psycho-analytical practice, which is fundamentally an interpersonal relationship. 'Anxiety has a "dialogic" nature and rises up as the result of an obstructed relationship of coexistence.' This inconsistency between the theoretical Freud and Freud the therapist, and the necessity of having an anthropological (I would venture to say personal) instead of a bioenergetic conception of psychic life, have been highlighted by Ludwig Binswanger. Moreover, J. Suttie, in a critical and original study which was little noticed at first but has now come to be appreciated, treats as fundamental the need for protection and tenderness in the interpersonal relationship between mother and child, in opposition to Freud.[15] On the other hand, we have seen how Freud himself, from a position rigidly confined to the individual—man wrestling with society and with his own conflicting tendencies—moved towards an interpersonal concept of psychic life. This approach is stressed in Binswanger, Suttie

[15] I. D. Suttie, *The Origins of Love and Hate*, Penguin Books, London, 1960.

and Horney and is carried to its extreme consequences by Sullivan, for whom the person disappears in the interpersonal relationship. This concept of anxiety is closely related to religious experience which stands out as an encounter, communication, protection and submission involving man and another Being. Religious anxiety is the whip which forces a man to go beyond the raw data of life and urges him to seek something hidden beyond. It becomes extremely painful and unsparing to man when his search is blocked, broken or frustrated.

Action

Religion understood as a response to the need to understand and to the anxiety which accompanies that need, does not stop short at passive receptivity but demands action. If action does not take place the religious sense is impoverished and very serious general repercussions are the result, ranging from apathy to cynicism and to unresponsive and spasmodic anxiety. For this reason religion involves not only a certain interpretation of events and a characteristic sensitivity, but an entire manner of life. No action escapes its influence. We can call to mind many lives especially of humble and little-known persons who arouse our admiration (and even our envy), people to whom a simple and profound religious sense has given a calm and harmonious balance, even in face of the most disconcerting trials, in silent but consistent and resolute activity. But this fortunate possibility is not the only one. It is an almost incredible fact that there is no action, no matter how insignificant or even unworthy or wicked, which has not in one circumstance or another been considered to be religious, that is, dictated by the conviction that a higher than human power demanded it. Likewise individual and social fanaticisms are fed and stimulated by an ideology with a religious background, while conversely apathy or *taedium vitae* is associated with a dearth and inertia of the religious sense.

The religious sense is personal in its origin and development and this also applies to its practical activity. In this it is not differentiated from other psychological activities which, although seemingly dissociated from a practical reference, are really saturated with it. The imagination itself depends for its content on relations already established with one's environment and signifies relationship to the environment even when this is unrealizable. Religious action can be judged in widely varying ways but it invariably expresses a manner of being and communication with something which is different from the subject and which imposes itself upon him. It can be manifested in an attempt to escape, to defend oneself either in solitude or within the community. It can, on the other hand, take the initiative in an endeavour to know the mysterious powers with which it is faced or to propitiate them even in quite absurd and incongruous ways which are believed to be effective: incantations, magic, conformism and cultic practices. From this point of view technical knowledge, by which man has triumphantly mastered unknown forces, can assume religious characteristics. We may even wonder whether man could ever have achieved so much without a constant and blind faith in technical knowledge. But the fact remains that, however wonderful the technical invasion may appear to us, it has reached only a small sphere of the mysterious universe and has left untouched and perhaps more acute than ever some insuppressible human needs. These needs too are obliged to adapt (and it remains a mystery how far this adaption can endure) to the increasingly urgent demands of technical progress.

The need which religion has to express itself in action gives rise to two further problems: the search for a human social environment in which it can operate and expand; and its relation to evaluative standards of action, that is to say, the social and ethical relations of religious experience.

Sociality

The dimension of psychic activity which consists in relationship with other human beings is also present in religion. There is much discussion as to what is inborn and independent in the individual and what is due to his relations with other men. We cannot describe this by a clear-cut definition, for while psychic activitives are inherent in the individual, their actualization, their development and the pattern they assume depend to a certain extent on the social environment in which they operate. One of the strongest impulses of religious activity in the individual is manifested towards others who share in this activity. Moreover, the religious sense in the individual is also due to his association with other religious individuals. There is therefore a communication, a tendency to grouping, in which the religious sense finds stimulus, expression, approval and continuity.

Religious grouping calls for certain measures such as the establishment of rules, institutions and methods of action. Besides, the very creation of the bonds between individuals makes it possible to distinguish one group from another and involves duties of membership and fidelity on the part of the individual. At the same time the need arises to extend the group and to proselytize, which produces conflict with other groups but also makes for greater cohesion in the group itself. The bigger the group becomes the more exacting does respect for institutional observances become, while individual participation becomes less profound. If a social form of religion, dynamic and operative, is to stimulate the religious sense of the individual, it must be continually on the alert to prevent its expressive forms from losing their significance. Greater religious vitality is to be found in smaller groups, although membership of very widespread and powerful groups confers a particular prestige on the individual. All this applies to individuals in their reciprocal relations. But the religious sense also entails a relationship of these individuals with the Unknown.

The point raised by MacMurray is very important, namely, that a large proportion of the terms employed to describe religion bear the stamp of social origin and are in fact the very words we use to describe interpersonal relations: company, communion, enmity, withdrawal, guilt, pardon, reconciliation, admiration, respect, fear, trust and love.

All the varied forms in which religion has expressed itself are to be found directly in the forms of such simple and commonplace human relations; and most of the paradoxes which have puzzled the minds of theologians and philosophers, and which have seemed to many people to show that religion is a fantastic tissue of irrational conceptions, are merely the description of facts which are so common and universal in our daily experience that we hardly notice them. Religion, in fact, is simply the universalization in reflection of this central factor in human experience.[16]

Martin Buber has offered a profound explanation of the I-Thou relationship in religion as opposed to the I-It relationship. The former is encounter between two persons as distinct from encounter between a person and a thing.[17] Anton Boisen uses a very simple and meaningful expression in describing his own experience of the anguish of solitude when he had just recovered from an attack of schizophrenia. 'What is needed,' he writes, 'is forgiveness and restoration to the fellowship of that social something which we call God.'[18]

Morality

The qualities of pervasiveness and commitment which characterize religion bring it very close to moral obligatoriness. 'The human being, sick or well,' E. de Greeff has written, 'is aware of but one fundamental problem—the problem of good and evil.'[19] I would add, to be more exact: the propensity to

[16] J. MacMurray, *The Structure of Religious Experience*, Faber and Faber, London, 1936, p. 37.
[17] M. Buber, *The Eclipse of God*, Harper, New York, 1957. Also available in a new Harper paperback edition, 1967.
[18] A. Boisen, *The Exploration of the Inner World*, 1936, quoted in O. Hobart Mowrer, *The Crisis in Psychiatry and Religion*, Van Nostrand, Princeton, N.J., 1961, p. 25.
[19] Et. de Greeff, 'Péché et maladie' in *L'homme et le péché*, Plon, Paris, 1938, p. 37.

G

what appears to him to be good and aversion from what appears to him to be evil. This is where moral obligation lies, in deciding —when a choice is possible—in favour of what is considered good. In this sense moral obligation is the opposite of the forcible obligation by which I am compelled to do something even if I do not recognize it as good and even see it to be evil. It is curious that while we Italians have only one verb for the two forms of obligation, the verb *devo*, the Germans have two: *ich soll, ich muss*, as also the English *I ought* and *I must*.

But we Italians, while stressing the common character of actions determined in a single sense, also recognize the difference between the situation in which we are constrained to act and that in which we are not; we recognize occasions on which we submit and others where we act freely. There is a difference in structure, in *Gestalt*, between the two situations even though the ultimate act may be the same. There is a qualitative difference which permits the coexistence of the two situations, even though the final act is identical in each case. I can be constrained without approving what I do. Conversely, I can approve and be free from constraint. The consequence of the transgression differs also: in the case of external compulsion there is a penalty, also external, while in the case of the moral obligation there is interior disapproval. While I can submit to the penalty without interior disapproval of my action, I can disapprove of what I have done although I do not suffer a penalty. While I realize that the external penalty proceeds from another, in the case of interior disapproval it is my own ego which accuses itself.

This leads us to believe that the experience of moral compulsion, although accompanied by cognitive, affective and conative factors, has a particular manner of being in psychic activity, not so much on account of characteristic 'contents' as for the particular character they assume. That morality is inevitable in the general economy of psychic activity is moreover apparent from the general 'tone', from the sense of self-control, which its observance confers and from the innumerable and subtle deceptions by which men try to justify its transgression, even representing this as a moral requirement. This typically distinctive and constantly operative activity is a characteristic and ineffaceable feature of human life.

Psychological interpretations of morality, religion and the social sense

In the second chapter of this book reference was made to Freud's theory that 'religion, morality and the social sense— the noblest elements in human nature—were originally one and the same thing'. We saw that Freud considered the affective bond, the libido, to have been differentiated in the course of phylogenesis into religion and morality by the Oedipus complex, and into social feeling by interpersonal relationships in the family. It will be well for us to follow up these developments separately.

'Identification is known to psychoanalysis,' writes Freud,

as the earliest expression of an emotional tie with another person. It plays a part in the early history of the Oedipus complex. A little boy will exhibit a special interest in his father; he would like to grow like him and be like him, and take his place everywhere. . . . At the same time as this identification with his father, or a little later, the boy has begun to develop a true object-cathexis towards his mother according to the attachment (anaclitic) type. He then exhibits, therefore, two psychologically distinct ties: a straightforward sexual object-cathexis towards his mother and an identification with his father which takes him as his model. The two subsist side by side for a time without any mutual influence or interference. In consequence of the irresistible advance towards a unification of mental life, they come together at last; and the normal Oedipus complex originates from their confluence. The little boy notices that his father stands in his way with his mother. His identification with his father then takes on a hostile colouring and becomes identical with the wish to replace his father in regard to his mother as well. Identification, in fact, is ambivalent from the very first;

it can turn into an expression of tenderness as easily as into a wish for someone's removal.[20]

The superego is the result of the dissolution of the Oedipus complex; it is the heir to this complex. As substitute for the desire for the father it contains the seed from which religions have sprung. When the child grows bigger, the father-role is taken over by his teachers. Their injunctions and prohibitions remain in the superego and in the form of conscience they continue to exercise moral censorship.

The social sense also originates in social relations within the family. The social group reproduces the pattern of the primitive family horde: the father is the leader feared by all; the sons kill him in order to take his place and they identify themselves with him, taking on his superego which becomes the superego of each member of the family. This primordial event is repeated in every family, where the father is obeyed but also feared. The superego is not exhausted in the exhortation: 'You must be like your father', but also includes the prohibition: 'You cannot be like your father', that is to say, you cannot do all that he did. Even in family relationships the bond is created by the libido. This plan is reproduced in the various forms of religious grouping: a father or a leader imposes the same superego, the same ideal, which must be followed inexorably by all members of the group. Here we have duty, religious sense and social sense. Since the process of identification is a childish process, according to Freud, its appearance in the adult is to be understood as an infantile residue or a regression, and hence religion is considered to be a universal obsessional neurosis.

It is really difficult to express a critical judgment in regard to this reconstruction. Perhaps what strikes us most by its tragic and dramatic quality, namely, the setting up of an individual and ancestral Oedipus-scheme of psychic life, is the most uncertain and questionable aspect of the theory. But on the other hand we find here some partial intuitions of enormous

[20] S. Freud, *Group Psychology and the Analysis of the Ego*, in Standard Ed., vol. XVIII, p. 105.

importance: affective organization in early childhood and within the family; the inevitability of cohesion and leadership in a group; the moulding of moral, religious and social needs in the family; the ambivalence of relations between individuals (love and fear). What leaves us perplexed is the exclusiveness of the genetical interpretation, which is most questionable and in complete contrast with the *prima facie* presentation of the situation. Are the religious sense and the social sense therefore the result of an instinctual failure, of a withdrawal of energies which originally ran in a different or even an opposite direction? Is the superego or ideal ego merely 'the total of the prohibitions to which the ego must adapt' and against which it endeavours to rebel? Or may not morality, religion and sociality be the actualization of positive potentialities which have a process of development and are closely associated among themselves and with other psychic activities? The psychoanalytical explanation, in order to reduce everything to the *primum movens* of the libido, is obliged to treat as a 'secondary process' that which also possesses a distinct primary meaning of its own, by recourse to transformistic meta-morphoses. We are given to understand that a negative condition, repression, is really the only artificer of the 'noblest part of human nature'.

It is undoubtedly true that in every man's life there is an attempt at self-assertion and independence and an effort to overcome obstacles. In the history of mankind the rebellion of man against man is a general and recurring fact. The idea of a 'primordial rebellion' is found in psychoanalysis just as it is found in many religions, particularly Christianity. But the problem with which we are dealing here is a different one, namely: Is filial respect born of rebellion, is the religious sense the result of parricide and the social sense the outcome of rivalry? Or is there in these negations an emergence, a deeper and more personal experience, of something that was formerly only vaguely guessed at, something that was shattered and is lacking, a love, a condition of dependence, a reciprocal attach-ment? Personally I believe that these positive qualities are real and primordial, just as sexual attraction and aggression are real and primordial, and that conflict is inevitable, precisely because they coexist and cannot be derived one from the other. Perhaps this is the meaning of Freud's contrapositioning of Eros and Thanatos.

Learning-theory offers us another interpretation. The repetition of socially acceptable acts corresponding to expectations and therefore gratified by approval and success is reinforced and definitively established. It may be so. Actually, the fact that an act followed by success is reinforced is a datum of experience rather than a conclusion of research. The question here is whether the range of learning is unlimited or circumscribed by the possibilities of the learner. In the case of animals a type of learning (by imprinting) without any reward or reinforcement and therefore due merely to an innate tendency has already been demonstrated. We have the example of a raven reared in captivity showing patterns of behaviour towards a man which ravens reared in normal conditions only manifest towards others of their own species. But in the case of man it has been clearly and authoritatively shown that the principles of satisfaction and reinforcement, while adequate in the case of learning at an elementary level (sensorimotor learning), constitute at most an incentive of altogether secondary importance, whereas the interests which comprise the structure of the individual ego have a decided predominance.[21]

Remarks

Morality and the religious sense are considered both by psychoanalysts and by learning psychologists to be the result of a process of interiorization, of 'introjection' as psychoanalysts call it, or 'internalization' of social norms, as the learning psychologists have it. This crucial point is not at all clear. Psychoanalysis speaks of identification with the parental superego, while learning theory speaks of the passively

[21] G. W. Allport, *The Nature of Personality*, Addison-Wesley, Cambridge, Mass., 1950, p. 170.

experienced imprint of a pattern of conduct, without any light being thrown on the fact that there is a necessary consistency between what the subject *is* and what he *makes his own*. No organism can assimilate or make its own that which does not correspond to the needs and limits of its own structure. In the psychological sphere, a difficult discourse cannot be assimilated by one who is mentally deficient even if he learns the words in which it is formulated; a feeling cannot be imposed or provided even if the subject is capable of learning the signs which express it. Hence moral and religious obligation is not 'created' by constraint, repetition or success. These are conditions which can accompany it, facilitating or obstructing its development, but they can accomplish nothing at all unless the subject has a genuine capacity to experience it. The appearance of the relationship between good and evil, right and wrong, must and must not, constitutes the question to which doctrines of mechanical psychology are unable to furnish any answer. An assertion made by the psychoanalyst J. C. Flugel in regard to 'sublimation'—the unconscious process which transforms the instinctive impulses—seems to me to be full of meaning. 'We can establish the conditions for sublimation,' he says, 'but we cannot bring it about.'[22]

Social, interhuman relations undoubtedly exert a strong influence in the sphere of moral obligation. But to consider them decisive because the same actions (considered separately) in one cultural environment are judged to be good and in another to be bad, and to conclude that moral obligation can be reduced to the assumption and execution of social norms through the play of 'expectations' and 'sanctions', would be to overlook the central question: how, namely, there can be awareness of an obligation, whatever its concrete form, unless there exist, at least for the adult man, the capacity and the primordial need to feel himself obliged and not passively constrained, in a word, the sense of responsibility. Social habits and conventions only become norms when a moral obligation

[22] J. C. Flugel, 'Sublimation: its notions and conditions' in *British Journal of Ed. Psychology*, 1942.

is involved. To 'keep oneself clean' is a very different thing when done of one's own accord or when imposed by others. It can in the latter case become a habit but it still remains mere drilling. Only when it becomes a possibility which is preferred to others on a basis of what is judged to be good even in a mistaken or superficial way does it become an object of moral obligation.

With reference to 'reductive' theories of moral obligation it may be remarked that those who hold them, in their anxiety to explain its development, confuse its successive phases with their conclusion; they try to derive the greater from the lesser, to derive something possessing a certain characteristic from something possessing a completely different one. Here we see the congenital inadequacy of evolutionist theories, also called transformist theories (and in a certain sense rightly so). Are we to exclude completely the possibility that psychic (endogenous) development and the conditions for this development (exogenous conditions, particularly social relations) prepare the tools or instruments which will be utilized quite differently according as they are employed in abstract thought or in autonomous activity? Does this not seem to be an extraordinary novelty in the development of organisms, in which we observe that organs are fashioned prior to their use, or have a transitory function before assuming their final one? L. Carmichael has formulated a 'law of anticipatory function', which may be 'demonstrated experimentally in many action systems of the growing organism well before the time when the function in question is normally called upon to play an active and significant part in the vital economy of the organism'.[23] A. Dalla Volta proposes a 'law of preparation and anticipation' with reference not only to individual organs but to 'fundamentally important psychic activities which require an adequate period of preparation and anticipation in order that they may respond to the demands of social adjust-

[23] L. Carmichael, 'Ontogenetic Development' in Stevens, *Handbook of Experimental Psychology*, Wiley, London and New York, 1951, p. 292.

ment'.[24] Hence I believe that moral obligation and the religious sense are two genuinely primitive ways of psychological being, even if they make use of preconstituted materials and only fully appear when conditions of development are favourable to their actualization.

Nevertheless I consider that a distinction ought to be made between the moral and the religious sense. The moral sense implies the possibility of assent or refusal in face of various courses of action, even when there is nothing inherent in the object itself to determine the answer given, but simply because a situation demands that answer. On the other hand, the religious sense, while maintaining this character of option, is concerned with something mysterious, something higher, something transcending (in the etymological sense) the objective conditions of human life. Hence the character of particular commitment which the religious attitude assumes and which pervades the subject's entire psychic activity, especially his moral activity, which depends on 'principles of behaviour' that 'qualify' the raw data of experience. While there is a close reciprocal relationship, then, between morality and the religious sense, they do not necessarily coincide.[25]

An immoral action can take on the garb of religion. We may recall moral aberrations connected with certain cults and the sophistries of the Pharisees which Christ so ruthlessly unmasked. A moral action, on the other hand, can be performed

---

[24] A. Dalla Volta, *La legge della preparazione e della attesa nello sviluppo sociale dell'uomo*, Accademia Medica, Turin, 1961.

[25] In his book *Morality and Beyond* (Routledge and Kegan Paul, London, 1963), Paul Tillich maintains that 'the relation of religion and morality is not an external one, but that the religious dimension, source and motivation are implicit in all morality, acknowledged or not. Morality does not depend on any concrete religion; it is religious in its very essence. The unconditional character of the moral imperative, love *agape* and not *eros* or sexual love, as the ultimate source of the moral commands, and grace as the power of moral motivation are the concepts through which the question of the relation of religion and morality is fundamentally answered' (p. 64). For Tillich the fundamental concept of religion is 'the state of being grasped by an ultimate concern, by an infinite interest, by something one takes unconditionally seriously' (p. 30).

without reference to religion, from habit, because of a certain philosophy of life and even as a protest against religious practices which have lost their moral sense or encourage an immoral one. There are indeed people who hold that only morality is truly our affair and that religion is just a lifebelt to hold on to in time of trouble and a convenient cloak for the selfishness of believers. From this they conclude that religion does more harm than good to man because it lessens his sense of personal responsibility. This judgment contains a certain amount of truth, but it fails to recognize that morality is defined as such precisely because it respects an Absolute, that it is not regulated purely and simply by personal satisfaction and social expediency. Obviously, then, morality and religion must derive their criterion from something more than mere subjective experience; actually there is a relation of mutual consistency and complementariness between them. From the psychological standpoint we can only verify an attitude of dependence towards objectified ideals or norms, but we have no standard by which to decide what they are. We can ascertain the presence of morality and religion, but we have no way of establishing if these are true, right and good. They might be said to be 'signposts' which cannot be ignored, but we have no means of knowing whether they point to a right goal or to a wrong one.

My treatment of religious experience from the psychological point of view is likely to be found unsatisfactory, especially by those endowed with keen religious sensitivity. It may well be felt that a vital human experience has been deprived of its dignity by submitting it to a technical examination. It may also appear that while its marginal characteristics have been pointed out insistently and its inevitability and power debated, no answer or rather a discouraging answer has been forthcoming when it was stated that religious experience as a human fact points to an attitude or a manner of behaviour but has no means of justifying this behaviour. These observations are appropriate, but they reveal a fact of great importance. They show us that psychology which must study religious experience just as it studies any other human activity is completely at a loss when it deals with the characteristics and psychological dynamics of religious experience. It gropes its way along a dark and difficult path where there are possibilities of progress but also possibilities of being delayed or of going astray. Psychology may be able to explain the mechanism of religious experience but it fails to tell us *what it is*.

This situation is a painful one for the psychologist himself who has got thus far and feels he cannot stop here, but at the same time is unable to go forward. This explains why psychologists who have advanced cautiously and in continual danger of error up to this point now launch forth defiantly into assertions and denials which are all the more categorical the less consistent they are. The philosopher Etienne Gilson has remarked that when scientists begin to scrutinize the depths of their special field of study they seem to pose metaphysical questions without expecting answers of a metaphysical nature. The psychiatrist Gregory Zillboorg, referring to this observation of Gilson, writes:

> This solution of the scientists in untenable because when we penetrate into the field of ontology we cannot repudiate metaphysics. This is a symptomatic fact—they reach the boundaries of science without recognizing that they are facing Mystery. At that stage scientists manifest a devotion and a faith which go further than science, or else an intellectual contempt which rejects every solution of the problem they have created for themselves. In other words, they are afraid of metaphysical answers and their science becomes a neurosis of defence.[26]

This drastic clinical diagnosis applies particularly to the psychologist who studies religious experience. Actually it is bitter but necessary for him to admit that his raids into areas beyond the psychological field reveal his limitations rather than his abilities.

[26] G. Z. Zillboorg, 'Dénegations et affirmations de la foi religieuse' in *Foi, raison et psychiatrie moderne*, Paris, 1957.

6. Religion in Human Life

Religion in childhood

Our attempt to describe certain aspects of religious experience has shown us that it affects all psychic activity in a particular way. We have been obliged to appeal to an 'experience' already more or less clearly constituted and characterized. But how is religion manifested in the various phases of human life? How does it originate and develop and how does it decline? Here too we are faced with a complex problem, but one which arouses particular interest at the present time as a result of studies which fix attention on the development of psychic activity rather than on the nature and meaning of the forms in which it is actualized. Our starting-point must therefore be child psychology.

Development of children's thinking according to J. Piaget.
As far as mental development and particularly the development of thought are concerned, I appeal to the studies made by Jean Piaget. Even though he has remained in a certain sense isolated and is only beginning to be known, appreciated and discussed at present in the great world of American psychologists, his researches and his doctrine introduce a distinctly original note, I should venture to say a personal note, which is nevertheless closely connected with the psychological problems of our day. Piaget himself has told us how his philosophical interests and his passion for collecting and classifying shells emerged at an early age:[1] and (without

---

[1] J. Piaget, 'Autobiography' in Murchison, *A History of Psychology in Autobiography*, Clark University Press, Worcester, Mass., 1952, vol. IV.

considering this to be a proof of the guiding influence which childhood interests exercise over the development of later interests), his entire work may be said to reflect the effort to reach a synthetic understanding of observed data and to classify them. Piaget has also told us how, in order to satisfy his curiosity concerning the psychological processes of thought, he followed the lectures of E. Bleuler. To oblige himself to exercise observation and escape the danger of autistic thinking, he decided in favour of naturalistic studies (ending with the work of classifying shellfish).

After his university studies Piaget went to France and remained in close touch with Dr Simon who had cooperated with Binet in devising a scale for intelligence testing, and here he devoted himself to the psychological study of children's verbal reasoning. The task which Piaget set before himself was the discovery of the relations between nerve structures and degrees of intelligence. The method he used was fundamentally clinical, similar to that adopted by psychiatrists, who endeavour to discover the hidden thread which connects their mental patients' apparently disjointed thinking. In children's thinking it is a question of discovering the psychological structure underlying verbal expression. The psychologist begins with a question relating to the spontaneous statements made by the child and the reply is followed up by further questions regulated by the answer itself, while great care is taken to avoid influencing the child directly and to guide him by degrees and without any jolts towards the subjects which interest the interrogator particularly. From the whole series of answers received will result either confirmation or negation of the hypotheses the observer has formulated beforehand.

This would appear quite a simple and easy procedure, but such is not the case. Piaget emphasizes the continued effort required in order to formulate the questions adequately and to catch not only the apparent but the deeper meaning of each reply. He also speaks of the difficulty of establishing reciprocal understanding in conditions which can vary from one moment to the next, and the danger of extreme interpretations, either judging everything the child says to correspond with real conditions or considering everything to be the product of unconscious thought.

According to Piaget, the development of thought proceeds from the child to the adult through successive characteristic stages, each of which utilizes the preceding phase and reaches greater efficiency and is gradually detached from concrete and particular conditions. 'Logical thinking is the apex of intellectual development and forms the conclusion of an actual building process and of discussion with the environment which lasts all through childhood. The intellectual building which terminates in logical thought is initially based on sensorimotor activities. At a later stage it is based on symbolic images of a plastic nature employed to interpret reality, and finally on logical mental operations.'[2]

Piaget describes this triple aspect of the cognitive processes and the 'building of reality' (physical objects, space, number, time), the process of representation (games, imitation, drawing, language) and the process of feeling (elementary feelings, moral judgment, will). I shall refer merely to some points relating to our own problem. Particularly in his earlier books Piaget stresses the tendency to egocentricity in children's thinking. The child is incapable of realizing that different points of view from his own can exist. He therefore places himself at the centre of his world and interprets things and events according to his own subjective experience. The sensorimotor behaviour of the first months of his life has given him the capacity to direct and connect the movements of his body in relation to circumstances, and when he begins to take part in events he interprets them as though they were regulated in the same way as the happenings of his subjective experience. Hence we have 'objectivization' in the child, or rather 'realism' (understood as the almost exclusive supremacy of immediate perception over representation), so that he attributes a real existence to

[2] J. Piaget and B. Inhelder, 'La Psicologia della prima infanzia' in D. and R. Katz, *Trattato di psicologia*, Boringhieri, Turin, 1960, p. 273.

subjective facts (dreams, imagination, words, rules) and believes they depend upon a guiding activity (animism) and an intentional activity (artificialism).

It is ordinarily observed that the child at a certain stage fails to distinguish dreams and phantasy from reality and that he attributes life to things and intentionality to events (the ball goes where it wants to go: the stone is naughty because it made me fall, the pillow is hurt when it is beaten). Simultaneously objects can acquire an imaginary significance (the stick is ridden as a horse, the chairs are the carriage). But here it is a question of extension of the outlines already constituted in sensorimotor behaviour, transferred to the symbol (the meaning in place of the thing). By his gestures the child acts the part of the cat, the aeroplane, his grandfather reading. The action gives meaning to the object. Acts and words can thus take on a 'magic' character: the child considers, that is, that he can obtain what he wants by this means.

Piaget recalls how his own little girl, upset by seeing him go off with a friend, put her fingers in her mouth in a strange new way and said to her mother: 'I'm putting my fingers like this so that Daddy will come back'; or kicked the door of her room because she thought that if she didn't the soup would not have tasted good. Moral judgment is also more bound up with the material consequences of the act than with a critical evaluation of the intention. To the question whether it is naughtier to break a lot of glasses by accident than to break one on purpose, the child answers that it is naughtier to break a lot of glasses. In all these cases it is obvious that the child's thinking remains tied to 'mental diagrams' (perceptive-motor or explanatory) without modifying the diagrams themselves. Thus the child's thinking takes the single direction indicated by the event.

Finally, from Piaget's collection of conversations between children under seven years of age, it is evident that child language is used much less to communicate information and thoughts to others than as an accompaniment and commentary on a subjective experience. The child speaks of himself and is readier to engage in monologue than in dialogue; his tendency to self-centredness prevents him from understanding and sharing the point of view of others. After seven years of age, when he participates more fully in the human community (socialization process) a new phase begins. This phase culminates in logical thinking in which the child, by contact with objectual and social reality, undergoes a disintegration of the subjective world which he had built up and in which he had shut himself up. He now begins to acknowledge the force of other points of view from his own (and therefore the possibility of explanations which no longer pertain to animism or artificialism). As a result, the adolescent has to adjust his mental diagrams to reality, detach his thinking from merely perceptive data and rearrange these in more general schemata of abstract and productive thinking. At the same time the way is opened up to reciprocal understanding and conscious, effective cooperation. Logical, deductive thinking culminates in autonomy of the will and independent moral judgment.

This brief sketch of Piaget's reasoning furnishes a far from adequate picture of his complex and systematic theoretical analysis. Criticism of his work has not been lacking. V. Hazlitt already pointed out in 1930 that Piaget's contrast between child and adult thinking is the effect of overestimation of verbal expression as a means for measuring thought.[3] Piaget himself recognized that side by side with a 'level of verbal thinking' there exists a 'level of concrete thinking', which is more primitive and sometimes precedes verbal thinking. Hence he extended his method of observation to include the use of concrete objects which could be handled by the child. E. Pichon considers that the essential difference between child and adult is not to be found so much on the plane of greater intellectual fecundity as on the plane of a better didactic faculty, a better introspective knowledge of intellectual processes, or what is rather narrowly called 'better logic'.[4] This explains how

[3] V. Hazlitt, 'Children's Thinking' in British Journal of Psychology, 1930.
[4] E. Pichon, Développement psychique de l'enfant, Paris, 1947, p. 20.

children understand adults more easily than adults understand each other.

With reference to animism and artificialism it has been remarked that they are not exclusively confined to children. W. Dennis has observed them both in children and in adults.[5] As regards moral judgment, A. Brenco has observed that when the quantitative disproportion between two actions is reduced in the question asked (breaking a lot of glasses and breaking one glass) and the motive is placed in greater evidence, a genuine moral judgment is the result. In point of fact, if children are asked to judge a child who steals two buns to give them to a poor hungry companion and another who steals them to satisfy his own gluttony, almost all of them answer that the second is more guilty than the first.[6] Finally, American psychologists in particular object to the lack of satisfactory statistical proof in Piaget's results. However this may be, I consider the position of R. I. Watson to be very sound: 'Piaget is dismissed,' he says, 'because his own research rightly is not considered as sufficient evidence. . . . It is his ideas which are stimulating, not his evidence.'[7]

Piaget's theory has a direct bearing on the question of religion. A short-circuit conclusion (not Piaget's own) would be that logical, deductive thinking inevitably demolishes the animistic and magical structures of childhood, that it is the only one which guarantees security and that religious ideas are therefore destined to collapse as soon as logical adult thought appears. There is some truth in this judgment, since many religious crises occur in adolescence when logical thinking asserts itself. But we must ask ourselves if in these crises it is not merely a certain childish concept of religion which breaks down to make room for a more adequate expression of the religious sense. From the purely descriptive point of view it is

[5] W. Dennis, 'Animistic thinking among College and University Students' in *Scientific Monograph*, 1953.

[6] Cited in G. Petter, *Lo sviluppo mentale nelle ricerche di J. Piaget*, Ed. Universitaria, Florence, 1960, p. 486.

[7] R. I. Watson, *Psychology of the Child*, Wiley, New York, 1959, p. 359.

true that traces of childhood thinking survive in religion. Self-centredness, artificialism and notions of magic creep into man's monologue in the presence of an invisible being in whom he seeks gratification of his own needs and desires, a being he tries to influence to his own advantage by absurd formulas or acts, by observance of the letter rather than the spirit of certain prescriptions, by establishing with this being the social relations he had with his parents or others. But at this point we wonder if survivals of the same kind cannot be discovered also in the thinker, the scientist or the artist, who lives in a world of his own where dialogue is reduced to monologue and who arrives at assertions which to the uninitiated appear absurd.

The question therefore hinges rather on the meaning of the 'infantile characteristics' indicated by Piaget and on their incorporation into successive periods of life. Self-centredness is in itself a one-sided position, but we must recognize it as an inevitable phase in the building up and establishment of subjectivity, of the ego and its distinction from the objects around it. I would venture to say that artificialism and animism indicate the priority of perception of forces and persons over perception of objects. It is only by this enrichment of raw experience that the way is opened up to detachment from concrete situations which marks the deep distinction between man and the animal. We cannot establish the precise moment in which an experience becomes religious and can be qualified as such, but it is true that in childhood the features of the religious sense are outlined decisively: relations with powers generally personified, attraction towards these, fear of them and the effort to enter into communication with them. To critical logical thinking all this is enlarged and can appear false, yet it is a meaningful and sound initial approach. There is a danger that logical thought itself, by its determined elimination of infantile survivals, instead of proceeding to reintegrate them, may spell its own ruin. This is the fate of radical intellectualism. On the other hand, it is true that continued attachment to an infantile formulation closes the door to ampler and more adequate concepts. But anyone who demolishes indiscriminately, in his holy zeal to destroy the superstructures which may obstruct the harmonious growth of the edifice, runs the risk of being buried beneath the ruins, or, if he survives, of having nothing left on which to rebuild. If we were to attempt to eliminate imagination from the adult's realistic thinking because it predominates in the child, man would be reduced to an automaton incapable of any initiative whatsoever. Likewise, if we attempted to abolish the religious sense, man would be deprived of such an indispensable support that he would create substitutes which would be just as exacting and dangerous.

Piaget believes that instead of having recourse to a heritage of archetypes to account for the universality of some manifestations of thought it is simpler to suppose that 'the same genetic mechanisms which account for the development of the thought of the child of today were in action also in the minds of those who . . . were just emerging from mythological and prelogical thought'. He recalls

the striking resemblances between the beginnings of rational thought in the child of from seven to ten and in the Greeks. We find, for example, explanation by identification of substances (stars which are produced by air or clouds, air and earth coming from water, etc.), by atomism resulting from this identification and the use of the ideas of condensation and rarefaction, and even the exact explanation of certain movements by reactions of the air *(antiperistasis)* used by Aristotle.[8]

The meaning of mythical thought is only partially and insufficiently explained by comparison with children's thinking. Mythical thought grasps a unity and an intimate relationship between events which critical logical thinking will never achieve, although it will endeavour to do so by immensely involved and complex structures, or by allowing mythical

[8] J. Piaget, *Play, Dreams and Imitation in Childhood*, Heinemann, London, 1951, pp. 197-8.

thought to re-emerge unchecked. But if Greek thought is really infantile thought, it is to be regretted that we, who claim to be adults, have lost this capacity, because it is there that we find outlines of all developments of modern thought which very often gets no further than sterile lucubrations. If this is the case, then it is equally to be regretted that the religious sense of primitive peoples has today been overpowered by an inexorable technical advance which leads man to believe that he can subject everything to his power, but leaves him isolated and alone, more woefully alone than an abandoned child.

Development of character and affect

Psychoanalytical theories are concerned with development of character and affect and their influence on the study of religious feeling is undoubtedly strong and stimulating. Although all these doctrines spring from a single source, there are now so many ramifications that it becomes really difficult to follow all of them and express an opinion on the original contribution made by each. I may be permitted all the same to try to furnish an overall view of these psychoanalytic doctrines. All of them agree in maintaining the decisive importance of the early years of development, and this is so strongly stressed that we are led to believe that it is only in early childhood that structures can be formed which are sufficiently stable and definitive to endure or re-emerge in later years. The key which opens the door to adult man is his development as a child. But how is this process to be reconstructed?

Psychoanalysis has begun to discover the child in the adult person, indeed in a particular type of adult, the neurotic. Freud's only study of a child is his *Analysis of the Phobia in a Five-Year-Old Boy*, written in 1909.[9] In order to treat little Hans, Freud had suggested to the boy's father (already subjected to analysis) the interpretation of his behaviour, so that he might make the child understand. 'No one else, in my

[9] S. Freud, *Analysis of the Phobia in a Five-Year-Old Boy* (1909) in Standard Ed., vol. X, p. 5.

opinion,' writes Freud, 'could possibly have prevailed on the child to make any such avowals; the special knowledge by means of which he was able to interpret the remarks made by his five-year-old son was indispensable, and without it the technical difficulties in the way of conducting a psychoanalysis upon so young a child would have been insuperable.' At that time, therefore, Freud did not consider it possible to carry out psychoanalytic investigation on children. Hence, his entire teaching on infantile sexuality is an interpretation or doctrinal construct which explains children's behaviour on a basis of study which was not carried out directly on the child but on the memories which re-emerged in the adult, especially the neurotic adult. It was only from 1930 onwards that Freud's daughter, Anna, began to study children of three or more years of age by observing what they said spontaneously, the tales and dreams they related and their favourite games. Her interpretation was conducted according to the doctrinal principles of psychoanalysis, but it bore in mind that the child's situation is very different from that of the adult, both because he is still developing and because he reacts to the present situation without reproducing the past, that is to say, he does not present the behaviour patterns of the neurotic patient who transfers his infantile reactions to the analyst.

Melanie Klein, another of Freud's pupils through K. Abraham, pushes analysis back to the first two years of life, in which she considers it possible to discover the manifestation and development of anxiety and aggressiveness by observing the child's imaginative behaviour at play.

Freud himself has discussed the origin of religious feeling in reply to a reader of *The Future of an Illusion*, who, although agreeing with Freud's judgment on religion, considered that he had not properly appreciated the true source of religious sentiment which he called a 'sensation of eternity', a 'feeling of something limitless, unbounded, as it were oceanic'.[10] Freud replied that although he himself had not experienced this

---

[10] S. Freud, *Civilization and its Discontents*, Standard Ed., vol. XXI, p. 64.

'oceanic' feeling, this gave him no right to deny that it does in fact occur in other people. But he questioned whether it is being correctly interpreted and whether it ought to be considered as the *fons et origo* of the whole need for religion. According to Freud this feeling is a shrunken residue of the child's ego which has not yet been marked off distinctly from the external world. 'Originally the ego includes everything and later it separates off an external world from itself . . . a much more inclusive feeling than the adult's ego-feeling, indeed an all-embracing feeling which corresponded to a more intimate bond between the ego and the world about it.' 'The derivation of religious needs from the infant's helplessness and the longing for the father aroused by it seems to me incontrovertible,' writes Freud. He continues:

I cannot think of any need in childhood as strong as the need for a father's protection. Thus the part played by the oceanic feeling which might seek something like the restoration of limitless narcissism is ousted from a place in the foreground. The origin of the religious attitude can be traced back in clear outlines as far as the feeling of infantile helplessness. There may be something further behind that, but for the present it is wrapped in obscurity.[11]

It is rather striking that Freud sees the father as the almost exclusive object of the child's desires. Ian Suttie's criticism, conducted on the psychoanalytic plane, attacks this onesidedness of Freud's doctrine. He accuses Freud of inability to admit the social significance of the mother and of denial that any love exists which does not originate in sexuality.[12] In criticizing Freud, Suttie clearly asserts his own conviction that mother attachment and maternal tenderness lies at the root of religion and of psychotherapy.

Concerning the origin of religious feeling, Piaget remarks:

Sublimated sexual love does not account for all religious feeling. The key to the problem is found on the contrary in

[11] *Ibid.*, p. 72.
[12] I. D. Suttie, *The Origins of Love and Hate, op. cit.*, pp. 176-9.

primitive filial feeling. The essence of religious feeling is in fact a mixture *sui generis* of love and fear which we call respect. Now this respect cannot be explained unless its source be found in the relation between the child and his parents. It is therefore a truly filial sentiment.[13]

Here Piaget is following the theory advanced by Pierre Bovet, who, while appreciating psychoanalysis (especially in the 1952 revised edition of the book he wrote in 1912), does not accept the reduction of the various types of love (parental, filial, religious) to sexuality and maintains that they are differentiations of filial love. It is true, as Freud asserts, that in sexual relations between adults infantile feelings and satisfactions re-emerge, but this does not cancel the differences. Bovet perceives 'a double origin in the more characteristic manifestation of filial love: veneration and respect: tender love and admiring love, that is, the same origins which we see attributed to religion'.[14] The child attributes divine qualities to his parents: omnipotence, omniscience, eternity and even ubiquity. (Piaget sees in this a close connection with infantile artificialism and realism.) The first 'religious crisis' is reached when the perfections attributed to parents are belied by daily life (between six and seven years of age, in a period which Bovet calls rationalistic and philosophical).[15] This collapse of the spontaneous and instinctive 'divinization of the parents' is necessary in order that the child may rise to the conception of a spiritual and paternal God; still, especially when it coincides with the communication in brutal terms of information regarding the sexual act, it can constitute a serious trauma.[16]

Freud's doctrinal conception starts out by asserting the existence of a single primordial energy, the libido, which has

[13] J. Piaget, *La formation du symbole chez l'enfant. Imitation, jeu et rêve, image et représentation*, Dalachaux and Niestlé, Neuchâtel-Paris, 1945, p. 383.
[14] P. Bovet, *Il sentimento religioso e la psicologia del fanciullo*, La Nuova Italia, Florence, 1956, pp. 15-16.
[15] *Ibid.*, p. 29.
[16] *Ibid.*, p. 34.

the qualities of sexual attraction, 'invests' objects and persons and can 'transfer' itself to other objects and persons. The undifferentiated world which surrounds the newborn infant is gradually differentiated and articulated according to the libido's 'choice' of objects. The libido, at first diffused throughout the body, is at a later stage localized in the mouth, then in the anus and finally in the genital organs. While in the oral and anal phases satisfaction is confined to the subject himself (autoerotism), in the phallic phase it demands an external object. At about the age of three the libido turns to the parent of the opposite sex, but since it cannot be gratified it turns in upon itself. In this way an interior judge is set up who imposes what must be done and what must not be done (superego). Simultaneously the child 'projects' towards the father an aura of greatness, power and authority, and later on he 'transfers' this also to an invisible being of whom the parents speak to the child and of whom he himself creates a mental picture as an idealized copy of his father. Side by side with this there is an impulse towards the desired person (identification). The religious sense, therefore, is the result of these processes of projection, transference and identification inherent in the libido.

I may perhaps be pardoned for this rough-and-ready, incomplete and perhaps even clumsy presentation of Freudian doctrine when it is understood that my intention has been to simplify it as far as possible. Substantially the fundamental elements seem to be the following: 1) the libido, understood as the basic element of psychic activity; 2) direction, 'investment' and 'projection' upon objects and persons; 3) self-adjustment of the superego; 4) transference to objects of its own making (duty, values, the divinity, etc.).

Freud's own attitude towards religion was clearly and decidedly negative and it is only right to respect it. This does not mean, in principle, that sexual and emotive development cannot take place from the psychological point of view according to his schema. He points to the manner in which the religious sense develops, without being able to assert or deny anything in regard to its meaning, just as the description of growth of the father-image does nothing to solve the problem of its meaning, that is to say, whether in saying 'my father' I am simply projecting a feeling of my own or whether I am expressing a real, objective relationship with another being. Here we have a repetition of the eternal equivocation which makes the conditions of a phenomenon coincide with its nature. In the present case it is stated that the supposed condition of psychological development is also the cause of the phenomenon. We must add that the primitive psychoanalytic diagram sketched by Freud was continually revised by Freud himself and even more so by his followers.

In the sphere of orthodox Freudianism today, at least two trends have taken shape. The first began with Anna Freud, who strongly stressed the ego and defence mechanisms, with a broader consideration of environmental conditions, always supposing the formation of the superego as the result of the Oedipus conflict and the substantial immutability of the libido. The other trend began with Melanie Klein and sought to explore the stages preceding the Oedipus complex, finding traces of the superego already in these earlier stages. This trend maintains the precedence of aggressive impulses and considers environmental factors to be of secondary importance; already in the pre-Oedipal phases there are signs of schizoid, maniacal and neurotic situations to which the adult can revert. In England this second trend preponderates today, supported by Ernest Jones, Susan Isaacs and R. Money Kyrle.[17]

Among the dissident Freudians there is a disconcerting

[17] The chronological anticipation of developmental phases proposed by Melanie Klein is so daring that some are inclined to think she oversteps the limits of Freudian orthodoxy. Against the background of the aggression instinct she traces 'initial innate phantasies' which guide the child in his choice of objects to satisfy his needs. Even in the first months of life when the child has no ego by means of which he can delimit himself and his environment, there is a conflict between reality and the symbolic constructions of the child's phantasy. This is the 'paranoid-schizoid state' which marks the first three or four months of life during which the subject lives entirely in his unconscious phantasy without being able to distinguish between himself and the reality around him. In the second half of the first year of life, as his ego becomes

variety of theories. C. G. Jung stands out on his own and as far as religion is concerned he reverses the Freudian situation. For him the religious sense is not a by-product of the libido but the mainspring of psychic dynamism. The accentuation of the importance of interpersonal relations is very significant in the doctrines of two orthodox psychoanalysts who emigrated to America, namely, K. Horney and Erich Fromm, as well as in the doctrine of Sullivan, an American, who also associates himself with Freud. Also worthy of note is the employment of psychoanalytic concepts by anthropologists in their study of primitive peoples, particularly for the purpose of demonstrating the influence which methods of rearing children (enormously different from one people to another) have on the character of adults (M. Mead, C. Kluckhohn).

It is impossible to go into the various theories in any detail in the present work, but in general it can be said that the predominantly biological and instinctivist trend of the orthodox Freudians has been supplanted by the environmentalist-sociological-cultural trend of American psychoanalysis. From this point of view the religious sense is to be understood as an acquired behaviour, indispensable for the individual's socialization. The child's relationship of dependence on his parents, especially on the mother, is interpreted as the expres-

stabilized and as he becomes aware of other people (of his mother in the first place), the 'depressive state' emerges: the child is subject to contradictory impulses and is ambivalent in his affections. In these states the Oedipus complex and the superego already begin to appear. The power of construction serves to liberate the child from the depressive state, enabling him in his play to express and compensate for his destructive desires. According to Melanie Klein the paranoid state from the religious point of view corresponds to animism. The depressive state is the necessary path leading to higher forms of religion (guilt sense, reparation, disinterested love). An objection to this theory is that in the early oral phase (to which both the states she describes belong) the child is not yet capable of forming representative images and that the fear he experiences of being attacked by the world involves fear of an external object and not the anxiety produced by an interiorized object (Pasche, 'Regression, perversion, névrose' in *Revue française de Psychologie*, 1962). Melanie Klein's theory is supported by F. Fornari (*La vita affettiva originaria del bambino*, Feltrinelli, Milan, 1963).

sion of a need for security rather than a sexual manifestation. Anxiety is considered to be the fear of detachment and isolation.

The Oedipus process, on which Freudian doctrine hinges and which is the obligatory turning-point at which childhood is left behind, is no longer accepted as initially formulated, but is reduced to a process of weaning, of change in the interpersonal relations between parents and children, decidedly moulded by cultural conditions. The main problem in neurosis is a question of solitude, of difficulty in communication and of socialization. From this point of view religion is seen as dependent on interpersonal conditions, influenced by the direction taken by infantile needs, rather than as a genuine human characteristic. Hence there is research into basic 'needs', basic 'personality', basic 'anxiety' and basic 'trusts'. Briefly, Freud's principle remains: the explanation of all things is to be found in the beginning and not in the destination: in predetermination and not in contemporaneity with the necessity of action: in the past and not in the present or the future.

What perplexes us about psychoanalytic concepts of childhood is their partial aspect. They can be very useful for the purpose of explaining an aspect of psychological development. I would venture to say with reference to religion that these theories enable us to understand the human projection—man's most instinctive projection—of a God 'in man's image and likeness' into the Olympus of the gods and the myths or into the world. But this, as we have already seen, pertains merely to the manner in which the religious sense is expressed. The deficiency in psychoanalytic concepts of infantile religion lies in the fact that they consider the negative aspects (a religion of utility and convenience) rather than the positive aspect (the overcoming of limitations and the need of the Absolute). Perhaps this is a general quality of human psychic activity as compared with that of animals: the continual urge to get beyond sensory, affective and social conditions, to pass on from what appears to be acquired and reach out to new conquests.

It is probable that the religious sense is situated in the antagonism between man's limitation and restriction to himself on the one hand and his impulse towards an immutable Unknown on the other hand. To reduce this to illusory consolations which help us to endure life in this world would be to raise a preliminary issue which psychology lacks the means to affirm or deny. To conceive religion, on Darwinist lines, as a mere defence produced by the struggle for existence, as a manifestation which will continue until natural selection eliminates it, would lead us to wonder what useful purpose is served by religion if it merely turns aside from the danger instead of facing up to it. To take refuge in illusion is certainly not a note of efficient vitality but rather of deficiency. Yet this is where psychoanalysis leads.

Meaning and importance of infantile characteristics

To conclude, it seems important to establish that the religious sense in children, like all infantile psychic activity, has certain characteristics of its own: a marked egocentricity, an anthropomorphic expressivity dependent upon domestic, social and cultural environment and bound up with particular verbal expressions and rigid and ritualized behaviour. These qualities may be summarily judged as signs of deficiency in the child's mentality. This is true in one sense, for the child really lacks what the adult possesses; he cannot fend for himself and has need of others. But it would be a mistake to assert that the child possesses no other mental qualities than these. Children have qualities of genuineness, spontaneity, constructiveness and capacity for admiration which the adult unfortunately loses to his own detriment. Egocentricity is not such a very negative quality, since it is the inevitable phase in which the ego is differentiated from its environment and the friction set up between ego and environment continues all through life. Imaginative activity also lasts all through life, either setting the individual free or enslaving him.

In comparing the child with the adult, we usually confine

ourselves to the more apparent qualities, asking ourselves if these qualities are the exclusive property of child or adult. It does not occur to us that they may be just two different positions, the first that of a being in process of formation and development, and the second that of a being who, at the end of a certain type of development, has attained relative stability but is all the time reaching forward to something beyond him. As long as life lasts, the position of the human being in the world consists, not simply in his more or less adequate adaptation, but in the constant need to assert himself and to build. Mere adaptation to immediate elementary needs or to the so-called derived needs produces frustration instead of satisfaction, both for the child who is forbidden to transcend himself and for the adult whom we think we are making happy when we leave him to vegetate in an institute run on model lines.

Psychoanalysis, by having recourse to the persistence of infantile experiences or to regression towards them in order to explain patterns of adult behaviour, seems to justify the disparaging use of the phrase 'infantile behaviour'. More harm has been done to psychoanalysis by the stupid certainty with which some counsellors tell their patient that he has an infantile mentality which must grow up and become mature, than has been occasioned by technical and doctrinal difficulties. Childhood is a period of waiting, the expectation of a future which lasts all through life and only ceases with death itself. When a man's interest in the future grows weak and when he is prevented from looking forward, when the future appears to him as a wall against which he hurls himself in vain, there is good reason to suspect that his mental balance is upset. That is why the eagerness of childhood years is considered to be the first expression of a fundamental human activity.

In religious feeling this eagerness is always present more or less strongly and to reduce it to a psychic *vis medicatrix*, automatic and deterministic, is quite a mistake. It is much easier than is generally believed for the psychologist to condemn himself to 'rationalizing' events in order to fit them into his theory. While the eagerness of which we spoke is initially expressed in apparently strange and inadequate forms, it would be a serious error not to follow it up and not to cultivate it as other human capacities are cultivated. Such a privation would be just as dangerous and just as certain a forerunner of trouble as the neglect of personal hygiene or of emotional control.

If a comparison may serve to bring out the importance of infantile psychic activities, we may recall the fetalization theory proposed by Bolk and supported by Buytendyk, De Beer and Portmann. This theory presents the distinctive characteristics of the human organism as resulting from a prolongation of primitive qualities into what Portmann calls the period of 'extra-uterine gestation'.[18] By this he means the period in which the child is under parental care, when human 'novelties' develop from qualities which had remained longer in their primitive state (standing erect, intentional movement, the rudiments of speech). According to Bally, Freud also approaches this conception by situating in preadolescence, in the so-called refractory period, the sublimation of repressed infantile impulses.[19] Characteristics surviving from infancy would therefore distinguish the development of the human organism from that of the other vertebrates and afford it incomparable possibilities of development.

The decisive importance of the first five years of development appears much more fully justified when they are considered as the beginning of a vital impulse destined to last all through life, rather than as crystallized in patterns to be reproduced. K. Horney considers that latter position to be one of the most serious errors of Freud's doctrine (and rightly so). 'It is one thing to say that the experience of birth is the original anxiety-producing situation and quite another to suppose that later anxiety is the same thing all over again.'[20] Piaget has

[18] A. Portmann, *Zoologie und das Neue Bied des Menschen*, Hamburg, 1956.

[19] G. Bally, *Einführung in die Psychoanalyse S. Freud's*, Hamburg, 1961, p. 141.

[20] K. Horney, quoted in J. A. C. Brown, *Freud and the Post-Freudians*, Penguin Books, London, 1964, p. 136.

advanced the same objection to Freud: 'The continuity in internal development which we stress does not by any means oblige us to believe that the feelings as such remain identical. It is not the feelings which are transferred from a known situation to a new one but only the acquired affective attitude.'[21] The religious sense is not, then, a survival from infancy destined to disappear in adulthood, but an attitude which continues in the adult although its form of expression changes and it is not immune from the danger of decadence.

Several psychotherapists have openly attacked the exclusively genetic conception of adult psychic capacities. M. Boss is their spokesman in his report to the Fifth Congress of Psychotherapy in Vienna.[22] He maintains that the great power of machinery is the cause of neurosis and of its false interpretation by psychologists. Man has the sensation of being a mere cog in a mechanized system, of being compelled to take his place in the vast social machine. The psychologist judges that neurosis derives from the faulty functioning of the more delicate and primitive pieces of the human machine, both individual and collective, and that when these are set in order the rest will right itself. According to this theory what goes before is the cause of what appears later: the anguish of birth is the cause of anxiety in the eight-month-old in the presence of a stranger, of anxiety with reference to parents, to teachers, to authority and to God; the sense of guilt is aroused in the child by the parents' orders and punishments: their image is interiorized in the superego and later projected on to teachers, authority and God, and on to the parents themselves, and this produces the sense of guilt in the adult.

The psychotherapist must discover the kernel of the neurotic terrors and demolish them as infantile fears devoid of any foundation.

Some flaws are to be found in this mechanism. There is nothing to show that what appears first in the course of life,

[21] J. Piaget, quoted in D. and R. Katz, *op. cit.*, p. 303.
[22] M. Boss, *Lebensangst, Schuldgefühle und psychotherapeutische Befreiung*, Bern, 1962.

merely because it comes first, is to be considered the cause of what follows, and that what appears later is to be degraded to the rank of a secondary product, a sublimation, an epiphenomenon. The technical approach which imagines forces and causes underlying phenomena diminishes the possibility of understanding the phenomena themselves in their immediacy. They are lost in a hypothetical and questionable succession of events deriving from an initial one which it is generally impossible to verify. Moreover, in actual practice, 'on the basis of these theories psychotherapy, despite its premises, has not succeeded in setting any man free from anxiety and a sense of guilt'.[23]

This last statement made by a psychotherapist of such worth as M. Boss is a very serious one. He recalls how Freud himself observed that the most successful analyses were those in which the analyst had laid aside his ambition to succeed as a therapist, a pedagogue or a scientist, to give place to human participation with the patient—lending himself to him as a *Tummelplatz*, or riding-track, so that the patient might express in all freedom the impulses which up to that time he had repressed. 'We, as psychotherapists, want to be "more Freudian" than Freud,' says Boss, 'when, for example, we attribute to our patients' spiritual and religious experiences which emerge during treatment the same originality, genuineness and reality as we attribute to the phenomena of the so-called impulse sphere.'[24] The patient must be led and guided in this way to regain his freedom by facing up to the problem of his own existence.

Play and ritualization.

Closely linked with the 'infantile mentality' are problems which arise from interpretation of play and ritualization. These we shall mention briefly. It is difficult to give a definition of play. All sorts of different definitions and interpretations have been proposed: recreation, giving vent to superfluous energy, survival of atavism, anticipation of movements and 'roles' to

[23] *Ibid.*, p. 22.   [24] *Ibid.*, p. 60.

be performed in later life, the mere need to be occupied. Miss Meyer Holzapfel, to whom we are indebted for a valuable synthesis on mammals at play,[25] has outlined the difference between play and instinctive action as follows: 'The readiness to do something not exact, but just something, and to change at will the manner of behaviour, is the essential criterion of activity in general and also of play, as one of the forms in which it is actualized.'[26]

In a famous book Gustav Bally, a broad-minded psychoanalyst, has seen in play the primitive expression of that freedom which the higher animals enjoy to a limited degree and which man, by his prolonged need of parental care, can maintain in a much wider sphere.[27] Man runs the risk, however, of losing the enjoyment, either because of social regulations which he elaborates to make sure of possessing it, or by defences which he himself must erect to withdraw from instinctual pressure. According to Bally (II, 1961), 'play, for the growing animal, is an action which enables him to become acquainted with his environment *(Umwelt)* in a particular way, and thus it not only discovers objects but creates them'.[28] Then he appeals to Merleau-Ponty: 'It is the game which makes the ball: the ball is known as an object which can be played with in one way or another.' In this perspective play appears as an authentic taking possession of the world, according to the capacities of the various living beings. In play the general environment is delimited into the 'private' environments of each living creature, as Uexküll has it. Here we are obviously approaching the borderline of the 'play' concept in so far as it is confused with instinctive action and with innate capacities. It is well to point out that play is distinguished from these by

[25] M. Meyer Holzapfel, *Kukenthal zool. Handbuch*, vol. VIII, Berlin, 1956.
[26] M. Meyer Holzapfel, 'Über die Bereitschaft zu Spiel und Instinkthandlung' in *Z. Tierpsychologie*, 1952, pp. 442-62.
[27] G. Bally, *Von Ursprung und Grenzen der Freheit: eine Deutung des Spiels bei Tier und Mensch*, Basle, 1945.
[28] G. Bally, *Le jeu et le propre de l'homme*, Archivio di Filosofia, Rome, 1961.

the fact that it always permits freedom of expression. As Huizinga has demonstrated in a famous book entitled *Homo ludens*, play is to be considered one of man's most characteristic and productive activities.[29]

But play also has its rules. It is not tumultuous and uncontrolled activity. It requires a form, it needs to be ritualized. The freedom of the game demands a delimitation, a meaning, a rhythm. Ritualization therefore appears as a regulating and constructive principle in which the activities of various individuals converge. It is not a solitary pastime but becomes personal participation for a collective, social purpose.

It is evident all through the history of mankind that the religious sense inspires play and ritual, that it finds expression in these forms and gives a meaning to the world, as Huizinga has shown magnificently. One of the most profound chapters of Romano Guardini's book *The Spirit of the Liturgy* is devoted precisely to the liturgy seen as play, as the institutionalized expression of man's freedom and jubilation in the presence of God.[30]

It will be remembered that Freud began by comparing ritual with neurosis and then proceeded to define religion as the neurosis of mankind and neurotic constraint or obsession as 'private religion'. Concerned as he was with the question of neurosis, he stressed the element of obligation in play and in ritual without realizing that neurosis is the unhappy formal survival of a free and constructive activity that has disappeared. Neurotic ritualization, with its burden of constrain and gloom, is the very opposite of free and untroubled play. The neurotic can no longer play and this is the tragedy of his state.

Religious ritualization can also degenerate and harden into mere formalism. This is to be observed in all religions and it is continually stressed in the Bible. The formalist religious sense is no longer capable of communicating with God; it builds a

[29] J. Huizinga, *Homo ludens: a study of the play element in culture*, Beacon, Boston, 1955.

[30] R. Guardini, *The Spirit of the Liturgy*, Sheed and Ward, New York, 1940.

wall between man and God. But is any expressive activity of man immune from this risk? Science can become a closely woven fabric of rules and techniques in which man, a being aware of his own existence, is ignored. Even art itself can deteriorate until it becomes the object of learned and critical comment but has lost all poetic impulse.

Religion in adolescence

To define adolescence as a transition from childhood to maturity is basically correct when we bear in mind that these different periods of life are not separated by clearly defined boundaries and do not always imply the complete, proportionate and permanent acquisition of certain qualities. Adolescence therefore stands out in contrast to childhood which it follows and to adulthood for which it prepares the way, although some features remain unaltered all through.

Physiological and psychological changes in adolescence.

A fundamentally important biological event takes place in adolescence, when sexual maturity or puberty is reached. The activity of the genital organs is accompanied by changes in height, weight, bodily proportions and muscular strength. The gonads produce not only the male and female gametes, but also the particular hormones appropriate to each sex. Besides possessing a specific action of their own, these hormones alter the hormonic balance as a whole. Hence the physiological and emotional impulse towards union between the two sexes.

This new element which appears in adolescence is in itself so striking and meaningful that it has caused other exceedingly important circumstances to be relegated to the background. It was believed that there was a univocal and immediate relation between physiological conditions and psychological factors in adolescence. But this is not exact. Physiological puberty can occur either before or after the appearance of psychological characteristics proper to adolescence, and a great variety of constitutional and environmental conditions must be taken into account. While race and climate affect the beginnings of adolescence, social conditions also play their part. This fact, unexpected by supporters of the biological explanation, has been clearly proved by cross-cultural studies, that is, by surveys on adolescence in various cultures and social classes.

It would obviously be foolish to deny or underestimate the importance of the biological element: nevertheless it is not so immediately connected with the psychological situation as might seem inevitable. Moreover, what happens in emotion in general is also repeated here: a particular physiological condition is not sufficient to bring about an emotion. It must manifest itself and be recognized as typical: shivering, perspiration or tears do not give us emotion unless they have taken on a meaning, a recognized relation with a situation. As Cannon has shown, physiological conditions produce a state of alarm and affect the receptivity of certain stimuli. The restlessness caused by the new element which the adolescent vaguely experiences or notices without understanding it seeks to express itself in those 'patterns' which he finds close at hand in his family and surroundings. We understand, therefore, how new attitudes of behaviour can make their appearance later than physiological changes and also how they can precede them, by a process of learning, and can even speed up these changes. At any rate, the fundamental note of adolescence is the distress produced by the transition from the comparative stability of childhood experience to a new unknown world where nothing is clear.

As far as intellectual activity is concerned, the adolescent's increased capacity for logical and abstract thought enables him to break away from his own point of view (Piaget's egocentricity) and to accept that of others by a critical and more independent attitude. This means the 'disintegration of subjectivity', to use Osterrieth's rather ill-chosen expression,[31] but only in the sense of detachment from the predominantly subjective point of view. The ego, on the other hand, tends to

[31] P. Osterrieth, *Introduction à la psychologie de l' enfant*, Paris, 1957.

assert itself, anxiously and spasmodically in some cases, seeking, discovering and defending its own identity, or 'what it intends to be'.[32] This ego that had asserted itself so vigorously in childhood as a launching-base for world conquest, must during adolescence find its own place in the world.

According to the psychoanalytic interpretation, a distinctive feature of adolescence is the re-establishment of sexual interest and activity after the long period of latency subsequent to the dissolution of the Oedipus complex. Apart altogether from Freud, the anatomist Bolk has pointed out the discrepancy between delayed 'somatic' development and accelerated 'germatic' growth. Sexual development which had been precocious until the fifth year of age undergoes a decided interruption until the age of puberty. During Freud's 'latent phase' which coincides with this interval, the child's sexual impulses are successfully repressed or 'sublimated' in other activities, but the hormonic impulse causes them to break out violently when puberty is reached. The problem of adolescence is therefore the seeking of balance between sexual repression and emotional stability, and between expression of the sexual need and the restrictions imposed by the superego and by social conditions. Freud interpreted anxiety at first as a backwash of the repressed libido, and later on as an effect of the guilt-feeling caused by the superego's demands. On the basis of this second formulation Anna Freud saw the adolescent's repression as a defence against an uncontrolled sexual expression and against the anxiety which the very thought of it produces.

Danger of excessive repression arises when the adolescent character becomes too rigid, or when he embraces an ascetical life or becomes over-intellectual. The adolescent is a prey to intense anxiety, assailed by the sexual urge which becomes all the more pressing the more he pays attention to it, and harassed by interior and social prohibitions. Very often he thinks the only solution lies in yielding to these impulses or else in denying them obstinately and blindly. Here too, on the

[32] E. H. Erikson, *Identity and the Life Cycle*, International Univ. Press, New York, 1959.

whole, the psychoanalytic approach seems to be one-sided and not always tenable. As to the latent phase, according to Kinsey's report it would appear that preadolescents have a lively curiosity concerning sexual relations with which they are keen to experiment either for fun or for sexual gratification, while for the adolescent they can become an end in themselves, highly charged with emotion and sought as a proof of personal capacity. Sublimation towards higher activities seems to be demanded by the theoretical necessity of giving an outlet to every activity of the libido rather than by the objective facts of the adolescent's situation.

At most the facts reveal a certain contemporaneity between the appearance of artistic ability and religious experience in adolescence and the reawakening of sexual needs, but it is very difficult to prove that the former derive from inhibition of the latter. Unfortunately it can more easily be verified that the sexual impulse seeks an outlet in the sexual sphere itself rather than in other activities. If we are to reach a full understanding of adolescence we must necessarily bear in mind other facts besides sexuality. We have already mentioned that the overcoming of infantile egocentricity does not diminish the ego but develops and strengthens it. The adolescent thirsts for appreciation from others and aspires to a social status which will afford him prestige, which will acknowledge his capacity to act on his own initiative and with a certain independence. In our own culture the social environment stimulates him to competition, efficiency and acquisition, and we regret to say that it offers him a chaos of values, some of which are morally unsound. For instance, the conviction is only too widespread that the important thing is to get on in the world, without paying too much attention to the niceties of moral observance, and this conviction is readily accepted by the adolescent. Fortunately, though, he is also open to what is best in human nature. Enterprise, generosity, courage, self-denial and intolerance of what seems unfair are found in the adolescent, while too many adults have lost these qualities and often look on them with a superior air as the products of youthful idealism which must give way before the would-be mature man's realism. Adolescence, like childhood, is a transition phase, but a unique one from the point of view of personal development.

A final remark is fitting here. Although adolescence is a period of transition in which changes take place, there is also something which stands firm and indeed the change would not be noticed if it were not for the existence of something permanent. A young person enters on adolescence with pre-constituted structures which must adapt themselves to new situations but which cannot be completely overcome without causing disorder. These structures are formed in the interaction between individual and environment and they inevitably involve factors that are innate and acquired, individual and social. A need can be satisfied in various ways but among these the more habitually repeatable ones acquire a preference (G. Murphy's 'canalization'). In this way the number of possibilities of behaviour is limited and personal development is marked with a certain continuity. These 'habitual ways of responding' (as I believe they have been called by Goldstein) sensitize the individual to some aspects of the situation, and unless they are altered deliberately or by chance at some stage in the development of the personality, they will very probably decide the direction development is to take in the succeeding phase (Cameron). Even though there are unknown factors in adolescence it is neither independent of childhood nor without effect upon adulthood.

Social conditions and adolescence

The importance of social conditions, on which American psychologists insist particularly, has been pointed out by the anthropologico-cultural school (R. Benedict, M. Mead, C. Kluckhohn). In primitive societies, such as the Samoa Island community studied by Mead, the transition from childhood to adolescence, regulated by fixed customs, takes place without the emotional upset which we associate with this phase of development. W. D. Wall has pointed out that in Western civilization prior to Rousseau and the Romantic movement few traces of the adolescent crisis were to be found, although great writers had admirably described human passions.[33] It was only with the advent of Rousseau that adolescence presented itself as a psychological problem, described by the Romantic writers as 'storm and stress'. 'It is not without significance,' observes Wall, 'that this marked increase in the treatment of adolescence as a literary theme should coincide with the beginning of the industrial revolution. It lends colour to the view put forward by Trotter, Hollingworth and others, that in our culture there are, for the adolescent, provocations to upset not so strongly presented to the child or to the adult.'

Wall also mentions Terman's studies on young people of supernormal intelligence and concludes that a high level of intelligence tends to make its possessor have considerably more difficulty in making social adjustments since he is obliged to choose companions only from his contemporaries. Wall believes that many descriptions of 'storm and stress' in literature are due to the difficulty experienced by the supernormal adolescent in adapting to an environment largely peopled by those of lesser intellectual maturity than himself. There is a certain amount of truth in this theory as opposed to a tendency during recent years to dramatize adolescence. I suspect that this tendency sets more store on the attainment of a precocious but uninspired intellectual adulthood than on the pursuit of an ideal in adolescence. This kind of adulthood ends in depressing and dangerous ennui. But even in this case the importance of social environment would emerge, revealed by the monotonous insistence today on the topics of wealth, enjoyment and sex.

The religious crisis in adolescence.

Adolescence inevitably entails a religious crisis, a period of weaning and growth in the young person's religious sense. The adolescent is no longer satisfied with the ideas which sufficed for him as a child and he looks ahead eagerly yet fearfully to the demands of adulthood. He is no longer content to accept

[33] W. D. Wall, *The Adolescent Child*, Methuen, London, 1948, p. 11.

the secondhand mental furnishings prepared by others, but wants to choose them according to his own tastes.[34] He flatters himself that he is doing things his own way, while he is really following paths already trodden by others, and he is afraid of being considered still a child.

The adolescent's religious reactions can vary greatly. He may give up his religion completely or become excessively attached to it; he may choose an intermediate attitude of indifference and opportunism, or there may be a well-balanced revision of his life and deliberate dedication to an ideal. One thing would appear certain, namely, that religious feeling is one of the more delicate aspects of adolescence and perhaps for this reason all the more difficult. The process of religious adaptation in adolescence has a certain influence over later life. The sexual urge, with its subtle and upsetting effects on emotional life, is one of the most distressing elements, especially if the adolescent is deprived of suitable guidance. The struggle between impulse and prohibition can be exaggerated to an intolerable extent by the young person's erroneous evaluation of his situation, and religious motives almost invariably enter in to increase his distress. He seems to be faced with a choice. He feels he must either yield to the impulse and repudiate his religion or else accept the latter in its strictest form with the continual fear of real transgressions or, worse still, of moods and situations which he mistakenly considers sinful.

Father Mailloux mentions 'the extreme ambivalence which is concomitant with the kind of defensive reaction described by Anna Freud under the name of adolescent asceticism. When failing in their energetic attempts to control their instinctual impulses through total renunciation, adolescents may be expected to swing alternately from an intensely religious attitude to an equally violent rejection of all religious practices.'[35] This sort of behaviour has been observed by Father Mailloux in so-called scrupulous persons who have been

---

[34] G. W. Allport, *Religion in the Developing Personality*, Academy of Religion and Mental Health, New York, 1960, p. 34.
[35] N. Mailloux, *ibid*., p. 41.

meticulously conscientious in moral and religious practice but later slip into complete indifference and declare that they feel at peace only when they steer clear of moral problems and forget about their faith. Actually, an excessively insistent guilt sense in regard to sexual life can be the prelude to abandonment of religious practice, which is considered an intolerable burden.

Cognitive and social aspects of adolescent religion.

Another characteristic aspect of adolescence is the broadening of the cognitive horizon by the use of abstract thought and deductive logic which leads to emancipated judgment and a critical sense. The adolescent becomes aware that many religious explanations which he accepted as a child are no longer tenable. Gifts and little brothers are not brought by invisible angels. Prayers do not always obtain the desired effect whereas petitions addressed to parents, possibly backed up by tantrums, meet with greater success. In the world things happen which a good master and ruler, if he existed, would not tolerate.

The adolescent now 'knows' that things do not proceed as he had been led to believe as a child. He is aware, too, that the very people who taught him knew that these things were untrue and he is not yet capable of distinguishing between religious intuition and the form in which it is expressed. The certainty with which he previously accepted what he was told by grown-ups is now transferred to the things he believes he has found out for himself but which are still mainly supplied by others. His relations with his parents are difficult. He discovers that they are not as perfect as he imagined and that he has a right to his freedom. Religion as practised in his childhood, largely dependent on the relationship with his parents, undergoes a process of liberation at this stage. His rejection of childhood religious ideas is at times accompanied by a sense of hostility towards his parents who are considered guilty of having imposed these ideas on him. Over-exacting and formalist religious observance on the part of parents leads to rebellion against their authority and at the same time against the religious practice itself. The adolescent's criticism is inevitably directed towards the religious behaviour of his co-religionists and the emancipation of his own age-group is an idea that strongly appeals to him.

The adolescent's place in society is also affected. He longs to reach a stage of equality with the adults around him and this impulse is perhaps even stronger and more decisive than the sexual urge itself. The latter very often receives a further stimulus from the desire to convince himself and others that he is now independent.

Where there is rivalry between various religious creeds, membership of a certain church or sect can be considered by the adolescent as an occasion to assert himself and fight with others, and therefore as a means of demonstrating his ability. Ausubel maintains that despite the general belief that American adolescents give up religious practice, this has not been proved. He declares that 'a majority of American adolescents belong to a church, usually the same church as their parents, attend church services once a month or more, have a favourable attitude towards the church, rely upon prayer and believe in a personal, omnipotent, omniscient God who, although bodyless, participated in the writing of the Bible and guides the affairs of men and nations'.[36]

In support of this statement Ausubel brings forward the results of numerous researches. We suspect, though, that the religious practice to which he refers is of a clearly institutional character. On the other hand, Allport points out that surveys on the religion of young people belonging to institutionalized religions indicate a meaningful correlation between racial prejudice and a religious feeling still very much bound up with general motives of personal advantage. This goes to show how difficult it is for the adolescent as well as for others to take stock of his religious sense and reshape it without allowing dangerous egocentric tendencies to get the upper hand.

The 'search for identity' which Erikson considers to be a

[36] D. P. Ausubel, *Theory and Problems of Adolescent Development*, Grune and Stratton, New York, 1954, p. 268.

typical quality of adolescence is expressed in the question 'Who am I?' involving the alternative 'Am I a child or an adult?' This aspiration is manifested not only in the search for social status but also in the young person's definition of his own existence in relation to the invisible 'Socius' whose presence is sensed even in a child's experience of religion. Although 'conversion' in adolescence is no longer the fashion nowadays, the adolescent's violent reaction against the religion of his childhood is an explicit or an implicit sign of his need to find something sure and immovable and absolute as a basis for his life. We are not surprised, then, to find in the young person at this stage a reawakening of the religious sense even though this may not last. There is danger that he may aim at too high an ideal and that failure to reach it may produce discouragement, a sense of guilt and petrifaction. But it is also possible that when the religious practices of childhood have been left behind the religious sense may continue in full vigour and become one of the most decisive factors in personal development.

The adolescent has not, of course, acquired perfect balance in the religious sphere as yet and he can only acquire it by repeated effort, by experience and exploration. But a religious sense which develops along these lines will be marked by deep conviction although it may not appear on the surface nor be easily moved to enthusiasm. Adolescence is a dangerous and difficult turning-point in the young person's life but it affords him possibilities of deepening and reinforcing his religious sense. Hence, while religious deprivation during early years diminishes the child's potentialities, an adolescent abandoned to his own devices—either through negligence or for fear of interfering with his freedom of decision—will be deprived, at a time when he is seeking personal identity in the continuity of subjective experience, of what is required to give life the meaning so necessary to him at this stage and also in his adult life later on. It is perfectly normal and right that he should be allowed to form his own personal convictions, but it is essential that he should be properly instructed in religion which constitutes such an important area of his life. This can be done tactfully, with due respect for his right to freedom, but firmly and surely to avoid all risk of misunderstanding on his part. Otherwise there will be a vacuum in his psychic life, unfilled by religion but open to the invasion of 'infantile survivals' in the most dangerous sense of this expression, even though they may be disguised beneath the appearance of independence, achieved or won, as the adolescent gives the impression of having asserted himself at last.

The values in adolescence.

During adolescence the young person must undoubtedly make an effort to get his bearings and to establish himself in an unfamiliar world where new and bewildering prospects open up before him. But this phase of development has another aspect, for it is now that life's ideals become strikingly evident. Beauty, personal capacity and justice appeal vividly to the young person and seem more exacting than biological needs themselves which he is ready to forgo for their sake. These ideals constitute a new need which induces him to break with everything that is a hindrance to their fulfilment, and they likewise oblige him to make a choice. This is the origin of the adolescent's daring and rebellious behaviour, his search for a hero whom he can imitate. But all this is far from clear to the young person himself and tends to upset him, for he is in danger of being deceived by these new capacities.

The meeting with a person of the opposite sex and the discovery of love appear to him in a beautiful and ecstatic light and he is perturbed rather than satisfied by the sexual urge. Sexual intercourse between adolescents, who seek immediate satisfaction like greedy children intent on having their sweets today and unwilling to wait till tomorrow, is in danger of settling down into sheer erotic enjoyment which becomes more and more demanding as time passes and is never really satisfied. The possibility of sublimation of sexual activity is therefore very doubtful, the possibility, that is, that the ideals and values of human life can spring from the repression of a primordial sexual energy.

The current interpretation is perhaps to be reversed: it is through the emergence of new requirements that adolescence channels sexuality and bestows on it its full human meaning. If the sexual encounter takes place on the purely biological and instinctual plane it is deprived of an essential factor and consequently engenders dangerous lack of balance. Psychoanalytic treatment deals with the control of instinctive impulses but remains sterile and ineffective if it fails to establish a right balance between values. Sexuality has a stimulating function upon the adolescent's new capacities but it cannot be identified with these.

Adolescence also opens up new horizons where the religious sense is concerned. At certain moments the adolescent is filled with an inexplicable feeling of joy and admiration, a sense of belonging to something great and mysterious which is certain and secure. This feeling can coincide with all sorts of different and unforseen circumstances. It can make itself felt in the contemplation of nature or of a work of art, in moments of recollection or solitude, but it can also surge up on quite ordinary and commonplace occasions, on hearing a popular song or passing down a street where one has frequently been before without receiving any impression in particular. There is a peculiar charm in this feeling which some describe as cosmic or mystic and it is impossible to express it adequately in words, which would in fact deprive it of its essential note.

It might appear that few people experience this feeling, but this is not so. It is true that few people experience it frequently and with particular insistence but on the other hand many and perhaps all have had at least some fleeting experience of the kind. Such feelings cannot be reproduced at will even when we place ourselves in the identical conditions in which they previously made their appearance. Some may consider them to be just one of the many odd things that occur in the course of life and may turn to other more easily accessible forms of pleasure, hankering after the transitory and elusive experience of joy in varied and vehement forms of so-called amusements or in the use of intoxicating substances ranging from the most harmless to the most injurious. (Man has an incredible, insistent and often exasperatingly monotonous need to escape from himself and to seek a sensation which he experienced at a certain moment but which he tries in vain to recapture.)

In some people, though, the so-called cosmic or mystic experience leaves lasting traces, and these feel the need to examine it more deeply so as to give it a meaning and an expressive outlet.[37] Here we have the torment which usually

---

[37] A most interesting book is *The Physical Basis of Personality*, by the physiologist V. Mottram (Penguin Books, London, 1949). After having illustrated the determinism which regulates the development of functions of the human organism (hereditary genes, nervous system and endocrine system) the author devotes the final chapter to mystical experience. The point is, says Mottram, that these mystical experiences are much more common than is generally imagined and they have appeared among all peoples. Although they are expressed in different forms, 'there is a fundamental agreement in what they say', and 'behind all phenomena there is a unity'. It is not a question of something abstract, like intellectual knowing, but concrete, like sense experience. 'I know, for instance, that "I am" much more certainly than I know that the pen with which I am writing these words "is". I know of the existence of the pen only through the sense impressions I obtain from it. But I need no sensory approaches to tell me that I am.' So also, in the case of mystical experience. The fundamental agreement in the mystical experiences of people in all parts of the world convinces us that these, like the principles of science, physics and chemistry, are everywhere the same although expressed in different languages. Mystical experience points to a single Reality, by different expressions. In this light the 'familiar thing which we call self, this assertive, greedy and sensual thing, compact of egoism, selfish desires, odd moods and passions and of outstanding characteristics, which we dub personality is an imposture and a delusion. So I throw out the suggestion that the real "I", the core of our being, that thing so alien from the everyday "I", is a spark, an atom of the fundamental Reality in the universe, but that its activities are conditioned by inheritance and nurture. . . . Man is divided against himself and only becomes whole . . . when the everyday "I" becomes one with the inner I' (pp. 137-47).

It is rather surprising to hear these ideas expressed by a man who spent his life in a laboratory, occupied with experiments and calculations which require to be tested and verified. But it may be the outburst of one who feels that the accumulation of facts cannot throw light on the Mystery which envelops and permeates us. As well as Mottram we may recall the appreciation of mysticism by the biologist Alexis Carrel, in *Man, the Unknown* (Harper, New York, 1939; paperback edition,

accompanies artistic, literary, religious or even scientific intuition. Religious feeling is accentuated when related with a Being whose presence is felt in an atmosphere of mystery and adoration. The place in the world sought by the adolescent appears in this perspective as belonging to a great and splendid order. But everything remains vague as in a dream (one of Freud's correspondents described his religious sense as oceanic), and it only assumes concrete form when subjective experience comes into contact with objects, which also have their meaning in the cosmic order and become symbols and expressions of power or of beings. Note once more how both theistic and pantheistic religion is due to the need to give a meaning to ourselves and to the universe: it is the sign of a state of insecurity and therefore emerges more fully in critical periods of our lives. From this point of view Father A. Bertocci defines religion as 'creative insecurity'.[38]

The reader will readily understand that there has been no attempt here to explain religion as manifested in individual adolescents, but merely an effort to understand its general terms. The religious ceremonies of most 'cultures' dwell on this turning-point in man's life, just as they draw attention to the decisive moments of human existence: birth, marriage and death. Even the most secularized cultures are obliged to stress these events.

Burns Oates, London, 1961) and by the surgeon K. Walker, in *Diagnosis of Man* (Penguin Books, London, 1962). But it is to be noted that mystical experience does not necessarily lead people to accept a religious belief. It can mark the starting-point for a deeper examination and articulation of religious feeling, but it can also be abandoned as singularity or attached to futile behaviour, or it can even cause people to give up religious practice, which they judge to be sterile outward conformity. Genuine mystics have always been diffident in regard to sensational manifestations of mystical life. On the other hand, authors who practised no religion (e.g. H. G. Wells and Aldous Huxley) have reported personal mystical experiences, and people are not lacking who have mystical experiences and become fanatical preachers of animal protection or vegetarianism.

[38] P. A. Bertocci, *Religion as Creative Insecurity*, Association Press, New York, 1961.

The religious sense in adult life

Psychological maturity.

In describing 'religious experience', or religion as it is subjectively lived, we have been obliged to deal with it in the complete form in which it is manifested during adulthood. But now that we come to examine its presence in the 'mature man' we must acknowledge that it is difficult to define psychological maturity. Yet this expression is now so generally employed as a discriminating criterion that we cannot avoid it. When we speak of maturity we have in mind the manner in which a living organism develops, moving up to a culminating point and then declining. Maturity coincides with the highest point and therefore implies full development of all capacities: the process leading up to the peak point is called 'becoming mature' or 'maturation'.

In the psychological field the term 'maturation' lends itself to a great many different interpretations. There is much discussion as to whether this process is guided by internal causes or by environmental factors and psychologists who accept the influence of both elements have not succeeded in determining the precise part played by each. They speak of maturation with reference to the anatomo-physiological structures indispensable for the regulation of behaviour, with reference to the succession of psychic structures and with reference to possibilities of learning. We are faced with the same interpretations as in the case of embryonic development: the theory of preformation, epigenesis and ideal type.

If we are to start off, then, from a genetic presupposition, the situation is not only complicated but confused. We remain at the stage where we ask 'how' is maturity reached but we cannot define it, while we are convinced that the entire process of development must lead to maturity and otherwise has no meaning. When we propose to state what we mean by maturity the situation is equally confused. We generally make use of three criteria: a criterion of time: at a mature age certain characteristics are manifest; a criterion of level: the majority of people at that age possess these qualities; and one of efficiency: the actualization of these qualities must take place smoothly, harmoniously and without hindrance. But I hasten to add that in the case of fundamental aspects of psychic activity it is evident that each of these can achieve its own maturity with a certain degree of independence in regard to the others. Thus we distinguish intellectual, emotional, conative and social maturity, and tests have been devised for an evaluation of each of these. All this obviously makes an overall appraisal of maturity between the ages of twenty-one and sixty-five extremely difficult and questionable. The general evaluation of maturity used in comparing different individuals and the principle of appropriate and efficient adaptation are partly arbitrary and partly ill-defined criteria even though they actually constitute the framework of 'maturity tests'.

This does not necessarily mean that predominantly intuitive estimates of a person's maturity, because of their failure to reach exact results, are to be discarded completely. The Institute of Personality Assessment and Research at the University of California asked the various university departments to rate graduate students for 'all round soundness as a person', defined as 'the balance and degree of maturity which the individual shows in his relations with other people'. Eighty of the rated students were then brought together for an intensive period of testing. The results showed an adequate (though imperfect) correlation between the independent ratings and those obtained by means of technical methods and psychological study. The chief personality differences between sound and not so sound students were four in number ('sound' being understood in this context as 'mature'): effective organization of work towards goals; correct perception of reality; character and integrity in the ethical sense; interpersonal and intrapersonal adjustment.[39] It can be understood how the conceptual antithetic pairing 'maturity and immaturity' which

[39] G. W. Allport, *Pattern and Growth in Personality*, Holt, Rinehart and Winston, New York and London, 1964, pp. 278 ff.

we apply to personality is analogous to other conceptual pairs such as normal and abnormal, healthy and sick, which are indispensable for the purpose of rating but are very difficult to analyse. Moreover, the words 'mature' and 'immature' have a strong emotive tonality. Nobody likes to be considered immature.

The psychoanalytic theory, according to which immaturity coincides with abnormalities (since these are said to be caused by stoppages or deviations in development), has increased the anxiety of a great many people desirous of being assured of their complete maturity and immunity from infantile survivals. In response to the question: 'What is psychological maturity?' a psychiatrist has given the following subtle reply:

> One might say, paradoxically, that it is immature to imagine that any human being could be completely mature. The more one becomes grown-up oneself, the more one realizes that there are no grown-ups. Nor am I certain that, as most people conceive it, maturity is even a very satisfactory ideal at which to aim. For, if we succeed in overcoming or discarding all our childish characteristics, are we not throwing out the baby with the bath-water? When one describes this condition of maturity, life itself escapes. There are certainly some people who, by middle life, seem to have stopped developing. They have reached a kind of stability and one knows that they will never change. But the price of their stability is ossification. They have become impervious to new experiences and they tend to talk in clichés, for their life has become stereotyped. . . . They might be said to have lost the child within, the child whose incomplete development is necessary if life is still to be a process of growth and still to be spontaneous.[40]

These considerations, very much to the point, open up before us a different view of maturity. It is not a state acquired by

[40] 'What is Psychological Maturity?' by a psychiatrist, in *The Listener*, London, 14 June 1962.

reaching a certain age, something which we then continue to possess without any further upset, a state which can be defined once and for all, which can be estimated in the individual and used to evaluate individuals. Rather it is a general condition marked by a particular manner of being, by a style which cannot be measured objectively but is still characteristic of the individual, a configuration recognizable not so much by its elements as by the manner of their arrangement. (But this statement is not to be taken as a profession of faith in the Gestalt theory.)

Traits of psychological maturity.

What are the features or attributes, then, which distinguish psychological maturity? If we were to endeavour to list them all, we would find that every author gives a list of different length. Fromm mentions a dictatorial attitude as a trait of immaturity; Freud gives two traits of maturity—the ability to love and to work; M. Jahoda mentions three attributes: control over one's environment, unity in one's personality, the capacity to see the world and oneself in the right light; Barron lists four traits, Shoben has five and Maslow mentions fourteen. Allport lists six qualities and shrewdly remarks that this 'seems to give a reasonable balance between distinctions too fine and too coarse for our purpose'.[41] We can take this as a fair standard, a well-balanced solution. In point of fact all the lists deal with the same things fundamentally while stressing some traits more or less exclusively. Allport's list runs as follows: extension of the sense of self; warm relating of self to others; emotional security; realistic perceptions, skills and assignments; self-objectivation, insight and humour; the unifying philosophy of life. We shall try for a moment to illustrate this list by a description of the mature personality.

The mature person has overcome the tendency to refer all things chiefly to himself and reaches out to an understanding

[41] G. W. Allport, *Pattern and Growth in Personality, op. cit.*, chapter 12.

of those around him. His understanding and his active sharing in the life of others is based on an affective relationship which combines intimacy with respect. Where he himself is concerned the mature person has arrived at a degree of self-mastery which is not just the elimination of impulses and conflicts. He is not in a permanent state of blissful calm but is capable of bearing trials and opposition coming from others and even more so his own interior trials, with a basic sense of security which keeps enthusiasm and anxiety within proper bounds. He has a realistic outlook on the world. He deals suitably with circumstances as they come and is efficient in his work commitments. He can observe his own life without indulging in useless or depressing self-analysis, aware of his own personal contribution to each situation and of the part played by others, with a certain sense of detachment. He is undoubtedly concerned about his own affairs and those of others, but is able to keep smiling. He is capable of consistent behaviour in every sphere of his life, basing everything he does on certain principles and values among which there is one which predominates.[42]

This descriptive translation of Allport's list is uninspiring and colourless, but it is sufficient to make us ask at once: where is the man who possesses all these requisites to the full? *Quis est iste, et laudabimus illum?* We can only remark that there is no question here of individual men, but of a kind of reference table which we can apply to men in the flesh without

---

[42] Each of the criteria of maturity listed by Allport, taken separately, could be interpreted in an unfavourable sense: extension of the sense of self could be a sign of swollen egoism and the desire to turn everything to one's own satisfaction; emotional security, subjectively considered, could coincide with the conviction that one cannot act otherwise; realistic perception, with more fully developed artificialism; self-objectivation, with an exaggerated opinion of one's own sentiments and judgement; the unifying philosophy of life, reduced to ordinary terms, could signify utility, enjoyment and personal well-being. Each of these qualities can be traced to a typically infantile source: egocentricity, dependence and basic trust, instinctual immediacy, realism, myth-making and identification; seeing everything in terms of the agreeable or disagreeable; narcissism.

going too deeply into their complexity, their capacity or their shortcomings. Any description of the mature personality, as we have already seen, is doomed from the outset to this limitation.

The religious sense in adulthood.

We are faced with a similar difficulty when we set out to describe the religious sense in people of mature age. Religion cannot be reduced to a more or less genuine final colour-wash applied to the personality. It is very often a meaningful expression of personality and its emphases as well as its deficiencies penetrate deeply into the structure of personality. It is true that few people reach full religious maturity, but if we are to recognize its possibilities we must appeal to its more harmonious and complete expressions so that we may compare these with strikingly or partially deficient forms.

The traits of adult personality are coloured in a particular way by the development of religious feeling. The tendency to refer everything to ourselves is overcome by the need to place ourselves in the presence of something bigger and more masterful than the individual. Interpersonal relations are deepened by personal and social religious adherence; emotional stability is fostered by the sense of participation in security; we are more independent in our perception of things, of men and of ourselves because we start off from the presupposition of something which surpasses the individual; our objectivation of ourselves is clear and more decided by reference to something outside the subjective; the unifying concept of life is greatly accentuated, for religion is really the attempt to find a meaning and an answer for the problems of existence.

Here too we can present a rough sketch of the mature religious person. The central point of his religion is not himself but God. 'The man who wants to have a sound religious sense,' said Meister Eckhart, 'must act as one who draws a perfect circle: his centre must be God and he must consider all things including himself as contained within the circle which he traces from this centre point. God is no day-labourer at

your beck and call. He cannot be treated like a cow to be led
to pasture so that you may have milk.'[48] And Socrates, to the
statement 'All things are measured by man', retorted: 'All
things are measured by God.'

The religious person's horizons are broad and radiant. His
vision is therefore a unitary one but it is also articulated and
differentiated. He does not fall into over-simplification: he
sees lines which suggest a design but do not present it fully,
like embroidery seen on the wrong side. This applies to others
and also to himself. He sees other people's failings but also
their abilities; he is painfully aware of his own defects but is
not overwhelmed by their manifestations or by the vexation
they occasion. Hence he is tolerant without being indifferent.
He is cheerfully and confidently enthusiastic but guards against
fanaticism which he considers to be a sign of weakness rather
than of strength. He is eager to see justice and goodness and
beauty flourish around him, but he is neither immobilized nor
embittered when he realizes that this is never fully and flaw-
lessly accomplished. He has a keen desire to share his convictions with others but his efforts in this direction are marked
by discretion and courtesy. His religion makes demands upon
him from the point of view of moral behaviour and indeed
religion and morality are fused, but this does not involve him
in puritanical attitudes. Although calm and cheerful, he is not
self-satisfied, but constantly seeks to understand more fully
and participate more deeply in the mystery of life by which
he is surrounded.

We could continue in this strain, but unfortunately this
picture errs in one respect: It is too good to be true!
Undoubtedly. But can we not set against it a slightly less
pleasant picture corresponding more closely to reality?
Religious people live in a world apart, into which they conveniently retire with the satisfaction of feeling themselves more
perfect than others, the possessors of a defence of which others
are deprived. It is true that they see things from a higher point

[48] Cf. O. Karrer, *Meister Eckhart Speaks*, Bloomsbury, London, 1957.

of view, but where their own interests are involved they act exactly like other men. Their self-control depends to a greater extent on the pride they take in being esteemed than on their forbearance. They expect a great deal of others and criticize them freely while finding little or no fault with themselves. They point out the close connection between religion and morality but in practice are adepts in the art of cloaking their own shortcomings with the mantle of religion, or if they acknowledge their defects they seek to set things right by convenient devotional practices. They can be very eloquent when it comes to describing the beauty and grandeur of religion, but when their emphatic declarations are put to the test they dissolve into thin air. The religion of mature persons, of 'respectable' people, is a convenient means of escape from personal responsibility. Besides, all the failings that we condemn in other people exist in religious people too. Religious feeling therefore makes no difference.

We could continue further along these lines, but at all events it must be acknowledged that there is some truth in criticism of this kind. However, this admission brings us no further. We are faced with two pictures, an optimistic and a sceptical one, both of them unreal. The second is probably the more convincing, since defects are more readily noticed than positive qualities. But the question still remains: Is religion more complete and mature in the first case or the second?

A comparison may be suggested. A great many people enjoy popular illustrated magazines, frivolous reading, light music, while they fail to appreciate pictures by the great masters, are bored by classical literature and fall asleep during the playing of good music, although they may loudly proclaim their admiration for these things. Are we to consider their artistic sense mature or insufficiently developed? I believe the same thing can be applied to the religious sense. In the vast majority of men this sense is poorly developed; it remains at the stage in which its possibilities are only partially manifested and not always in the best way. Mature religious behaviour requires a training which few people have received and a commitment which many of those who have been trained fail to practise.

Most people lack a really keen desire for the things they admire but consider too arduous for themselves; their social environment, moreover, fails to stimulate them to anything higher than purely conventional religious practice. Particularly in an acquisitive and competitive society such as our own there is a stimulation of qualities which do not conduce to mature religious activity. On the other hand it is incredible how tenaciously the religious sense clings to outdated forms and how it rebels against any direct attack on these. It slumbers peacefully once the outer forms are respected even though it is threatened from within.

An inadequately developed religious sense can coexist with patterns of behaviour which are contradictory to it and for which it serves as a cloak, exactly as in the sceptical picture of the mature religious person previously outlined. Actually these camouflages exist and psychoanalysis has certainly not been the first to discover them, although it has interpreted them in a new way. As Rümke tells us, Freud has shown that an image of God exists to which properties are attributed that do not pertain to pure and genuine religion but to symptoms closely connected with what we call neurosis. Psychoanalysts are in daily contact with neurosis against a religious background.

Rümke himself goes on to say:

It cannot be denied that in belief and its observances repressed ambitions are still satisfied in a sort of distorted way: from the remotest times up to today . . . the wish for meddling, intolerance, pseudo-religious slander (which also exists!) . . . the conviction of having found God sometimes misused in the service of vanity and unbridled narcissism. He who doubts that repressed sexuality may sublimate itself in pseudo-religious adoration lacks psychological discernment (let him read the esoteric writings on bridal mysticism). In fact, in the domain of religion, all human passions—

including the corrupt ones—are exhausted in a monstrous, sometimes unrecognizable way.[44]

Even some less dangerous forms of religious feeling, which are however strongly tinged with childishness, create an obstacle to deeper and more life-giving religion. An excessively human mental picture of God, of an over-indulgent or implacably harsh God; exaggerated familiarity or fear in his regard; the need to receive immediate satisfaction of the requests we present to God in prayer; expectation of an immediate reward for what we do: all these are images and attitudes which must be overcome if the religious impulse is not to be suffocated. We find all this set forth magnificently in the Bible, where we are given a strikingly realistic picture of the aberrations and meannesses opposed continually by men to the religious practice required of them by God. But this antagonism towards a God made to our own image and likeness, towards a God who runs counter to our plans, is a daily experience even in the life of deeply and genuinely religious men. There is therefore a discrepancy between what the religion of an adult can and ought to be and what it actually is. Adult religious behaviour is one thing and the religious behaviour of adults is quite another.

Religious 'maturity'.

What are the psychological causes of this disparity? We have already seen how social pressure stops at conformism, how it stimulates the development of other human abilities to a greater extent and how the subject's aspirations turn towards goals within easier reach. But it may be added that religious instruction ceases for all practical purposes when a man grows up and all that remains to him are the few notions acquired but not assimilated when he was a child with a child's mentality. So he either rejects these notions or holds on to them from habit or for convenience, or else he merely keeps them without

[44] H. C. Rümke, *The Psychology of Unbelief*, Rockliff, London, 1952, pp. 31-2.

examining them critically for fear of destroying them. But we must also bear in mind the incredible varieties of temperament and differences in education and social environment. If the religious sense is to ripen, it must undergo a time of trial. But even when trial and crisis bring about a religious awakening, progress does not always follow, either because the subject is ready to accept some compromise or because he finds it really difficult to separate the religious content from a mistaken formulation of it and fears that the acceptance of a more adequate statement of religion will result in rejection of the content itself.

Up to the present in speaking of development and maturation it may seem that I have not been very clear or have even contradicted myself by defending in the first place the survival of some infantile traits as a condition for complete maturity and subsequently admitting that the survival of other infantile qualities interferes with harmonious development. An explanation is therefore called for at this point. Development implies, as well as increase, a differentiation between the various developmental phases. Childhood differs from adolescence and adolescence from adulthood. If there were merely a transition of identical characteristics from one period to the next, how could we speak of difference or of newness? This is one of the weak points in Freud's theory that the 'id never changes', that infantile patterns of behaviour pass on to the adult and that anomalous behaviour in the adult is to be interpreted as infantile behaviour.

We can perhaps apply to Freud the opinion Manzoni expressed of Machiavelli when he said:

Machiavelli was perhaps the first of the moderns to go in search of remote causes of great historical events, a method which leads to fine discoveries when one works on a basis of truth. But it leads to wonderfully wild suppositions when we are led away by the happy connection we are pleased to find between a fact in the past and some later events and when we fail to examine separately the character and origin of the later events, so that we connect them with nothing but the earlier fact.[45]

If we believe instead that each phase implies something new, we are bound to acknowledge that a rearrangement has taken place, that there is a new articulation of pre-existent facts. Each phase possesses its own balance and its own maturity. We can speak appropriately of maturity in the child, of adolescent maturity and of adult maturity. When this equilibrium is lacking we ought first of all to try to discover the cause of the disaster in some contemporary event. If this investigation produces negative results, then we may presume that something in the previous period has become petrified and inflexible and has not been assimilated. In this sense we can speak of survivals from childhood, although the structure and general resonance of the adult's neurotic or antisocial behaviour are very different from the behaviour of a child.

Those very qualities of childhood that are indispensable to the adult, namely, enthusiasm, spontaneity and trust, can become an obstacle to maturity if they are not assimilated. Thoughtlessness, boastfulness and foolish credulousness are these very qualities which fail to harmonize with adult requirements. Maturity does not consist in successful adjustment, which can even slow down the movement towards maturity. People who are said to be eternal children or eternal adolescents, and certainly not as a title of honour, have been satisfied with a process of adjustment and have gone no further. Maturity, on the other hand, is marked by effective and well-balanced mastery of one's own life, and this does not mean suppressing the sources of trouble but dealing with them effectively. It is not the jarring notes and conflicts of life which obstruct the path to maturity, but our own attitude towards them. If we have gained the mastery over these things, then we have reached maturity, even though our attitude be merely one of forbearance.

[45] A. Manzoni, 'Discorso sopra alcuni punti della storia longobardica in Italia' in *Opere varie*, Milan, 1845, p. 273.

With reference to religious maturity what has just been said is particularly important. The religious man who has reached an Olympian serenity which carries him unperturbed through upheavals in his environment and through personal mental stress is not necessarily mature. But the man who is painfully aware of his own inadequacy yet does not rebel or become disheartened is mature, for he views himself and all things against a background of ineffable certainty and grandeur. The religious sense of an adult can be defective, paltry, contradictory and even cowardly, but there is no religious maturity unless these deficiencies occasion suffering, a keen desire to eliminate them, the resolute will to resist them and a sense of confidence even when results fall short of what was desired.

Our preconceived ideas concerning infantile survivals must not cause us to treat with lofty contempt the many simple and humble folk who manifest their religion in apparently childish forms, but who have none the less reached genuine religious maturity of a refreshing and often heroic kind which ought to be the object of our admiration. A poor woman saying her prayers and placing flowers before the statue of Mary, a neurotic and even a criminal, can possess a more mature religious sense than an intellectual who parades his knowledge of 'religious problematics' and a mystic who takes pride in his state. 'Why do you recite the prayers in the prayer books when you don't even understand the words?' a cynical young Jew used to ask his grandfather who said his prayers regularly in the Hebrew tongue which he did not know. 'Why do I have to understand if the One Above understands?' was the old man's habitual reply. A perfect example of genuine religious maturity.[46]

Irreligion

The religious sense undergoes a process of development. Why does this process sometimes fall short of completion? Why

[46] D. Bakan, *Sigmund Freud and the Jewish Mystical Tradition*, Van Nostrand, Princeton, N.J., 1958.

does it become petrified and decline? What do faith and incredulity mean? This is a complex problem that has been discussed in a book written by the Dutch psychiatrist, H. C. Rümke, a densely packed work which for that reason is not always easy to understand.[47] I shall refer here mainly to Rümke's treatment of this subject.

Rümke points out that 'if we define "beliefs" as something we consider true, something we are in agreement with regardless of being unable to supply a sufficiency of intellectual reasons for it, we may immediately conclude that there are no people who do not believe'.[48] All are obliged to take many things on trust and if we decided to act henceforth on objective knowledge alone, life would be undermined by the paralysing doubts which are typical of certain pathological cases. Religious unbelief has the typical characteristics of religious belief, including the negative ones of rigidity, narrow-mindedness, fanaticism and persecution.

On the basis of his practice as a psychiatrist and psychotherapist Rümke formulated the following working hypothesis to serve as a point of departure. Belief is something which accompanies us in our psychological development in various forms; unbelief is an interruption in development. This hypothesis reverses Freud's theory that religious belief is a survival from childhood. According to Rümke such a hypothesis is scientifically as fully justified as the hypothesis that religious experience is not a primary experience but something we can reduce to some other experience. Moreover, the hypothesis of religion as a process of development accords with the facts of mental development from childhood to adulthood. In the question the child asks about the world, in his animistic attitude, in the way he listens to stories, he is already exercising a form of faith. After his sixth year he readily accepts the explanations he is given. It is only later on, at the age of puberty, that there is a faith which looks for reasons and therefore a personal, religious faith. Rümke therefore believes that

[47] H. C. Rümke, *The Psychology of Unbelief, op. cit.*
[48] *Ibid.*, Introduction, p. ix.

faith develops according to the child's mental development and that on purely empirical grounds we may speak of degrees or phases in religious experience which must follow each other in a set order.

The basis of religion is to be found in the vague sense of being 'linked up with the whole of being'. This 'whole of being' makes itself felt as the cause of being in all things and the cause of personal individual existence. This realization comes about at the age of puberty but its roots are already present when the child becomes aware of himself as distinct from the world around him (in early childhood) and when he becomes detached from his parents (in later childhood). Religious faith properly so-called is born when the young person realizes that the source of all being and of his own personal existence is God. This may come about through verbal learning, but the words are laden with deep cognitive and emotional significance. Religious faith then proceeds to develop in the form of obedience to an urgent question, the response to which involves the responsibility of giving or refusing unconditional allegiance. A great many people fail to get beyond a vague religious sense limited to a few infantile symbols and bound up with an irrational impulse which they jealously defend against all possibility of attack.

Those who get beyond this stage by acquiring deeper knowledge and a richer personal experience of their religion pass on to a broad, all-embracing and harmonious religious belief and complete dedication to this ideal. From the numerical point of view there is a gradual falling off at this stage but there is an enrichment of religious qualities in those who continue.

The itinerary traced by Rümke is not really as clear as may appear from this description and he himself points out the psychological conditions which favour it on the one hand or create obstacles on the other.

Because of the close connection between psychological development and religious growth, both are subject to traumas, conflicts, stoppages and regression. Rümke repeats in psychological terms the observations already made by the moralists concerning the duplicity of human passions and he goes on to describe the more noteworthy neurotic complications which can mark religious development.

Rümke says:

> I have treated many people by psychoanalysis, and in the course of analysis I have never seen real belief founder, but repressed belief—which occurs quite often—has been liberated through analysis. A second argument is the experience I have had so often, that so-called unbelief shows a much stronger affinity with neurosis than real belief. We see this, first of all, in Freud's work: he describes, in fact, unreal belief.[49]

Infantile superstructures constitute an obstacle to religious development: excessive stress on the father-image; rebellion against God; an over-familiar attitude towards God; exaggerated desire of reward; excessive fear; a sense of frustration when prayers go unanswered.

Certain neurotic traits can also bar the way: prohibitions based on ambition; a tendency to interfere in other people's business; intolerance; slander with a religious background; religious vanity and narcissism; sexuality sublimated into pseudo-religion.

Doubt is not a factor of unbelief. If it is free from a sense of guilt and is not the object of boasting, doubt is a stimulus to liberation and purification of motives and leads to deeper religious conviction.

On the other hand faith is greatly endangered when a person delights in seeking out and laying bare the inadequacies and weaknesses of religion and goes no further. He thus practises a purely negative psychology, or a 'critical' one—by which description such people seek to justify their attitude. When people stop at the first deficiencies in religion and pay attention chiefly to its negative aspects, they are prevented from observing the positive and much more important aspects which only reveal their meaningfulness when deeply and thoroughly

[49] *Ibid.*, p. 34.

examined. Hence this attitude tends to degenerate into sceptical irreligion.

The question of religious unbelief has been studied from the psycho-social point of view by Gustav Jahoda.[50] The vast majority of people receive at least a limited degree of religious instruction during childhood, yet a great number abandon or neglect their religion when they reach maturity. What is the psychological explanation of this fact? By observation of people in the mass and in groups and with the help of a questionnaire, Jahoda has sought to establish *what* changes come about in the religious attitude, *when* and *why* they have taken place, in the opinion of the people concerned, and *what persons and groups* have contributed to these changes. The general conclusion is that the vast majority of unbelievers come from families devoid of deep religious convictions. A third of the existing non-believers recall a sense of guilt which became violent in the period between six and nine years of age and to which the parents paid no attention. Religious indifference begins with separation from the family for one reason or another and in particular circumstances (working environment, change of residence, marriage). The reasons advanced are generally very superficial; they denote insufficient religious knowledge and reflect the opinions and prejudices picked up from the environment. Although individuals and social groups evidently contribute much to this situation, most non-believers are unaware of this fact. At most they will admit that one person or another has influenced them but they refuse to acknowledge the part played by social groups.

A survey carried out by Gillespie and Allport in various ethnic and social groups shows with surprising regularity that seventy per cent consider it necessary to give a religious meaning to their lives, even if their religious practice is inadequate or takes the most varied forms.[51] This would lead us to con-

[50] G. Jahoda, 'The Genesis of Non-Belief' in *New Outlook*, vol. I, London, 1952.

[51] J. M. Gillespie and G. W. Allport, *Youth's Outlook on the Future*, Doubleday, New York, 1955.

I

clude that the actual irreligion of the vast majority of people is not a rejection of religion but a rudimentary form of religion containing a strong though unconscious emotional element. This is often diverted towards substitute objects and possesses the primitive and dangerous qualities of unconscious activity inherent in the individual or consequent on relations between individuals.

7. 'Scientific' and 'Secular' Religion

Science and faith, science and religion, have all the appearance of two enemies engaged in mortal combat: reason versus illusion, progress versus immobility, freedom versus slavery. When we observe them more closely we may describe them rather as *zwei feindliche Brüder*, two hostile brothers who detest each other because they have many things in common over which each is determined to rule supreme. Is there any science which does not rest on faith? Or any faith which is not bound up with some science? We greatly doubt it when we consider how, prior to the birth of the two hostile brothers, knowledge and religion lived side by side during a long and by no means sterile period; and when we realize, moreover, that science has necessarily many religious aspects while religion is a compendium of knowledge, or in other words, a science. Both religion and science, after all, are seeking to paint a picture of the world and of man.

It may be interesting, then, to examine some forms of religion which have developed in the realm of science, or, rather, in the various realms into which it is now being subdivided. What concerns us here is to grasp its characteristics rather than to review it exhaustively.

Religion and the concept of the physical world

Newton was responsible for the first impressive plan which unified the physical forces at work in the universe. To him the world no longer appeared as directly ruled by extraneous entities but as subject to a universal law. He visualized God as the irremovable remnant of mystery, as the great Architect of the universe, the manager of this immense establishment which is the work of his hand, who dwindles to a mere hypothesis which can be dispensed with or replaced, without detriment, perhaps, or indeed even to man's advantage. Not that Newton himself expressed such ideas, for he was a man of deep religious faith and devoted much of his time to studying the Bible. But the wave of naturalistic deism and illuminism which has swept over the world from the eighteenth century up to the present day is largely the repercussion of the new concept of the physical world introduced by Newton. One of its religious expressions is freemasonry.

In the deep study which Bernard Fay has offered us, supported by ample documentary evidence, freemasonry appears as a 'thinking society chiefly concerned with acting on men's hearts and minds, and whatever it may have to say for itself it is a form of religion'.[1] The great invention of freemasonry was 'the establishment of an era of comradeship in the name of fraternity and brotherly love as a substitute for Christian charity, just as its great intellectual and mystical achievement was the replacing of dogmatic religions with a spiritualist mysticism, a scientific religion, a cosmic mysticism'.

By means of its initiation rites, by the mysterious atmosphere of its lodges and by its vague belief in a supreme Being, freemasonry created bonds of solidarity between men whose ideas differed widely but whose aim was to reach certain concrete objectives. In some countries, particularly in England, it fulfilled a philanthropic and moralizing function and numbered among its supporters a number of ecclesiastics. Benjamin Franklin was one of its more representative and influential leaders in America. After a wild and adventurous youth he reached a religious crisis and became a freemason. A good deal of the prestige attached to his name in France during the period leading up to the Revolution is to be attributed to the activity of the masonic lodges.

[1] B. Fay, *Le franc-maçonnerie et la revolution intellectuelle du XVIII siècle*, Ed. de Cluny, Paris, 1935.

Religion and the biological world

Another event which produced deep reverberations, this time in the field of the biological sciences, was Darwin's theory of evolution. It challenged the literal interpretation of the Bible and was fiercely opposed by Protestants, for despite their principle of free examination they were not prepared to sacrifice the literal veracity of the Bible. Moreover, Darwin's evolutionism eliminated the barrier between man and the animals. It presented man as a more complex form of animal organism, derived from a numberless succession of other animals, all subject to fortuitous changes, in which individuals possessing unfavourable qualities were eliminated and those with useful qualities survived. Man was therefore stripped of the superiority which he had always considered himself to possess in relation to the animal world and his appearance on the earth was attributed to a process of development in purely natural life.

Darwin himself realized at a certain stage that his theory was in no way opposed to the greatness of the Divinity. Actually in *The Origin of Species* he concludes by saying: 'There is grandeur in this view of life, with its several powers having been originally breathed by the Creator into a few forms or into one; and that while this planet has gone cycling on according to the forced law of gravity, from so simple a beginning endless forms most beautiful and most wonderful have been and are being evolved.'[2] But this intuition vanished from the life of Darwin at a later stage, and towards the end of his days he declared that he had lost all interest in art and religion.

The evolutionary theory popularized the principle that man is a natural being like others and only differs from the animals by the fact that his organism is richer and more complex. It held that since evolution is the effect of fortuitous changes, God was no longer obliged to exercise control over it, just as

[2] C. Darwin, *The Origin of Species*, Dent and Sons, London, 1958, p. 463.

it is no longer necessary for him to control the movement of the sun, moon and stars. Sir Arthur Keith, one of Darwin's disciples, declared that Darwin 'had done more than anyone to lift the "pall of superstition" from mankind' and that by the discovery of natural selection he had brought about a total revolution in ideas about man and all living creatures. Keith considered Darwinism to be 'a basal doctrine in the rationalist liturgy'. These words contain all the elements of a new religion: liberation, a new concept of the world, and the exaltation of reason.

One of Darwin's most enthusiastic followers, Thomas H. Huxley, who combined astute reasoning with the zeal of a propagandist, when arguing with theologians and non-theologians about the five days of creation, about Noah's Ark and Jonah and the whale, had no difficulty in propagating a liberal, agnostic and scientific religion in a society in which respect for formalities was merely a cloak for a deeply sceptical and utilitarian mentality.

Huxley's earliest book, *Man's Place in Nature and Other Essays*, published in 1863, was followed by an endless series of works by other authors on the same subject. Huxley himself writes:

> Our reverence for the nobility of manhood will not be lessened by the knowledge that Man is, in substance and in structure, one with the brutes; for he alone possesses the marvellous endowment of intelligible and rational speech, whereby, in the secular period of his existence, he has slowly accumulated and organized the experience which is almost wholly lost with the cessation of every individual life in other animals.[3]

These words contain a statement which is undoubtedly correct. But it is only a partial statement and it embodies the programme of a current of thought which is still very strong today.

[3] Thomas Huxley, *Man's Place in Nature and Other Essays*, Macmillan, London, 1901, pp. 155-6. The preceding quotation is from W. R. Thompson in the Introduction to C. Darwin, *The Origin of Species*, London, 1958, p. xxii.

Thomas Huxley's own case (which reminds us of B. Franklin's) is an interesting one from our point of view. He relates in a letter:

Thrown out into the world as I was without guidance or experience, I confess that I tasted sin as few people have done. Fortunately I was stopped in time, before I came to destruction, and I spent many years climbing back uphill, slowly, painfully and with many relapses. Looking back, what do I see as the factors of my redemption? The hope of an immortal life or a future reward? I must honestly declare that in all those years such a consideration never entered my head. No, and I shall tell you exactly what was at work within me: *Sartor resartus* has taught me that a profound religious sense is compatible with a complete absence of theology. In the second place, science and its method has offered me a firm basis independent of the principle of authority and tradition. Third, love has opened up to me a new vision of the holiness of human nature and has impressed upon me a deep sense of responsibility. If today I am a human carcass, a corrupt and dissolute man, if my destiny has been and is to be to further the advance of science, if I have today the slightest right to the love of those around me, if in the supreme moment when I looked down into the grave of my little boy my sorrow was full of submission and free from all bitterness, this is due to these three factors at work within me, and not because I ever worried as to whether my poor personality was to remain eternally distinct from that All from which it was born and to which it will return.[4]

This is a beautiful page, touching in its sincerity. The psychological motives of a scientific religion could not be more effectively indicated than they are in these phrases: the independence of personal religious experience from a doctrinal

[4] Quoted by E. Padoa in the Italian edition of T. Huxley, *Man's Place in Nature*: Letter of Huxley to a friend in 1860 in reply to a letter of sympathy on the death of Noel, Huxley's firstborn son.

content; the capacity of science to take the place of religious doctrine; love, with which religion is always and necessarily linked.

'Scientific humanism' pursues the path opened up by Thomas Huxley with his grandsons Julian (the zoologist) and Aldous (the writer). A recently published collection of essays entitled *The Humanist Frame* begins with a programmatic essay by Julian Huxley and ends with an article by Aldous.[5] The collection comprises contributions by many authors, who set forth the point of view of scientific humanism in their respective provinces.

Huxley's thinking may be summarized as follows. Science and human nature constitute the inevitable antinomy of our times. Intimately connected, they nevertheless give rise to profound conflicts. Man benefits by science but he is also damaged by it. Science offers us a picture of the world that is so extensive and yet so pulverized, both in what is infinitely great and what is infinitely small, that the elementary ideas of daily life are absolutely incapable of holding their own before it. Even the most gifted imagination is unable to depict a world of which the supreme rulers are abstract things. It is an unreal world in comparison to the one in which men live and operate and which is 'real' to them. The idea of an unreal world fills them with consternation, with a sense of nothingness, of personal annihilation.

On the other hand science has penetrated deeply into the very 'world' of human experience which it has not only modified but transformed. Think of how men live today in large cities and even in more scattered human communities. How different is their life in all that concerns nutrition, defence, conveniences and possibilities of communication from the life of the savage and even the life of men of a few centuries ago. It is a life bound to all the things science has discovered and utilized. Science comes forward as the gradual, certain and inevitable conqueror of the world around us and of ourselves who live in

[5] Julian Huxley and others, *The Humanist Frame*, Harper and Brothers, New York, 1961.

it. Yet science does not furnish the answer to all human requirements. Its cold, methodical intellectualism takes no account of man's affective and religious needs. In contrast with the 'dehumanized' scientific theory of the world, we have the idea which hinges on man himself who is the author of science and controls it for his own benefit, but who feels pulsating within him a life which science seems to ignore.

This is the humanist concept of life, but it runs the risk of petrifaction in defensive attitudes towards conventional realities (religious factors of a doctrinal or prohibitive nature) and of clinging so tenaciously to these attitudes as to obstruct science in the discovery of far from illusory realities. While science, then, is impersonal, humanism is decidedly personal, for even when it uses general concepts it expresses the relation of a person to other persons or to individual objects. A picture is not a combination of technical rules: it is *that* picture which reveals the man who created it. A man one loves or hates is *that* man and not the general idea of a man. A thing to be done or not to be done is *that* particular thing and not the category to which it belongs.

Religion, inevitable in the world of human beings, has a really particular appeal. Huxley defines it as a complex emotional attitude of the human personality towards the universe.[6] It is therefore something that man feels deep within him, in the place he knows to be his in the world, and it is bound up with his destiny. It is his *raison d'être*, 'no more and no less a function of human nature than fighting or falling in love, than law or literature'. '. . . sometimes noble, sometimes hateful, sometimes intensely valuable, sometimes a bar to individual or social progress'.[7] But religion has been dealt a mortal blow by science. In the scientific view of the world the religions have receded from a position of absolute truth to that of legend, and the supernatural factors operating in them have become 'projections' or hallucinations of the human mind.

Yet something has emerged unscathed from the assault of

[6] J. Huxley, *What Dare I Think?*, London, 1931.
[7] *Ibid.*, p. 187.

science, and this something is religious experience. It continues to be a reality both in its more intense manifestations (in mysticism) and in the less apparent ones which are nevertheless undeniably and necessarily present in every human life. When God and theistic ideas are taken away, what is left of religion? Two very important things remain, says Huxley: the typical emotional reaction to destiny and the sentiment of the 'sacred' or *numinosum*. In the present situation, concludes Huxley, there are two dangers: the danger of a philosophical mysticism completely cut off from science and the danger of desperate, complacent rationalist destruction, utterly regardless of human nature.

Where is the solution to be found? Huxley believes it is to be found in scientific humanism. Science is now able (through psychology and anthropology) to examine even religious experience by scientific methods, to control it and use it to breathe life into its discoveries. A religion is thus visualized which assumes an attitude of reverent agnosticism before the mystery of the world but is determined to shed light upon it by slow and sure methodical procedure. It is a religion which makes men face up to reality and defends them from the danger of mistaking it or exchanging it for their own desires; a religion that stimulates a richer, freer and more intense human life in all its manifestations. The clash with constituted religions is inevitable, but this will be very valuable because it will oblige these religions to give up everything ephemeral that obstructs and diminishes their deep and precious worth. Scientific humanism, even when it demolishes, is more genuinely religious than conservative attachment to doctrine and ritual.

The doctrine of evolution is the central theme of scientific humanism. It presents us with a continuous, progressive development from inorganic matter to living organisms and to man. We are not to think that the inclusion of man in the animal kingdom is equivalent to dethronement, to a reduction of his dignity to the purely biological level. This might have been true of the first men whose life was necessarily employed in the satisfaction of bodily needs alone. But in the history of mankind something completely new in the sphere of living creatures takes place.

The type of life lived by all animals is necessarily determined according to their anatomical and physiological structure, and the acquisitions of the individual animal are not transmitted to the next generation. But in man's case, with his capacity for thought and speech, a completely new type of acquisition is established, namely, cultural tradition. It might be said, in the current language of information theory, that while dumb animals are capable of transmitting only those items of information that are 'encoded' in the species, man transmits information by social means, from one person to another and from one generation to the next by teaching and learning processes.

Organic evolution ends with man and psychological evolution, as Huxley calls it, begins. This is socio-genetic evolution, as Waddington prefers to term it. In the realm of organisms, then, man is a being apart: man stands alone. This does not mean that there is a stoppage, since man's psychosocial acquisitions proceed with inevitable rhythm, with considerably greater rapidity than is the case in organic evolution. There is another fundamental difference: while other organisms are passively subject to evolutionary determinism, man is able to control socio-genetic evolutionary processes and to direct them towards the goals he has in view. Consequently, when man reaches this stage of evolution a particular task is incumbent upon him, the task of controlling and developing the values which give meaning and joy to his existence.

The constitution of values and of a scale of values and moral judgment are the consequence of man's characteristic capacity as compared with other living creatures. Values are the product of psycho-social evolution and they 'can' regulate its development (Waddington expresses this opinion more strongly, declaring that they 'must' influence its development since they are part of the mechanism of socio-gentic transmission). In this light religions are to be considered as organs of psycho-social man concerned with human destiny and with experiences of sacredness and transcendence. Man, the product of evolution, becomes its master and must take care that it be progressive and not regressive, that it go straight on without deviation. God is a vain projection into the heavens and must be replaced by the reality of men. 'The disappearance of God means a recasting of religion, and a recasting of a fundamental sort. It means the shouldering by man of ultimate responsibilities which he had previously pushed off on to God.'[8]

The fundamental themes of religion, of religious concepts, beliefs and ceremonies must therefore be restated in humanist terms. The past history of religions makes possible a prophetic vision of the religion of the future. With the 'discovery and exploitation of the sphere of mental activities' which has just begun, it is possible to clarify a 'psycho-social ecology', that is to say, the whole network of man's relations with nature, with himself and with other individuals and all they have in common. It is possible to establish a psycho-social technology in order to regulate these relations. It is up to the religion of the future to organize and guide the indispensable manifestations of prayer, sacrifice, sin and love which at times become fixed in sterile formalism, while other tasks such as medical assistance, recreational activities, competitions and so forth will be taken care of by social organization.

Obviously Julian Huxley emerges as the theorist, theologian and prophet of a new religion: scientific humanism. His brilliant and categorical statements combine genius and discernment with paradoxical, superficial and trivial assertions and leave us bewildered and disconcerted.

The Humanist Frame ends with an essay by Aldous Huxley, Julian's brother, on 'human potentialities', a vague but peculiarly fascinating expression since it couples 'what man is capable of doing' with 'what he may do'. Aldous Huxley is one of the most noteworthy novelists and essayists in contemporary English literature. His criticism of conventionalism is severe and caustic. He is sceptical in describing the lack of

[8] J. Huxley, *The Uniqueness of Man*, Chatto and Windus, London, 1941, p. 283.

humanity in the Utopian ideals of science. He faces religious and mystical problems openly but brings to them an empirical attitude which is typically English. He declares that 'anatomically and physiologically man has changed very little' and that the 'native or genetic capacities of today's bright city child are no better than the native capacities of a bright child born into a family of Upper Palaeolithic cave-dwellers'. It is therefore the favourable or unfavourable environment that determines the development of human potentialities (a process of 'becoming more and more a human being') or obstructs this development.

Every adult human being is a multiple amphibian who lives in three different worlds: the electro-chemical world of his body, the world of first-order subjective experiences and the world of symbols, of which the most important is language which can be applied on the higher levels of abstraction, in science, art and religion. The latter is the world of which civilized man is particularly aware. Man intervenes to regulate these three worlds by various means, by instruction and propaganda in the symbolical world, by conditioning, auto-suggestion and the refining of tastes in the world of first-order subjective experience, by employing electro-chemical means in the world of the body. Today pharmacologists are learning to synthesize drugs which powerfully affect the mind on the level of first-order experience. Particular psychological states can be foreseen and controlled. We therefore possess the means by which to foster and regulate the development of human potentialities.

This feeble effort to summarize Huxley's ideas may perhaps serve to indicate his position in regard to religion. He sees it chiefly as a direct experience of a sensory and affective nature. The diversity of doctrinal content in the various religious creeds, according to Huxley, goes to show that their formulation is not the essential element in these religions. They have a common base on which they all meet, a basic religious sense in its pure state. This is an encouraging element, since it shows how souls that have passed beyond the limitations of personal existence and reached the 'integrating principle of the universe' converge on the joint basis of a religion devoid of dogmas. Huxley refers to this as *The Perennial Philosophy* and has given this title to one of his more important books.[9]

In this work he has collected the sayings of writers and mystics of many different religious creeds in order to show that the truth they are enunciating is fundamentally the same although their forms of expression differ. This book undoubtedly contains a vast store of information. Its literary style is refined and stimulating but also terribly elusive. The work is undeniably valuable as a testimony to the presence of mystical religious feeling in all peoples of all ages, but it evades the issue when it comes to stating precisely the meaning and value of religious experience apart from the purely subjective fact. Huxley has a decided leaning towards the religious ideas of Buddhism which he brings forward as the only way to prevent the decline of Western civilization. He is particularly interested in direct religious experience, psychological experience, I would go so far as to say sensory-affective experience, and towards ascetical methods by which it is achieved.

This line of study is apparent in a recent book of his entitled *The Doors of Perception*, in which he describes his own experiences produced by taking mescalin.[10] The Indians from time immemorial had made use in their religious festivals of a substance extracted from a cactus plant (peyotl, *Anhalonium Lewinii*) which they venerated as though it were a deity. Mescalin is alkaloid extracted from the peyotl plant, synthetically prepared nowadays. Jaensch, Havelock Ellis, Enrico Morselli and D. Cargnello have described the effects of this drug which has a most particular influence on the conscious mind and produces moods considered similar to those of schizophrenic patients.

It has also been discovered that the chemical composition of

[9] A Huxley, *The Perennial Philosophy*, Collins, London, 1958.
[10] A. Huxley, *The Doors of Perception*, Penguin Books, London, 1960.

mescalin is close to that of lysergic acid, a derivative of which produces hallucinations, and to that of adrenochrome, a product derived from adrenalin. Huxley relates how, intoxicated by mescalin, he experienced hallucinations very similar to those of which the mystics speak. He distinguishes broadly between three types of experience: the transfiguration of natural objects into objects of unimaginable beauty; experience of the transfigured objects and simultaneously the feeling of one's own identification with them; sudden panic when the vision appears irresistibly real and presents a situation which must be faced. We therefore have the *fascinosum* and *tremendum*, the identification with the universe which Rudolf Otto points out as characteristic of the sacred. This explains why the Indians considered the peyotl tree to be a god.

The habitual use of the drug in their religious feasts does not seem to have produced any particular disorders among the Indians. Huxley wonders, then, if a methodical and controlled use of mescalin might not be advisable in order to reach those states of ecstasy (in the sense of getting outside ourselves) which people seek by painful ascetical practices (concentration, fasting, scourgings), or by recourse to inebriating substances or drugs (alcohol, opium, hashish and cocaine).

The urge to transcend self-conscious selfhood is a principal appetite of the soul. When, for whatever reason, men and women fail to transcend themselves by means of worship, good works and spiritual exercises, they are apt to resort to religion's chemical surrogates: alcohol and 'goof-pills' in the modern West, alcohol and opium in the East, hashish in the Mohammedan world, alcohol and marijuana in Central America, alcohol and coca in the Andes, alcohol and barbiturates in the more up-to-date regions of South America. In *Poisons sacrées, ivresses divines* Philippe De Felice has written at length and with a wealth of documentary evidence on the immemorial connection between religion and the taking of drugs. . . . The modern Churches, with some exceptions among the Protestant denominations, tolerate alcohol;

but even the most tolerant have made no attempt to convert the drug to Christianity or to sacramentalize its use. The pious drinker is forced to take his religion in one compartment, his religion-surrogate in another. . . . This does no harm to the distillers, but is very bad for Christianity. Countless persons desire self-transcendence and would be glad to find it in church. But, alas, 'the hungry sheep look up and are not fed'. They take part in rites, they listen to sermons, they repeat prayers; but their thirst remains unassuaged. Disappointed, they turn to the bottle.[11]

Religious experience ought therefore to be encouraged by the use of harmless drugs.

We cannot but feel a sense of regret when we compare this book with certain admirable pages, certain really noble passages of Huxley's *Perennial Philosophy*. The bitter irony of *Brave New World* seems to fall here into the icy scepticism of one who appreciates religion solely on account of a certain type of emotional enjoyment. But unfortunately this attitude is only too logical if man's task is the cultivation of his potentialities, as the horsebreeder acts with breeds of horses, striving to obtain the maximum yield with the minimum damage to the animal. Pills in place of prayers!

As to Huxley's offhand manner of dealing with 'psycho-

---

[11] *Ibid.*, pp. 55-7. Havelock Ellis had already expressed ideas very similar to these, identifying religion with the entire field of man's liberation from oppressive states of mind. 'The simplest functions of physiological life,' he writes, 'may be its ministers. Everyone who is at all acquainted with the Persian mystics knows how wine may be regarded as an instrument of religion. Indeed, in all countries and in all ages some form of physical enlargement—singing, dancing, drinking, sexual excitement—has been intimately associated with worship. . . . Whenever an impulse from the world strikes against the organism, and the resultant is not discomfort or pain, not even the muscular contraction of strenuous manhood, but a joyous expansion or aspiration of the whole soul—there is religion. It is the infinite for which we hunger, and we ride gladly on every little wave that promises to bear us towards it' (*The New Spirit*, p. 232, cited by W. James, *The Varieties of Religious Exerience*, p. 49). These remarks are fundamentally true, but what food for thought there is in the final sentence: 'It is the infinite for which we hunger. . . .'

chemistry', we might remind him that those who deal with it as a profession—and conscientiously—do not share his enthusiasm, nor do they consider that the panacea has been found for all sick and healthy men. They are aware that in spite of all the discoveries that have been made the problem of psycho-physiological relations is no less obscure to the men of our day than in the past.[12]

'So far as I can see,' Julian Huxley writes, 'the only chance of securing a religion that will unite humanity instead of dividing it is to build it around the concept of evolutionary fulfilment, with belief in human possibilities as its central core and scientific method as its chief weapon.' The tasks, or rather the duties indicated by scientific humanism are, first of all, birth-control, since population-increase can only lead to frustration and misery; then the combat against monotonous uniformity and all that causes it—'the extermination of wild life, over-mechanization, the boredom of mass-production and conformity, the spoiling of natural beauty, the destruction of cultural traditions'; then 'trans-national cooperation with a view to world unity' and against the threat of atomic destruction; finally, reform of educational systems and principles, so that 'the idea of the Welfare State must be supplemented by that of the Fulfilment Society'.[13] As we pass on from the lyrical presentation of scientific humanism to its concrete proposals, we are subjected to a miserable prosaicness which has no more agreeable religious aims to propose than birth-control, landscape protection, idle talk on the policy of world unity and mescalin pills.

It seems significant to me that the antinomy between nature and man, between science and humanism, should give rise to the assertions that man's qualities as a living being are so singular as to be likened to those that the religions attribute to their divinities and even take their place. Science which is the

[12] Cf. I. H. Page, 'Chemistry of the Brain' in *Science*, Washington, D.C., April 1957.
[13] J. Huxley, *The Destiny of Man*, Hodder and Stoughton, London, 1959, pp. 88-91.

work of man consequently possesses religious qualities: it has a universal outlook, it necessarily takes account of religious experience, and scientific values are reconciled with humanity and suffused with a religious light. Moral obligation guides evolutionary possibilities towards a more complete realization of human capacity. Everything remains, as it were, in the material and pragmatist sphere, but with an undeniable religious afflatus. The Huxleys do not acknowledge God but they cannot escape from religion.

In the recent *Magna Carta* of scientific humanism, Huxley and his collaborators refer continually in enthusiastic chorus to Father Pierre Teilhard de Chardin, the Jesuit, a man who is truly admirable for the nobility and purity of his religious convictions and for his Christian life. How can this be?

A connection exists which deserves our attention. Teilhard was a geologist and a paleontologist of more than ordinary worth. He devoted his entire life to research as an explorer and a scientist. He was a deeply religious man who pondered ceaselessly on the great problems which science disclosed to him. It would be unjust and disloyal to describe him as a believer who, when faced with the collapse of concepts considered indispensable to his religion, became a desperate and fanatical apologist. Quite the contrary, for he accepts unreservedly the entire evolutionary system of the universe.

Teilhard's fundamental work is *The Phenomenon of Man* and in it he states his programme. The scientist devotes himself to the study of phenomena and cannot exclude the phenomenon of human life. How does this fit into the network of all the other phenomena that make up the universe? The theory of evolution, says Teilhard, has opened up a new vista which was not understood at first but which must be followed up in all its consequences. In a universe which we know to be formed of fine cosmic dust, of energetic particles in the most varied conditions of amalgamation and dispersion, we find inanimate bodies, living bodies and human beings existing side by side. Man alone by virtue of his mind is capable of reaching and understanding them. He has discovered with certainty that the universe was not always thus and he can foresee the various possibilities of future evolution. He knows that inanimate bodies were formed from cosmic dust, that living bodies appeared at a later stage and finally man himself. He is also aware that although the human body has remained practically identical down through the centuries, man has lived his own unmistakable history.

How has the history of the universe come to pass, how has human history happened, what does the future hold for the universe and for man? Man is certainly at a focal point in this history since he alone has been aware of its unfolding; but in what way has the transition taken place in the course of thousands of centuries from nebulous matter to human life? He must acknowledge a general datum: a gradual increase of complexity and at the same time of efficiency: from energetic particles to atoms, molecules, molecular groupings, and then to molecular groupings capable of reproducing themselves, to more and more varied organisms and finally to human beings.

When we retrace the path beginning from man, the only intelligent being, and explore the various organisms, we observe that complexity and efficiency are bound up with psychic capacity (from the conscious autonomy of man himself to the capacity of animals to master their environment and act independently), and that psychic capacity is in turn related to the extent and complexity of the nervous system. When we proceed in descending order, complexity, autonomy and efficiency diminish as the nervous system becomes less complex and psychic capacity is reduced. At a certain point the nerve cells also disappear, while full mastery and perfect organization of the molecular groups in the living body remain, ensuring its stability and continuity.

Proceeding further upstream to the point at which we no longer find life but merely molecular interaction, complexity is still present and even when we reach what is considered to be the elementary power charge we do not find this isolated but always in a complex dynamic relationship with other elements. When we trace back the line of events to their very beginning, when we go up to the sources of this great river at the mouth of which we human beings are to be found, we discover a gradual attenuation of that complexity which is bound up with overt psychic activity and biological control. Then we find that psychic activity and biological control cease but complexity continues up to the unsurmountable 'limit' of the dynamic relationship between power charges.

We may therefore conclude, by a legitimate process of extrapolation, that from the molecular state to the radiating state of inorganic matter there is a continued organization, a fundamental complexity of a psychic nature. This is the guiding thread that explains the whole increasing succession from the electric charge to the atom, to the molecule, to the living cell, to the organism and to culmination in man with the unique acquisition of consciousness, the capacity, that is, to observe and control himself.

Man is evolution become conscious, according to Huxley, and Teilhard accepts this opinion. Like Huxley he asserts that the human phenomenon is a milestone in the history of evolution, just as the appearance of the atom and the dawn of life were milestones. Precisely because of the appearance of consciousness, evolution which had exhausted all its biological possibilities on reaching the human organism (whose somatic variations, although considerable, are negligible in comparison to the fact of consciousness), continues by means of social tradition in which are repeated fundamentally the same themes of growth, differentiation and extinction which had appeared in organic evolution.

A new element becomes characteristic of the human being, namely, socialization. Teilhard attributes a particular meaning to this term and it is worth our while noting this at the present time. He sees it as the enrichment and complication of inter-human relations both at personal and group level. With convergence towards a human totality, or mankind, socialization is an unavoidable necessity or destiny. It is the drifting movement by which evolution is prolonged in the human race until men have occupied every corner of the earth, until the human race is 'planetized'. It is not possible, however, to suppress differences of race and individuality, and there must therefore be an intimate complementariness between races and between men, determined by what unites and not by what separates, namely, by love.

If socialization were merely self-evolutive it would be destined to shut itself in, to end in general stagnation, and it would put an end to evolution itself. The joy of living, the desire for progress, the need of action (which for Teilhard have their roots embedded in what is earthly and continue the evolutionary drive) would peter out at the end of a long period of laborious and insensate progress. But there is an inherent quality of irreversibility in evolution, passing from the simple to the complex, from separation to union, from humanity to what is above it and can confer unity upon it.

The various paths of evolution have led to different conclusions. In the stasis characteristic of the inorganic state there was an aperture from which the highly improbable combination which is life emerged to spread over the earth (the biosphere). In the biosphere innumerable branches of development died out and only one, a highly improbable one, culminated in man, and the noosphere rules the earth. In the noosphere the coalescence of extension and unity is accentuated, and if evolution is not in the end to stand self-condemned, it must turn towards an omega where the tension becomes gratification and not death. Hence the evolution of man cannot be enchained within man himself. It cannot survive unless it is directed towards the omega which is the term, the goal, of human evolution and of the entire universe.

For Teilhard evolution is not a blind succession of events but implies a central stream with a well-defined course. The goal gives a meaning to the way that leads to it. The omega which on the plane of scientific phenomenology is of a 'speculative and postulated nature' becomes for the believer the supreme reason of the universe, which is God. The Christian religion itself is clearly distinguished from other religions by the fact that, although it began in a narrow environment and under unfavourable conditions, it has spread throughout the world, aims to unite all men, and possesses a vitality which overcomes the internal or external obstacles it encounters in the course of its development. It repeats in sacred fashion the rhythm of evolution: complexity, consciousness, hominization, socialization and ultimate convergence in God. 'Even if I were not a Christian, but only a man of science, I think I would ask myself this question [of this coincidence].' These are the concluding words of *The Phenomenon of Man*.

Here, too, when we have finished reading, we cannot avoid a feeling of bewilderment. Side by side with scientific methodology and a wealth of information we have the most daring extrapolations. Hand in hand with a continual wariness towards the metaphysics of principles goes a 'metaphysics' in the etymological sense of the word (what is beyond nature), or, as Teilhard calls it, a 'hyperbiology', justified by the assertion that there is no science if data are not linked up. We are fascinated by the passion of a visionary or a mystic who expresses himself masterfully and overthrows the scientist's scaffolding, because he 'sees and makes others see'.

The fact that Teilhard is so widely discussed today is not without significance. He is discussed by scientists who consider him a poet; by theologians who refuse to recognize the arguments of one who invades their field with a method and phraseology proper to the naturalists; by a vast public who read him eagerly for the sake of an emotional thrill, but who understand very little of what he has written. It is impossible to offer a critical judgment here, but it is interesting to note that both an atheist (Huxley) and a believer (Teilhard) in dealing with the 'phenomenon of Man' follow the same road in their evolutionary interpretations of man's origin. Both acknowledge that man occupies a unique place in nature and recognize that religion, the sense of being bound up with the universe and the attempt to explain it, is an irrepressible human quality.

Thus far Huxley and Teilhard follow the same road, but then their paths diverge. Huxley attributes divine qualities and powers to man and makes him responsible for the fate of mankind, while Teilhard sees in man the continuation of the evolutionary impulse which must be channelled in its essential direction, towards the Absolute, towards God. While Huxley has nothing to say about the meaning of man's attitude towards God, Teilhard sees this as the indispensable condition for the enrichment of man's personality. Huxley is the prophet of a utilitarian religion and sees in religious experience an advantage for man and nothing more. Teilhard preaches a religion which is rooted in human nature but which cannot abdicate from dedication to something higher than man and the universe.

We have to ask ourselves at this point if science, with its methods of observation and induction alone, is qualified to say all that has to be said about religion, and if the ideas of Huxley and Teilhard which are so close yet so divergent do not really point to an impossibility on the part of science to do more than recognize the existence of religion and the conditions in which it exists. If science is to pronounce judgment admitting of no appeal on this subject, it is bound to embark on intellectual adventures whose material and spiritual consequences are in danger of injuring reason itself. Reason is more inclined to accept a mystery (containing an invitation which is felt to be genuine) than to cling to fictitious explanations such as science is capable of offering. Evolutionary thinking in particular has the bad habit of doing away with the limits of the categories which Nature presents to us. It gives us unverifiable speculations and invokes historical arguments 'to establish the continuity required by theory even though historical evidence is lacking'.[14]

Can a radically evolutionary theory correspond to the categories of 'Absolute' and 'relative' which are so strongly stressed in religion? I doubt it, because it would be necessary to make evolution absolute, to hypostatize it, and we should be obliged to make an act of faith in a cosmic evolution possessing divine qualities. Teilhard's thinking, so decided as a whole, but containing many nuances when it comes to detail, is less simple

[14] W. R. Thompson, Introduction to C. Darwin, op. cit., p. xxiv.

and tangible than Huxley's and can quite easily be misunderstood. 'The surprising success of Teilhard de Chardin,' writes
A. Vergote, 'is not explained by any literary or scientific
consideration, but solely by his religious message.'[15]

Religion and the psychological world

In endeavouring to ascertain 'man's place in nature' we come
face to face with a religious problem: the meaning of man's
life in the unfolding of events. But even when we consider man
by himself and in his inner life, the religious problem necessarily
arises. We must look for the meaning of his knowing and feeling
and acting, and the question is all the more urgent since man
is directly and simultaneously both spectator of and actor in
his own states of mind.

Psychologists who are interested in the religious question
are almost unanimous in asserting that psychology as a science
is unable to establish or deny the truth of a religious statement.
They add that in studying religious feeling they are faced with
the same psychic processes which are normally observed in
other fields, although in the case of religious feeling these
acquire a characteristic tone. Finally, they agree that apart
altogether from the question of passing judgment on the
problem of religion, there is no doubt whatever as to the reality
of religious emotion.

In *The Future of an Illusion* Freud pointed out the
advantages which religion offers to the individual: the possibility of dealing with the forces of nature as one would deal
with people; the continued sense of parental protection; the
satisfaction of taking an active part in events by influencing a
Being who rules us and to whom we can present our requests;
a sense of dignity in view of our relationship with this Being;
having at our disposal a force opposed to the ever-present
threat of death, in virtue of our belief in personal immortality;
possessing a ready and convenient explanation of all events

[15] A. Vergote, 'De l'expérience religieuse' in *De l'expérience à l'attitude
religieuse*, Brussels, p. 82.

and of the world by referring it all to God's action. Against these advantages, according to Freud, there are two serious drawbacks: faith, which has the qualities of an illusion (of thinking according to our desires and not according to reality); and the manner in which divine prescriptions oppose and deny human needs. The tenacity of religion in face of opposition is due to the advantages it offers, especially in difficult circumstances. But it is impossible to go against reason all the time and the conclusive decision must be made by reason, even if it takes time to bring this about. Science alone 'has shown itself not to be an illusion', and it is only science that can conduct us safely and surely.

To Freud psychoanalysis appeared to be the only way to free ourselves from 'illusions' and give us a measure of serenity and joy compatible with our state. 'This last representative of rationalism, Freud, this ambitious man who lacked self-confidence but was honest and courageous, was seen as the messianic leader of an intellectual revolution, of a new scientific religion for an élite who were to lead mankind.' This is how E. Fromm expresses himself and his judgment would appear to be fundamentally exact.[16]

It is man, then, who can establish what men are to do, by studying and discovering mankind, without any recourse to illusory entities. But even if we accept this canon and seek to set men free from the obsessional neurosis of mankind, the crusade itself by which we endeavour to overcome it becomes a religion, with all the risks and disadvantages of constituted religions. Freud himself wondered if this could possibly be avoided. The psychoanalytical movement as it appears in Ernest Jones' biography of Freud savours strongly of religious conspiracy. We find in it the indisputable authority of the head, dogmas, the privilege of membership, penalties of expulsion, and even a few harmless magical practices.[17]

[16] E. Fromm, *Sigmund Freud's Mission*, Harper, New York, 1959.
[17] D. Bakan's book *S. Freud and the Jewish Mystical Tradition* (Van Nostrand, London, 1958) is enlightening in regard to Freud's religious sense. Freud was deeply conscious of belonging to the Jewish race. Biblical themes, and even more so references to Jewish tradition

When the fundamental principle of every man's duty to cooperate for the betterment of mankind is accepted and perhaps imposed, a particular type of religion is not only envisaged but actually exists. Let us listen to J. C. Flugel, one of the psychoanalysts who followed Freud most faithfully while being open at the same time to other psychological currents. 'The religious emotions must be largely or entirely secularized and be put in the service of humanity. The religion

(from the ancient and modern Kabbala to the teachings of the Chassidim) recur continually in his teaching. There are also resemblances to the attitudes of rebellious prophets (Sabatai Zevi and Jacob Frank). The figure of Moses stands out in Freud's thinking. E. Jones asks whether Moses was for Freud the all-important father-image or if Freud identified himself with him (*op. cit.*, II, pp 364-5) and adds: 'Probably both, at different periods of his life.' In Moses he saw the 'non-Jew' who imposed a heavy yoke of monotheism on the Jews and was assassinated by them in the desert. Freud imagined himself to be the victim prophet who rebels against tradition to become the head of a new religion, 'the new Moses who comes down from the mountain with the law of personal psychological freedom' (*ibid.*). Freud shows a weakness for the Devil over and over again—the symbol of the tempter who breaks the chain of obligation (the permissive superego) and who, through magic, confers exceptional powers of mastery over others.

Bakan also points out that in biblical tradition sexual relations have always been fully appreciated and that in the Kabbala the origin of being is traced to sexuality. According to Freud, the first problem with which the child occupies himself is not the question as to the difference between the two sexes, but the riddle 'Where do children come from?' He discovers the explanation of his own creation in the sexual union of his parents. 'The Oedipus complex,' writes Bakan, 'is a profound metaphor which catches at the deep mystery of human existence' (p. 276). There is therefore in Freud a religious impulse but also a note of rebellion. 'The most important sin which Freud committed was the breach of the first commandment—the sovereignty of God—which he achieved by its translation into the fifth commandment—honour thy father and thy mother—and his nullification of the latter by an appeal to "natural law" . . . a denunciation by a Jew of his God' (p. 317).

Neither did his rebellion go unpunished, remarks Bakan. Freud, who had placed himself outside the Jewish tradition to fight against the Father and free the community of Israel, sought the final comfort and safety of his life in his belonging to the Jewish race, the Holy Shekinah, the community of Israel (p. 317).

of humanity is surely the religion of the near future.'[18] He
continues: 'Of the modern psychologists of religion, Cattell
would seem to have given by far the most thoroughgoing,
consistent and courageous exposition of this view.' Let us turn,
then, to R. B. Cattell.

In a work entitled *Psychology and the Religious Quest*,
written in 1938 while he was still living in England, he asserts
that

> a single-minded devotion to truth, no matter into what
> emotional difficulties it leads its followers, is (for the pure-
> bred scientist) the most important value in life. . . . No
> scientist worthy of the name will follow any escapes to
> religion, no matter how great his sympathy with a society
> in torment or individuals in extremities. For he holds the
> search for truth to be the noblest aim—and as for human
> suffering, he knows that no people have ever been
> permanently happy or successful by cherishing an illusion.
> He recognizes in such pragmatic arguments as that men will
> return to religion in their troubles an argument equally
> applicable to drink and drugs. . . . Stoically to follow science
> into its bleak altitudes is the only course left to us.[19]

Cattell endeavours to show that our relations to the Group
Mind—which, from the religious point of view, he suggests,
can be appropriately called the Theopsyche, and which Flugel
prefers to call Humanity—are in many all-important ways
similar to our relations to God, and that we can find in them
an adequate outlet for our religious needs and aspirations
without recourse to any form of supernaturalism. Flugel
summarizes Cattell's arguments under eight headings.

1. The individual depends upon his fellows, upon his social
group, in much the same way as, according to revealed religion,
he depends ultimately upon the will of God.

2. He is to a very large extent spiritually created by the

[18] J. C. Flugel, *Man, Morals and Morality*, Penguin Books, London,
1955, p. 335.
[19] R. B. Cattell, *Psychology and the Religious Quest*, Nelson, London,
1938, pp. 42-3, 49.

Group Mind, i.e. his ideals, his goals, his frames of intellectual reference, his whole outlook upon life are profoundly influenced by the 'mental atmosphere' of the society in which he grows up and in which he lives, just as according to the supernaturalist view, his spiritual being is guided and influenced by God. Even his physical existence is largely determined by the social conditions of his group, his actual parents, essential as they are, being indeed on both views only the immediate instruments of a greater creative purpose.

3. The group, as the 'cumulative reservoir of super-individual wisdom', provides the ultimate commands of morality (incorporated in the superego), just as God does on the theological hypothesis.

4. The individual can find his own purpose in life in service of the group, just as he can in service of God's will. His 'need to be needed', his desire for cooperation in something larger and higher than his own immediate and personal concerns, can be satisfied in this way perhaps even more effectively than in trying to fulfil the often mystifying and inscrutable intentions of a supernatural God.

5. This service may often call for personal sacrifice (even for the 'supreme sacrifice' of life itself) in ways that are at least intellectually more satisfying than the sacrifices usually demanded by the religious rituals of the past.

6. The continuance of the group after the individual's death gives him the necessary faith to carry on with the tasks valuable to the community which personal chance or accident may interrupt.

7. The fact that the individual has during his life influenced the group—for good or ill, and of course in varying degree according to his abilities and eminence—inevitably confers on him a sort of immortality, which is independent of any strictly personal survival.

8. If he has children, he gains a further and more direct immortality through them and their descendants—both in virtue of his physical parenthood and of his special moral influence as parent.

Such a substitution of the 'group theopsyche' for the God of revealed religion can hardly function satisfactorily without some provision for the aim and purpose of the group. Cattell finds this aim or purpose in progress, the gradually increasing realization of the aspirations of mankind, from the biological (eugenic) and psychological points of view. Mankind will, in fact, engage in an applied science of itself, which may be called 'the experimental study of God'. Flugel does not fail to point out the formidable difficulties to be faced in this religious project. In particular it involves relations between the various groups themselves and relations with mankind as a whole. It also implies the need of arriving at some degree of consent as to the nature of human progress, before controlling it. He also mentions the sacrifices involved and the means which might be devised in order to avoid them.

Perhaps it was not worth our while dwelling so long on these ideas of Cattell and Flugel, for we have here just one among innumerable projects, or, as we should say today, one of the countless examples of planning that issue forth copiously from human intelligence. But we have singled it out from the rest because it serves to illustrate some important facts.

Note, first of all, the uniformity between this scheme and Huxley's: unconditional trust in science; contempt for religion, which is accused of connivance with selfish habits or of constituting a dangerous distraction from real problems; appreciation of religious emotion unrelated to institutional religion; constitution of a supra-individual entity (evolution, society, progress) with divine attributes; prediction of an efficient and happy regeneration; unconditional commitment with a view to this reform which is planned with scientific certainty and is functionally consistent with real human potentialities. The absence of warning against the harmful potentialities of man is to be noted: they are disposed of as 'inefficient adjustments' which can be corrected in 'more functional' planning.

Here we have a rationalist and optimistic illuminism. But it must also be remarked that this programme, item by item, expresses convictions widely spread among psychologists today: the priority and creative capacity of the group and culture in regard to personality; the constitution of cultural patterns as standards of moral value; personal expansion, maturity and identity conditioned to participation in the group; overcoming frustration by a broad outlook; the satisfaction of intellectual and emotional needs in an atmosphere of individual freedom and social valuation; the projection of the continuity of individual life on to biological and cultural life. Even today, a quarter of a century after its formulation and with all that has happened in the meantime, this programme could be presented as something new.

When he published his book in 1945, Flugel overlooked the fact that the programme had already been tried out and in that very year had reached its tragic conclusion. In this same book Flugel reproduces with indignant disapproval one of the numerous Nazi rigmaroles on the occasion of 'Mother Day'.

> The national revolution has brushed aside everything that is small and petty. Ideas lead us once more. Family, Society, People! The idea of Mother Day is intended to honour that which is the symbol of the German idea—the German Mother. Nowhere has the woman and the mother such a profound significance as in modern Germany. She is the protection of a family life from which the German people cull the strength which shall lead them upwards. She—the German Mother—is the sole carrier of the German folk thought.

Membership of the German people, this people's conquering and regenerating mission, the 'scientific' certainty of progress and victory, were continually staged by Nazism with subtlety and with recourse to trivial expedients. But we can substitute for 'Mother Germany' the creative, conquering theopsyche, the unquestionable source of morality, which in the name of progress calls for sacrifice to this ideal; and on propagandist grounds equivalent humanist rigmaroles can be composed which, unfortunately, are destined to meet with success among people of superficial, mediocre culture, to the detriment of the human race.

One hundred and fifty years prior to the fall of the Nazi gods, there had been another fall of other divinities who thirsted for human blood. On 10 November 1793, Chaumette, pro-curator and mayor of the commune of Paris, organized and celebrated a festival to honour the Goddess of Reason. In Notre Dame Cathedral a cardboard mountain was erected with a Greek temple at its summit. A procession of girls ascended the mountain by a path flanked with busts of Voltaire, Rousseau and Franklin, to enthrone the Goddess of Reason, impersonated by a ballet dancer. On 1 April of the following year, Chaumette was beheaded.

At Pentecost of the same year, on 17 June, Robespierre presided over the festival of the Supreme Being. After a hymn had been sung to the 'Father of the universe, the supreme intelligence', Robespierre, the revolutionary who had never worn the Phrygian cap on his carefully powdered hair and who on this occasion stood out from the crowd in his elegant blue evening jacket, set fire to the tow effigy of atheism in the Tuileries, on the remains of which the statue of Wisdom stood out, tallow-stained and incombustible. On 28 July, Robespierre too climbed the ladder to the guillotine.[20]

This grim and ghastly pageantry also proceeded from the need to give 'religiously emotional' content to the speculations of scholars and the idle talk of intellectuals which had issued forth from books and salons to be spread abroad by a few people greedy for popularity and proselytism, who fomented and directed the discontent of the populace towards a mirage of regeneration. There is no need to follow up contemporary events where a science which had a dignified awareness of its successes, its limitations and its ignorance has been replaced by a science which, in the effort to meet human demands for a better life, considers itself authorized to impose with all its might the truth of which it claims to be the only possessor. A

[20] P. Gaxotte, *La révolution*, Paris, 1928.

scientific secular religion is as mercilessly demanding—and even more so than a religion that professes faith in God. Neither is it anything new to see celebrations in honour of humanitarians and pacific ideals marked by military parades in which all the most terrifying weapons of destruction are exhibited. Unfortunately, it is the fanatical upholders of humanism who have recourse to the sword more readily than those who are 'numbed by the opium of the people'.

In the field of psychology itself, and particularly in so-called depth psychology which takes a bolder interest in religious facts, some interesting elements are to be observed. Jung's recent book of *Memories* affords us a starting-point.[21] Jung relates how, in his first personal meeting with Freud (in 1907, several years after he had come to know, appreciate and defend Freud's theories), he was greatly struck by Freud's attachment to the sexual theory and by his attitude towards the spirit. Whenever in a person or a work of art an expression of spirituality came to light, he suspected it and insinuated that it was repressed sexuality. 'I could see that his sexual theory was enormously important to him,' writes Jung.

> When he spoke of it, his tone became urgent, almost anxious, and all signs of his normally critical and sceptical manner vanished. A strange, deeply-moved expression came over his face, the cause of which I was at a loss to understand. I had a strong intuition that for him sexuality was a sort of *numinosum*. . . . Freud never asked himself why he was compelled to talk continually of sex, why this idea had taken such possession of him. He remained unaware that his 'monotony of interpretation' expressed a flight from himself, or from that other side of him which might perhaps be called mystical. . . . There was nothing to be done about this one-sidedness of Freud's. . . . He remained the victim of the one aspect he could recognize and for that reason I see him as

[21] C. G. Jung, *Memories, Dreams, Reflections*, Pantheon Books, New York, 1963. Also available in a new edition as a Fontana paperback, 1967.

a tragic figure; for he was a great man, and, what is more, a man in the grip of his daimon.[22]

Jung relates how Freud said to him later, the second time they met in Vienna, in 1910:

'My dear Jung, promise me never to abandon the sexual theory. That is the most essential thing of all. You see, we must make a dogma of it, an unshakeable bulwark.' He said that to me with great emotion, in the tone of a father saying: 'And promise me this one thing, my dear son, that you will go to church every Sunday.' In some astonishment I asked him, 'A bulwark—against what?' To which he replied, 'Against the black tide of mud . . . of occultism.'

By 'occultism' Freud did not mean exclusively what the rising science of parapsychology had learned about the psyche, but also what philosophy and religion had to say of it. 'First of all,' continues Jung, 'it was the words "bulwark" and "dogma" that alarmed me, for a dogma, that is to say, an indisputable confession of faith, is set up only when the aim is to suppress doubts once and for all. But that no longer has anything to do with scientific judgment; only with a personal power drive.' And he adds:

I was bewildered and embarrassed. I had the feeling that I had caught a glimpse of a new, unknown country from which swarms of new ideas flew to meet me. One thing was clear: Freud, who had always made much of his irreligiosity, had now constructed a dogma; or rather, in the place of a jealous God whom he had lost, he had substituted another compelling image, that of sexuality. It was no less insistent, exacting, domineering, threatening and morally ambivalent than the original one. . . . The advantage of this transformation for Freud was, apparently, that he was able to regard the new numinous principle as scientifically irreproachable and free from all religious taint. . . . The lost god has now to be sought below, not above. . . . Much later, when I

[22] *Ibid.*, pp. 149 ff.

K

reflected upon Freud's character, these thoughts revealed
their significance. There was one characteristic of his that
preoccupied me above all: his bitterness. It had struck me
at our first encounter, but it remained inexplicable to me
until I was able to see it in connection with his attitude
towards sexuality. Although, for Freud, sexuality was
undoubtedly a *numinosum*, his terminology and theory
seemed to define it exclusively as a biological function. . . .
Basically, he wanted to teach—or so at least it seemed to
me—that, regarded from within, sexuality included spirituality and had an intrinsic meaning. But his concretistic
terminology was too narrow to express this idea. He gave
me the impression that at bottom he was working against
his own goal and against himself; and there is, after all, no
harsher bitterness than that of a person who is his own worst
enemy.[23]

It is difficult to say whether we can fully accept this diagnosis
of Freud's character. However, anyone who reads Freud
receives the impression of an excessive insistence on sexuality
(at least in his early works), of a bitter diffidence towards everything that can be called spiritual and of a defensive stiffening
every time the religious question is broached. We may venture
to say that psychoanalysis was Freud's religion and that it
completely subjugated him.

But it is interesting to follow up Jung's relationship with
him. Jung saw in Freud a repressed religion and in sexuality
he saw a symbol of the religious sense. In the book which
determined his separation from Freud *(Symbols of Transformation)*, he interpretes the theme of incest which frequently recurs
in myths and dreams, not as the frustrated aspiration to sexual
union, but as the need to reunite with the primordial vitality
of the universe, with the libido in the sense in which Jung
understands it. Freud clung to the literal interpretation of
incest and was unable to grasp its symbolic significance.

But why on earth should a religious significance be attributed

[23] *Ibid.*, pp. 150-2.

to such a repugnant representation? Because, says Jung, when a human being is faced with products of the unconscious he undergoes a religious experience, a thrill of mystery and terror and fascination, an experience of the *numinosum*.

Numinous experience elevates and humiliates simultaneously. . . . Wherever the psyche is set violently oscillating by a numinous experience, there is a danger that the thread by which one hangs may be torn. Should that happen, one man tumbles into an absolute affirmation, another into an equally absolute negation. . . . The *numinosum* is dangerous because it lures men to extremes, so that a modest truth is regarded as *the* truth and a minor mistake is equated with fatal error.

This is what Jung says of Freud. In another chapter of his *Memories*, in which he tells of his own personal religious experience, Jung writes:

Such experiences have a helpful or, it may be, annihilating effect upon man. He cannot grasp, comprehend, dominate them; nor can he free himself or escape from them, and therefore he feels them as overpowering. Recognizing that they do not spring from his conscious personality, he calls them mana, daimon, or God. Science employs the term 'the unconscious', thus admitting that is knows nothing about it, for it can know nothing about the substance of the psyche when the sole means of knowing anything is the psyche. Therefore the validity of such terms as mana, daimon, or God can be neither disproved nor affirmed. We can, however, establish that the sense of strangeness connected with the experience of something objective, apparently outside the psyche, is indeed authentic.

The three terms mana, daimon and God

have the great merit of including and evoking the emotional quality of numinosity, whereas 'the unconscious' is . . . too neutral and rational a term to give much impetus to the imagination. The term, after all, was coined for scientific purposes, and is far better suited to dispassionate observation which makes no metaphysical claims than are the transcendental concepts, which are controversial and therefore tend to breed fanaticism. Hence, I prefer to use the term 'the unconscious', knowing that I might equally well speak of 'God'. . . . I am aware than 'mana', 'daimon' and 'God' are synonyms for the unconscious—that is to say, we know just as much or just as little about them as about the latter.[24]

Thus is was through 'the clinical case of Freud' that Jung first became aware that forces possessing the characteristics of religious experience are at work in the sphere of consciousness. If for Freud God is sex, for Jung God is the unconscious. We cannot follow Jung in his detailed treatment of the psychological reality of the religious imprinting of man, but we are anxious to stress the fact that the unconscious, which began as an explanatory idea, a 'working hypothesis', was deified by Jung at a later stage.

In Adler, too, we can discern a far from negligible religious 'understudy'. The tireless enthusiasm with which this formerly bashful man, immersed in his books, after his separation from Freud and after the experience of the first European war, set out to make proselytes for individual psychology and for socialism, leads us to suspect some much stronger motive than the calm, cautious, detached observation and organization of facts required in the scientist. This activism made Adler intolerable to many people. He was described by them as a *Streber* (social climber) and a *Schwindler*. In his book *The Individual Psychology*, Adler expresses the following ideas in a chapter on 'The Psychology of Religion'.[25]

God can be recognized and manifest only within a thought process which moves toward the quality of height and greatness, and only within feelings which experience greatness as

---

[24] *Ibid.*, pp. 336-7.
[25] A. Adler, *The Individual Psychology*, Basic Books, New York, 1956.

redemption from oppressing tensions and inferiority feelings. The idea of God . . . is the concretization . . . of the human recognition of greatness and perfection, and the dedication of the individual as well as of society to a goal which rests in the future and which enhances in the present the driving force towards greatness by strengthening the appropriate feelings and emotions.[26]

'The fact that the form of the ideal varies is not essential. Whether the highest effective goal is called God or Socialism or, as we call it, the pure idea of social interest, it always reflects the same ruling, completion-promising, grace-giving goal of overcoming.' Mankind, having undertaken to be the centre of earthly and even universal events, can bring this task nearer to fulfilment if men consider the physical and spiritual well-being of all as the incontestable factor in all their valuations of life.[27]

We might conclude that Adler has installed yet another God in the psychological Olympus: the god of 'community feeling'. But it is interesting to observe how his pupils, Allers and Künkel, have given a Christian version of individual psychology, and how Allers follows the path of scholastic philosophy. V. Frankl, too, the leader of the logotherapy school which advocates the medical care of souls according to a spiritualist concept and with emphasis on the religious aspect, goes back to Adler through Allers. Erich Fromm also has considerable leanings towards Adler.

Among Freud's immediate disciples, Otto Rank, although less well known, occupies a special place. In the first place he was highly esteemed by Freud, for whom he in turn had a deep admiration. Secondly, although not himself a doctor but an ardent student of socio-cultural problems as well as an artist, he was admitted to the 'inner council' of psychoanalysis where he fulfilled the role of secretary. Rank's name is linked with the 'birth trauma' on which he wrote a study. Anxiety in its more serious forms, he maintains, tends to be accompanied by

[26] *Ibid.*, p. 460.   [27] *Ibid.*, p. 461.

emotional manifestations very similar to those which accompany the process of birth. The shock of birth consists fundamentally in separation from the mother and reappears in manifestations of anxiety every time a separation takes place or is even feared. Neurosis has its origin in the trauma experienced at birth and the Oedipus complex occupies a secondary place.

Although Freud himself did not react at once against this assertion, his other disciples disapproved of it. Rank, who was not only excessively sensitive to this criticism but also tormented by deep-seated dissatisfaction, broke away from Freud and his group, moving first to Paris and later to America. This separation was very painful for Rank but it spurred him on to choose a path that was to lead him far from Freud.

Rank's personal problem was perhaps the problem of artistic creativeness with all the torment which the preparation of a work of art entails. Freud's psychic determinism with its fatal dynamism did not explain to him how artistic creativeness came to be marked by a sense of direction towards a recognized and actively desired goal. The mainspring of action, according to Rank, is not found in submission to necessity but in a resolute will even when the aims are only gradually identified and classified. Hence in treating neurosis one cannot be an onlooker but must help the patient to aim resolutely at the solution of his own case, even by establishing in advance the duration of the treatment.

The voluntary act is accompanied by a sense of self-assertion and even though it may have an impulsive and therefore instinctual aspect, it is nevertheless inseparable from the awareness that one is acting as an individual with a personal identity. 'The individual will, as the united and balancing force between impulses and inhibition, is the decisive psychological factor in human behaviour.'[28] 'The psychology of the unconscious unveils itself to us as one of the numerous attempts of mankind

[28] O. Rank, *Beyond Psychology*, cited in I. Pogroff, *The Death and Rebirth of Psychology*, Julian Press, New York, 1956, p. 206.

to deny the will in order to evade the conscious responsibility following of necessity therefrom.'[29] 'Mankind's civilization, and with it the various types of personality representing and expressing it, has emerged from the perpetual operation of a third principle which combines the rational and irrational elements in a world view based on the conception of the supernatural.'[30]

The aspiration to immortality is the third principle which provides the key to the whole man as an individual and to his history. It is not a biological but an ideological and social continuity that is qualified as belief. The effort to attain immortality assumes an infinite variety of forms: identification of personal existence with the life of the group; belief in personal survival after death; dedication to some work whether great or small, but considered as one's own; heroic action in time of war or in the cause of politics, religion or science. All this is invariably sustained by a faith which derives from the community and from the living conditions of the individual.

The desire for immortality is fundamentally unconscious and irrational but it is also rationally formulated and reaches out beyond individuality. It is to be noted that despite the stress placed on 'faith', the desire for immortality does not reach a theistic concept (as Rank's use of the term 'supernatural' might lead us to believe), but remains in the sphere of psychology, in the sphere of the study of states of mind and of the forces which determine their formation, their alteration and their influence on behaviour. Rank has introduced yet another divinity into the psychological Pantheon, namely the desire for immortality.

An interesting aspect of Rank's thinking is his destructive criticism of psychology, which he sees as a self-sufficient explanation of the human problem. He holds that psychology explains human beliefs without having any faith of its own. 'This is why the psychological ideology has never been alive. It came into the world, so to say, with an old mind. It was

[29] O. Rank, *Will Therapy, ibid.*, p. 199.
[30] O. Rank, *Beyond Psychology, ibid.*, p. 230.

produced from the neurotic type and corresponds to it.'[31] 'How presumptuous and at the same time naïve is the idea of simply removing human guilt by explaining it casually as "neurotic".'[32] 'Psychoanalysis is psychological knowledge only to a minor degree; it is principally a translation of old animistic spiritual values into the scientific language of the sexual era.'[33]

> Freud, without knowing it, interpreted the analytical situation in terms of his world view and did not, as he thought, analyse the individual's unconscious objectively. . . . The materials of psychology are not facts, but ideologies, such as spiritual beliefs, which again are not simply facts related to a definite reality, but ideologies related to a definite mentality. . . . Psychology . . . is a predominantly negative disintegrative ideology . . . an ideology of resentment in Nietzsche's sense. It destroys illusions and ideologies, which can no longer withstand its progressive self-consciousness. It becomes progressively unable to maintain itself, and finally, as the last natural science, ideology, it destroys itself.[34]

The various types of analytical psychology call for a further step beyond their own position; otherwise they tend to mow down the conscious analysis of themselves.

> When Rank wrote in the preface to *Beyond Psychology* 'that people, though they think and talk rationally—and even behave so—yet live irrationally', I thought that 'beyond' individual psychology simply meant social or collective psychology until I discovered that this too is generally conceived of in the same rational terms. Hence my recognition of the ideologies—including those determining our psychological theories—was not sufficient to complement our understanding of individual behaviour because they too were stated in terms of the rational aspect of human life. In fact these ideologies more than anything else seem to carry the

[31] O. Rank, *Modern Education, ibid.*, pp. 221-2.
[32] O. Rank, *Beyond Psychology, ibid.*, p. 222.
[33] O. Rank, *Psychology and the Soul, ibid.*, p. 223.
[34] O. Rank, *ibid.*, pp. 224, 226.

whole rationalization that man needs, in order to live irrationally.[35]

There has been an attempt to achieve the impossible, to rationalize the irrational whereas man lives irrationally beyond psychology.

In referring to these ideas of Rank it has not been possible to trace the full connection between them. But one aspect has perhaps been made sufficiently clear, namely, the impossibility of reducing man's entire nature including the unconscious to merely rational terms. Affect also eludes this constraint and religion even more so. We are all the time imprisoned in subjectivity and relativity and there is an irrational need to escape. Why? How? Where? Psychology can give us no answer.

From certain points of view the thinking of Erich Fromm is linked up with Otto Rank's attitude. Born and educated in Germany, Fromm practised psychoanalysis in the psychoanalytical institutes of Munich and Berlin and moved to the United States in 1933, where he continued his activity as a psychoanalyst and professor. His books, which have aroused and continue to arouse discussion on a wide scale even beyond the sphere of psychology itself, are chiefly of a critical and doctrinal nature. His orientation is distinctly social although he professes faith in psychoanalysis.

Strict psychoanalysts do not consider Fromm a genuine psychoanalyst. They accuse him of superficiality and of diluting Freud's principles. Still, he is an effective writer who gives us food for thought. His basic theme is human isolation and solitude as a result of man's separation from Nature and from other men: the privilege and torment of a being who has diminished the direct action of instinctual impulse and realizes that he is 'set apart while being a part'. As he becomes more civilized man is increasingly cut off from Nature, but he experiences an intolerable loneliness from which he flees *(The Flight from Freedom)* and against which he has no resources except within himself *(Man for Himself)*.

[35] O. Rank, *Beyond Psychology, ibid.*, pp. 249-50.

Self-awareness, reason and imagination have disrupted the 'harmony' which characterizes animal existence. Their emergence has made man into an anomaly, into the freak of the universe. He is a part of Nature, subject to her physical laws and unable to change them, yet he transcends the rest of Nature. He is set apart while being a part, he is homeless, yet chained to the home he shares with all creatures. Cast into this world at an accidental place and time, he is forced out of it, again accidentally. Being aware of himself, he realized his powerlessness and the limitations of his existence. He visualizes his own end: death. Never is he free from the dichotomy of his existence: he cannot rid himself of his mind, even if he should want to; he cannot rid himself of his body as long as he is alive—and his body makes him want to be alive. . . . He must give account to himself of himself and of the meaning of his existence. He is driven to overcome this inner conflict, tormented by a craving for 'absoluteness', for another kind of harmony which can lift the curse by which he was separated from nature, from his fellow men and from himself. . . . He has to strive for the experience of unity and oneness in all spheres of his being in order to find a new equilibrium. Hence, any satisfying system of orientation implies not only intellectual elements but elements of feeling and sense to be realized in action in all fields of human endeavour. Devotion to an aim, or an idea, or a power transcending man such as God, is an expression of this need for completeness in the process of living.[36]

Fromm's ideas are expressed here in beautiful literary style enlivened by an inner passion. They contain a note of romanticism and existentialism, a note of typically German *Sehnsucht*. We certainly should not be scandalized by his 'offence to psychology' in not employing the usual jargon. Fromm's definition of religion, however, has a psychological timbre and style: religion is 'any system of thought and action . . . which

[36] E. Fromm, *Man for Himself*, Routledge and Kegan Paul, London, 1960, pp. 40-7.

gives the individual a frame of orientation and an object of devotion'.[37] Fromm comes to the decided conclusion that religion is inevitable. 'The question is not *religion or not* but *which kind of religion*, whether it is one furthering man's development, the unfolding of his specifically human powers, or one paralysing them.'[38]

Here the psychologist and psychoanalyst enters in as an arbiter to discover the sources of religion and determine its value. Fromm makes a fundamental distinction between authoritarian and humanist religions. The former hinge upon obedience, reverence and worship and therefore presuppose the existence of a power higher than man which exercises dominion over him. In the humanist religions, on the other hand, the centre is man himself and his powers: man must develop his mind and recognize truth; he must love others so as to reach, by reason and love, the experience of participation in the All.

In the authoritarian religions God is the symbol of power and dominion over man; in the humanist religions he is the symbol of the power by which man actualizes his own life. Fromm stresses this antagonism although he acknowledges that the distinction can also exist in the sphere of a single religion. What counts is not the doctrinal system but the human attitude beneath it. He decides in favour of the humanist religions and has a particular leaning towards Zen Buddhism because of its anti-authoritarian attitude. He considers that humanist religions are the only ones that improve man and stimulate him to spiritual progress, while other religions reduce him to outward conformity and slavery.

These two types of religion, humanist and authoritarian, reflect the fundamental dichotomy in man, his need to be free and his need of bonds. The task of the community is to mould the character of the individual members by processes of socialization and assimilation. Every society therefore develops

[37] E. Fromm, *Psychoanalysis and Religion*, Yale University Press, 1961, p. 21.
[38] *Ibid.*, p. 26.

a particular social character in its members. Fromm prophesies a sane society, an ideal type of society which he suggests should be called Humanistic Communitarian Socialism. In this type of community 'man relates to man lovingly, rooted in bonds of brotherliness and solidarity'. It is a society 'which gives him the possibility of transcending nature by creating rather than by destroying, in which everyone gains a sense of self by experiencing himself as the subject of his powers rather than by conformity, in which a system of orientation and devotion exists without man's needing to distort reality and to worship idols'.[39]

This too is an attractive project, but has man shown himself capable of carrying it out? Or rather, do we not see the humanist religions, in fanatical pursuit of their ideal, becoming more oppressive than the authoritarian religions? The three words by which Fromm denotes the sane society evoke very grim and tragic historical echoes. The necessity of religion is effectively expressed by Fromm but in a way that embodies the same pattern and the same fate as the concepts of scientific humanism. Man is exalted as the supreme end and becomes not only his own idol but his own despot.

In the sphere of psychology itself and of the various types of depth psychology, then, we find a rather unexpected religious note. Although its tone is a subdued one, it is in point of fact insistent and pretentious to the point of claiming sovereignty and of imposing itself exclusively. In an Olympus of gods (theopsyche, sex, the unconscious, society, immortality, the solitary man) there is but one Jove, man himself. Dogmas and authority have been banished, but other dogmas and another authority have taken their place, merely presenting themselves in different attire. The flock of believers in these ideas is fortunately a small one.

Psychology actually has an almost religious attraction for people, because it places man face to face with himself and seems to reveal to him what he is and what he can and must

[39] E. Fromm, *The Sane Society*, Routledge and Kegan Paul, London, 1963, p. 362.

do, while setting him free from bondage. It gives the impression that it is placing him on the road to a better future and introducing him to a judicious and reasonably tranquil life. It affords a 'care of souls' in a human way, possibly backed up by the prestige of a doctor. It is a 'scientific' and secular religion. But it is a remarkable fact that in the field of psychoanalysis itself the religious sense has gradually come to be positively acknowledged and in a more and more compelling manner as time goes on. It is important, also, to observe the men who represent the psychoanalytical movement and to see it in its historical setting.

With the exception of Jung, the more prominent psychoanalysts are all Viennese Jews (Freud, Klein, Adler, Allers, Frankl, Rank). Among the emigrants to the United States, Alexander and Rapaport are of Hungarian origin, J. L. Moreno is a Rumanian, Erikson an Austrian, Horney and Fromm are Germans, and all of them are Jews. In addition to its subtlety and detachment in observing interior conflicts, a quality with which the Jews are particularly gifted, psychoanalysis possesses a note of universal participation, of aspiration to liberation and a new order of things, combined with an aura of mystery, all of which are characteristic of the Jewish religion. It is not surprising, then, to find the religious note emerging even in the psychoanalysts' denials of religion.

Secular religion, which occupies itself with man and sets God aside, is linked up with the natural sciences and with the sciences which deal with life and human nature. It shares the vicissitudes of science but confers on science itself such supreme and absolute dignity as to turn it into a despot. Science actually has many things in common with religion. It transcends individual facts and persons, presents a picture of the world and in this setting tries to give a meaning to human existence, and demands commitment and sacrifice. Thus we can have a religion of agnosticism or even atheism.

But considerable inconsistencies are evident in secular religion. It vaunts the patronage of reason and freedom from dogma, but actually it is a rational construction which possesses all the sophistications of the theologies which it deprecates, yet it has none of their enthusiasm. It posits presuppositions no less debatable than the dogmas which it rejects, while it appropriates all the intransigence of such dogmas. Fixing its attention all the time on feeling and undervaluing the rational aspect, it lowers religion from the level of sentiment to sentimentalism, to the sentimental gratification of religious experience. But it assumes no active commitment and fails to conform its behaviour to what is indicated by this experience. It is a utilitarian compromise in the interests of the individual and of society. Consequently it fails to maintain a religious attitude in regard to man, who from the state of sovereignty attributed to him initially, comes to be considered as raw material to be made more efficient and more functional, whether he likes it or not.

Science cannot tell us what man *is worth*; it can only tell us how far he can *serve* his own practical ends and those of the community. But despite all this, secular religion appeals continually to general categories of right and wrong, reasonable and unreasonable, humanitarian and authoritarian, progressive and reactionary and so forth. Since it cannot appeal to an Absolute, secular religion is open to all possibilities of good and of evil. All the failings and mistakes with which it finds fault in various religions—and often with reason—can be attributed to secular religion itself. It is guilty of intolerance, fanaticism, and outward conformity, which are all the more implacable and ruthless the more it realizes how fragile and how exacting is the principle from which it started. It should also be remembered that the possibility of separating religious experience from a doctrinal context, which Thomas Huxley declared he had learned from Carlyle's *Sartor resartus*, can be an indication of psychic dissociation of which Carlyle himself was a victim.

When we observe a man dedicated to science we note the intertwining of the same religious and irreligious attitudes. The scientist is usually spurred on by an increasingly keen curiosity to observe in order to make discoveries, by a need to understand the universe and by a lively sense of wonder at his own littleness and at his own capacities. These are qualities which we find also in the religious man. On the other hand, the scientist's continual effort to 'reduce' complex entities to their elementary components dims his vision of the whole and possibly develops his view of partial data. The temptation to 'technicize', to exercise control and dominion, blunts his religious sense of mystery. An excessive thirst for power blinds him to the realization of how little he can really do. He may flatter himself that he has created a new world, whereas he is just a poor foreigner who has had the courage to visit it, in order to exploit it rather than to know it.

In face of a science which professes to take the place of religion and thereby runs the risk of being a false science and a wretched religion, we may well find ourselves inclined to return to the old-fashioned idea of religion overtaking science precisely in its most appropriate function, which is the search for truth and the reverence for what transcends human capacity. Though science in the course of fifty years has offered man more discoveries than religion has done in as many centuries, it cannot introduce eternal man, the man of all centuries, into the mystery—today more profound than ever—of the world around him and of his own inner life, unless by a spellbound admiration, a *pietas* that bows its head before a great invisible power.[40] A religion which sees man against the background of a great and mysterious Absolute and a science which bides its time respectfully and vigilantly while courageously endeavouring to approach this Absolute, can and must coexist if man is really to understand himself and his place in the world.

[40] Newton's words shortly before his death are equally topical today: 'I do not know what I may appear to the world; but to myself I seem to have been only like a boy, playing on the seashore, and diverting myself in now and then finding a smoother pebble or a prettier shell than ordinary, while the great ocean of truth lay all undiscovered before me' (E. N. da C. Andrade, *Sir Isaac Newton*, Collins, London and Glasgow, 1961, p. 118.)

8. Religion

Reality

When children have listened with interest to a fairytale they turn to you and ask: 'Is it a true story or did you make it up?' This is the eternal question man asks in regard to religion. Here, too, we find children in the forefront. Allport gives an account of some young Unitarian ministers who had related with complete impartiality to a group of children the cosmogonies of various religions.[1] 'But are they true? Which one is true?' was the unanimous question. Children expect an immediate explanation, remarks Allport. It is the simplest and cheapest way to obtain information and it implies full confidence in the informant.

This manner of obtaining information is also adopted by the adult, for even though he feels the need of forming his own ideas during adolescence, he is merely transferring his confidence to other persons considered by him to be competent. But the question 'Is it true?' persists in a particularly pressing manner in those who want to get to the root of things. If we were to heed everything that has been said, even science would seem to be an accumulation of utterly conflicting statements, each of which was once considered to be true. The desire for truth is invariably present even when it does not show itself. There is nothing more intolerable than to discover that something we considered true is false, or, worse still, to uphold something which we know or suspect to be untrue. In this case there is an attempt to cover it up with plausible pretexts and obstinately to defend the false position.

But what is truth? *Quid est veritas?* This question expresses

[1] G. W. Allport, *Religion in the Developing Personality*, *op. cit.*, p. 37.

a cynical attitude but at the same time a problem from which there is no escape. The whole of philosophy has sought an answer and men have all the time continued to contrast a true with a false, without paying much attention to the arguments of philosophers. The alternative true-false is one of the most primordial standards of measurement, which we cannot abstract from even though we are unable to define it. The alternative real-apparent is a particular instance of the true-false alternative, even though it is less distinct, and we merge true with real in contrast to false and illusory.

But what do we mean by real? The definition is a difficult one, as is obvious from the numerous books written on this subject. Scientists seem to have come off best in the whole matter. By 'trying and trying again', by putting statements to the test and subjecting them to control, they have achieved progress in science and have extended the range of man's dominion. But if we consider the continual succession of scientific discoveries we have to admit that what was asserted as reality has often turned out to be merely apparent since it has been supplanted by new discoveries. Those who are clearly worst off are the psychologists, who have been obliged to complicate what was already far from clear by introducing the further alternative of subjective-objective. What is directly experienced and is therefore in a certain way confined to the subject is said to be subjective, while what can be observed and verified by others is said to be objective.

The anxious desire to make use of data which are indisputable because they admit of a more rigorous verification from many angles has led a large number of psychologists to deal only with objective facts. But alas for the facts. Taken by themselves they shed very little light on real experience. In addition, like objective facts to which all the sciences direct their attention, they presuppose the existence of the subjective fact which it is so difficult to capture and bridle. It is true that we can hardly question the result registered by an instrument since various observers can verify it. But this presupposes that the observers know the nature of the instrument and are able to read the results it produces; and these are facts inherent in the subject and therefore subjective.

Strictly speaking, says Köhler, there is no such thing as conclusive proof of the existence of a physical world, just as no proof exists to show that we have direct subjective experience of other people.[2] But we can go further. If we make 'what is apparent' coincide with the subjective fact and that which 'is' with the objective fact, we shall make no headway at all. A stick immersed in water under certain conditions appears to be broken while it is really unbroken. A wheel appears to us to be round while the image of it formed by the eye is only occasionally so, that is, when the wheel is directly in front of us. A person appears to us to have the same stature when he is close to us as when he is not very far away, but in point of fact his image as seen by the eye must necessarily be larger in the first than in the second case. When we go to the cinema people and objects appear to us to be moving on a screen which is luminous all the time. In reality we are looking at a succession of stationary pictures and the screen in a regular succession of extremely brief intervals is alternately luminous and dark.

In order to study the perception of causality Michotte made an apparatus that allowed him to determine, in the case of two pictures, the conditions under which one appeared to be the cause of movement in the other. Michotte himself tells us how a colleague of his, a philosopher with a sense of humour, drew the following conclusion after he had seen the experiments: 'To put it briefly, you start out from an illusion to prove the reality of the causal impression and to demonstrate its objectivity.' These words, comments Michotte, contain the entire justification of the method we have followed in our researches.[3]

Actually psychology confines itself to establishing the

[2] W. Köhler, *Gestalt Psychology*, Mentor Books, New York, 1947. Also available as a New English Library paperback, 1966.
[3] A. Michotte, *The Perception of Causality*, Basic Books, New York, 1963.

conditions and relations in which a given psychic act comes about, but psychology unaided is unable to establish whether the act has really taken place or not. The perception of movement or of causality can take place where there are either real or apparent movements or causal relations. It is true that we have a 'sense of reality'. A dream is distinguished from reality but unfortunately only when we are awake. While we are sleeping the dream is so vividly and forcefully present to us that we are unable to reject it and it makes a deep impression on us. Hallucinations appear real despite the assurance that nothing of what we see and hear is real. Even when we are wide awake and can control our perceptions we cannot escape from the emotional repercussion of what we know to be only apparent.

We can visit the *Hexens-schaukel* (literally, 'witch's see-saw') in a fair-booth where we get the impression that the room has turned upside down, and though we know how the trick is worked we can find ourselves obliged just the same to grip our chairs during the performance and come out with a sense of nausea that is anything but apparent. We may go to the cinema perfectly aware that the screen is not a window through which we witness real events, yet we participate fully and consistently in the fictitious happenings. The emotional attitude is often of decisive importance in our summing-up of a situation.

It has been said that our passions blind us, precisely because we are readier to behave according to our feelings and what appears to us subjectively than in a realistic way in accordance with actual facts. Depth psychology has pushed the question of 'psychological reality' to its most extreme consequences. Freud went so far as to assert that dreams, fancies and even memories are appearances which conceal but also express deeper and more decisive events. Reality does not consist, therefore, according to Freud, in facts of which we are subjectively certain, but in those of which we are quite ignorant. Jung is perhaps even more radical than Freud. According to his view what works is real: *es ist wirklich, was wirkt*. That which is charged with emotive significance is real.

It might appear that Freud's ideas on the 'investiture' of objects by the libido and by the reality principle suggest a reality distinct from the psychological reality. But the premises leading to this conclusion are lacking. 'Freud is always dealing with the reality of experience and not with that of the objects to which that experience has reference,' remarks Grensted.[4] Freud confines himself to testing symbolic judgment and the solution of conflict in the experience he is considering. 'In psychoanalytic writings,' says Erikson,

> the terms 'outer world' or 'environment' are often used to designate an uncharted area which is said to be outside merely because it fails to be inside the individual's somatic skin, or inside his psychic systems, or inside his self in the widest sense. Such a vague and yet omnipresent 'outerness' by necessity assumes a number of ideological connotations and, in fact, assumes the character of a number of world images: sometimes 'the outer world' is conceived of as reality's conspiracy against the infantile wish world; sometimes as the (indifferent or annoying) fact of the existence of other people; and then again as the (at least partially benevolent) presence of maternal care. But even in the recent admission of the significance of the 'mother-child' relationship, a stubborn tendency persists to treat the mother-child unit as a 'biological' entity more or less isolated from its cultural surroundings, which then again become an 'environment' of vague supports or of blind pressures and mere 'conventions'.[5]

The psychologist is therefore not in a position to decide whether there is a reality distinct from psychic reality. He confines himself to establishing how the real is constructed in the case of psychic reality.[6]

[4] L. W. Grensted, *The Psychology of Religion*, Oxford University Press, London, 1952, p. 160.

[5] E. Erikson, *Identity and the Life Cycle, op. cit.*, p. 150.

[6] This subject is dealt with by C. L. Musatti, *Condizioni dell'esperienza e fondazione della psicologia*, Universitaria, Florence, 1965.

This conclusion sets the limits to the psychologist's possibilities as a student of psychic facts. But we must admit that this is very unsatisfactory for the psychologist, who aims at fitting psychic facts into the world around them and cannot escape from the insistent question of a reality distinct from the psychological one. In practice he behaves like the rest of men, convinced that there are other things in the world besides himself and aware that he must deal with them, and this unspoken conviction is present all through his work. Stimulus and response, situation and behaviour, aggression and frustration as well as many other binomials postulate a twofold reality.

This state of affairs is also reflected in the psychology of religion. The psychologist begins by asserting that he is not competent to deal with anything beyond the range of psychic facts, and rightly so. But when his work is done he concludes that all religious facts can be explained in psychological terms and that in the psychological chain there are no gaps suggesting other than psychological causes. Consequently, since there is no trace of a transcendental cause, religion is not true. This is more or less what Leuba has to say on the subject.[7] Freud's version is that religion is a psychological construction for the satisfaction of natural desires and needs and is therefore an illusion. Durkheim and the sociological schools assert that religion is always conditioned by social situations of transmission and learning and that it therefore expresses a social reality to which there is no corresponding factual reality.

All these statements throw light on only one aspect of religion, and the conclusions are all short-circuited. Our entire conception of reality, it is said, is in psychological terms. Does this exclude a priori the possibility of non-psychological causes, of non-subjective realities? Religion is an expression of human needs. But is it nothing more and are we to exclude a priori the possible connection between need and reality? Religion is a social institution. Does this necessarily mean that

[7] J. H. Leuba, *The Psychology of Religious Mysticism*, Harcourt Brace, New York, 1925.

social institutions have no reality of their own which responds precisely to individual needs?

We are therefore faced with the necessity of re-examining the question of reality as previously posited by the psychologists. Is not this, after all, a lawful question even for the psychologist? It is a question which we find at the very beginnings of experimental psychology, although stated in a different way. While Wundt fixed his attention on the constituent elements of psychic processes and on the laws which regulate their reciprocal connection, Franz Brentano argued that the psychic phenomenon has a distinctive character which is lost to view when we concentrate on psychic 'contents' alone.[8] When I perceive 'red' it is not the 'red', that is, the content of my experience, that constitutes the psychic fact, but the act of seeing 'red'. The content (the colour I see) may change. It may be red or yellow or purple, but I cannot suppress the 'seeing'.

If I say I am fond of red, or that I prefer red to yellow, I am speaking of an experience which is different from mere seeing, because I am saying how it affects me and how it affects me in comparison to other colours. It is not, therefore, the content but the act that qualifies psychic activity. It is not the noun but the verb. It is not the raw material but the way I treat it. On the other hand, psychic acts must necessarily have a content: it is not possible to see without seeing something, nor to love without loving something, nor to want without wanting something. In the psychic fact there is therefore a fundamental duality and the two terms of this duality are united by a relationship of direction: the act is directed towards the object and the object is 'intentionally' inexistent in the act. If we wanted to use a mathematical term we might say that the psychic act has vectorial properties, that is, it cannot be defined by a number alone (the content) but by a number plus a direction (the act).

In psychological language we find these characteristics

[8] F. Brentano, *Psychologie vom Empirischen Standpunkt*, Leipzig, 1874.

continually. We distinguish a subject from an object, an impulse from the end to which it is directed, a state of passivity from one of activity. We distinguish an 'I' who observes from a 'self' who is observed; an 'I' from a physical object, an 'I' from another person, an 'I' from a 'you', an individual from society, an individual from the world. The general conviction is that just as the first term in these relationships is real, so too is the second. It is only when the psychologist points out that the first 'real' can produce the second which is therefore a fictitious fact created by the first that we come to a halt and are obliged to agree that from the strictly psychological point of view we have no possibility of proving the real independent existence, *sui juris*, of the second term. But there is also a sense of reality and unreality, undoubtedly very fragile as an absolute criterion, since a real object may be experienced as unreal and an unreal one as real.

We have the emotional charge, a force that moves us (Jung), but this too is far from being a sure criterion: unreal objects can move us deeply and real objects can leave us indifferent. On the other hand we cannot assert that our emotional and affective participation is detached from the situation in which it is expressed. It is, in fact, the situation itself that moves us and stimulates us to understand what it means. Fear or anger drives us or 'motivates' us to discover the meaning of the situation (danger or opposition).

There is usually a consistency between the situation and the emotive response. We are not moved by a stone nor do we feel ashamed in the presence of a horse. When we are hungry we do not feel disgust for food and we do not respond to a spontaneous act of kindness with an insult. It is true that in particular cases even necessary food can produce in us a sense of nausea and that we can, in particular circumstances, consider a kindness to be an offence, or that we can be attached to a useless object. But in such cases there is a mistaken interpretation and one tries to rectify it by every possible means, although the attempt is not always successful. The effort of doctor and psychotherapist to re-establish consistency between situation and subjective experience is not without meaning. Even when the psychic fact is studied as such we must not 'fall into the error of isolation', as Goldstein has said.[9] Subsidiary criteria have to be used.

Religious experience is marked by a sense of participation in something different from ordinary sensory experience, something ineffable, to which fear, attraction, mystery, but also peace, confidence and love communicate a note that is not to be confused with anything else. Can we say with certainty that no reality distinct from sensory reality corresponds to this experience? Even the exclusion of this possibility obliges us to employ subsidiary arguments and criteria which differ from the psychic datum.

In addition religious experience takes place not so much as an action on the part of man, but as the action of something external which he admires and with which he endeavours to establish contact. 'Objectification' (in the psychological sense) reaches its culminating point in religious experience. We are not dealing here with objects to which psychic acts and tendencies are directed, but with an object which differs from those to which these acts and tendencies are applied and which emerges as the foundation of all objects and from which the subject cannot escape. It is something 'beyond', something that transcends the human being and the world because it is totally different from both.

It may be remarked from the psychoanalytical point of view that the creation of a substitute for the object of tendencies, an imaginary outlet for them when their natural flow is obstructed, is a quality peculiar to human psychic activity. Religion would therefore be a product of the unconscious that the ego is unable to recognize directly. But even if we accepted this point of view, a question would still remain unanswered. How can it be that whereas neurotic 'transformation' reaches a very unstable condition, religion (the conviction, that is, of the existence of extra-psychic realities) is so tenacious that it can

[9] K. Goldstein, *Human Nature in the Light of Psychopathology*, Schocken, New York, 1963.

oppose and overcome obstacles at a decisively biological level?

Finally, as Thouless has rightly pointed out, the effort made by religion to state its doctrine in rational terms (an attempt that could immediately be disqualified as 'rationalization') aims at a reality to which it seeks to draw near by a standard and a method adopted precisely by the experimental sciences.[10] Here the sequence of doctrines (for example, regarding the constitution of matter) expresses a more and more penetrating approximation to a given reality and not a denial of this reality.

To sum up, we may say that psychological investigation, as is the case with the empirical sciences, reaches partial, detached or isolated results from which a rapid and impatient process of extrapolation can lead to negative conclusions where religion is concerned. But these very results, which when taken singly fail to achieve indisputable probative force, do when subjected to a critical examination acquire a circumstantial and cumulative force in favour of religion which is not to be minimized. The psychologist is not necessarily obliged, then, to assume the position of the last desperate defence which William James raises in *The Will to Believe*.

According to James, man is obliged to make a forced and most serious choice between agnosticism and faith. He cannot defer this choice because not to make it would involve a decision *sui generis*, since faith has an immense practical importance from the psychological point of view. It may be remarked that this alternative is not absolute, for atheism and agnosticism can assume typically religious qualities and can even become religions themselves. As to the 'functionality' of religion for the efficiency of its members, considered as a criterion of validity, we wonder if this is not just a vicious circle: the declaration that to 'have a belief' is equivalent to considering it to be true, and that a belief is true because it offers advantages. This would amount to saying that we can believe in everything, true or false, as long as this belief has a practical value for which it should be upheld.

[10] R. M. Thouless, *The Psychology of Religion*, *op. cit.*, pp. 279-80.

For Don Ferrante astrology had an unquestionable value and perhaps also a practical one, since it concealed his fate from him. However, 'his fretus, or in other words, on these good grounds, he took no precautions against the plague: he was stricken by it and went to bed to die like a hero of Metastasio, laying the blame on the stars'. To attribute to religion mere 'psychological truth' or utilitarian value is to bar the way to an understanding of its meaning. There are signs in religion, though, which must not be overlooked. First, its need of turning to something real and independent instead of something imaginary and fictitious; second, the note of the presence of something quite different from ordinary objects of experience; third, its receptive rather than active attitude in face of this 'something' that is at work; fourth, the effort to make contact with this something and to understand it rationally; and fifth, the closeness of the relationship with the mystery, a secret and gladdening closeness, terrible in some cases, imperceptibly and gently but firmly persuasive in others.

Further elements might be added, but those mentioned suffice to introduce the questions which follow. Are we really to deny the existence of other realities than psychological ones and are we to deny that the latter have a meaning only when they lead us to recognize further realities? Does not the sensation of 'difference' between the subject and religious reality point to something higher than man, something that transcends him? Does our receptivity in regard to a religious reality, as also in regard to a work of art, quite exclude the existence of an appropriate stimulus? Is not the translation of religion into intellectual terms, as far as this may be possible, an indication of criticism and refinement analogous to those of the psychologist when he tries to describe and understand the psychic act? Does the impression of nearness to something not point to other types of discovery, as in the case of psychic activity itself and scientific investigation?

This series of questions shows that the strictly and severely psychological approach is not to be considered the only or the definitive one. Hence, anyone who wants to form an idea of religion cannot refuse to approach it by other paths. Philosophy, the natural sciences and the sciences which deal with man all have something to say on the subject. History also has something to contribute, for in describing the various religions it can penetrate beneath their formal differences to reveal a convergence of outlines and can even lead us to examine a possibility that is clearly maintained by some religions, the possibility of revelation.

A final point is worthy of mention. An exhaustive, critical and complete study of religion according to scientific methods does not necessarily involve assent to it. The approach to religious reality and participation in it do not take place according to the schemata of logical deductive reasoning, such as we use in the sciences, but by a personal relationship. When I am personally committed, I first of all experience the situation as a consistent whole and later I analyse it and examine the parts and relations involved in it. I move by intuition, I have an insight into it and I see my way without explanations. Intuition may involve risk, exposed as it is to the possibility of erroneous interpretation, but it contains the nucleus from which approach begins.

Intuition has different qualities from logical reasoning, but it is also a process of reason or intelligence. A symphony or a work of art proceeds from an intuition but they are the fruit of reason and intelligence just as fully as logical reasoning or calculation. In religion we are not faced with a mental construction to be followed and evaluated step by step with the cold detachment we bring to our examination of things. We are in the presence of a mystery and feel the need to participate in it. That is why its most primitive manifestation is anthropomorphic, since a colloquy presupposes an 'other' and we picture him as other men appear to us. Anthropomorphism, although it has a 'projective' aspect, or an aspect of subjective production, is perhaps the most primitive phase of the symbol, the substitution of a sign for the reality.

Mankind's great images of the divine, writes M. Buber, are not born of his imagination but of real meeting with real divine power and majesty.[11] To the same degree that we lack the capacity to meet realities that are independent of us but are accessible to our research and commitment, our human power to picture the divine is also defective. 'Without the reality of encounter, all images are play and deception.'[12] The religious world does not appear to us in the icy coldness of the scientific world, but in the dramatic and even tragic fervour of the human world.

The symbol[13]

Closely connected with the problem of 'reality' is the question of the 'symbol'. We live in contact with the world, we have information about the world, we communicate with the world, and thus we establish its 'reality' through our organs of sense and movement, of reception and action. I say that an apple is there because I see it and bite it. I say there is an apple on the tree even if I cannot reach it to pluck it. I say 'I ate an apple' and the apple is in this case neither touchable nor visible. The apple may be there or not, and I treat it as something apart from myself. However, when we see, touch and bite an apple, we also refer to what happens within us, to information that filters through our sense, passes through our nerve cells, arrives at nerve centres and causes action on our part. A series of signals, quite different from the apple, succeeds in determining a meaning and behaviour, causing us to bite the apple. The

[11] M. Buber, *The Eclipse of God*, Harper, New York, 1957. Also available in a new edition as a Harper paperback, 1967.

[12] *Ibid.*

[13] An adequate treatment of symbolism and of questions relating to it is not possible here. A. Miotto has pointed out succinctly the interpretative stages in symbolism (social perspective, problematical valuation, relation between conscious and unconscious, dialectic valuation and global valuation: A. Miotto, *Il simbolismo nelle comunicazioni di massa*, Ist. A. Gemelli, Milan, 1965). I myself am referring in these pages to the symbol as a means of expressing the religious sense. See F. N. Dillistone, 'The Function of Symbols in Religious Experience' in *Colston Papers*, XIII, London, 1960, and also two books by the same author: *Christianity and Symbolism*, Collins, London, 1956 and *Christianity and Communication*, Collins, London, 1955.

signals converge in a meaning, in a word, so that we say that an apple is there.

Helmholtz already drew attention to this fact when he spoke of a 'sign language' of the senses *(Die Zeichensprache der Sinne)*, and Woodworth pointed out that although we make use of this sign language continually in our daily life we skip it in order to get immediately to the meaning.[14] We are immediately concerned with the apple and we do not stop to consider the stimuli by which it provokes, stimulates and excites the corresponding signals in our nervous system. The mere word 'apple', a succession of sounds that have nothing to do with physical qualities of the apple, presents a very clear image to our mind. We may denominate the apple by various sounds, as occurs in different languages, but the final meaning is the same. The word formed by sounds represents an object, without however always producing the image constituted by the object's signals. I can speak and think of apples without necessarily picturing them every time I hear or pronounce the word.

Our mental work does not therefore deal with the physical condition of objects but with the signs and signals by which they are connoted. In our thinking and speech we also have continual recourse to signs of a particular kind—that is, to signs of things which we never see in concrete form. When we speak, then, of length and height and depth, of light and darkness, we are indicating conditions which do not exist in isolation but only in relation to certain objects. We are then referring to abstract qualities apart from objects. Moreover, these indicators of abstract qualities can be transferred to other objects which are also abstract.

When we say of someone, for instance, that 'his talk is superficial, long and far from clear', we are attributing qualities found in concrete objects to a person's whole manner of expressing himself, which is separate from the physical conditions in which it takes place. Our everyday language has continual recourse to abstract expressions and to displaced

[14] R. S. Woodworth and D. G. Marquis, *Psychology*, Methuen, London, 1949.

connotations and only in this way does it become speech instead of a mere list of words. Verbal signs enable us to give explicit expression to the things that make up our subjective world and the world in which we live. There is therefore a succession of signs which vary as to their properties and complexity. We pass on from the 'sign' as a sensory imprint to the sign which indicates an actual object (which we may more suitably call a 'signal'), or which indicates actual behaviour. Thence we proceed to the signal which denotes an abstract object or abstract behaviour separated from its physical concreteness. We then reach the signal which is abstracted from a concrete object and is transferred to other abstract realities. There is a gradual detachment from concrete conditions up to the point at which the 'sign' and the 'signal' achieve, as it were, an autonomous existence, and here we have symbol.

It is essential to distinguish between signs and signals, on the one hand, and symbols on the other. This distinction is far from easy, since all of them have an element in common, namely, the fact that they are not the object but an indication of it. In other words, they denote something different from what they are.

A sign or signal is an indicator of the presence of something without telling us anything of its nature, just as the galvanometer indicates an electric current or the colour of litmus paper reveals the acidity of a solution, although they tell us nothing of the nature of these elements. A flag denotes a nation but tells us nothing of the characteristics of that particular state, and a certain sound on a trumpet denotes an event or an act to be performed without explaining their meaning. In animal life we find a series of signs and signals: light and darkness which attract an amoeba or cause it to withdraw; optic and olfactory interindividual communication among insects (von Frisch's 'bee language');[15] the smell and the gesture of his master that makes a dog run towards him or even keep the dog in an attitude of expectation.

[15] K. von Frisch, *Bees, their Vision, Chemical Senses and Language*, Cornell, Ithaca, N.Y., 1956.

The understanding of these signals may be innate (amoeba, bees, ants) or acquired (the dog). To man a signal can be conventional, variable, and therefore learnt. When red appears on traffic lights it means that traffic is to stop, while red on an electric switch signifies that the current is on. It is therefore necessary for us to learn somehow what the signal means and this we achieve by the use of words as well. When we learn a foreign language the signals change but the sense remains. Signals, however, telling us that a certain object is present or that we are to behave in a certain manner, only indicate something which we already know either by an innate or an acquired capacity.

A symbol in itself is less direct than a signal, but it carries with it a cognitive and emotive value for the thing it symbolizes. In the sentence 'That person's talk is superficial, long and far from clear', the adjectives are derived from symbols which have a meaning of their own. To a man born blind we can convey some idea of what a colour is like by a transposition of sensory impressions: red is like a sharp sound or a strong scent. In this way fire, light, the sky, are employed to indicate connotations proper to an event and to enable us to know and feel it. For example, we speak of clear thinking, fiery action, a calm mind, a state of mind.

Poetic and religious language is only possible by the use of symbols, but even our everyday language cannot do without them. The symbolic meaning is not always conveyed by some particular symbols; but it can be attributed to some signs. There are, accordingly, conventional symbols which vary from one culture to another, from one type of interest to another. White, which is a symbol of serenity to the European, is a symbol of sorrow to the Chinese. Mathematical symbols should more properly be called signs, since their symbolic character depends on the fact that they are instruments for a type of thought that would otherwise be inexpressible. The mathematical symbol is a fixed one and the symbol is therefore impoverished and returns to the condition of a mere indicator.

According to Ernst Cassirer signals and symbols belong to

two different worlds. The signal belongs to the physical world while the symbol belongs to the world of intellect. Signals are 'representative' while symbols are designative. Signals, even when understood and adopted as such, have, however, a type of physical and substantial existence, but symbols have a functional value only.[16]

If we want to illustrate the increasing complexity which finds an outlet in the symbol, we can present the following succession: stimulus or electro-magnetic oscillations on a certain wavelength; sign, or the nervous condition aroused by the stimulus and experienced by the subject who sees the colour red; signal, or red understood as indicating that the road is not clear; symbol, red signifying ardour, blood or life. The symbol is more immediately understood than the signal.

In myth and allegory the symbol is adopted as a means of expression. Both myth and allegory are intended to convey a meaning through a narrative. The myth is further from reality but has a deeper meaning, while the allegory adheres more closely to reality but is more rationally constructed and more superficial.[17]

A myth is ordinarily understood to be an imaginary construction, like a fable, but beneath the veil of fiction it possesses something of the dramatic vitality of human experience and it is permeated with a religious sense, a sense of admiration and awe in the presence of mystery. By comparing myths with documented history, there has been an attempt to purge history of myths (demythologization) with the possibly undesired result that history has been made arid and meaningless and that myth has been deprived of its roots. It is certainly right and proper to distinguish between what is supported by documentary evidence and what is not, but this does not imply the necessity of suppressing what is vital in myth. Myth is born again when its head has been cut off. It is all the stronger for the fact that its strength is not recognized and in this it is very

---

[16] E. Cassirer, *An Essay on Man, op. cit.*, p. 57.

[17] Huizinga, cited in Erikson, *Young Man Luther*, Norton, New York, 1958; and Faber, London, 1959.

similar to religion. A radical demythologization such as people think to accomplish by mathematics ends up in the myth of man's dehumanization (R. Dubos).[18]

In parenthesis we may add that the word 'demythologization' is widely used today to indicate the purification of history from legendary elements so as to reach the literal truth. But this interpretation corresponds only partially and inexactly to what Rudolf Bultmann means by the word *Entmythologisierung*. He proposes as far as the Bible is concerned to discover the genuine meaning (the *Kerygma*, or proclamation of the message) which was of necessity expressed in forms understood by the mentality of the age (myths, e.g. the sky, the earth, the infernal regions, the kingdom, judgment, etc.), which today are unacceptable and devoid of religious meaning. To demythologize is to reach the true interpretation of the myth, and the theologian's task is to find an adequate interpretation of it for the man of today. Bultmann leans on Martin Heidegger's philosophy of existence and asks what the myth tells us of human existence in God's sight and of man's understanding of himself. The New Testament posits the existential alternative between the world and God. Demythologization is therefore an existential interpretation.[19]

Returning to what we have been saying, it would appear that the line of demarcation between sign and symbol is that which divides the capacity of animals from that of man. Animals act in accordance with signs and configurations of signs (Tolman's *sign Gestalt*),[20] but they do not reach the level of symbol. In recent years an attempt has been made to discover symbolic thinking in animals, but only some initial efforts in this direction have been made, without further development. Even when monkeys have learned to distinguish a particular quality in the use of substitute instruments (for instance, a coin to set

[18] R. Dubos, *I sogni della ragione*, Turin, 1962.
[19] K. Rahner-H. Vorgrimler, *Concise Theological Dictionary*, Herder-Burns Oates, Freiburg, London, 1965, pp. 121-3.
[20] E. C. Tolman, *Purposive Behaviour in Animals and Men*, Century, New York, 1932.

L

a slot-machine in action), they cannot make this explicit in language and therefore cannot transcend the concrete situation. They remain at the level of indication and are unable to set up something on its own. Geometrical figures, numbers and the coins represent concrete situations, but cannot become abstract and general entities. On the other hand it is remarkable how language assumes a general significance for man. In the case of the deaf, dumb and blind (Helen Keller and Laura Bridgmann) the tactile sign, as soon as it was understood, became at once symbolic.

'Non-human beings seldom produce the signs which influence their behaviour,' writes C. Morris, 'while human individuals in their language and post-language symbols characteristically do this and to a surprising degree. Here is a basic difference between men and animals, and until the behavioral theory develops a semiotic adequate to this difference it will remain what it is today: a careful study of animals and a pious hope for a science of the human person.'[21] Quoting this statement of Morris, Allport comments: 'Morris seems to be saying with fine candour that there is a world of difference between signal and symbol, and that even his own careful system of semiotic fails adequately to bridge the gap. . . . In any case, it is clear that Morris, like many other psychologists, is enamoured of the phylogenetic model.'[22] While the cases of H. Keller and L. Bridgmann illustrate the extraordinary power of the symbolic function, Kurt Goldstein's psychopathological cases show us the possibility of decadence and loss of the abstract attitude to objects, while the concrete attitude persists tenaciously. The subject is still able to use objects correctly even though he has lost the power of verbal indication or of developing abstract concepts and principles in regard to concrete objects. This concrete attitude seems very close to the intelligent behaviour of animals.

In human behaviour the symbol acquires a full and decisive

---

[21] C. Morris, *Signs, Language and Behaviour*, cited in G. W. Allport, *Personality and Social Encounter*, Beacon Press, Boston, 1960, p. 64.

[22] G. W. Allport, *ibid.*, pp. 64-5.

existence of its own. 'What disturbs and alarms man,' said Epictetus, 'are not things, but his opinions and fancies about things.' Cassirer describes as symbolic those forms by which human awareness transforms 'the world of impressions received into the world that is the expression of the human spirit'. Without symbolism, he says, man's life would be similar to that of the prisoners in the cave in Plato's famous allegory. Human life would be confined within the limits of man's biological needs and practical interests. There would be no access to the 'ideal world' which is opened up to man on various sides by religion, art, philosophy and science.[23]

The psychologist's position in regard to symbolism is very difficult and embarrassing. He himself more than anyone else is committed to the use of symbols and these, as he uses them, become for him instrumental signs. He declares that we should not speak of attention, perception or feeling but of attending, observing and feeling, and he then has to determine these processes and express them concretely in such a schematic way that he seems to be describing an apparatus or an organ rather than a global activity. Moreover, the psychologist is greatly perplexed if we ask him 'Who attends, who observes, who feels?' If, in order to reply, he acknowledges an elusive 'I', he immediately places this 'I' on the dissecting table, since he must explain how it is formed, how it works, how it degenerates. The psychologist's entire lexicon is composed of symbols to indicate realities which can only be tackled by abstract thought. On the other hand, he needs something on which to work and thus, more frequently than he realizes, he falls into the error of treating his symbols as real objects.

Probably no other science possesses such an abundant and complex heterogeneity of symbols as psychology. Let us take at random some of its most ordinary terms. Psychology has borrowed from mathematics the terms quantity, gradient, vector; from physics action, reaction, field, energy; from chemistry valency, reactive, sublimation; from biology survival value, instinct, phases of development; from physiology

[23] E. Cassirer, *An Essay on Man, op. cit.*, p. 25.

stimulation, reflex, inhibition; from mythology Eros, Thanatos, Oedipus, libido, etc., and from ordinary experience seeing, remembering, learning, dreaming, feeling, desiring. Sad to say, it is these last elements, which in the last analysis are irreplaceable and are proper to psychology, that are sacrificed in favour of the others for fear of falling into what Newton called 'occult qualities', which are not the object of science.

It has been said that reduction to a common denominator is the condition for the development of science. The unification of physical forces in energy has enabled us to link up apparently different facts (mechanical, optical, electrical) in a unitary concept. In the same way it is believed that the reduction of psychic phenomena to simpler and more general facts accessible to scientific methods of quantification and measurement ought really to give us a psychological science. We wonder if this would not lead to the elimination of psychology by psychological means, that is to say, if it would not eliminate awareness or the knowledge of knowing, as an 'occult entity', though this is indispensable for the utilization of number and measurement.

What is said of physical reductionism can also be applied to biological reductionism. When we have accounted for man as we account for an animal, we may be allowed to ask if we are not left with the animal, while man has disappeared. It is precisely the multiplicity of the symbols used by the psychologist that inclines us to think that various levels of reality exist, each of which has an appropriate symbolism that is inadequate at other levels, and that psychology ought to make an attempt to delimit them. When Tolman proposed his famous distinction between molecular behaviour and molar behaviour, he was pointing out a difference of level.

Colours are certainly due to stimulation of the eye by luminous oscillations on various wavelengths, but we cannot replace colours by their electromagnetic equivalent and perhaps conclude that since colours are caused by stimulations produced by the same energy all colours are the same. It is precisely the psychic fact that qualifies, articulates and gives a meaning to events, and for this reason the psychic fact has dimensions that are lacking in the physical fact which has been carefully purified from 'occult qualities' and made worthy of science. Light and darkness themselves—two physically definable events— assume the clear symbolic connotation of freedom and joy (light), of isolation and fear (darkness), which enter much more deeply into subjective experience than the theories which science has offered one after another to account for light (corpuscular, oscillatory or quantum theories).

Precisely because it operates by symbols which penetrate more deeply into human life, psychology cannot fail to observe that the importance of the symbol is not merely phenomenal or apparent but pertains to real experience. The psychologist is thus faced with an opposite alternative to that of reductionism. He asks himself whether symbols may not open up communications with reality, ways of communication that elude the grasp of logical thinking or that this thinking glimpses but is unable to grasp completely.

This is particularly true of religious symbolism. The psychologist and the religious man must speak of things which can only be expressed symbolically. Why be surprised, asks Philo, if the Supreme Reality is inapprehensible to men when even the mind in each one of us is something we cannot know?[24]

The religious symbol gives expression to a real human experience which has no appropriate sensory elements to go by and is permeated by a profound affective state: the experience of the sacred, of the *numinosum fascinans* and *tremendum*, as Rudolf Otto calls it. This immensity and indefinibility of religious experience involves the danger of going to two extremes. There is the risk of objectification, of attributing the sacred quality to sensory or imaginary objects, an idolatry that can invest any object whatsoever (hence the chaos of religions). At the other extreme there is the danger of stripping the 'sacred' of all determination, even symbolical, to the point of agnosia where it is lost in the 'cloud of unknow-

[24] Cited in E. Bevan, *Symbolism and Belief*, Collins, London, 1962, p. 20.

ing' of the mystics or in the agnosticism of modern philosophers, reaching 'the paradox of religious atheism', as Tillich has said.[25]

The symbol is indispensable, but it must not be degraded to the level of an idol, nor is it as a matter of principle to be declared false and illusory. The psychoanalyst, who is more closely tied to symbols than any other psychologist, is faced with a similar difficulty. He encounters certain contents in dreams which cannot have their origin in the mature life of the dreamer and must turn to childhood thinking and prelogical language, to myths and lengends, to folklore, to the wisdom of the various peoples,[26] to a primordial hallucination which when it comes up against reality (through sensory experience) is delimited in particular ways and takes on particular affective tones. The symbol is thus constituted in the unconscious and acquires a psychological reality of its own.

A process of projection lies at the roots of the construction of the real. It would not, then, be inappropriate to say that anthropomorphism is inherent in psychoanalysis. But we might well ask ourselves if any human activity is possible in the sphere of thought or affect which is not anthropomorphic. Even the most abstract activity is the privilege of human beings and is therefore in a certain sense anthropomorphic. A derogatory connotation of relativism is usually attached to the term anthropomorphism, which is considered to falsify reality. The real problem is to avoid an uncritical anthropomorphism, but only man himself can exercise criticism.

As to the religious symbol, it it clearly anthropomorphic by the very fact that it deals with human experience, but man is capable of distinguishing the symbol as an object from that which it signifies. By passing on to the meaning of the symbol man in a certain sense overcomes anthropomorphism even if it is formally present all the time. As E. Bevan points out, those religions which have no conception of a personal God form an idea of God from the elements which are known as qualities

[25] P. Tillich, *Blätter für deutsche Philosophie*, 1928, p. 288.

[26] G. Bally, *Einführung in die Psychoanalyse S. Freuds*, pp. 129-35.

proper to the human person, and hence we have the joy of Vedantic Hinduism, the wisdom of the Stoics and the natural laws of the materialists.[27]

Since everything we encounter in this world is related to the ultimate ground of being, namely, to the Holy, the history of religions, as Paul Tillich says, develops in apparent chaos in which it is nevertheless possible to find order.

The key which makes order out of this chaos is comparatively simple. It is that everything in reality can impress itself as a symbol or a special relationship of the human mind to its own ultimate ground and meaning. So in order to open up the seemingly closed door to this chaos of religious symbols, one simply has to ask, 'What is the relationship to the ultimate which is symbolized in these symbols?' And then they cease to be meaningless and they become, on the contrary, the most revealing creations of the human mind, the most genuine ones, the most powerful ones, those which control the human consciousness, and perhaps even more the unconsciousness, and have therefore this tremendous tenacity which is characteristic of all religious symbols in the history of religion.[28]

While the absolutizing of symbols leads to idolatry, the recognition of their meaning puts us in touch with ultimate Reality which is a mystery, and which is therefore beyond the symbol and cannot itself be a symbol. Still the symbol necessarily remains as a means to be used in our relations with mystery. It enables us to draw near to mystery in the highest form of self-expression, by the 'I-Thou' relationship, as Martin Buber has shown us. Genuine symbols therefore preserve the mystery and 'otherness' of God and enable us to draw near to him as one person to another. Here we have adoration and prayer, two fundamental notes of religion.

In the presence of the mystery of God, while the negative

[27] E. Bevan, *op. cit.*, p. 23.
[28] P. Tillich, *Theology and Culture*, Oxford University Press, New York, 1959, pp. 59-60.

form: 'God is not like other things' constitutes the first most secure and most convenient means of knowing, the affirmative form in which we acknowledge his attributes and his works can only come about by means of symbol, since it must express something indefinable but none the less existent. All religious language is symbolic: fire, light, sky; love, anger, pardon; shepherd, healer; water, bread, wine; eternal, beautiful, perfect. When we say that God 'has created the world', or 'has sent his son', or 'will fulfil his word', in all these temporal, causal and other expressions we are speaking symbolically of God, says Tillich.

Tillich then proceeds to examine the one short sentence: 'God has sent his Son.'

> Here in the word 'has' we have temporality. But God is beyond *our* temporality, though not beyond every temporality. Here we have space; 'sending somebody' means moving him from one place to another. This certainly is speaking symbolically although spatiality is in God as an element in his creative ground. We say that he 'has sent'—that means that he has caused something. In this way God is subject to the category of causality. And when we speak of him and his Son, we have two different substances and apply the category of substance to him. Now all this, if taken literally, is absurd. If it is taken symbolically, it is a profound expression, the ultimate Christian expression, of the relationship between God and man in the Christian experience.[29]

This should not surprise us, for all our speech as man to man is symbolic, both in our reference to 'real' things and in our general, abstract statements. If it is reduced to a series of operative propositions it risks becoming absurd, just as on the other hand a symbol varies in its formal expression and can be out of place with reference to the one who uses it, so much so that it is only by explaining the meaning we intend to attach to the symbol that it becomes comprehensible. We probably find it more difficult to understand the language and art of

[29] *Ibid.*, pp. 62-3.

other epochs than to understand the religious symbols that
have spoken to the men of all ages.

As regards the use of symbols, we are faced with a big
problem which has already been debated at length in the
philosophical field. Does the use of symbols reveal to us various
levels of reality by way of analogy or through some other
mental process, for the sake of rapid expression, for logico-
deductive reasons, or because of a primitive intuition which
seeks a means of expression? It is not my intention to dwell
on this problem here. I mention it in passing, however, because
of the fact that the two processes, often considered to be
antagonistic, are perhaps complementary, while a greater or
lesser intensity marks one or the other.

From the strictly psychological point of view the relationship between symbol and reality is assumed but cannot be
resolved. We ought, however, to bear in mind that when
affirmation and negation alternate, the sum total of probability
points towards affirmation rather than negation. Religious faith
is not only concerned with mysteries but is in itself a mystery,
since it points to our participation in the mystery of the sacred
and in its action upon us.

God

'Was Moses right, or Xenophanes? Did God make man in his
image, or is it not rather man who has made God in his?' This
is how the eternal problem is restated today by the theologian
Henri de Lubac.[30] The psychologist sides with Xenophanes.
That which man calls God, he says, possesses, symbolically,
characteristics which are typically human, which appear already
in the concepts of childhood, are firmly established in interpersonal relations and come to light in the observation of the
events and the conflicts of subjective experience.

The multiplicity of ideas of God in the various religions, he
continues, in different individuals professing the same religion

[30] H. de Lubac, *The Discovery of God*, Darton, Longman and Todd,
London, 1960, p. 11.

and even in the same person in different situations or at different stages of his life, indicates that God is a construct or a projection of human psychic activity which is maintained and transmitted by tradition and serves to express particular states of mind, but does not stand up to logical and critical thinking. From the psychological point of view, moreover, this construct obstructs the free development and progress of man's psychic capacity. In order to make progress and reach that modest share of happiness to which he has a right, man must rid himself of this spectre just as he has already rid himself of many others. This will involve the sacrifice of something he holds dear, but it will also mean the acquisition of something that is true.

'Appearances, certainly, are on the side of Xenophanes,' continues the theologian, 'yet it is Moses who is right. And at bottom Xenophanes agrees. For they are not speaking of the same God or of the same image; which is why the argument is unending.' Xenophanes, using psychological terminology, is right in one way. It is quite true that the idea of God is expressed by symbols derived from human experience in the most varied circumstances, that it reflects a particular attitude of the subject and that it therefore has the appearance of a projection rather than of an objectively recognizable datum.

It is also true that the concept of God is closely bound up with the learning process or a cultural tradition and that a religious idea that has been ossified in institutional forms can be an obstacle to progress and be unreasonably inhuman. But in making these statements, asks the theologian, is the psychologist who takes the side of Xenophanes speaking 'of the same God and of the same image?' No, he argues; the psychologist is referring to what men say about God and to the way they represent him to themselves. He is therefore mistaken when he concludes that since men express certain opinions about God and since psychologists have identified the conditions and reasons of these statements, God is what men declare and believe about him, that is to say, a creation of men themselves.

The psychologist is speaking, then, of the God of men and,

we may add, of the God of psychologists. But is he speaking
of the same God who is present in the idea of God? No,
because the psychologist remains on the empirical plane, con-
centrating his attention on 'how' the idea of God is formed
and expressed, while the theologian remains on the plane of
ideas, on the plane of 'being'. To clarify the position we may
recall the fact that geometry has come down to us from the
Egyptians, who, it has been said, discovered it through their
need to irrigate the Nile delta. The conclusion might be drawn,
then, that geometry is merely the projection of a concrete
problem in a supposed world of general principles. 'But,'
observes M. Eliade, 'we do not see very clearly how the fact
of the discovery of the first geometrical laws, due to the
empirical necessity of irrigation, can have any sort of importance in establishing the validity or invalidity of these laws.'[31]

Newton warns us against confusing abstract space, true
mathematical space, with the space with which we are familiar
by means of our senses. People think of space, time and movement, he says, simply on the basis of the relationship between
these concepts and perceptible objects. But this principle must
be abandoned if we want to reach scientific or philosophical
truth. In philosophy we must abstract from data acquired
through the senses.[32] 'The points and lines of the geometer are
neither physical nor psychological objects; they are nothing but
symbols for abstract relations. If we ascribe "truth" to these
relations, then the sense of the term truth will require redefini-
tion. For we are concerned in the case of abstract space not
with the truth of things but with the truth of propositions and
judgments.'[33]

Einstein also asserts this. 'One is ordinarily accustomed to
study geometry divorced from any relation between its concepts and experience. This is satisfactory to the pure mathe-
matician. He is satisfied if he can deduce his theorems from
axioms correctly, that is, without errors of logic. The question

[31] M. Eliade, in *Témoignages*, 1951.
[32] I. Newton, *Principia*, L. I, def. VIII.
[33] E. Cassirer, *op. cit.*, p. 44.

as to whether Euclidean geometry is true or not does not concern him.'[34] For his part the theologian declares:

> It is really no easier to understand how the fact that the first emergence of the idea of God may possibly have been provoked by a particular spectacle, or have been linked to a particular experience of a sensible nature, could affect the validity of the idea itself . . . the problem of its birth from experience and the problem of its essence or validity are distinct. The problems of surveying no more engendered geometry than the experience of storm and sky engendered the idea of God. The important thing is to consider the idea in itself; not the occasion of its birth, but its inner constitution.[35]

Actually the problem lies in the fact that the idea of God has been formulated in a vast variety of ways. Substantially, however, all of them intend to express something definitive and absolute. The idea of God does not therefore originate from the circumstances to which it is attributed, but it is this very idea that interprets and gives a meaning to the circumstances. What is essential is not the manner in which the idea of God is formed, expressed and made explicit. What matters is the meaning of the idea of God and its quality of absoluteness, which cannot be derived from mere objects. Hence it is necessary to distinguish between 'principles' and 'origins', not to look for principles in origins, not to seek causes in the first empirically verifiable manifestations.

The idea of God can be manifested in the most varied circumstances, but the principle it expresses is not to be derived from these circumstances. So, when the psychologist asserts that God is the infantile residuum of a concept of omnipotence, the expression of a desire to return to the mother's womb, a feeling caused by fear and solitude, or by astonishment in the presence of exceptional phenomena, and that he is a myth

---

[34] A. Einstein, *The Meaning of Relativity*, Princeton University Press, New Jersey, 1950, p. 8.

[35] H. de Lubac, *op. cit.*, pp. 19-20.

handed down by tradition, he immediately incurs the theologian's censure: *Ignoratio elenchi!* You, the psychologist,
are falling into the sophism which Aristotle declares to be at
the roots of many errors in logic, namely, ignorance of the
subject in question. The subject is criticized and said to be self-
contradictory when in fact the meaning of its terms has not
been grasped.[36]

A clash of this kind might suggest that relations between
the theologian and the psychologist have been broken off
altogether. But this is not the case. The same theologian already
quoted resumes: 'Xenophanes has no intention of denying the
divinity; on the contrary, his purpose is to recall man to the
divine when he loses himself among the gods he has
fashioned.'[37] The antagonism between God the Creator and the
creature gods is already evident in the great biblical assertion:
'I am the Lord your God; you shall have no other gods before
me', and the entire history of religions and of mankind tells
of the opposition between the idea of an absolute being and
the deification of dependent beings.

At this point the theologian becomes the psychologist's ally.
'Away, then, with all the projections, sublimations and creations
of our passions of our dreams, of our fears or anger, of our
nightmares or desires! Away with the gods who "seem to have
been invented of set purpose by the enemy of mankind in
order to sanction crime and turn the divine to ridicule"!
(Fénelon). Away with the gods of nothingness which leave us
to ourselves and keep us in bondage! Away with all false
gods!'[38]

Not only does the theologian associate himself with the
psychologist in doing away with 'false and lying gods', but he
draws near to him in vindicating the power of reason over the
madness of deification. 'All our representations of the divine,'

[36] On this point see S. Stebbing, *Thinking to Some Purpose*, Penguin
Books, 1959.

[37] H. de Lubac, *op. cit.*, p. 11. He is referring to W. Jaeger, *The
Theology of the Early Greek Philosophers*, Oxford University Press,
New York, 1947.

[38] *Ibid.*, pp. 11-12.

he writes, 'are woven of elements taken from our world, whether from the natural or the social world; but there is a faculty or a power in man which always drives him on beyond them: the power of reason itself.' And the psychologist asserts: 'We may insist as often as we like that man's intellect is powerless in comparison with his instinctual life, and we may be right in this. Nevertheless, there is something peculiar about this weakness. The voice of the intellect is a soft one, but it does not rest till it has gained a hearing. Finally, after a countless succession of rebuffs, it succeeds.'

Who is the psychologist who speaks thus? It is Freud, in *The Future of an Illusion*.[39] But once again a fundamental difference comes to light. In Freud's conception human intelligence is bound in an inconsistent way to the premises. It leaps forth from the irrational dynamism of instinct. It has the appearance of a defensive weapon in the struggle for existence, rather than an impulse towards transcendence, and it asserts itself against religious illusion. But the theologian says of man:

In his most intimate being, made in the image of God, there is always something which he is quite unable to represent to himself, though he is not without experience of it. 'He bears within himself a source of wonder, a source of infinite self-transcendence' (Fénelon); and that, in the last analysis, is what allows him to know God in truth. . . . Christian tradition adds that man, made in the image of the incomprehensible God, is ultimately incomprehensible to himself. 'Who can enter into himself and understand himself?' . . . It does not mean substituting another principle in the place of reason; rather it means going back to the source.[40]

The theologian's attitude may seem to be aprioristic and influenced by prejudice, while the psychologist appears to advance without prejudice, on a basis of objective facts. But

[39] S. Freud, *The Future of an Illusion*, in Standard Ed., vol. XXI, p. 53.

[40] H. de Lubac, *op. cit.*, pp. 12-13.

the strange thing is that the psychologist who has dismissed God as an illusion prepares for himself and finds himself face to face with another god, no less mysterious and dangerous than the one he has driven away. He is face to face with the god of human reason. In Freud himself we find an attachment, a decided and demanding commitment to his convictions, which has all the appearance of a religious belief. There is just one difference—in place of God there is man, self-sufficient and alone, not real man but a symbolic man into whom men's desires are projected.

It is significant, even from the psychological point of view, that we cannot create a void where God should be, and that when we believe we have eliminated him we have merely set up another in his place. How many divinities have succeeded one another in the course of human history! Leaving aside the divinities of the various religions, we have only to think of some of the 'ideologies': matter, the 'spirit', reason, society, the state.

This instability and this continual recurrence of the need for a supreme, fundamental, irreplaceable principle justifies the theologian's conviction that God is different from what we think him to be. When we think we have defined him fully and with certainty or believe we have established an absolute and universal principle, we are no longer speaking of God, but of the wretched image we ourselves have created of a being who is always beyond us and for whom our definitions and symbols are necessarily inadequate.

There is always a danger that God may become an idol. Hence the continual intransigent admonition of Jewish-Christian tradition: 'I am the Lord your God; you shall have no other gods before me', taken up again at the present time by Christian theologians such as J. Maréchal, H. de Lubac, E. Przywara, Karl Rahner, Karl Barth, A. Farrar and Paul Tillich, with varying kinds of stress but fundamentally with complete unanimity. The theologian's stand cannot be attributed to prejudice. The theologian asserts that man must necessarily seek an absolute, which the psychologist also has to grant; but the theologian goes further than the psychologist in asserting that a unique Absolute exists and that man absolutizes other beings which prevent him from reaching this one Absolute.

The theologian moreover agrees with the psychologist that the decline of the abundant myths which obscure the *Majestas Dei* may encourage man to approach the true God. But on the other hand, with the disappearance of myth, the glimmer of truth it contains may also vanish. It is not in processes of imposition or suppression that religion gives of its best, but in the inner torment of purification and the ceaseless desire for the true God which it awakens in man.

One of the religious assertions that meets with greatest opposition from scientists is that of a personal God. This question was taken up by Einstein in a lecture delivered at a congress on Science, Philosophy and Religion in 1941.[41] His arguments echo substantially those of the general mentality today and are particularly acute for those who live in a world in which events seem the very opposite to what might be expected from a most perfect ruler of all things.

Einstein attacked the idea of a personal God from four angles: The idea is not essential for religion; it is the creation of primitive superstition; it is self-contradictory; it contradicts the world scientific point of view. Translated into current language the first two objections can be rendered as follows: we can be upright men without believing in God; the idea of God is a construction of a primitive mentality. But religion is something different from morals, and while mythological imagination is capable of creating gods it is incapable of creating the idea of God, who surpasses all the elements of human experience that enter into mythology.

The third objection, that the idea of a personal God is self-contradictory since God cannot will the good and evil that exist in the world, refers to the eternal problem of evil. Einstein appears to conceive omnipotence as panenergeticism of a physical nature. This concept does not take into account

[41] P. Tillich, *Theology and Culture, op. cit.*, pp. 127-32.

the existence of other forms of activity. It suffices to mention that God's action does not suppress the activity of individual beings according to their particular nature, whether they be inanimate, animal or human, and that the concept of omnipotence expresses the religious conviction that nothing can remove men from the action of God. In the Bible, it was precisely the exiles in Babylon (Isaiah 40) and the slum dwellers of Rome (Romans 8) who were told that nothing could remove them from God's power even if human powers were to overcome them. 'If the idea of omnipotence is taken out of this context,' writes Tillich, 'and transferred into the description of a special form of causality, it becomes not only self-contradicting—as Einstein rightly states—but also absurd and irreligious.'[42]

Einstein's fourth objection is that the idea of a personal God contradicts the scientific interpretation of Nature. Here the question depends on the meaning we attribute to the word 'personal'. Excluding crude anthropomorphism, the assertion of a personal God is ordinarily understood to mean that in the same way in which a person intervenes actively to regulate events, God intervenes or may intervene in natural events as a cause independent of them.

The deists' 'great architect of the universe' was already considered by Laplace to be a 'superfluous hypothesis'. Einstein's argument belongs to the same order of ideas and indicates a certain tendency towards projection. In this way God is set on the same plane as natural causes and objects, with the sole difference that he is treated as a special and more comprehensive case. But here, too, there is failure to recognize the essential character of God which is his 'otherness' and absoluteness. God does not 'intervene', he does not enter into a scene that is working itself out in its own way in order to set it right. God 'is', and what we say 'happens' does not come from outside but is already necessarily ascribed to God who is the reason of being. When we say that he changes a pre-ordained order so as to be more fully present to us, we must

[42] *Ibid.*, p. 129.

not imagine that he brings about a change in the same way as men make changes in things or in themselves, but that a change is effected in us, a ray of light makes us more aware of his presence and his action.[43]

What does the appelation of 'person' mean, then, when it is applied to God? It indicates the possibility of an 'I-Thou' relationship with him, as one person to another, but all the time in a particular atmosphere of mysterious diversity. Tillich reminded Einstein of something he had written, namely that the true scientist 'attains that humble attitude of mind towards the grandeur of reason incarnate in existence, which in its profoundest depths is inaccessible to man'.[44] And Tillich comments:

> If we interpret these words rightly they point to a common ground of the whole of the physical world and of supra-personal values, which, on the other hand, is hidden in its inexhaustible depth and is announced by the experience of the numinous, by the religious experience. This experience can occur in connection with intuition of the 'grandeur of reason incarnate in existence', it can occur in connection with the belief in 'the significance and loftiness of those suprapersonal objects and goals which neither require nor are capable of rational foundation' as Einstein says.

And, let us add, the same experience occurs at least transiently in every human life, in the most varied and unforseen circum-

[43] I am not referring here to the theological problem of the possibility of exceptional events through an extraordinary manifestation of the Divinity. I mean to say that from the psychological point of view it is not sufficient that they take place, but it is necessary that they be judged to be such. That is to say, that they must be recognized as resulting from a divine action. Here, in fact, lies the difference between a believer and a non-believer. The parable of the rich man ends thus: 'If they do not hear Moses and the prophets, neither will they be convinced if some one should rise from the dead' (Luke 16: 31).

[44] Einstein also wrote that 'the finest thing we can experience is Mystery. It is the fundamental emotion that is at the roots of true science. Those who do not know it, those who cannot admire, those who are no longer capable of experiencing a sense of wonder, might as well be dead.'

stances, when men become aware that something supremely great has taken command of them.

Why speak of a personal God, then? Precisely in order to stress his character of superiority as a 'person'. Symbols inevitably start out from human concepts and for this reason tend to impart a human meaning to that which is mystery. This leads Tillich to declare, paradoxically, that 'without an element of "atheism" no "theism" can be maintained'. A 'personal God' means that God is a person 'above the person' and not 'beneath the person', as he is considered to be in monism and pantheism, in which the intimate 'I-Thou' relationship that unites God to men is destroyed.

This personal relationship, because of the very intimacy which marks it, has a severe aspect. The God who revealed himself as the Lord and commanded man to have no other gods before him was the God of tremendous majesty, and man did not dare approach him for fear of dropping dead. Something of this holy fear is to be found even today in those who draw near to the God who admits of no other gods. He is not a convenient God, providing for human needs, the 'labourer prompt to fulfil man's desires' (or the cow that must be well treated so that she may yield milk, as Meister Eckhart said), just as he is not the distant and indifferent architect of the universe. He is the God of the burning bush, and man fears him and takes to flight.

'If there exists a "constant" in the history of human religions,' writes M. Eliade, 'it is flight from the supreme God', whose place is taken by human divinities.[45] This 'flight from God' continues today also.[46] It is painful for man to realize that he is known through and through, always and everywhere, when he is so very reluctant to know himself and continues to deceive himself by looking at the image of his 'ideal self'. The knowledge that he is always face to face with one who surpasses him is bitter to man. Yet even when he thinks he has withdrawn from God, man finds himself continually in his

[45] M. Eliade, *Témoignages, op. cit.*
[46] M. Picard, *Die Flucht vor Gott*, Freiburg, 1958.

presence. He cannot live in the icy region of an empty scepticism. Illusions, subversive ideas, doctrinal dogmatism and faith
in utopias step in and place their yoke upon the man who flees
from God.

Erich Fromm has spoken of a 'flight from freedom' and Max
Picard, more correctly, of 'flight from God'. Does not the worship of technical achievement conceal a wild and desperate
flight from God towards the refuge in human inventions? Is
there then no way out? David Hume made a shrewd remark
when he said:

> . . . the most natural sentiment, which a well disposed mind
> will feel on this occasion, is a longing desire and expectation,
> that Heaven would be pleased to dissipate, at least alleviate,
> this profound ignorance, by affording some more particular
> revelation to mankind, and making discoveries of the
> nature, attributes, and operations of the divine object of our
> Faith. A person, seasoned with a just sense of the imperfec-
> tions of natural reason, will fly to revealed truth with the
> greatest avidity.[47]

Man turns to constituted religion to find a revelation of God.

Institutional religion

In contrast with the vagueness of subjective religion the sense
of reality, symbol and the Absolute become explicit and are
'objectified' in institutional religion. At one and the same time
institutional religion stimulates, expresses and moulds the individual religious sense. Every man has his own 'religious
experience' but this is necessarily expressed and manifested in
the forms belonging to a given 'culture' in a given 'religion'.
When they come into the world men find a 'cultural tradition'
already awaiting them (language, social relations, instruments
of various kinds), and they make this their own without having

[47] D. Hume, *Dialogues concerning Natural Religion*, Part XII.

to discover all over again what has already been discovered. In the same way they find an institutional religion already prepared, which they take up and make their own.

This does not mean that institutional religion creates the religious sense. Language does not create the need to communicate with other men, nor does the existence of the automobile create the ability to use it. Indeed in many cases the individual refuses to accept the traditional institutional religion and his religious sense goes out in search of other means of fulfilment. However, institutional religion with its teachings and practices does assume a particular character for the subject—a certain sacredness which evokes respect and continuity. In this way religious laws and customs themselves become sacred, binding and inviolable. True religion is ill served when institutional forms become an end in themselves and evoke institutional idolatry. This kind of idolatry gets established when the forms are reduced to a framework supporting inveterate habits and customs which have a religious veneer but are not sustained by personal religion.

Institutional religions are a particularly durable sociocultural construction and their collapse can signify the ruin of a civilization. We can therefore understand the obstacle they constitute to the introduction of those innovations which we call by the general name of progress. It is widely believed that in order to place the advantages of progress at the disposal of peoples living in misery in forms of civilization which we consider backward, we must make a clean sweep of all former customs, beginning with religion.

There is something to be said for this opinion. In India, for example, projects for the improvement of agriculture are obstructed by veneration for the cow. The caste system based on religious traditions raises another barrier in the path of social reform. Still the danger is there that the introduction of new technical and economic methods, imposed or made inevitable by new conditions of life, may bring with it, through the collapse of institutional religions, an appalling religious void in which a degenerate and inhuman kind of religion may develop—idolatry of the state in nationalism, of race in racism, of equality in Communism.

Lucretius' bitter exclamation *Tantum religio potuit suadere malorum* does not only apply to ancient times: it is perennially topical in the history of mankind. The eternal tragedy of man is inherent in religion—his inability to do without God and his attempt to eliminate God in order to take his place. When God becomes the man-made idol, made to man's own image and likeness, all the wickedness of human nature breaks out beneath the shadow of this idol. Protected by inviolability, greedy for success, blinded by the illusion of power and thirsting for victims, such wickedness rears its head in the great events of human history and likewise in the small affairs of each man's life, which are no less important. 'Turning to God without turning from self' is William Law's trenchant description of this phenomenon.[48] How subtle, attractive and easy it is to believe we are looking towards God when we are merely looking to our own interests.

It is a mistake to look on institutional religion from this point of view and no other. It has a much greater claim to admiration than to contempt. It is religion that bestows a note of greatness on human existence, raising it up above the satisfaction of immediate needs and giving a meaning to man's life and to his world. Even when it is dominated by formalism it still has the power to attract us to the *mysterium tremendum et fascinans*, in the presence of which man becomes aware of his own weakness and aspires to overcome it.

The world of the sacred could not endure, at least in its primitive pagan form. The gods had to die (though one could wish that the process had not often been so cruel). But this death of the gods has left a terrible void in human life. This is surely the source of the feeling, which is now so widespread, that life has lost its meaning. The inner mystery, in which all meaning is to be found, has been lost and we are

[48] W. Law, *A Serious Call to a Devout and Holy Life* (first published 1728), Collins, London and Glasgow, 1965, quoted in Aldous Huxley, *The Perennial Philosophy, op. cit.*, p. 250.

left with the surface of life. This again surely explains the loss of the power of creative art. The artist is left either to copy the surface appearance of things, or wildly to explore the unconscious in an attempt to reach a deep level of reality. Thus the great need of our time is to recover the sense of the sacred.[49]

Institutional religion, then, as seen from the outside, appears to be a paradoxical tangle of ideals and of facts opposed to them. It is face to face with mystery, yet it deceives itself into thinking that it can dominate mystery and subordinate it to human interests and human greed. It shows men a world pervaded by order and peace, yet it nourishes discord and war. It claims to possess the truth, but exhausts itself in subtleties and miserable deviations. It proposes justice but becomes an *instrumentum regni*.

Christianity

Christianity is an institutional religion and it calls for brief mention here, if only because the writer is a Christian and has a duty to state his own view with precision.

Christianity introduces itself with the clear assertion that it is a religion revealed by God and hence it lays claim to the truth, reality, mystery and absoluteness proper to God. It is therefore a revelation in the strict sense. It does not unfold itself and gradually take form through a vague sense of the sacred or an amalgam of theophanies finding concrete expression in certain objects, places and powers. Its historical beginning goes back to the faith of a small nomadic people in a unique Being, the true God, inaccessible in his majesty but also inexorably present in the affairs and the history of men.

This means that man has passed from a state of fleeting significance in the cosmic process, in which he is bound up with conditions of life and society but unable to overcome

[49] Dom Bede Griffiths, O.S.B., 'The Sense of the Sacred' in *Good Work*, Cambridge, Mass., XXVI, 1963, 2, p. 37.

them, to the dignity of a creature that among all other creatures is the only one to have the privilege of knowing God, of entering into relations with him and thus surpassing everything around him. In biblical history the assertion of one supreme God is continual, categorical, and I venture to say even fierce, in opposition to the continual pullulation of more convenient gods made to human measurements. Biblical monotheism is therefore quite different from the monotheism of the Greek and Roman world which was derived from the attribution of a sovereign and mysterious superior to the particular gods or from an intellectualist overcoming of the contradiction between separate divinities.

Biblical monotheism persists intransigently in Judaism and in Islam. Christianity, for its part, claims to be the continuation of the revelation of the one only God, the God of the Patriarchs, of Moses, and of the Prophets, which culminates in the full revelation, the Incarnation, of Jesus Christ, God and Man. Christ in his teaching and his life is the invisible God become man. The mystery of God is emphasized by this participation in humanity, for although it enables us to draw near to him it certainly does not allow us to understand him. God's participation in humanity is continued in the constitution of an intimate communion between believers, in other words, the Church.

These doctrinal outlines of Christianity emerge from the totality of biblical tradition in which we find a history—a sacred history in the strictest sense of the word, since it is a history of God's revelation—but nothing that can compare with a scientific or philosophical treatise or even with a historical treatise in the current sense of the term. It is not without reason that the Church, although proposing the mysteries of revelation to our belief, resolutely defends the value of reason, since any religion or homage rendered to God which would deny or doubt man's highest capacity, the power of knowing him, would not be a true religion.

The history of dogma, as Cardinal Newman has shown in a classic work, far from being the result of a blind and desperate

defence of irrational assertions, or the abdication of reason
in favour of authority, is the development of fundamental
principles of the Christian message, whose importance is more
clearly understood and affirmed as time goes on. Christianity
does not present itself all bright and shining to our gaze. It is
full of dramatic contrasts that make us reflect on its meaning
even when we accept it as valid.

The Bible certainly offers us no idyllic picture of humanity.
Human passions and wickedness, acts of rebellion and of madness, human tragedies, are all described there with striking
realism, and even the most prominent characters in its pages
are not immune from these things. The one figure that stands
out in incomparable perfection, Jesus Christ, nevertheless
shares man's most painful limitations (poverty, suffering and
death) and appears in human history to succumb to injustice
without having changed anything in the situation of the human
race to which he merely bequeathes a religious and moral
message. Furthermore, at certain periods the Church seems to
have betrayed her mission. Worldly interests, divisions,
persecutions and wars cannot be cancelled from Church history.

Yet this dark side of Christianity imparts to it a note of
realism and greatness which distinguishes it clearly from human
ideologies and causes its religious validity to stand out in bolder
and more conclusive relief. It is not a replica of the countless
myths and utopian aspirations that have dreamed of a golden
age. God's work is present in the midst of human misery, at
times frighteningly so, but always intimately consoling. God
is no wicked and cruel stranger to our world, but in Jesus
Christ, the victim of what is most detestable to us, he opens up
the way to himself. Nothing is more foreign to the Gospel than
the universal happiness of men on this earth. In God alone
(and therefore in conditions we can only express symbolically
and in an utterly inadequate manner) does man find fulness of
life. It must be acknowledged that Christianity does not escape
the danger of institutional religions, the danger of turning what
is merely a means into an end. But whenever human greatness
threatens to take the place of God's majesty and to banish

man's misery, a catastrophe comes about. God is eclipsed but he does not disappear. And perhaps it is necessary for us to descend to the depths of misery to recover what we had thrown away.

All great Christians have found themselves face to face with the *mysterium iniquitatis* that exists in the world and that appears to gain the upper hand, at times in sensational fashion, at times by subtle penetration that silences the 'divine torment' under an appearance of well-being. They warned Christians of their responsibility in adopting a mentality and behaviour so different from and even contrary to Christian principles. In some of these reproving voices a note of sincere sorrow is heard, in others there is an element of hostility that avails itself of failings on the part of Christians in order to attack their religion. In Kierkegaard there is an almost blind and enforced acceptance of Christian principles, but denial of everything that savours of ecclesiastical organization. Bonhoeffer, a genuine Christian who was hanged by the Nazis, predicted a 'Christianity without religion', a Christianity freed from the burden of institutional traditions but fully committed to dedication and sacrifice.[50]

It must be granted that many formulations of doctrine are couched in terms that suggest a different view of the world from that of contemporary science, and that legal or ritual norms have at times usurped the place of religion and annulled the supremacy of love. But despite their antiquated terminology, do not the formulations of dogma admirably express the synthesis between the 'otherness' of God and our relations

---

[50] Bonhoeffer's ideas, with references to the ideas of R. Bultmann and P. Tillich, were recently popularized by J. A. T. Robinson, in *Honest to God* (S.C.M. Press, London, 1963). This book, though severely criticized even in the Anglican communion, had a wide circulation outside as well as in England. Its exceptional success is perhaps due to the fact that it gives an exposition and criticism of religious problems in terms of the secular mentality of today and tries to find a solution of them in this same mentality, while preserving a filtered and 'essential' Christianity. Ambiguity and controversy were therefore inevitable. *Honest to God* was a rude blow to Christian inertia and somnolence but was hardly a harbinger of true revival of Christianity.

with him which is a fundamental element of Christianity? On the other hand legal and ritual norms that do more harm than good ought to be appropriately modified, though not suppressed, for the precise purpose of guaranteeing the supremacy of love. Genuine religion needs norms but norms divorced from love lose all their value.

We may also ask if the most serious danger for Christians today may not lie in contempt for the human expressions of Christianity, in which there is always and necessarily some defect since they are the work of men in a changing world. Such Christians may turn to a Christianity devoid of religion, but this dwindles down to vague sentimentalism or to a rationalist and abstract religion. We cannot overlook the fact that many people today boast that they profess a truer Christianity than the one that is tied in with the Church, merely because they do not accept the Church's dogmas and rites. Here we have a new Romanticism which asserts its respect for religious values of an intuitive and affective kind (love, equality, idealism), but is decidedly sceptical about the doctrinal content of Christianity. This too is a religion of convenience—and a religion of convenience that lapses into indifference is the most subtle and irreparable form of irreligion.

But we would not be Christians if we did not accept and suffer the 'scandal' of the Church, if we did not remember that Christ compared it to a field in which weeds grow up side by side with the wheat, but cannot be gathered without uprooting the wheat as well. The final sorting will take place at harvest time. Not without reason does the Bible—God's word in the language of men—which opens with Genesis, the book of origins, close with the Apocalypse, the book of Revelation. The intricate and hermetic symbolism of the latter makes it very difficult reading for present-day people, but when we go back to the times in which it was written, we discover that it describes with incomparable artistic power the struggle between good and evil beneath the sovereignty of God the Redeemer, and the ultimate victory of good. The inevitable intertwining of good and evil in the history of man and of the world and the continual effort required to overcome evil by good is itself part of Christian teaching.

Christianity, then, gives us an unchangeable order of doctrine and practice: God the Creator, the created world, man a privileged creature 'made in God's image and likeness' with the capacity to understand and to act on his own free will. It is precisely this special characteristic of man, his initial participation in God, his having within him a divine afflatus, which has given him two divine qualities: knowledge and freedom. But these very qualities offer him the alternative of adoration or rebellion. This accounts for his continual temptation to reverse the situation and put himself in God's place. But just as God created man in his own image and likeness he created him over again as a son in the image and likeness of Christ.

In creation and redemption God remains supreme. Man, a creature of God, a rebel against him, but pardoned by him, finds his fulness in God alone; everything he has comes from God as a gift. Christianity therefore proclaims a full, intimate and perfect humanism. The psychological dimension of life is in no way suppressed, but it cannot be taken in abstraction from God and confined within man himself. Human intelligence in its anxious search for truth, for the Absolute, deceives itself when it asserts that it can subject everything to its own dominion, but it is fully in line with truth when it acknowledges something which surpasses it, when it recognizes the existence of a Mystery.

God's presence is announced in Christianity not only as a majestic reality but as an ineffable plenitude of love. Redemption offers the Christian the possibility of drawing near to God, of communication and communion with him, not only in the form of personal experience of him but also in the act of participation and communion in the life of other men.

In this the love of God was made manifest among us, that God sent his only Son into the world so that we might live through him. In this is love, not that we loved God but that he loved us and sent his Son to be the expiation for our sins. Beloved, if God so loved us, we also ought to love one another. No man has ever seen God; if we love one another God abides in us and his love is perfected in us. By this we know that we abide in him and he in us, because he has given us of his own Spirit.

This is what we are told in a text of the earliest Christian preaching, in the First Epistle of St John (1 John 4: 9-13).

There is a basic social rapport, if we care to make use of such terminology, between God and the Christian and among Christians themselves, and the Church is simultaneously the cause and the expression of this social relationship. For this reason the Church describes itself as a 'supernatural' society, for in the theological sense God alone and what leads to participation in God is supernatural. In its charismatic mission the Church transmits the gift of God (grace), which is communion with God and communion among believers. The Christian therefore believes that there is not merely a love (Eros) which comes from the urge to procreate or from the need for protection and dependence which man has in common with the animals, but another love (Agape) which begins with God and calls forth the Christian's love, just as a bridegroom's love elicits love from his bride.

This religious symbol of marriage is frequently and powerfully used in the Bible. This is at first sight strange since it seems to point to a human sensual content in the relationship of God and man. True, the Bible everywhere shows a realistic appreciation of full normal sexual relations between man and woman and is rich in sexual symbolism; but there is no place in it for feminine divinities or for the divinization of sex. In fact, however, the symbol of marriage between God and man has a deeper and more precise meaning. It indicates a love of predilection, an exclusive love which finds fulfilment in monogamous marriage, while adultery is rebellion and betrayal. God loved his people (and the idea of people has developed by degrees to include 'every nation . . . all tribes and peoples and tongues' (Revelation 7: 9), as the husband loves his wife, but the wife betrayed him and plunged into unbridled satisfaction of her sensuality.

Man's rebellion against God is, in the Bible, an event of all generations. Man is tempted to rebel and to abandon the 'living and true God' who loves with an abundant but demanding love, and to go in search of other loves which appear more satisfying but which become harsh, cruel and demoralizing. Thus men run away from the 'God who sees us and calls us by name' in pursuit of human ideals, apparently fine and noble but in reality vague, impersonal and disappointing. Sin—the breaking of our friendship with God—seems to have vanished from the consciousness of men today, who picture to themselves a God according to their own convenience but flee from the just and powerful and loving God. Yet sin is not irremediable, since it can be overcome by pardon.

Much more rigid and inexorable is the sense of guilt which spreads among men who have lost faith in God, who feel themselves to be at the mercy of forces they are unable to subdue, against which they cannot rebel, and which do not pardon. There can be rebellion and pardon when we are dealing with a person, but not when we are dealing with impersonal, blind and fatal powers. Man remains alone, at the mercy of his own instincts, with a desolate sense of inferiority even if he succeeds in bending the forces of nature to his will and to his service. Here we understand the decisive importance of historical revelation: God makes himself known, he loves and pardons.

Revelation does not tolerate contamination of any kind: God is the Lord, human ideals without him become idols, and the most cunning and dangerous is the idol of ourselves. This precise assertion might appear to be an instigation to intolerance and hatred among men. It has been interpreted as such in the past and this can happen again. But the Christian revelation itself corrects and condemns this distortion. 'You have heard that it was said "An eye for an eye and a tooth for a tooth". . . . You have heard that it was said "You shall love your neighbour and hate your enemy". But I say to you, Do not resist one who is evil. . . . But I say to you, Love your enemies and pray for those who persecute you. Be merciful as your Father in heaven is merciful.'

If the Gospel distinguishes, then, between children of light and children of darkness and points to their incompatibility, the Christian must follow the Light that 'did not come to judge the world but to save the world' (John 12: 47). Judgment is reserved to God and if man dares to take it upon himself to judge he falls into darkness. The call to God's kingdom is a responsibility, not a convenient privilege. Firm in his conviction that the Church assembles the faithful and the children of God, the Christian must look with respect upon the other religions, in which he admires the common aspiration of mankind towards God, although this is manifested in a disorderly, chaotic and often contradictory manner. He knows that the Church is the not yet perfect fulfilment of that which in other religions is only roughly outlined, with striking vigour in some cases but submerged by human wretchedness in others. And if his proselytism has had an aggressive and contemptuous tone in the past, the Christian is now convinced that his attitude is not true and genuine unless he has transcended this degenerate attitude and is obedient to Christ's injunction that he should put up his sword, since all those who take the sword will perish by the sword. It is inevitable that human lapses and inconsistencies should continue to show themselves, since the very condition of the Church is a human condition, a transitory one on the way to perfect fulfilment.

9. Homo religiosus

The characteristics of religion according to modern psychology were outlined at the end of the first chapter and some questions were formulated at that stage. These questions have guided the development of the subsequent chapters either directly or indirectly. In the second and third chapters the religious phenomenon was shown to be genuinely human, irreducible and constant, even though expressed in many different ways. In its social aspect (chapter three), in its individual aspect (chapter five) and in the course of human life religion maintains a characteristic quality of its own. It reappears even where it has been openly dispensed with or where it has been 'explained' by reasons outside its own orbit (chapter seven). Up to this point we have been dealing mainly with the 'religious sense' understood as a general attitude of man in the face of Mystery. In chapter eight we examined religion in itself, that is to say, the religious sense translated into practice in the form of a relationship between man and the ultimate Reality, and in institutionalized form, where the subjective and strictly psychological facts cannot be confined to man himself but involve acknowledgment of another Reality and relations with it.

We remarked how the study of psychic activity in the religious field, while it enables us to identify a typical attitude, does not authorize us to establish its nature and meaning, namely the value of religion, and that when we attempt to do so we are exceeding the limits of psychology. There is a religious sense in religion and there can be a religious sense in unbelief, since one and the other are based on psychological reasons as conceived by a human mind. But this does not mean that religion and unbelief can impose themselves in an irrefutable manner. In both cases decision ultimately rests on faith and not on science. Science investigates, describes and explains, but it cannot furnish understanding.

Here we meet the distinction which, at the beginning of his famous book, William James makes between two types of judgment when we undertake any investigation whatsoever. The first type replies to the questions: 'What is it, how was it formed, what are its constitution, its origin, its history?' This is an 'existential' judgment. The second replies to the questions: 'what is its meaning, what importance has it?' This is a proposition of value.

As we saw in chapter one, according to James the Bible can be studied as a literary work by investigation regarding its authors, customs, ideas, the reliability or otherwise of what is written there. Here we have an 'existential' judgment. But what is the meaning of the Bible as it is today, what importance has it, what is its spiritual and religious content? Here we have the proposition of value which is not contained in the 'existential' judgment—even though it must take this into account—but goes further and expresses a particular attitude and a particular valuation.

Some people will say: 'The Bible is one of the many mythological narratives which have come down to us from ancient times, but it does not interest me.' Others will say: 'The Bible is a highly valuable work from the poetical point of view, but it is a human work.' Still others will say: 'The Bible, despite its different mentality and its reference to different conditions of life, contains a precious religious teaching which, though expressed in human language, is a revelation of God to all men.' The same applies to the psychologist in his study of the phenomena of religion. He can and he ought to study them according to the canons of his science so as to reach an 'existential' judgment. But when he passes on to a proposition of value, although maintaining his 'existential' judgment, he is appealing to the criteria of another kind.

The scientific psychology of religion has directed its attention to facts which can be observed and described and it has been

M

particularly insistent in seeking out the aspects which lend themselves to elaboration. Just because the superficial manifestations of religion emerge in a vast variety and with many contradictions (let us not forget that philosophical theories are destined to do likewise!) it has been thought possible to find a valid explanation of them in irrational instead of intellectual motivations. Social relations, therefore—in the broad or narrow sense—emotional conditions, feeling and impulses, to which man is subject without knowing their origin, have been mentioned with particular and almost exclusive insistence, so much so that we seem obliged to conclude that poor human reason enters into religion for the sole purpose of elaborating more or less plausible pretexts to make religion presentable.

But motives are not reasons and a religion to which valid reasons are denied on principle is degraded to the level of an illlusion. An anti-intellectual procedure, though, is dangerous here. When reason is banished from 'awareness' it becomes a tyrant in the unconscious. When emotions and affect are allowed to rule they lose their consistent relation to reality. Those qualities of which the individual is deprived are attributed to society and to the unconscious. It is not necessary to be extraordinarily shrewd to perceive that all this is the result of absolutization of a principle, and that there must be a rearrangement of idea so that complementariness and not elision may mark the relationship between the various aspects of religion. It strikes me that modern psychology has skidded dangerously in its devaluation of the cognitive aspect of religion.

It is true that there are real reasons and fictitious ones and that men cling more readily to the latter than the former as long as they find it convenient to do so. Freud was successful in this respect, although he was merely elaborating in a new light some facts which had not escaped the notice of the great moralists. However, the fact that he defined religion as an illusion and a projection of human desires produced a disastrous effect, since it deprived religion of its original and genuine character and reduced it to an expedient for defence and vain consolation. The concepts of Schleiermacher and B. Constant, who attribute primary importance to feeling, gives us a religion that has been beheaded and has no other justification than the fact that it exists among men. Since no rational validation is furnished, the individual is asked if it is moral to do something for which he does not know the reason.

Sociological theories which explain the human being by his social relations must necessarily see in religion a dangerous by-product of human interaction which protects group interests and hinders social progress. But if religion is an expression of man's relations with absolute Reality, independent of himself, then narrowness and exclusiveness are no longer possible: reason, affect and social intercourse are necessarily interdependent and form a totality. When we observe religion in the individual we get a clear impression of this unity. Still, there are different emphases in individual religion and different aspects of it can become disjoined and independent. This happens in neurotics and is the basis on which Freud built his doctrine.

Reason is an extremely valuable but extraordinarily delicate instrument which enables man to know himself and the world and which is frequently subject to errors which it can also correct. With these reservations, reason is fundamentally the necessary reference point for man's existence and for his actions. When man fails to understand or to be understood, then he staggers, and here we have the kernel of his anxiety and one of the most apparent causes of neurosis. Religion invariably implies more or less adequate effort towards knowledge, and when this is taken away or reduced to mere gratification, when it loses its impulse towards truth, it vanishes in illusion. The same fate, however, also awaits man's other spiritual needs. There is an attempt to safeguard science, but when it is reduced to an accumulation of information and 'technical improvements', what can it offer man but the illusion of omnipotence?

In the course of the present work we have been obliged to keep to the rules of the game by discussing the psychological interpretation of religion. But this does not mean failure to acknowledge the rational justification of religion. Ontological and cosmological arguments do not lose their value because the roots of religion are sought *in interiore homine*. One thing is certain: religion is neither pure reason, nor a vague feeling, nor a continual state of agitation, but coordination and commitment of the entire man. Unfortunately, just as there are unbalanced men there are also unbalanced forms of religion.

One of the most recurrent and insistent notes in the study of religion is the search for its earliest beginnings and, in these beginnings, for the cause and explanation of its more conspicuous forms. The study of the child and of primitive man, in whom the scholars presume to find in a more genuine and simple state what is later reproduced in the complicated behaviour of the adult and civilized man, is taken to be the only reliable method. It is true that there is a continual and 'historical' succession from the cave-dweller to the inhabitant of the skyscraper, but we wonder, all the same, if the cave-dweller would have been able to treat the world around him as the man of the skyscraper treats it, or if the latter could treat it as the cave-dweller did. It is not, therefore, in the cave-dweller that we come to understand the mentality of the dweller in the skyscraper.

There is a continual succession from the seed to the plant, the bud and the flower; from the egg to the embryo and the foetus; from the newborn babe to the youth and the adult, but this does not mean that we understand the flower from the seed or the adult from the germ-cell. It is more consistent to declare that the flower enables us to understand the seed and the adult enables us to understand the embryo, because in the flower and the adult we find complete development ('perfect' in the etymological sense) of what is still in a state of becoming in the seed and the embryo. The seed and the embryo have meaning only in relation to the flower and the adult and we would really be unable to establish their derivation if we could not follow the various phases of development in which the maturity of the final stage is still lacking.

Even if we were to presume equality of environment, we would still be faced with the enormous difference in the relations of the living being to this environment in the various stages of its development. Hence it is doubtful whether identity of psychological qualities can be established in child and adult and whether the initial manifestations of these qualities can be ascertained in embryonic form in the child without taking account of the vastly different situations from both the objective and the subjective points of view. Furthermore, the recognition of emotions is already so difficult in relations between adults that we wonder if in the case of children there is not a huge risk—when we go further than broad generalities—of interpreting them in terms of the adult or even according to the personality of the observer.

In modern psychological theories there is, on the contrary, a categorical assertion of the derivation of secondary motives and needs from primary motives and needs. The latter are considered to be fundamental and the former are taken to be a superstructure built upon them. This shuts us into a blind alley: the uniqueness and continuity of infantile patterns does not explain the variety, multiplicity and contemporaneousness of adult patterns.

Nevertheless, the effort of psychologists to go back to the sources (especially Freud and his followers) affords an indication which seems to be quite meaningful.

Freud went right back to earliest childhood and made the phases of psychic development coincide with physiological activities to which he attributed sensual pleasure of an erotic character. He established steps and stages, events and processes in development (Oedipus crisis, formation of the superego, repression, sublimation, etc.) which, however, according to his pupil Melanie Klein should be antedated. As regards religion, Freud maintained that the oceanic feeling, the sensation of cosmic participation which some consider to be the essence of religion, is nothing but a residue of the ego feeling in the child 'who initially contains everything within himself and later distinguishes the world from himself, is more intimately bound to his immediate environment and, frightened by his own powerlessness, seeks paternal protection'. Religion is not, therefore, a 'primary' feeling, but is derived from the need for the father. It is a dramatization on the universal plane of the emotions aroused by the child's relationship with his father.

This infantile feeling breeds the prerogatives which are attributed later on to the divinity, namely, omnipotence, omniscience and ubiquity. This not an altogether transitory feeling. It re-emerges in the adult although in reduced form when what were considered to be insurmountable boundaries between the ego and the outside world disappear. According to Freud 'there is only one state—admittedly an unusual state, but not one that can be stigmatized as pathological—in which it does not do this. At the height of being in love [in the sexual embrace] the boundary between ego and object threatens to melt away. Against all the evidence of his senses a man who is in love declares that "I" and "you" are one and is prepared to behave as if it were a fact.'[1]

Obviously, this way of looking at the matter brings up once more the questions already raised as regards the validity of our interpretation of infantile affective states, their repetition in the adult and the attribution of cognitive processes to the unconscious. Instead of dwelling on this aspect, I intend to deal with the convergence of cosmic participation which Freud attributes to the child and Lévy-Bruhl to primitive man and which more recent authors (the psychiatrist Rümke and the anthropologist M. Mead) consider to be a typical quality in the adult also. All psychologists presume a primordial condition in which the child does not distinguish between himself and the world.

Freud says that the feeling of 'cosmic participation'—of man's having an intimation of his bond with the cosmos— 'sounds so strange and fits in so badly with the fabric of our psychology' that one is justified in seeking a genetic explanation of such a feeling. But when he has explained it as a partial

---

[1] S. Freud, *Civilization and its Discontents*, in Standard Ed., vol. XXI, p. 66.

survival of the child's ego feeling he has antedated the main problem, namely, what is the meaning of this ego feeling which is primitive or genuine in the child but reappears only on rare occasions in adult life 'in an unusual state but not one that can be stigmatized as pathological'?

We can well believe that just as the organs intended for an independent life are prepared in the embryo within the maternal womb, so too in the child's psychological evolution the psychological structures are formed which are to remain in the adult. But why judge them as strange? We might consider strange, if need be, the presence of a feeling so disproportionate to the child's state. But it is not so strange that this feeling of bewilderment due to the fragility of one's own life, this longing for protection, this need of union, even though it does not fit in with 'the fabric of our psychology' should appear at critical moments or even in unexceptional conditions (for Freud did not take into consideration the whole gamut of religious feeling from its less apparent forms to the mystical intuitions of religion).

We should be inclined to think that this feeling is consistent with man's condition and that its absence would indicate a lack of harmony, as happens in the case of the neurotic, whose emotional reaction does not respond to the actual situation. I am wondering if Freud's appeal to the ecstasy which crowns the sexual embrace in which the boundaries of the ego disappear could not be used to emphasize the substantial fact of gratification in union, the joining together where there was formerly separation.

The note of return to the origins is repeated in various keys in psychoanalysis: desire to return to the mother's womb, desire to return to the inorganic state (death instinct). Freud gets no further than crude physiological symbolism, that is to say, than reference to a concrete biological condition. These references are certainly present in the symbol: father, mother, sexual union, maternal womb, etc., but does their meaning end here?

It seems unlikely, since the desire for a return that is

impossible and biologically opposed to the 'vital impulse' (return to death) induces us to think of a broader and more distant source. Not the desire to go back to the foetus or to inorganic matter, but the desire to be once more protected, happy and satisfied in a plenitude which knows no limits, in an 'oceanic' fulness. This, and not the biological reference, is the meaning of 'return' just as hunger does not consist in knowing we must eat a certain food ration but in the aspiration to a state of agreeable satisfaction. In the impulse to return to the origins there is therefore something essentially different from return to the concrete states in which these origins are manifested. There is nothing 'strange' in thinking that an innate demand of human nature is its need of mystery, of true fulness, its need of God.

Freud stopped at biological symbolism. His strength lay there, since this afforded him a material reference, but here we also find his weakness, since it marks a boundary line which must necessarily be crossed if we are to go back from beginnings to origins.

The child, observes Freud, does not at once notice the difference between the two sexes, but asks 'why' children come into the world and discovers that this comes about through the sexual union of his father and mother. But in this manner the 'how' and not the 'why' is reached; the beginnings and not the origins; there is 'explanation' but not 'understanding'. 'With the metaphor of the Oedipus complex,' writes Bakan,

Freud was able to seize upon the much more critical question that is in the life history of each person, the question 'Where did I come from?' If the Oedipus complex does not exist cross-culturally in its limited form as Malinowski believes, it exists cross-culturally in the more general form of the sense of wonder at one's own being. The Oedipus complex is a profound metaphor which catches at the deep mystery of human existence. That this sense of mystery should be referred to the sexual is one of the great insights Freud provided. But this insight, that being has its origins in the sexual, that the sexual is thus one with the meta-physical and the theological, is central to the Jewish tradition of Kabbala.[2]

According to Bakan, then, Freud invests sexuality with a religious value, indeed with a theological and metaphysical value. In this way Freud, without realizing it, stepped across the boundary between physical and metaphysical, between science and religion, between the explanation of 'how' and the understanding of 'why'. On the other hand, experienced analysts and psychotherapists of undoubted ability are not lacking (Jung, Maeder, Boss, Rümke) who assert that if the analyst explored further after the discovery of sexual and aggressive tendencies, 'he would find with many—perhaps even with all—the primal forces of the spirit, the primary urge to express their link with God'.[3]

This does not mean that religious indoctrination, or worse still, the imposition of religious practice, causes the immediate disappearance of the neurotic disorder. It means that in the gradual re-establishment of the patient's balance it can be ruinous to abstract from his religious sense. Accurate psychological observation, therefore, discloses much more of the religious sense than we might suspect: a poor and undeveloped religious sense, repressed, displaced, on the defensive in the 'reactive formation' of ostentatious irreligion. This goes to show that religion is incorporated in man perhaps even more deeply than his biological needs.

The sense of cosmic participation has been judged by Lévy-Bruhl to be a typical trait of primitive peoples and he stresses this so excessively that he was obliged to tone down his assertion in his later writings, although he did not withdraw the statement. Actually the anthropologists maintain that to primitive men religious 'realities' are present and decisive as much as and even more so than material 'realities'.

'Man in so far as he is *homo religiosus*,' writes Gerardus

[2] D. Bakan, *S. Freud and the Tradition of Jewish Mysticism, op. cit.*, pp. 275-6.
[3] H. C. Rümke, *The Psychology of Unbelief, op. cit.*, p. 61.

van der Leeuw, 'has fully awakened from the sleep of undifferentiated embryonic life, but is invariably and continually attracted towards it: the foundation of every religion is unity of subject and object, the primal identity that is often sought as a final identity. The foundation of all religion is mystic life.'[4] Although this may appear to be a hyperbolic assertion, it corresponds to the statement of a need on man's part. Freud himself who bows low before the 'splendid myths' of Eros and Thanatos has indicated in the latter instinct the impulse of living matter to return to organic unity, and he saw the 'oceanic feeling' as an illusory consolation to evade the danger to which the ego feels itself exposed. But for Freud, too, there is a return to a 'primal identity sought as final identity'.

If man's origin and destiny, known or unknown to him, are the meaning of his existence, there is nothing surprising in the fact that a religion which presents God as the Alpha and Omega of man and of the universe, as Christianity does, should maintain that man knows himself only when he knows God. Vivified by this belief, Christian philosophy as developed from St Augustine to St Bonaventure, from St Thomas to Rosmini, asserts that there is an 'imprint' of God in man which is a sign of his greatness, since it requires that he be reunited with the beginning.

I am thinking here of Rosmini's idea, misunderstood and too little appreciated, of a 'divine in nature' which is not to be mistaken for God. The light is not mistaken for the sun from which it proceeds; nevertheless, when it is received by the eye it enables us to see, to evaluate and to act. The light of reason, the 'divine in human nature', enables us to discover a meaning, an order, a Uni-verse. Even when man is unaware of it this constitutes the link with his origin, with God. Thus the human being is necessarily religious, with the dignity of belonging to the 'living and true God', but also with the risk of making a god of himself and becoming the slave of an 'idol made by his own hands'.

[4] G. van der Leeuw, L'homme primitif et la religion: Etude anthropologique, op. cit.

The 'divine' in human nature therefore constitutes a terrible power, an absolute from which there can be no derogation, which can be the beginning of completeness *(perfectum opus)* but also of the most cruel and merciless tyranny. If man projects himself into this 'divine'—if he thinks he is God and that he can subjugate God to his own will—there is no human monstrosity which cannot be disguised as religion. Massacre of innocent victims for sacrificial purposes, slaying of men so that their strength may be incorporated in other men, prostitution to obtain fertility, extermination of an enemy, imposition of one's own power for the sake of gain—these are horrors which we consider have now been conclusively overcome. But the elimination of men judged to be harmful or a burden to society, either in extermination camps or by deportation; imprisonment, violation of the person, civil war, class hatred, revolution, the stirring-up of national egoisms are all affairs of the day and all of them are justified by some superior reason in homage to the powers which regulate man's destiny.

It has not been possible to eliminate these degenerate aspects from institutional religions, which have tried to keep them within bounds. Zen Buddhism, for example, is the official religion of a very warlike people. Christianity itself, both Catholic and Protestant, has known dark and terrible episodes. Still in Jewish tradition (the prophets) and in Christian tradition, there is a continual, uninterrupted prosecution and unmasking of religion which abandons God and ties itself to man. It is in the Bible that we catch a glimpse of the final goal of men's desires, namely, union with God. Christianity, the Church, is dragged down by human instincts, but it rises again, just like the individual Christian, who does not succeed in reaching complete and steady perfection but whose very weakness induces him to yearn for it continually and to implore it as a gift bestowed on one who does not deserve it.

Discussing the concept of 'soul', Cesare Musatti wrote:

Here we have a great monumental edifice, a temple, a Gothic church which launches its spires heavenwards in a network of marble shapes and forms. The technician, the builder or the engineer sees it as a complicated problem of statics: he calculates stress and resistance, thrust and limits of weight; and each single arch represents a separate problem within the whole complex problem, so that his approach is analytical. He can get lost in the examination of single details and nevertheless he can always reconstruct the unity of the whole by taking these details as his starting-point. The whole great mass is made up of weights which lie heavily on the foundations of the building and on the ground which supports it, in an equilibrium of forces so arranged as to prevent the building from collapsing.

But the artist or the architect who contemplates the same temple or pictures it in his creative fancy sees something quite different. The weight vanishes and the whole pile becomes light; the forces which in the first instance all flowed downwards now seem to be reaching upwards; gravity no longer exists; the girders and stay-rods and the entire inner framework of the building are cancelled; all that remains is the play of shapes and forms which complete each other and arrange themselves in indissoluble unity; and the different materials, the various types of stone and marble used in the building, lose their own character and remain as mere tones of light which cause these forms to stand out in relief. Meanwhile, in the half-light of the nave, the believer, oblivious of the world, is deep in reflection and feels close to God. For him the temple is the way to this meeting with God, the oasis of peace, the one secure stronghold in life's storm, the sacred spot where every solemn act of his existence from birth to death is consecrated.

The same can be said of the soul, which is seen by the psychologist on the empirical plane, by the philosopher, the artist and the historian on the plane of human values, by the religious man on the plane of transcendence.[5]

---

[5] C. L. Musatti, 'Anima' in *Archivio di psicologia, neurologia e psichiatria*, Milan, 1948.

The matter could not be more clearly and correctly stated. But if this is the soul, can the psychologist be a psychologist— that is to say, can he know and understand the soul—if he remains so bound down to his technical office as to be no longer capable of admiring the beauty of the temple, of opening its door and kneeling down to pray?

'Where does God live?' was the question Kozker sprang on some learned men who were his guests. Derisively the scholars answered: 'What are you talking about? The world is full of his glory.' But Kozker replied to his own question: 'God is to be found where he is allowed to enter.'[6]

[6] M. Buber, *Hundert chassidische Geschichten*, Berlin, 1933.

Bibliography

General

Allport, G. W., *The Individual and His Religion*, New York, 1950

Anwander, A., *Wörterbuch der Religion*, Würzburg, 1962

Berguer, G., *Traité de psychologie de la religion*, Lausanne, 1946

Clark, W. H., *The Psychology of Religion. An Introduction to Religious Experience and Behaviour*, London, n.d.

Conklin, E. S., *The Psychology of Religious Adjustment*, New York, 1929

Cruchon, G., *Dynamic Psychology*, New York, 1965

Dunlap, K., *Religion: Its Function in Human Life*, New York, 1946

Goldbrunner, J., *Cure of Mind and Cure of Soul*, London, 1958
Realization, New York, 1967

Grensted, L. W., *The Psychology of Religion*, Oxford, 1952

Gruehn, W. D., *Religionpsychologie*, Breslau, 1926

Hellpach, W., *Grundriss der Religionpsychologie*, Stuttgart, 1951

Herr, V., *Religious Psychology*, New York, 1966

Johnson, P. E., *Psychology of Religion*, Nashville, Tenn., 1959

Kaam, A. van, *Religion and Personality*, London, n.d.

Leuba, J. H., *God or Man?*, New York, 1933

Lewis, H. D., *Our Experience of God*, London, 1959

Meissner, M. W., *Annotated Bibliography in Religion and Mental Health*, New York, 1961

Pratt, J. B., *The Religious Consciousness: A Psychological Study*, New York, 1920

Spinsk, S., *Psychology and Religion*, London, 1963

Strunk, O., *Readings in the Psychology of Religion*, New York, 1959

Strunk, O. Jr, *Religious Psychological Interpretation*, New York, 1962

Thomson, R., *The Pelican History of Psychology*, Penguin, London, 1968

Thouless, R. H., *An Introduction to the Psychology of Religion*, Cambridge, 1923

Valentine, C. H., *Modern Psychology and the Validity of Christian Experience*, London, 1929

Wunderle, G., *Der religiöse Akt als seelisches Problem*, Würzburg, 1948

Main journals

Archiv für Religionspsychologie, Vandenhoeck and Ruprecht, Göttingen

Journal for the Scientific Study of Religion, Colgate Rochester Divinity School

Journal of Religion and Mental Health, edited by the Academy of Religion and Mental Health, New York 16, N.Y.

Lumen Vitae (an international review of religious education, published in French and English), 184 rue Washington, Brussels 5

Chapter 1

(Other major works of James, Freud and Jung are given in the text and footnotes of chapter 1)

FOR WILLIAM JAMES

James, W., *The Will to Believe* (1897)
        Pragmatism (1907)
        A Pluralistic Universe (1909)

Knight, M., *William James*, Penguin, 1950

Perry, R. B., *The Thought and Character of William James*, Oxford, 1935

FOR S. FREUD

Brown, J. A. C., *Freud and the Post-Freudians*, Penguin, 1961

Freud, S., *Two Short Accounts of Psycho-Analysis*, Penguin, 1962

Jones, E., *The Life and Work of Sigmund Freud*, London, 1957

Lee, R. S., *Freud and Christianity*, London, 1948 (also Penguin)

Stafford-Clark, D., *What Freud Really Said*, Penguin, 1968

FOR C. G. JUNG

Fordham, F., *An Introduction to Jung's Psychology*, Penguin, third ed. 1966

Hostie, R., *Religion and the Psychology of Jung*, London, 1957

Jacobi, J., *The Psychology of C. G. Jung*, London, fifth ed. 1951 (also paperback)

White, V., *God and the Unconscious*, London, 1952
        Soul and Psyche, London, 1960

FOR PSYCHOANALYSIS

Görres, A., *The Methods and Experience of Psychoanalysis*, London, 1962

Nuttin, J., *Psychoanalysis and Personality*, London, 1954

Rycroft, G. (ed.), *Psychoanalysis Observed*, London, 1966

Storr, A., *The Integrity of the Personality*, Penguin, 1963

Chapter 2

Bakan, D., *Sigmund Freud and the Tradition of Jewish Mysticism*, Princeton, 1958

Bally, G., *Der normale Mensch*, Zurich, 1952

Baruk, H., *Psychiatrie sociale, expérimentale, individuelle et sociale*, Paris, 1945

Duykaerts, F., *La notion de normale en psychologie clinique*, Paris, 1954

Flugel, J. C., *Man, Morals and Society*, London, 1945 (also Penguin)

Frankl, V., *Ärtzliche Seelsorge*, Vienna, 1948

Hadfield, J. S., *Psychology and Morals*, London, 1923

Jaspers, K., *General Psychopathology*, Manchester, 1963

Jones, E., *The Life and Work of Sigmund Freud, op. cit.*

Laing, R. D., *The Divided Self*, London, 1960 (also Penguin)

Lorenz, K., *On Aggression*, London, 1966 (also paperback)

McDougall, W., *An Outline of Abnormal Psychology*, London, 1926

May, R., *Existence: A New Dimension in Psychiatry*, New York, 1952

Stern, K., *The Third Revolution*, New York, 1954

Storr, A., *Aggression*, London, 1968

Zillboorg, G., *Freud and Religion*, Westminster, Md, 1958

Chapter 3

Albright, W. F., *From the Stone Age to Christianity*, New York, 1957

Bouyer, L., *Rite and Man*, London, 1963

Cassirer, E., *The Philosophy of Symbolic Forms*, 3 vols, New Haven, 1953-57
    An Essay on Man, New Haven and London, 1944

Dubos, R., *The Dreams of Reason*, London, 1961

Eliade, M., *Patterns in Comparative Religion*, London, 1958

Evans-Pritchard, E. E., *Theories of Primitive Religion*, Oxford, 1965

Frankfort, H., *Kingship and the Gods*, London, 1948

Frankfort, H., and others, *Before Philosophy*, Penguin, 1949

Frazer, J. G., *The Golden Bough*, second ed., twelve vols and supplement, London, 1936 (also abridged paperback)

James, O. E., *History of Religions*, London, 1956

Karrer, O., *Religions of Mankind*, London, 1936

Kerényi, K., *The Religion of the Greeks and Romans*, London, 1962

Koenigswald, G. H. R., *The Evolution of Man*, Ann Arbor, 1962

Koppers, W., *Primitive Man and his World Picture*, London, 1952

Lévi-Strauss, C., *La Pensée sauvage*, Paris, 1962

Lévy-Bruhl, L., *Les fonctions mentales dans les sociétés inférieures*, Paris, 1910
    Les carnets, Paris, 1949

Malinowski, B., *Magic, Science and Religion*, London, 1948

Marrett, R. E., *The Threshold of Religion*, London, 1909

Otto, R., *The Idea of the Holy*, London, 1923 (and Penguin)

Steiner, F., *Taboo*, London, 1956 (also Penguin)

Suttie, I. D., *The Origins of Love and Hate*, Penguin, 1967

Chapter 4

Allport, G. W., *The Nature of Prejudice*, Cambridge, Mass., 1954

Dawson, C., *Religion and Culture*, London, 1948

Durkheim, E., *The Elementary Forms of the Religious Life*, London, 1915
    The Rules of Sociological Method, Chicago, 1938

Erikson, E., *Childhood and Society*, Penguin, 1965

Gurvitch, G., *La vocation actuelle de la sociologie*, Paris, 1958

Kardiner, A., *The Individual and His Society: The Psychodynamics of Primitive Social Organisation*, New York, 1949

Krech, D., Crutchfield, R. S., and Ballachey, E. L., *Individual in Society: A Textbook of Social Psychology*, New York, 1962

Kroeber, A. L. (ed.), *Anthropology Today: An Encyclopedic Inventory*, Chicago, 1953

Lienhardt, G., *Social Anthropology*, London, 1964

Lindzey, G., and Hall, C. (ed.), *Handbook of Social Psychology*, Cambridge, Mass., 1954

Mead, M., *Coming of Age in Samoa*, Penguin, 1928
       Growing Up in New Guinea, Penguin, 1942
       Mind, Self and Society from the Standpoint of a Social Behaviorist, Chicago, 1934

Parsons, T., *The Social System*, Glencoe, 1951

Radcliffe-Brown, A. R., *Structure and Function in Primitive Society*, London, 1952

Religion, Culture and Mental Health, Academy of Religion and Mental Health, New York, 1959; 1961

Weber, M., *Gesammelte Aufsätze zur Religionssoziologie*, 3 vols, Tübingen, 1920-21

Wach, J., *Sociology of Religion*, Chicago, eighth ed., 1957

Yinger, J. M., *Religion, Society and the Individual: An Introduction to the Sociology of Religion*, New York, 1957

Chapter 5

Allport, G. W., *The Individual and His Religion*, New York, 1950
       Becoming, New Haven-Yale, 1955

Bertocci, P. A., and Millard, R. M., *Personality and the Good*, New York, 1963

Godin, A., and others, *De l'expérience à l'attitude religieuse*, Brussels, 1964

Grensted, L. W., *Psychology and God*, London, second ed., 1936

Happold, F. C., *Mysticism*, Penguin, 1965

Mouroux, J., 'On the Notion of Religious Experience' in *The Downside Review*, 1948

Mowrer, O. H., *The Crisis in Psychiatry and Religion*, New York-London, 1961

Spencer, S., *Mysticism in World Religion*, London, 1967

Stace, Walter T., *The Teaching of the Mystics*, New York, 1960

Strunk, O., Jr, *Religion: A Psychological Interpretation*, New York-Nashville, 1962

Underhill, E., *Mysticism*, London, 1912

Wach, J., *Types of Religious Experience*, London, 1951

Chapter 6

Allport, G. W., *Pattern and Growth in Personality*, New York, 1961
    The Roots of Religion, Boston, 1956

Ausubel, D. P., *Theory and Problems of Adolescent Development*, New York, 1954

Bovet, P., *The Child's Religion*, London, 1928

Erikson, E. H., *Identity, Youth and Crisis*, London, 1968

Flavell, J. H., *The Psychology of Jean Piaget*, New York, 1963

Godin, A. (ed.), *Adulte et enfant devant Dieu*, Brussels, n.d.

Goldman, R., *Religious Thinking from Childhood to Adolescence*, London, 1964

Hadfield, J. S., *Childhood and Adolescence*, Penguin, 1962

Huizinga, J., *Homo ludens*, Boston, 1955

Lee, R. S., *Your Growing Child and Religion*, Penguin, 1965

Rahner, H., *Man at Play*, London, 1965

Religion in the Developing Personality, Academy of Religion and Mental Health, New York, 1960

Sandström, C. I., *The Psychology of Childhood and Adolescence*, London, 1966

Valentine, C. W., *The Normal Child and Some of His Abnormalities*, Penguin, 1956

White, R., *Lives in Progress*, New York, 1952

Chapter 7

Berdiaev, N., *The Russian Revolution, Two Essays on its Implications in Religion and Psychology*, London, 1931

Blackham, H. J., *Humanism*, Penguin, 1968

Blackham, H. J. (ed.), *Objections to Humanism*, Penguin, 1965

Cuénot, C., *Teilhard de Chardin: A Biographical Study*, London, 1965

Huxley, J., *Evolution in Action*, London, 1953 (and Penguin)
    The Humanist Frame, London, 1961

Lubac, H. de, *The Drama of Atheistic Humanism*, London, 1964
　　　The Religion of Teilhard de Chardin, London, 1967
Mooney, C., *Teilhard de Chardin and the Mystery of Christ*, London, 1966
Speaight, R., *Teilhard de Chardin. A Biography*, London, 1967
Wildiers, N. M., *An introduction to Teilhard de Chardin*, London, 1968

Chapter 8

Adler, L., *Der Mensch in der Sicht der Bibel*, Basel-Zurich, 1965
Bertocci, P. A., *Introduction to the Philosophy of Religion*, New York, 1951
Bevan, E., *Symbolism and Belief*, London, 1938 (and paperback)
Bremond, H., *A Literary History of Religious Thought in France*, 3 vols, London, 1928-36
Brunner, E., *Man in Revolt*, London, 1939
Huddleston, T., *The True and Living God*, London, 1964
Hügel, F. von, *Readings*, selected by A. Thorold, London, 1928
Karrer, O., *Religions and Mankind*, London, 1936
Lewis, C. S., *Miracles*, London, 1960
Lubac, H. de, *Sur les chemins de Dieu*, Paris, 1956
Maréchal, J., *Studies in the Psychology of the Mystics*, London, 1967
Newman, J. H., *The Development of Christian Doctrine*, London, 1845
　　　Grammar of Assent, London, 1870
Rosmini, A., 'Il divino nella natura' in *Teosofia*, 1869, vol. IV
Tillich, P., *The Courage to Be*, Yale, 1952
　　　Love Power Justice, New York, 1960
　　　The Religious Situation, New York, 1932
　　　The Shaking of the Foundations, London, 1949 (and Penguin)
Zaehner, R. C., *At Sundry Times*, London, 1958

Index

361